Praise for *Mozarabs, Hispanics, & the Cross*

"This is a marvelous contribution, recovering necessary sources for U.S. Hispanic theologies and with exciting interdisciplinary and cross-cultural implications. In retrieving the Mozarabic story as well as reflecting on the experience of the contemporary Mozarab community, Gómez-Ruiz skillfully interweaves strands from liturgical and ritual studies, Christology, and popular religion, Iberian history and ethnography. This book explores the rich diversity of Catholic liturgical expressions and the complex contexts from which they arise and within which they thrive."

—*Carmen Nanko-Fernández, Catholic Theological Union, Chicago,*
President-elect, Academy of Catholic Hispanic Theologians of the United States

"*Mozarabs, Hispanics, & the Cross* is a significant work because it integrates diverse areas of study as well as methodological approaches. Persons engaged in the study of liturgy, popular religion, ritual studies, and Latino/a Catholicism will find something of interest in this book. Raúl Gómez-Ruiz explores the symbolism of the cross, in particular the *Lignum Crucis*, as it mediates religious, social, and cultural identity. He also constructs methodological bridges as he makes use of data from social and liturgical history to provide a context for the study of contemporary enactments of Good Friday rituals in Toledo. This is a fine example of an approach to liturgical theology that combines the study of ritual texts and performance."

—*Margaret Mary Kelleher, O.S.U., School of Theology and Religious Studies,*
The Catholic University of America

Mozarabs, Hispanics,
and the Cross

STUDIES IN LATINO/A CATHOLICISM

A series sponsored by the Center for the Study of Latino/a Catholicism University of San Diego

Previously published

Orlando O. Espín and Miguel H. Díaz, editors, *From the Heart of Our People: Latino/a Explorations in Catholic Systematic Theology*
Orlando O. Espín and Gary Macy, editors, *Futuring Our Past: Explorations in the Theology of Tradition*
María Pilar Aquino and Maria José Rosado-Nunes, editors, *Feminist Intercultural Theology: Latina Explorations for a Just World*

STUDIES IN LATINO/A CATHOLICISM

Mozarabs, Hispanics, and the Cross

Raúl Gómez-Ruiz, S.D.S.

ORBIS BOOKS

Maryknoll, New York 10545

Founded in 1970, Orbis Books endeavors to publish works that enlighten the mind, nourish the spirit, and challenge the conscience. The publishing arm of the Maryknoll Fathers and Brothers, Orbis seeks to explore the global dimensions of the Christian faith and mission, to invite dialogue with diverse cultures and religious traditions, and to serve the cause of reconciliation and peace. The books published reflect the views of their authors and do not represent the official position of the Maryknoll Society. To learn more about Maryknoll and Orbis Books, please visit our website at www.maryknoll.org.

Copyright © 2007 by Raúl Gómez-Ruiz.

Published by Orbis Books, Maryknoll, NY 10545–0308.
Manuscript editing and typesetting by Joan Weber Laflamme.

Manufactured in the United States of America.

Library of Congress Cataloging-in-Publication Data

Gómez-Ruiz, Raúl.
    Mozarabs, Hispanics, and the Cross / Raúl Gómez-Ruiz.
        p. cm. — (Studies in Latino/a Catholicism)
    Includes bibliographical references.
    ISBN 978-1-57075-733-4
    1. Mozarabs—Religious life. 2. Good Friday—Spain—Toledo. 3. Holy Cross. 4. Toledo (Spain)—Religious life and customs. 5. Processions, Religious—Catholic Church—Spain—Toledo. I. Title.
    BR1024.G66 2007
    282'.4643—dc22

                                                              2007007672

To my parents,
D. Pablo Gómez Aguilar
and Dña. Idolina Ruiz Flores

Contents

Abbreviations

AAS	*Acta Apostolicæ Sedis*
AMs	Autograph manuscript
BAC	*Biblioteca de Autores Cristianos*
BOAT	*Boletín Oficial de la Archidiócesis de Toledo*
CCC	*Catechism of the Catholic Church*
CCL	Code of Canon Law
CELAM	Consejo Episcopal Latinoamericano
CM	*Crónica Mozárabe*
Constituciones	*Constituciones de la Ilustre y Antiquísima Hermandad de Caballeros Mozárabes de Nuestra Señora de la Esperanza, de la Imperial Ciudad de Toledo, Capítulo de Toledo.*
CUA	The Catholic University of America
D.	Don (Lord, Sir; honorary title of respect)
Dña.	Doña (Lady, Dame; honorary title of respect)
DS	Henricus Denzinger and Adolfus Schönmetzer, eds., *Enchiridion Symbolorum: Definitionum et Declarationum de Rebus Fidei et Morum*
ICEL	International Commission on English in the Liturgy
LG	*Lumen Gentium (Dogmatic Constitution on the Church)*
LM	*Le Liber Mozarabicus Sacramentorum et les Manuscrits Mozarabes*
LMCP	*Liber Misticus de Cuaresma y Pascua*

LO	*Le Liber Ordinum En Usage Dan l'Église Wisigothique et Mozarabe d'Espagne du Cinquième Siècle*
LTP	Liturgy Training Publications
Martimort	A. G. Martimort, ed., *The Church at Prayer*
Missale	*Missale Hispano-Mozarabicum*
NCCB	National Conference of Catholic Bishops
PG	*Patrologiæ Cursus Completus, Series Græca*
PL	*Patrologiæ Cursus Completus, Series Latina*
Prot.	Protocol
SC	*Sacrosanctum Concilium (Constitution on the Sacred Liturgy)*
TLS	Typewritten letter signed
TMs	Typewritten manuscript
USCC	United States Catholic Conference
Vives	José Vives et al., eds., *Concilios Visigóticos e Hispano-Romanos*

Introduction

The ritual use of certain symbols forges a link between liturgy and popular religion. Symbols used in both realms mediate this link and take on a pivotal role. Such is the case of the Lignum Crucis, a seventeenth-century reliquary purportedly containing a relic of the wood of the true cross. This reliquary is used by a community of Christians known as the Mozarabs of Toledo, Spain, in the parish of Santa Eulalia y San Marcos. That the Lignum Crucis is used ritually in relation to other forms of the cross by the community in both the liturgical and popular realms also suggests that the cross is a key symbol in the Hispano-Mozarabic liturgy and in the self-identification of the Mozarab community. Such prominent use of the Lignum Crucis points to certain christological, soteriological, liturgical, and cultural understandings among the Mozarabs and prompted the research underlying this book.

Who are these Mozarabs? They form a community centered in and originally from Toledo, Spain, although many now live further afield in Madrid and scattered throughout the world. In Spanish the name for them is *muzárabe* or *mozárabe*, the latter spelling being the current usage. The origins of the name are variously interpreted. Some take *mozarab* to mean "among the Arabs" or "Arabacized." Some attribute it to the Arabic word *musta'rib* (like Arabs). Others note that the term was first used for the community after the reconquest of Toledo in 1085 by the new Christian overlords from northern Spain,[1] though interestingly Thomas Burman notes that the Muslim Arabic writers never used the term *musta'rib* for the Christians. They used words such as *rumi* (Roman, Byzantine), *nasará* (Christian, Nazarene), and *mu'ahid* (keeper of the pact). The term first appears in Christian texts beginning in the eleventh century as *musta'rab* or *musta'rib* or in Romance variants of *muzaraves, muztarabes,* and *mozarabes.*[2]

The modern-day Mozarab community of Toledo is one of many ethnic groups that make up what can in general be called Hispanic culture. The use of this term—*Hispanic*—has often been controversial, especially in circles of scholars who identify themselves as Latino/a. Yet to describe in broad strokes peoples who share certain cultural characteristics, the term *Hispanic* is more appropriate here than *Latino/a*. First, the term *Latino* is too broad a category to describe adequately those marked by Spanish cultural, linguistic, and religious influences. *Latino* in its derivation means "of Latin origin" and is most often used to refer to those who share the languages and cultures stemming from Rome. Thus it can encompass Italians, Portuguese, and French, as well as Latin Americans and Hispanics in the United States. Second, the term *Hispanic,* while also a broad term, better describes the peoples in the world who share history and familial connections derived from Spain, a key element held in common by those identified as Hispanic.[3]

I use the term from this viewpoint. I do not deny the differences among the peoples of these countries but instead focus on what they hold in common. I maintain this includes a general religious outlook that can be discerned among Mozarabs and in their use of the Lignum Crucis, the focus of this book. Though there are great commonalities in terms of world view among Hispanics and other Latinos/as, I understand *Hispanic* to be a more focused term and use it for my examination of the ritual use of the Lignum Crucis.

In the following chapters I go into greater detail about the present-day Mozarab community of Toledo, its origins, and of the use of the Lignum Crucis reliquary and the Hispano-Mozarabic rite as a source of identity for the community. The rite is one of several Latin language ritual systems developed in Western Europe during the first five centuries of the Christian era. As such, it has similarities to the better known Roman and Gallican rites in structure and theological underpinnings. In particular, the rite is centered on the celebration of the Eucharist, the divine office, and the sacraments.

The immediate liturgical context for the ritual use of the Lignum Crucis is the Hispano-Mozarabic Lenten celebrations. Unlike the Roman rite, the Hispanic rite begins this season with the First Sunday of Lent; as a result, the forty days encompass the liturgies of Good Friday. The Lignum Crucis reliquary is used only on Good Friday. Another important element in the euchology (prayer system) of the Hispano-Mozarabic rite is the stress on martyrs. The Proper of Saints lists 141 individual saints' days in the liturgical year; of these, 98 are dedicated to martyrs. This is significant because it is forbidden to celebrate saints' days during Lent. Therefore, their liturgical celebration occurs during the course of the rest of the liturgical year, including Christmas and Eastertide. This implies that martyrdom is a significant factor in the theology of the Mozarabic liturgy, and by extension, in Mozarab spirituality.

The Hispano-Mozarabic rite has been developed and reformed many times over the centuries. The most important shift has been its change of status from the principal liturgy of Christians in Spain to its confinement in 1085 to the Mozarabs of Toledo. Since 1988 it has become an optional liturgy for all Catholics in Spain. There have been three major contributors to the rite's preservation in the last millennium: Cardinals Cisneros (sixteenth century), Lorenzana (eighteenth century), and González Martín (twentieth century). The last has been particularly instrumental in the recovery of ancient texts, their actualization, and publication in new liturgical books (1991). The two liturgical events of Good Friday, at which the Lignum Crucis plays a significant role, represent a reintroduction of and renewed emphasis on the penitential aspect of worship on that day among the participants in the rite.

However, a critique of the most recent efforts at updating is related to the vision of a "classical period" in the rite's development. This period, ranging from the fifth to the seventh centuries, provided a baseline for the identification of the supposedly authentic structure and texts of the liturgy. The elevation of a certain period over others implies later periods are somehow inauthentic. As a result, in a bid for authenticity, developments introduced during the sixteenth-century Cisneros era, for instance, have been eliminated from the liturgy. One of these elements was a prayer to the cross recited by the priest and assembly during the preparatory rites of every Mass.[4] Moreover, members of the Mozarab community of Toledo have complained that their sensibilities and spirituality have been overlooked in the efforts to actualize the rite.[5] Though they like some of the changes, they feel their voice has been discounted.[6] This has led to conflicts between those who celebrate the liturgy in the parishes and those who celebrate it in the Mozarabic chapel of the cathedral.

The Hispano-Mozarabic liturgy is primarily destined for Mozarabs who have canonical rights to the rite. The most recent efforts to update the rite have recognized this fact and have led to the acknowledgment that Mozarabs are the canonical subjects of the rite. Even so, this recognition has resulted from the self-assertion of the Mozarab community of Toledo, which arises from its keen sense of its history and culture.

Beginning in the eighth century, Christians from northern Iberia slowly reconquered major parts of the peninsula under Islamic rule, establishing kingdoms along the way. In the early to mid-eleventh century, rulers of the kingdoms of Castilla, León, and Navarra initiated efforts to introduce the Roman rite into their lands to replace the Old Spanish rite in an effort to "Europeanize" their subjects. The rite had already been introduced into the County of Barcelona in the ninth century. By 1080, Pope Gregory VII's agents had exerted enough influence on King Alfonso VI of Castilla-León to have him call a special council at Burgos. The council officially replaced the Spanish rite with the Roman rite. However, the legislation only held sway in the reconquered territories. As a result, when Toledo was taken in 1085, Mozarabs were still celebrating the liturgy in their ancient rite.

Mozarabs resisted the substitution, claiming that their liturgy had sustained their faith through the long years of Islamic rule. They were helped by King Alfonso, who, in 1101, in order to ensure their cooperation in holding the territory of Toledo under his control, granted Mozarabs certain privileges by means of a *fuero* (agreement). This agreement not only elevated their social status to that of nobility, but also designated the six extant parishes of Toledo as sites for the continued use of their liturgy. In this way the rite was preserved for later generations.

The effort to preserve their liturgy depended on a strong connection between liturgy and culture. Indeed, in Chapter 6 I examine liturgy as a cultural event in and of itself. I understand culture to be a meaning system manifested in socially patterned thought and human behavior. As such, culture is linked to identity. Because cultures are dynamic, they have a history and context. The Hispano-Mozarabic rite, therefore, emerges from a specific cultural context. This context imbues the rite and its particular symbols with meanings that are discernable, given adequate identification and importance of the necessary elements—which in this case includes Mozarab history and religion, as well as the efforts to preserve and transmit Mozarab culture through the centuries.

Members of the Mozarab community have been conservative in their efforts to construct Mozarab culture and to preserve the Mozarabic liturgy. This has included asserting over time their privileges under King Alfonso's *fuero*. Once the *fuero* was abrogated in the nineteenth century as a result of the republican movement in Spain that led to repudiation of most church privileges, Mozarab culture was in danger of disappearing. A major reason was the elimination of *tazmías* (registers) for the purpose of identifying members of the community and the support of their six parishes in Toledo. However, the existence of the corps of Mozarabic rite chaplains in the cathedral at Toledo, the occasional celebration of the rite in certain parishes of the city, and the anecdotal recounting of family histories aided sufficient numbers of the community to remember their origins. In the 1950s the efforts of Mozarabic rite chaplains who were pastoring Santas Justa y Rufina and San Marcos, their remaining two parishes in Toledo, led to the renewal of Mozarab self-identification and to the efforts to update the Mozarabic liturgy. A primary result of this was the reestablishment of the *Hermandad Mozárabe*, a confraternity of Mozarab families formed to help them assert their culture and preserve their liturgy.

One way culture and identity develop is by means of cultural events. In order to examine this phenomenon I employ ritual studies theory[7] to show how the ritual use of the Lignum Crucis reliquary is a cultural event that helps construct Mozarab identity. I also examine how rituals can be subversive in that they provide members of the community with a catalyst to engage in the contention and negotiation involved in the appropriation of symbols.

Actions play a role in constituting who we are as persons. They are symbolic because they evoke commonly held feelings and reveal shared values, and thus embody meanings and participate in the construction of culture. When actions follow a particular, identifiable, and consistent pattern they are called rituals. Rituals are significant actions by which people perform their culture. In the case of the Mozarabs of Toledo, they have taken the rituals of the Hispano-Mozarabic rite Triduum to be significant to their distinction as a people. When rituals occur in the religious realm they relate the participants to an ultimate frame of reference that helps identify what is most meaningful and necessary for a particular people to be itself. Consequently, one of the values embodied in rituals is the identity of a people: rituals emphasize particular aspects of the identity of a people, inviting the participants to appropriate and to contribute to the identity presented. Rituals, as a result, are the necessary actions required for individuals to integrate themselves into their society and to constitute their culture.

Rituals comprise symbols and symbolic actions. Because of their symbolic content, rituals contain meanings that are seen and unforeseen. In this sense rituals are subversive because no one person or group of persons can control them completely, and this gives rituals much power. Catherine Bell approaches rituals as a form of praxis, a unity of consciousness and social being that has the power to transform real existence.[8] As a consequence, rituals construct and at the same time actualize meaning. When rituals occur in the religious realm, they not only point to the identity, social relations, and values at the core of a specific culture, but also point to who God is for that society. The ritual use of the Lignum Crucis reliquary by the Mozarab community of Toledo is especially apt for uncovering the identity, social relations, and values that are at the core of the community in relationship to itself and to God. As participants in and co-creators of Hispanic culture, their history, experience, and approach to liturgy is instructive in terms of Hispanic spirituality, especially in terms of who Christ is for the community and the role of the cross in salvation. I present my findings in this regard shortly. To do this we will consider the present-day Mozarabs and their origins, an overview of their liturgy and the Good Friday services at the parish of

Santa Eulalia y San Marcos. We continue by looking at the ritual use of the Lignum Crucis reliquary, studying the christological controversies, and analyzing texts used in relation to the Lignum Crucis. We complete the book with a consideration of the spirituality of the cross and its meaning for Hispanics in general and Mozarabs in particular. A selected bibliography rounds out the book.

A work such as this is never completed by one alone. Rather, with the encouragement, support, and help of others one is enabled to engage in the study, research, and writing needed to accomplish the task. Such is the case with this book. I particularly wish to acknowledge the following entities and persons for their part.

My thanks to the Center for the Study of Latino/a Catholicism at the University of San Diego for being willing to add this book to its series dedicated to theological research and reflection on Latino/a Catholicism. Though this work focuses on one very particular source emanating from the Iberian peninsula, namely, the Hispano-Mozarabic rite, it provides a reference for scholars to gain insight into some approaches to popular religion shared by Latinos/as throughout the world who trace one of their roots to Spain. I suggest these approaches, especially in relation to the cross, have a common origin and are linked to the celebration of Good Friday among Hispanic, Latino/a Catholics throughout the world. I am particularly indebted to Dr. Orlando Espín, director of the center, for his encouragement.

In addition, I am grateful to those who provided financial help during my research: to the Hispanic Theological Initiative for the much needed grant that helped me engage in on-site research in Spain; to my religious community, the Society of the Divine Savior, for the welcome living-expense funds while I was completing this work; and to Sacred Heart School of Theology for providing me with the funds to cover other expenses as well as allowing me to take time from teaching in order to study and write.

I am especially appreciative of the following persons for their extraordinary support. My sincerest thanks to D. Jaime Colomina Torner, president of the Instituto de Estudios Visigótico-Mozárabes of Toledo for opening doors for me in my research in Spain. Thanks to D. Mario Arellano García, Dña. Justa Margarita Córdoba Sánchez-Bretaño, D. Enrique Carrillo Morales, D. Julio Gómez-Jacinto, and the Mozarabic rite chaplains as well as the officers and members of the *Hermandad Mozárabe* for their cooperation in my research. Thanks to D. Ramón Gonzálvez Ruiz and the staff of the Archivo y Biblioteca Capitular de la Catedral, Toledo. Special thanks to the V. Rev. James Brackin, S.C.J., former president-rector of Sacred Heart, who encouraged me to pursue these studies and kept my position open at Sacred Heart while I was away. Thanks to Dr. Carmen Nanko Fernández, my highly esteemed colleague, for her confidence in me and in this project. Thanks to the late Rev. Patrick Matthias Craemer, S.C.J., for providing me with initial translations of most of the Latin texts examined for this study. Thanks to my confreres Rev. Joseph Henn, S.D.S., and Br. Albin Laga, S.D.S., for their technical assistance. Special thanks to Joan Weber Laflamme for her skillful copy editing and to Ulrike Guthrie for carefully editing this text for publication. Finally, I am greatly indebted to the Rev. Thomas L. Knoebel for his clear insights and attentive proofing throughout my work. Without your help I could not have accomplished such a formidable task.

1

Rediscovering the Mozarabs of Toledo

"Some people in Toledo don't even know anything about us or that we even exist. Some think we are the Moors. We are not the Moors, we are the Old Christians," asserted Doña Justa Córdoba Sánchez-Bretaño.[1] It takes an extraordinarily interesting bit of sleuthing to uncover the story of how so many inhabitants of one and the same Spanish city can have become completely unaware of the existence, never mind history and faith practices, of a once dominant part of their population. But such is the story of the Mozarabs of Toledo.

Present-day Mozarabs claim to form a community comprised of the descendants of those Hispano-Roman and Visigothic Christians who held onto their Catholic faith despite the vicissitudes of Islamic invasion and the need to adapt culturally to the dominant culture.[2] Through the centuries they mingled and intermarried with subsequent conquerors and inhabitants of Toledo including the Arabs, Berbers, Syrians, Castilians, Galicians, and French who made their home among them. During the more than 370 years of Islamic domination they spoke Arabic and acquired the cultural characteristics of the dominant Arabic culture: their building styles and techniques, agricultural methods and products, clothing styles and materials, stress on learning, and religious outlook. Thomas Burman notes that in the course of becoming Arabicized, Mozarabs became partially Islamicized through their familiarity with Islamic books, religious language, and patterns of thought; this is especially evident in their religious-apologetic literary output.[3] Since the reconquest of Toledo in 1085, Mozarabs have blended with the general Spanish populace due to the social pressures that occur when a subaltern population enters into the realm of a more dominant one. This process can be traced partially through the change from Arabic to Romance names during the eleventh and twelfth centuries.[4] Over the course of time, many Mozarab

1

families were subsumed into the dominant culture and disappeared as part of a distinct cultural group or forgot their origins, as Doña Justa asserted in the opening quotation. For long periods of time those who despite everything maintained their sense of identity have suffered marginalization and domination, as I will recount.

Since 1996 I have come to know personally various Mozarabs through interviews, and I have been present at some of their community events. Who, then, are these people? Mozarabs speak modern-day Castilian, though they at one time spoke a particular Romance dialect.[5] Both adult males and females work as shopkeepers, professors, government officials, lawyers, and in other professions. Economically they appear to fall within various economic levels, but those I have met range from the middle income to wealthy. Some own estates or farms, while others work as craftsmen or are in various ranks of the Spanish military. In terms of social class they rank in the upper-middle to the titled classes. I think of a widow I met at a ceremony in June 2000, a marquesa, whose husband had been a high-ranking military officer under Generalissimo Francisco Franco. Nonetheless, in language, appearance, dress, lifestyle, occupation, education, religious practice, and so forth they otherwise appear to differ little from the general population of Toledo, and in fact, as Doña Justa reminds us, many of them feel that most of their compatriots do not even know they exist.

So what makes them different from their compatriots? The key difference is their liturgy and the social status they have received. Both of these derive from their self-identification as the original Old Christians of Spain. Ildefonso, Juan, and Salvador, the sons of a couple who are prominent lawyers, when asked what it meant to be Mozarab, answered, "We feel proud because it means to be descended from Old Christians; to be heirs to (and carry) a tradition that is so ancient (and has been passed on for so many generations)."[6] Because of their ancestors' cooperation in the Christian reconquest of Toledo, King Alfonso VI of León-Castile (1065–1109) entered into an agreement or *fuero* with the Mozarabs of Toledo.[7] Alfonso's *fuero* granted them notable exemptions and immunities and also raised their social status to that of *nobleza e hidalguía*.[8] In order to identify Mozarabs and to ensure their support of the parishes, a system of *tazmías* (registers) and *diezmos* (tithes) was established under Alfonso VI and developed by subsequent rulers and church officials. The members of the community were taxed yearly and their support subscribed to the parish to which they were assigned. In this way a system of identification was kept in place until it was eliminated by the *desamortización* (divestment) of 1834. Doing away with it then necessitated significant reconstructive work later on, as we shall see.[9]

Over the course of time the original six parishes have come to be housed at two sites, Santa Eulalia y San Marcos and Santas Justa y Rufina. Nonetheless, all Mozarabs are still identified with one or another of the six parishes. Those ascribed to the parishes of San Marcos, Santa Eulalia, and San Lucas are assigned to the parish Church of Santa Eulalia y San Marcos. Those ascribed to the parishes of San Sebastián, San Torcuato, and Santas Justa y Rufina meet at the latter's church.

Despite a long history of conquest, despite cultural, social, religious, and ecclesial conflict, and despite suffering caused by alienation and limited resources, Mozarabs have persisted. Mozarabs of Toledo tend to be conservative politically and religiously. This was a trait upheld by various of my older informants, although some of my younger ones gave evidence of this in terms of a desire to pass on their heritage intact. Mozarabs call their conservatism *conservadurismo*.[10] They have worked at conserving a sense of self by appealing to the past as well as rallying around Mozarabic Catholicism. Mozarabs call this sense of self *mozarabía* (mozarabicity).

But how does a minority culture maintain this sense of self amid all the forces of change and even repression? The people passed on their *mozarabía* from generation to generation by means of the *tazmías*, the system of registers first established by Alfonso VI. Once these were eliminated, their family histories helped them remember. This was especially the case between the period from the end of the *tazmías* in 1834 until the 1950s; during this time grandparents told the stories of their ancestors to their grandchildren.[11] Various informants told me their grandmothers and great-aunts especially spoke to them of their *mozarabía*.

Through my interactions with them and by examining their literature I have discovered that the shape, purposes, and meanings of the contemporary Mozarabs of Toledo are particularly expressed in the following institutions, arts, and learning: the *Hermandad Mozárabe* (Mozarab Brotherhood); the Hispano-Mozarabic rite; the Mozarabic rite parishes of Toledo; the charting of genealogies; the recourse to Spanish and Mozarab history; Good Friday processions; the emblem they have created for themselves named the Cross of Alfonso VI; the Lignum Crucis reliquary; Mozarabic architecture and artwork in churches; the images of saints they have installed in the Mozarabic rite parishes; Mozarabic chant; the annual gathering of the members of the *Hermandad* (called a *capítulo*, chapter); and periodic congresses at which both Mozarab and other scholars make presentations about Mozarab culture, some of which have been published and which I cite in this book. This short list gives an idea of the depth and range of the institutions, arts, and learning that are being generated by Mozarabs. Together these institutions and rituals have helped Mozarabs form a social group or community that shares common characteristics and interests as well as perceiving itself as distinct from larger Spanish society.[12]

The construction of contemporary Mozarab culture is, of course, the result of the power exercised, and the choices and responses made, by the members of the community in relation to the larger Spanish society and church. And, of course, certain members of the community and of the larger society and church wield greater power in this realm. Among them is the archbishop of Toledo, who functions as the ecclesiastical superior of the Hispano-Mozarabic rite as well as of the *Hermandad Mozárabe*. This puts him in a position to check the exercise of power by those who rank below him in regard to Mozarabs, both clerical and lay.

And yet, for all of the archbishop's power, a certain negotiation of power nevertheless takes place between the archbishop and those subject to him. For the male and female officers of the *Hermandad* are able to influence decisions made about who is identified as a Mozarab and what is considered as *mozarabía*. Don Mario Arellano García[13] in particular has great power as the one who keeps the register of members; he also frequently publishes scholarly and popular articles, and edits the community's official chronicle, the *Crónica Mozárabe*. The original *Crónica Mozárabe* was written in 754 by an anonymous author who probably lived in Córdoba; it was written in Latin and intended as a continuation of Isidore of Seville's chronicle.[14] The Toledan community began the contemporary *Crónica Mozárabe* in 1968 in order to maintain contact among the Mozarab parishioners in "diaspora" as well as in Toledo.[15]

Others who wield extensive power in the construction of Mozarab culture include the Mozarabic rite chaplains, particularly those assigned as pastors to the parishes. Chief among these is Don Enrique Carrillo Morales, pastor of the parish of Santa Eulalia y San Marcos, who also functions as the co-prior of the *Hermandad Mozárabe*. But even regular members of the community and certain outsiders engaged in the study, promotion, and publication of works on Mozarab culture contribute to the construction of the culture. Likewise, in the civic realm, Mozarabs have acquired prominence through their interactions with city and provincial governmental authorities. Some of this is the result of asserting their status through the *Hermandad* as well as through their granting of *Hermandad* membership to high government officials by reason of their office.[16]

The gradual loss of Mozarab self-identity was to result in tremendous reconstructive detective work later on. In the early 1950s Mozarabic rite chaplains Don Anastasio Granados and Don Luis Casañas encouraged Mozarab parishioners to reaffirm their *mozarabía* and their canonical rights to the rite.[17] They began to gather names of Mozarab families and to visit them. In 1957, led by newly named pastors of the Mozarabic rite parishes Don Jaime Colomina Torner and Don Balbino Gómez-Chacón, members of the community continued this initiative by means of a census. They went from house to house to remind people of their Mozarab heritage and to encourage their registration in one of the parishes. They identified at that time five hundred parishioners of Santa Eulalia y San Marcos and fifty of Santas Justa y Rufina. Most Mozarabs still lived in Toledo then.

The census takers drew upon the network of relatives as well as on the surviving parish registers and records of marriages. Their work was made considerably easier by Colomina Torner, who discovered the *tazmías* of Santa Eulalia dating to 1830.[18] This facilitated the construction of family genealogies and the revival of interest in Mozarab history among the parishioners. By studying marriage registers and phone books, the register of Mozarab families with canonical rights to the ancient personal parishes of Toledo slowly came to be reconstituted. Yet of almost ten thousand families recorded in the first one-third of the nineteenth century, only five hundred families were counted in a census taken in 1958. This was because, first, people had lost interest in their old parishes when they were no longer required to pay tithes; second, their old noble status had been degraded under the Bourbons; and third, the Roman church had decided to count only the eldest daughter as Mozarab.

So in 1966 the community reorganized itself as part of the effort to identify Mozarabs and began to revitalize its old brotherhood as a way to help them recover their cultural and liturgical heritage. Don José Antonio Dávila García-Miranda (Dávila) reconstituted the register on behalf of the revival of the old *Hermandad*; he describes how he studied the marriage register of San Marcos from the end of the 1800s until 1966, thereby creating a genealogical record.[19] The original brotherhood was founded in 1513 as a confraternity at the parish of San Lucas. It was formed to foster devotion among Mozarabs to the Virgin by means of the Rosary and the *Salve* on Saturday evenings. In 1867 the city of Toledo became the official civil protector of the Mozarab confraternity, then called *La Ilustre y Antiquísima Cofradía-Esclavitud de Nuestra Señora de la Esperanza de San Lucas* (The Illustrious and Ancient Servitude of Our Lady of Hope of San Lucas). It ceased to exist shortly thereafter.

The community renamed the brotherhood *La Ilustre y Antiquísima Hermandad de Caballeros Mozárabes de Nuestra Señora de la Esperanza, de la Imperial Ciudad de Toledo* and its feminine branch, the *Damas Mozárabes*. The name was revised in 1999 to include the *Damas Mozárabes* in the title.[20] The new name of the confraternity translated into English is The Illustrious and Ancient Brotherhood of Mozarab Gentlemen and Ladies of Our Lady of Hope of the Imperial City of Toledo. The *Constitutions* of the *Hermandad Mozárabe* state that its purpose is "to perpetuate the piety and the ancient traditions of the Mozarabs."[21] The brotherhood also aims to gather Mozarabs in Toledo and elsewhere for the purpose of repairing the harm done materially and morally by the Spanish Civil War (1936–39); maintaining, dignifying, and actualizing the ancestral liturgy, including the use of Spanish in its celebration; and recognizing the nobility of its members.[22] Upon its reestablishment in 1966, the archbishop of Toledo resumed his role as titular head of the brotherhood and the mayor of Toledo resumed the role of its civil protector.

Another aspect in the reorganization of the community has been to record again the names of families and individuals who are members of the community "by birth" or lineage. The leaders of the community have taken periodic censuses based on the census of 1957 as well as the work done on behalf of the *Hermandad*. The names gathered through this process were recorded in provisional *Padrones* (census registers) in 1971 and 1973.[23] A definitive *Padrón de las Nobles Familias de Caballeros Mozárabes de Toledo (Census Register of the Noble Families of Mozarab Gentlemen of Toledo)* was published in 1982 with the approval of Cardinal González Martín.[24] Since then, three appendices have been published as part of the *Crónica Mozárabe*.[25]

Mozarabs wishing to claim membership must prove descent from families listed in the official register of the Mozarab families.[26] To describe categories of membership they use the terms *nato* (born or natural), *de estirpe* (by stock), *linaje* (lineage), *ascendencia* (descent), *ius familiæ* (by family right) and *ius sanguinis* (by blood right). If their forebears are not listed in the official register and subsequent appendices, they are to solicit "rehabilitation" *(rehabilitación)* through the pastor of one of the Mozarabic parishes by submitting appropriate birth or baptismal records and a detailed genealogy that show direct Mozarab descent either through the father's or mother's line.

The keeping of the *Padrón* has become the means to record the names of those who have rights to the rite by descent. It is updated periodically by Arellano García who, together with his wife, Doña Justa Córdoba Sánchez-Bretaño, engages in genealogical research in order to verify *calidad mozárabe* (Mozarab authenticity). This has resulted in the identification of over thirteen hundred Mozarab families so far in the world. The majority of the families live in Spain, and most of them, approximately one thousand, have been identified as members of Santa Eulalia y San Marcos. Arellano García estimates five hundred Mozarab families actually live in Toledo, another three hundred to four hundred families live in Madrid, and the rest are scattered throughout Spain.[27]

Initially Mozarab nobility and personal membership in the parishes were transmitted in Toledo and elsewhere to all of the descendants of the first generation acknowledged by King Alfonso VI's *fuero*, whether male or female. This was confirmed by the Sacred Roman Rota in 1551.[28] However, Pope Julius III in 1553 restricted this to Mozarabs living in Toledo.[29] As a consequence, only descendants in the male line could claim the right. This was done to resolve conflicts between Latin and Mozarabic pastors in Toledo regarding tithes due the parishes. In another reversed decision, Archbishop Luis María de Borbón of Toledo in 1815 restored *calidad mozárabe* once again to those living outside of Toledo.[30]

Today, adult male and female Mozarabs who wish to affirm their *calidad mozárabe* are invited to become members of the *Hermandad Mozárabe*. They are required to present genealogical proof of descent from any of the parishioners of the six Mozarabic parishes.[31] Their children may also become members of the *Hermandad* when they come of age. *Calidad mozárabe* is transmitted according to regulations set out by canon law.[32] Namely, Mozarabs must be direct descendants through the male line either of a Mozarab father or the eldest married daughter of a Mozarab family. All sons of a Mozarab family are considered to be Mozarabs. Daughters are also Mozarabs, but they retain their *calidad mozárabe* only if they marry a Mozarab or if their non-Mozarab spouse opts for membership in the Mozarabic rite at the time of marriage. He can acquire *parroquialidad mozárabe* (membership in a Mozarabic rite parish) at the time of marriage. The children are then considered Mozarabs as well. If the spouse decides not to join a Mozarabic parish, the children of the Mozarab daughter are not considered Mozarabs. However, if the wife is widowed, she may recover her *calidad mozárabe*.

Calidad mozárabe is dependent on descent and membership in one of the six parishes. Thus, recovery of status as a Mozarab requires enrollment in a Mozarabic rite parish, even if one lives outside of Toledo. The Mozarab is expected to support the parish and its assistance programs for needy members. Mozarab men and women who are members of the *Hermandad* may participate in the Good Friday processions and other public religious acts that are of importance to the community, especially if they are celebrated in the Hispano-Mozarabic rite.[33] Non-Mozarab men and women who contribute to the welfare of the community or promote knowledge of it and its rite can also join the *Hermandad* as honorary members after application and acceptance by the *Cabildo* (governing body) of the *Hermandad*. They do not, however, acquire *calidad mozárabe* nor *parroquialidad mozárabe*.[34]

THE LITURGY AS A SOURCE OF IDENTITY

The requirement that those wishing to recover their *calidad mozárabe* must enroll in one of the Mozarabic parishes raises the issue of the rite's role in the community's identity. Through speaking with various Mozarabs of Toledo I learned that they very much link self-identity to what they claim as their liturgical heritage. For example, Alicia Arellano, a Mozarab, wrote an open letter to the community calling upon it to take responsibility for passing on *mozarabía* by participating in the liturgy and by getting involved in its promotion.[35] Or as Doña Justa put it: "There is no difference in religiosity and culture; the difference is the liturgy and the fact that the Mozarabic parishes are personal and not territorial like the Latin ones."[36] This was affirmed by Don Felipe Jurado Puñal, who declared to me that being Mozarab "means to be the descendant of people who maintained their rite; the link is the rite."[37] The *Crónica Mozárabe* affirms this notion as well noting that the community is "conscious of the historico-liturgical treasure that encompasses the symbolism of Mozarabism."[38] Another member of the community, Don Antonio Muñoz Perea, declares in an article in the *Crónica Mozárabe* that "the defense and survival of Mozarabism depends basically on us; as long as there are faithful there will be worship and parishes; if one day there are no faithful it will be the end of the Hispano-Mozarabic rite."[39] He goes on to declare that if "our churches are filled we will be able to ask for the approval of our sacramentals so that we can celebrate the Sacraments in our proper rite, to which we have a right especially to Baptism, Confirmation, Marriage, and Anointing of the Sick."[40] So that the community is aware that the rite is for its use and forms part of its religious and cultural heritage, the 1984 *Constitutions* of the *Hermandad* explicitly attest to the importance of the liturgy to its identity, with Article 1 declaring that one of the main purposes of the *Hermandad* is "the conservation of the traditions of the historico-liturgical Mozarab community."[41]

The pastors of the community have encouraged it to hold on to this liturgical heritage as well as to participate in the rite's updating. In 1987 Cardinal González Martín affirmed the community's efforts by authorizing the Mozarabic rite parishes to celebrate the Mozarabic Mass on a regular basis. Since the approval of the new *ordo missæ* in 1991, Santa Eulalia y San Marcos does so every Sunday at noon as its only eucharistic celebration. By contrast, Santas Justa y Rufina only celebrates the Hispano-Mozarabic rite Mass on the first Saturday of the month.[42]

Mozarabs attribute the link between liturgy and their culture to the Islamic conquest.[43] The Mozarabic liturgy became the "all-encompassing literary expression of Mozarab culture, the best dispensed to all the social classes, and the fount and source of collective life, the living center of the community's resistance to the diverse centrifugal forces of assimilation."[44] Although they succeeded in living with the Muslims, their own culture, particularly in the ninth century, was centered upon and unified by the church, "which was not only the custodian and purveyor of learning and tradition from the past but also the educator and trainer for immediate tasks confronting the Christians."[45] Don Cleofé Sánchez, also a Mozarab, writes that "in *mozarabía* there is a line that has threaded its way through the melody of life's ups and downs and those difficulties inherent in a culture and that is the liturgy."[46] It appears that Mozarab genealogy, law, history, and art have revolved around and been subordinated to the Mozarabic liturgy. This link between the community, the church, and the liturgy has been strengthened over the centuries. What were the cultural forces that occasioned this link, and what efforts were made to preserve the liturgy?

PRESERVING THE CULTURE THROUGH THE LITURGY

Over the centuries the Hispano-Mozarabic rite has remained the distinctive liturgical celebration of Mozarabs. Even after Cardinal Francisco Ximénez de Cisneros (1436–1517) installed a corps of Mozarabic chaplains in the Corpus Christi chapel of the cathedral in 1502 for the express purpose of celebrating the rite, Mozarabs continued to celebrate it in their parishes. Cardinal Marcelo González Martín had the celebration by Mozarab parishioners in mind when he authorized its actualization in the 1980s. The rite is primarily destined for them. A commission established by González Martín is making efforts as far as possible to bring up to date the sacramental and other liturgical celebrations that compose the rite.[47] The eucharistic celebration has been the starting point. In addition, the marriage rite has been updated and has become an optional rite for all Spanish Catholics.[48] Currently the other sacraments are celebrated according to the Roman rite usage. Mozarabs themselves are keenly aware they are the canonical subjects of the rite and have made their thoughts and desires known in the efforts to update the rite. It is precisely the self-consciousness of Mozarabs of Toledo that is a key factor both in the actualization of the rite and its potential for continued survival.

2

The Origins of the Mozarab Community and Its Liturgy

The modern-day community of Toledo continues to name itself Mozarab despite the fact that for over nine hundred years it has not lived under Islamic domination. Clearly, the Islamic period was defining for the community. As for the Hispano-Mozarabic rite as an expression of culture, however, some of the cultural influences fostering its development can be traced to pre-Christian history as well as to the subsequent events that shaped Iberian Christian history. Identifying likely cultural influences can provide a way to explore the connection between Mozarab culture and its liturgy.

PRE-CHRISTIAN INFLUENCES

Archeological findings indicate that isolated family groupings had settled in Iberia beginning more than 500,000 years ago. There is evidence in Spain of Australopithecines as early as 700,000 years ago, Pithecanthropi 500,000 years ago, Neanderthals c. 200,000 BC, and Cro-Magnons, 40,000 BC.[1] Even so, clearly definable cultures did not begin to appear until c. 3000 BC when Neolithic cultures appeared. Archeologists and historians attribute much of the movement to and through the peninsula to its strategic location in the western Mediterranean forming a type of bridge between Europe and Africa.[2] Thus, successive waves of peoples made their way to Iberia over the centuries establishing control in distinct portions of the peninsula. These included Carthaginians (228 BC) who established themselves among Iberians such as the Tartessians, as well as earlier migrants such as Celts (1000 BC).[3] The Tartessians may have been the people of biblical Tarshish.[4] It is unknown exactly when the Tartessian culture began to develop in Iberia, but it appears to have been native to southwestern Spain, developing near the mouth of the Guadalquivir River. Tartessian society and influence collapsed at the end of the sixth century BC when the Tartessians began to intermingle with Phoenicians and Carthaginians who had settled in their region. The resulting people, the Turdetanians, supplanted them and were recipients of their cultural heritage.

The peoples from the eastern Mediterranean played a particularly important role in the history of Iberia. Literary sources reveal that Phoenician settlement began in the eighth century BC.[5] Communities, such as Gades (Cádiz), founded by colonists from modern-day Lebanon c. 1100 BC, traded with other Phoenician and non-Phoenician communities throughout the Mediterranean basin, including Carthage c. 184 BC. After the mid-sixth century BC, Greek colonists founded colonies all along the eastern coast of Iberia, using the primary colony of Massalia (modern Marseilles) as their base. "Carthaginian and Greek influences combined with local traditions to produce a brilliant regional culture that survived until the Roman conquest and formed the cultural basis of the Roman province of Baetica."[6]

By the onset of the second century BC, distinct cultural groups were dispersed throughout the peninsula and dominated different regions. The population of Iberia was never numerous and was widely dispersed in ancient times. The majority of peoples lived along the eastern Mediterranean coast and the southern part of the peninsula in mostly semi-urban settings. This allowed for the development of various cultures and isolation to some extent of peoples in the interior and the northwest, who tended to live in villages and rural settings. The Turdetanians held the southwestern region, the Celts the northwest and west. The Basques and Cantabrians could be found in the north, while the Greeks established themselves in the northeast and east. The Phoenicians and Carthaginians held sway in the southeast and south.

Diverse peoples inhabited other parts of the peninsula including the central *meseta*. In this region a mixture of Celts and other Iberians formed a culture called Celtiberian.[7] The Celtiberians comprised a number of tribes and inhabited the zone now encompassed by Zaragoza, Guadalajara, and Soria. Even so, there was no sense of firm territorial realms, for peoples of the different groups could be found in the same region. Rather, a federation of "city states" prevailed among some of the urban centers established by members of the same cultural group. Interaction among the various peoples of the peninsula as well as those outside of it ran the gamut from trade to warfare. Though cultural exchange occurred among the Iberians, differences were keen enough to result in a mosaic of cultures throughout Iberia.

UNITY UNDER ROME

Roman civilization began to influence the Iberians with the onset of the Roman conquest in 264 BC.[8] The conquest would take about two hundred years to complete, however. Roman soldiers entered Iberia to fight the Carthaginians three times in the renowned Punic Wars.[9] They occurred in 264–41, 218–201, and 149–46 BC. As a final result, Rome acquired territories in Iberia and North Africa. Victorious, the Romans stayed because Rome needed grain, slaves, metals, and so forth. Driven by political and economic need, Rome thus began to expand its sway, establishing the first Roman provinces outside of Italy. However, due to the dispersion of peoples there was no central authority. In 197 BC the Romans formally divided Iberia into two provinces: Hispania Citerior and Hispania Ulterior. The former was the larger of the two and comprised the Mediterranean coastal strip from the Pyrenees to the southern coast. Its capital was Carthago Nova (Cartagena). Hispania Ulterior in the south would eventually comprise most of modern-day Andalucía and Portugal; its capital was Corduba (Córdoba).

Under Julius Caesar (d. 44 BC) the Roman army in 61 BC incorporated the major portion of the Iberian Peninsula under the aegis of Rome.[10] Octavian Augustus (27 BC–AD 14), Caesar's adopted son and first Roman emperor, conquered the remaining north and northwest portion of the peninsula between 29 and 19 BC. He imposed Roman governmental structures on the various peoples and subdivided Iberia into three provinces: Tarraconensis encompassed the northeastern third with Tarraco (Tarragona) as its capital. Baetica covered the lower third of the peninsula with Hispalis (Sevilla) as its capital. Lusitania took up the rest with Emerita Augusta (Mérida) as its capital.[11]

Over a period of approximately seven hundred years Iberian peoples were culturally and politically integrated into the Roman Empire. Much of this occurred gradually and at times due to the sword. Hispania provided mineral and agricultural wealth to Rome, eventually becoming its granary. Thus, the first-century AD writer Pliny the Elder declared that Spain was next to Italy in importance to the Romans.[12]

Although not all of the Iberian peoples succumbed completely to Romanization, the vast majority did. This the Romans accomplished by a policy of toleration of regional and cultural differences as well as by applying a single code of law that helped to unify the far-flung empire. The forging of the Spanish provinces also resulted in a unique Hispano-Roman civilization. Roman authorities encouraged colonization by soldiers and citizens of Rome, further helping to integrate its peoples into the heart of the empire. For example, Julius Caesar and Augustus encouraged farmers, merchants, and retired soldiers from Italy to settle in various parts of the peninsula but especially in the south and southeast. This obviously increased ties to Rome dramatically.

Furthermore, the Romans treated their subjects as Romans. Granting the inhabitants of Iberian towns citizenship also broke down barriers between Iberians and Romans, contributing to further development of a unique Hispano-Roman culture. In this way people such as Seneca (55 BC–AD 40)[13] from Corduba (Córdoba) and Quintilian (c. 33–c. AD 97) from Calagurris (Calahorra) were able to contribute to the development of *Romanitas* (Roman culture). Over the course of time Hispania provided the empire with two pagan emperors, Hadrian (AD 98–117) and Trajan (AD 117–38).[14] In the Christian era, another Spaniard became emperor, Theodosius the Great (379–95), who was born at Cauca (modern Coca) in northwestern Carthaginensis, the son of one of the most successful generals of Emperor Valentinian I (AD 364–75).[15] Theodosius had returned to live in Spain shortly before becoming emperor.

The Romans in general showed great tolerance toward local religions. With time, however, many of the local Iberian religions mingled with Roman religion. Absorbing the deities and practices of the locals into the official cult afforded the Romans another means to control their outlying subjects. The Romans had their own traditional gods and rituals, much of which had already blended with Greek religion. These were supplemented after Augustus by the cult of the divine emperors and in the first and second century AD by so-called mystery religions that had entered into the empire from the east.

CHRISTIAN ERA

The Hispano-Roman Christians and their liturgy of the first two centuries of the Christian era are shrouded in obscurity. The expansion of Christianity was carried out by anonymous believers whose only motive was their deep conviction of the importance and necessity of being Christian.[16] Christianity probably reached Hispania in much the same way as some of the mystery religions had—by way of traders, soldiers, and travelers.[17] Missionaries must have been among them also. The construction of roads and the establishment of trade routes facilitated Iberia's incorporation into the Roman Empire. Roads and trade routes let intercommunication take place with other peoples and cultures also consolidated into the far-flung empire. This afforded an opportunity for exchanges in ideas, peoples, and religious practices as well as in goods. There were three other factors favoring the spread of Christianity in the first two centuries: the public spectacle of persecutions, the natural curiosity of people looking for something new, and a growing sense of the importance of "the beyond."[18]

In terms of the Christianization of the peninsula, the Jews who had settled in Jewish towns were one of the most important peoples to come. It is unknown when Jews first arrived in Iberia, though some scholars believe they had established themselves in the peninsula by the first century BC. Others say that Jews did not come to the peninsula until the destruction of Jerusalem in 70 AD. In any case, it is notable that Iberia came to be identified by Jews with Sepharad, mentioned in Obadiah, verse 20.[19]

Jewish communities in Hispania had gained sufficient fame to warrant the apostle Paul desiring to visit them around the middle of the first century, as noted in the Letter to the Romans, written after 50 AD.[20] Clement of Rome, also in the first century, says Paul succeeded in reaching the extreme west of the empire. Nonetheless, there is no evidence that any Christian community in Hispania attributed its foundation to Paul or to James, the apostle venerated today as the evangelizer of Iberia. In the case of James, attributions are made to him beginning in the seventh century in scholarly circles. However, popular devotion to him begins only in the eleventh century.

Christianity emerged in the first century AD as one of various forms of Judaism extant at the time. It quickly spread from Palestine to Jewish communities dispersed throughout the Roman Empire. As for its spread to Iberia, a tradition attributes the evangelization of the Jews and Hispano-Romans in the first century to seven envoys sent by Peter and Paul from Rome: Torcuato, Tesifonte, Indalecio, Eufrasio, Cecilio, Hesiquio, and Segundo.[21] Nonetheless, there is insufficient evidence to state definitely when, how, and who evangelized Hispania. This obscurity can be attributed to the fact that in the West, the first converts were those least likely to leave testimony of their existence, that is, merchants and soldiers. For instance, the VII Gemina legion, based near Astorga, may have been a source for the spread of Christianity in Iberia, particularly after its return from Mauretania (modern-day Morocco). Its base in Hispania became the city of León (from *Legio*, legion). One of the first "Hispanic" martyrs was a member of this legion, Marcellus, a Christian Roman centurion who died in Tangier in 298 after refusing to sacrifice to the emperor.[22]

The advance of the Roman army helped unify the different areas of the empire and facilitated the movement of peoples and ideas throughout it. Unification was gained even while particular cultural practices and characteristics continued to unfold. In Hispania these factors, along with the growing contacts and interdependence of the Christian communities, aided in the formation of an autochthonous church and liturgy.

The second century also offers little in the way of concrete evidence of the spread of Christianity in Hispania. The first historical document that mentions the existence of Christians in Iberia is Irenaeus's *Adversus hæresis* I 3, written between 182 and 188. He claims that the power of the tradition is one and the same "throughout the world" despite the diversity of peoples and tongues with which the message has arrived. He continues by naming various peoples, including those in the "Iberias."[23] There is also some reference in traditions to small isolated communities in the more Romanized Iberian cities of the first and second centuries.[24] Clearly the church organization evident there in the third century did not arrive full blown but must have developed over time from the foundations set in the first two centuries. Christianity began to take root to such an extent that "by the latter second century AD Christian communities flourished in many parts of the empire. As yet the communities were disunited and many preached their own versions of the gospels."[25] Most important, the church in Spain should not be considered as imported but rather as a communion of churches emerging and developing over time as the result of multiple evangelizing efforts by diverse elements in various sites beginning in the first century. In Iberia, as in other parts of the empire, Christianity advanced alongside Romanization.[26]

The third century provides better evidence of organized Christianity in the peninsula, for by AD 254 there were substantial communities at Emerita (Mérida), Asturica (Astorga), Legio (León), and Tarraco (Tarragona). Tertullian in the first decades of the third century notes the presence of Christians at "all the borders of Hispania."[27] Christians in general had a network of bishoprics throughout the empire by this time. There are also records of church leaders consulting one another. For instance, in this period the bishops of Hispania looked to the bishops of Carthage and Rome for guidance in resolving disputes among themselves.[28]

Furthermore, the third century is marked by growing conflict between Christians and non-Christians. Christians attracted persecution by Roman authorities because of their attitudes and practices.[29] Christians were generally noted in this era for their withdrawal from everyday life, their refusal to compromise their beliefs by praying to the Roman traditional gods or paying homage to the emperor, and their notable intolerance of nonbelievers.[30] In addition, the western empire was racked by civil wars and separatist movements at this time.

Apparently Christians were blamed for much of the trouble and concerted persecutions against them were unleashed by the Roman emperors Decius and Valerian. Decius decreed at the end of 249 or the start of 250 that all persons participate in the sacrifices of the official religion and obtain certificates *(libelli)* verifying this. Christians who did so were seen as apostates and excommunicated until rehabilitated. Valerian unleashed an even more bloody and far-reaching persecution in 258. Cyprian of Carthage was a victim of this persecution, while in Hispania, Bishop Fructuosus of Tarraco and his deacons Augurius and Eulogius were burnt to death in 259 for refusing to recant their beliefs. Their feast is on 21 January both in the Hispano-Mozarabic and Roman liturgical calendars.[31]

Periodic persecutions were not able to wipe out the church. By the early fourth century Christian communities in Iberia were flourishing and able to deepen their interconnectedness. "In 305 a church council at Illiberis was attended by bishops from towns in all the Spanish provinces."[32] This council, the Council of Elvira, condemned pagan processions, sacrifices, and more obscene public spectacles. Such Christian opinions were considered divisive by the Roman authorities, and so between 303 and 312 Emperor Diocletian (245–313), at the instigation of the deputy Caesar Galerius, began major persecutions against the Christians once again.[33] Martyred, among others, were Saints Felix, Cucufatus, Eulalia, Justa, and Rufina.[34] Only Constantine's conversion in 312 changed this state of affairs.[35] The Edict of Milan promulgated by Licinius, Augustus of the East, on 13 June 313, officially signaled the change. Licinius had met with Constantine, Augustus of the West, and agreed to religious freedom. However, persecution ended only after Constantine defeated him for control of the empire in 324. Soon the church could worship fully and openly. Later it would take on political and administrative power in public affairs.

VISIGOTHIC TRIUMPH

Tensions in the far-flung empire had been growing over the course of the centuries as the Romans assimilated more territories. In addition, invasions by so-called barbarian tribes from northern and eastern Europe beginning in the second century and continuing into the fourth century contributed to destabilization. Among these "invaders" were the Goths, who originated either in what is now lower Scandinavia or upper Germany.[36] Some time in the first century they inhabited the lands east as far as the Baltic Sea. On the eastern bank of the central Vistula of

Sarmatia (now a region in modern-day Poland and western Russia) they formed the core of the barbarian forces that crossed the Danube into the Roman Empire in the last third of the second century. In the third century they were also known as Scythians due to their prominence in the region of the Caspian and Baltic seas on the outskirts of the eastern empire known as Scythia. In the Baltic region the Goths split into two main bands, the Ostrogoths (eastern Goths) and the Visigoths (western Goths).

The Visigoths requested permission to enter the empire in 376 due to an invasion of Huns into their territories.[37] Emperor Valens (364–78) gave the necessary permission for them to settle in Thrace, but due to acts of treachery on the part of Roman authorities, the Visigoths began to rampage in Thrace. Emperor Theodosius I (379–95) was able to bring them under control by means of a *foedus* (treaty of federation) in 382; however, it was annulled with his death in 395. In 397 a new *foedus* was established between the Romans and the Goths that made them federates or members of the Roman military forces. However, civil wars between Roman military and political officials after Theodosius precipitated a breakdown of Roman control. As a result, the Visigoths under their leader Alaric I (d. 410) left Thrace to continue their rampage, causing great consternation by sacking Rome in 410. Only Alaric's sudden death ended the rampage.

The Visigoths made their way to the Iberian Peninsula and attempted to go through it on their way to Africa. They were stopped by their inability to cross the Strait of Gibraltar and surrendered to the Romans in 416. Constantius, Roman commander-in-chief of the west, then gave them the task of stemming Hispania's attempts to break away from the empire.[38] The Visigoths not only lacked the ability of seafaring but were also suffering from hunger. They had to provide hostages from among the nobility in exchange for grain; they then set about their task with enthusiasm and success. They were also to fight against the Suevi, Vandals, and Alans who had invaded the peninsula in 409. As a reward, in 418 the Roman authorities settled the western Goths first in Aquitaine and eventually in Spain and Italy as *coloni* (freemen and settlers). The Visigoths continued to serve Roman interests as allies, but chaos in the western empire continued unchecked, offering them greater possibilities of establishing their own rule of the territory. The chaos culminated in the deposition of Emperor Romulus Augustulus in 476, effectively ending Roman control of the West. As a result, the Visigoths in southern Gaul wrested control away from Roman officials in 466. They eventually established their own reign over most of the Iberian Peninsula as well as portions of Gaul.

In the late fifth century Toulouse became the capital of the most powerful barbarian state. The Kingdom of Toulouse developed between 418 and 507; it began as a *patria Gothorum* (Gothic land) of Visigothic federates within the Roman Empire. By 507 it was an independent Visigothic kingdom known as the *regnum Tolosanum*. From here the relatively small band of Visigothic overlords ruled the Gallo- and Hispano-Romans who formed the majority of the population.[39] The Visigoths over the course of time began to take on cultural traits of the dominant Roman culture including language, law, and social organization. This helped them consolidate their rule over their Roman subjects. Furthermore, the kingdom was governed under two legal systems. The Romans were governed according to the *Codex Theodosianus*, a compilation of Roman law promulgated in 438 and modified in 475, whereas the Visigoth subjects were ruled by the traditional Visigothic laws.[40]

After the Visigoths began to rule the Romans in their territory, the traditional Gothic customs were no longer enough to mediate the problems posed by Goths and Romans living side by side. Various attempts to rule by law following the Roman model led to the development of the *Codex Euricianus* (475) by King Euric (466–84) and the *Breviarium Alaricianum* (506) by King Alaric II (484–507).[41] The Visigothic codification, also known as the *Lex romana visigothorum,* formed the basis for the governance of the kingdom and was amplified by the series of church councils held under Visigothic auspices in Agde and Toledo, among other places, between 506 and 711. The most important compilation of Visigothic law was the *Liber iudiciorum*, completed and promulgated by King Reccesvinth (c. 654). It formed the basis of governance for Mozarabs under Islam and under King Alfonso VI's *fuero* with the community.

During Alaric II's reign, Clovis, ruler of the Franks (481–511), pushed the Visigoths out of southern Gaul, taking their territory as far south as Barcelona.[42] King Amalaric (510–31) was able to regain from the Franks only the northern provinces of Spain, Septimania, and a portion of the province of Narbonensis. The Visigothic kingdom survived, but the new capital was reestablished at Toledo under King Leovigild (568–86). Henceforth the Visigothic kingdom would be referred to as an *imperium* and Toledo would be the *urbs regia* par excellence of the Spanish national myth, for from here the Visigoths extended their rule to other regions of Iberia, forming an empire centered in the royal city of Toledo. The memory of the unity attained under them would motivate the warlords of the Christian *reconquista* in later times.

As for religion, the Visigoths had been converted to Christianity by the Arian bishop Ulfilas while in Scythia and Dacia, outside of the Roman

Empire boundaries, beginning in 332.[43] As Arians they believed Jesus became divine only after his death and resurrection and therefore was subordinate to God the Father, whereas Catholics believed Jesus to be both human and divine from eternity and co-equal to the Father. This created conflict with their Catholic subjects, since at times they attempted to impose their Arian Christianity on the peoples they came to rule, for the Gothic king was head of the Arian tribal church; after assuming governance over the Roman territory in 418 he also became head of the Catholic church of his Roman subjects. At first the Goths were tolerant of the religious differences, but after 466 hostility between the Arian rulers and the Catholic hierarchy ensued. After the defeat of the Roman armies the Catholic hierarchy was the only Roman institution still functioning on a large scale. The Catholics linked their *Romanitas* to their faith, which created cultural as well as political conflict. The Visigothic rulers linked unity of their territories to unity of religion. Thus, King Leovigild attempted to convert the Catholics to Arianism but proved unsuccessful. The conflict was resolved only by his successor's conversion.[44]

A trait of the Visigothic rulers was their centralizing tendency. Because they perceived a need to maintain political unity in their Iberian and Gallic territories through religion, King Reccared (586–601) and his magnates, as well as the leading Arian Visigothic bishops of his kingdom, converted to the Catholic faith in 589.[45] Reccared's conversion marked the integration of Visigoths and Hispano-Romans into one common liturgy. I suggest this influenced Catholic church leaders to seek uniformity to some extent in the celebration of the Eucharist as well. Significantly, it was under Visigothic aegis that the Hispanic rite had its greatest development. Under their auspices Saint Isidore of Seville (560–636) and Saint Ildephonse of Toledo (c. 610–67), among others, reorganized the Catholic liturgy of ancient Hispania in an attempt to bring greater unity to the various usages throughout the peninsula. Two main traditions resulted, which have been simply called by scholars Tradition A from the northern territories of the kingdom and Tradition B from the southern.[46] During this era new rituals, euchology, and hymns were added to the liturgical rites. This creativity was brought to an abrupt end with the onset of the Islamic invasion in the early eighth century.

BYZANTINE INFLUENCE

After the Visigoths asserted control over the majority of the peninsula, the Byzantine emperor Justinian (527–65), harboring great imperial ambitions, desired to reconquer all the lost western empire lands from their Germanic masters.[47] The Byzantines at this time saw themselves as the continuation of the Roman Empire. Thus, Justinian annexed the former Roman provinces of Carthaginensis and Baetica to form the Byzantine province of Spania. Even though the Visigoths claimed the south, the aristocracy of the highly Romanized region had resisted their power, effectively limiting their control. This allowed the Byzantines to gain a foothold in the peninsula. Spania endured from 552 until c. 621 when it was reconquered by the Visigoths.[48]

It is not clear what relationship Catholic Hispano-Romans had with the Byzantine rulers in the southeastern area of the peninsula. Tradition B of the Hispano-Mozarabic liturgy, emerging from the south, must have incorporated some Byzantine cultural influences in its formation, given the notable similarities in the use of certain terminology, language, structure, and other traits.[49] Byzantium exercised great influence over parts of the former Western Roman Empire under Justinian in the sixth century. For instance, Saint Leander of Seville (550?–601?) and John of Biclar (c. 540?–c. 614?) presided over Toledo III (589). Both had spent much time in Constantinople before the council; surely this would have influenced them to some extent. This council marked the religious unification of the Visigothic kingdom as well as legislating important changes to the liturgy.

There are notable Eastern characteristics to the Hispano-Mozarabic rite, such as the use of a more involved prayer style and the early incorporation of the Symbol of Faith.[50] Perhaps the two most famous church leaders of this era Saint Leander of Seville and his brother Saint Isidore, may have been of Byzantine origin; after all, their names are Greek and they were born in Cartagena, a southeastern port city under Byzantine control then. Even so, Leander and Isidore were in the Visigothic camp although they may have been influenced by the Byzantines. Isidore in particular saw Gothic Hispania as the heir to the Roman Empire.[51]

Byzantine influence extended to court life among the Visigoths. Leovigild (568–86) was the first Visigothic king to use Byzantine regalia such as a crown, a scepter, and a throne. Even so, he campaigned unsuccessfully against the Byzantines in southeastern Spain in an attempt to recover that territory from them. The expulsion of the Byzantine rulers was left to a later successor, King Swintila (621–31). The conquest of Spania by the Visigoths "marked the very end of active Roman involvement in Iberia."[52] The expulsion of the Byzantine rulers led to greater political unity in most of the peninsula, adding this achievement to the religious unity that had been won earlier.

ISLAMIC INVASION

The accession to power in 568 of King Leovigild was "a development that turned the Visigothic *regnum* into a Spanish *imperium*" that would emerge as the most complete successor state to the Roman Empire.[53] This would all come crashing down with the remarkably swift and complete victory of Islamic invaders in 711. These invaders, recently converted North African Berber tribesmen, were evidently led by equally recently converted Syrian overlords as well as Arabs.[54]

The Islamic overlords called their new territory al-Andalus. This name may conserve the memory of the Vandals who had inhabited the peninsula and northern Africa, or it may refer to the Atlantic region.[55] Once the Arabs lost the northern territories of the peninsula, al-Andalus would signify southern Spain. Toledo remained a part of this region until 1085. The Islamic overlords firmly established control over the greater part of the Iberian Peninsula. Only slowly and intermittently was it reclaimed by the definitive Christian reconquest in 1492.

The invaders had also taken parts of southern Gaul by 720, but the Franks expelled them in 759 and eventually pushed them beyond Barcelona in the northeastern part of the peninsula. Pepin the Short, Charlemagne's father, was the leader of the Frankish forces. Louis the Pious, Charlemagne's son, took Barcelona in 801. This gave the Franks a foothold in northeastern Spain that would prove important to various Spanish rulers as well as to the *reconquista*. Over time, many French influences entered Iberia through this area. In addition, Christians in Cantabria and Asturias in the north successfully established a kingdom independent of Islamic control in 722.[56] The Christians were led by Pelayo (718–37), supposedly a grandnephew of King Rodrigo, the last Visigothic king. Pelayo's resistance initiated the *reconquista,* which took seven hundred years to complete. It also laid the foundation for the Kingdom of Asturias; today, the Spanish crown prince carries the title Prince of Asturias. King Alfonso I (739–57), Pelayo's son-in-law, developed and expanded the kingdom to include Galicia, northern Portugal, Cantabria, Alava, and La Rioja, all in the north. Eventually other pockets of resistance led to the establishment of small, mostly isolated Christian kingdoms in the north from east to west.

The Berbers also revolted against their Arab and Syrian leaders in 740, prompting a withdrawal of Islamic forces from northern Spain. Nonetheless, the Islamic forces were seldom challenged successfully between 711 and 1031. Notably, "Christian triumphs were in direct proportion to Muslim strength or weakness, the greatest advances being made when al-Andalus was torn by internal crises."[57]

At first the territory was ruled by an emir as deputy of the caliph in Damascus.[58] The Islamic rulers established their capital on the Guadalquivir River, first in Sevilla and then in Córdoba, about 716–17. As a result, Toledo lost its privileged position. It was too far away from the coast and thus from communication with Africa, though it continued to be one of the more important cities during the 374 years it was under Islamic control. In the meantime, the emirate of Córdoba became independent from Damascus in 756. After his victory over the Berbers, Abd al-Rahman I (756–88), a member of the Umayyad family that had been deposed in Syria from the caliphate, was proclaimed emir in Córdoba. This was a novelty because it meant the establishment of the first independent emirate in the Islamic world of the time not based on dogma but on political differences.

Through the seven hundred years they ruled in Spain, the Muslims experienced waves of religious reformers as well as conflicts among themselves. This allowed the emirate of Córdoba to become a caliphate in its own right, rivaling the splendor of Baghdad and Constantinople. Abd al-Rahman III (912–61) took the title caliph in 929. However, the unity of al-Andalus ended with the death of the Caliph Hisham III (1027–31) due to increasing rivalries among the Islamic warlords. The caliphate itself would disintegrate after Hisham's death into numerous petty Islamic kingdoms called *taifas*.[59] Toledo became such a kingdom in 1031 and remained one until 1085.

Early in the eleventh century there were about twenty-three *taifas*, falling into three broad categories representing different ethnic strains. The Berbers held the southernmost portion of the peninsula; the *saqaliba* (slaves of northern European origin who had integrated into Islam) held the eastern coast; while elsewhere, indigenous Arab, Berber and *muwalladun* (converts to Islam from among the general populace) elements assumed power. A tenuous balance of power ensued between the *taifas* and the expanding Christian kingdoms. This balance shifted decisively in favor of the Christians after the fall of Toledo in 1085.

As Islam advanced from the Middle East westward and finally into Iberia, the indigenous peoples in its way were usually forced to convert. Peoples defeated as the result of the *jihad* (holy war) were given the choice of death or conversion.[60] The Islamic conquerors directed this policy toward polytheists and idol worshipers in general. However, the Muslims saw Christians and Jews as "People of the Book" and therefore allowed them to retain their religion within limits as "protected minorities." Since they were monotheists with written scriptures venerated by

Islam, the Muslim conquerors did not force them to convert. As "protected people" *(dhimmi)*, they enjoyed some internal autonomy. While People of the Book is an Islamic notion used to refer to Christians and Jews, this terminology does not take into account the fact that their religions go beyond the Book to include tradition, liturgy, theology, dogma, and other aspects that distinguish them from Islam.

Christians and Jews had their own magistrates and laws. At first they continued to live dispersed among the Muslim population, but gradually the Christian minority was forced to live in special quarters, often outside city walls.[61] There were important Christian communities living under Islam in Toledo, Sevilla, Córdoba, and Mérida. Some Christians continued to live in rural areas. As for converts to Islam, they were called *musalim* (converts) and technically enjoyed equality with all followers of Islam before God and the law. Though before God and law all were equal, in reality there were class differences and a hierarchy of power. At the top were those of Arab descent. Many Christians of the ruling class who converted tended to take Arab tribal names and invent Arabic genealogies in order to help them retain their status. The majority of the *muwalladun*, however, formed the lower classes. Conversion was discouraged at first because the Jewish and Christian protected minorities had to pay a type of tax in order to retain their religions and laws.[62] Conversions meant a loss in revenues for Islamic overlords. Nonetheless, many did submit to Islam and, though at first assimilation was superficial, with time it became authentic to the point that soon the majority of the adherents to Islam were native Iberians.

Christians who chose to remain as such in the conquered territories, including Toledo, the city of our focus, were allowed by their Islamic overlords to continue practicing their religion and celebrating their Eucharist, but with numerous restrictions. Indeed, there is evidence that Christians continued to live under Muslim rule in Spain as late as 1492, when Granada, the last outpost of Islam in al-Andalus, was captured by King Ferdinand and Queen Isabel la Católica.[63] However, resident Christians in Granada after the thirteenth century would have been few due to the shifting of Mozarabs northward as refugees.[64] Islamic authorities may also have sent some Christians to Morocco to minimize the possibility of military threat to the Kingdom of Granada. Christians remaining would have been resident foreigners, merchants, slaves, political refugees, and/or Castilian nobles seeking the backing of the rulers of Granada.

Christians under Islam eventually came to be known as Mozarabs. Periodically, some of the Christians of southern Spain migrated to Toledo both during the Islamic domination and afterward, thereby augmenting and becoming integrated into the original Christian population there. Mozarabs who migrated to the northern kingdoms beyond Toledo were well received, for they were seen as descendants of the Visigoths. Not all the refugees stayed in Toledo; some passed through on their way to other newly reconquered territories where they could serve as settlers and acquire land. The northern kingdoms were often sparsely populated in comparison to the southern part of the peninsula. Therefore, northern rulers frequently provided Mozarab settlers with incentives to go to areas where they were much needed. Mozarabs fleeing al-Andalus from the ninth century onward formed an especially important element in the Christian kingdoms because they tended to take with them a higher level of learning, new artistic styles, and improved techniques of farming and craftsmanship. These they acquired from the more dynamic Arabic culture of the south. In the eighth through tenth centuries the rulers of these kingdoms idealized the Visigothic *imperium* in their ambition to form their own empire. This was particularly the case in Oviedo, where King Alfonso II of Asturias (791–842) made a conscious effort to restore the civil and ecclesiastical order of the Visigothic monarchy.[65]

Despite the growing influence of Islam on the population, the church's structure and activities did not disappear. During this period the Mozarab Christians were an active part of the church, adding, among other things, new saints and feasts to the liturgical year.[66] In Muslim Spain they had established eighteen sees and had more than twenty-two bishops during the height of the ninth century, whereas there were fewer than a dozen in Christian Spain during the same era.[67] Though not all the sees survived into later periods, many were reestablished and reorganized as Roman rite sees as the *reconquista* advanced. At least seven sees survived into the age of the *taifas*. The record shows there was a Mozarab bishop of Granada who attended the Council of Sahagún in 1118 and one in Seville in 1144. The last known Mozarab bishop of Toledo was consecrated at León in 1058.[68] The evidence shows that the Christian population of Muslim Spain was sizeable, perhaps 30 percent, well into the eleventh century.

Earlier we learned about census efforts to reestablish the existence of Mozarabs in Toledo, and how through the census they were deliberately connected only to certain churches. The background to this is that early in Toledo, Mozarabs continued to worship only in certain church buildings, for others were either converted into mosques or synagogues according to their location in the areas taken by the Muslims or assigned to the Jews.[69] The seven churches that originally housed Mozarabs under Islam were Santas Justa y Rufina (c. 554), Santa María de Alficén (c. 555), Santa Eulalia (559), San Sebastián (c. 601), San Lucas (c. 625), San Marcos (634), and San Torcuato (c. 700). Of these, only parts of the original Santa Eulalia and of Santas Justa y Rufina remain; these two have been reconstructed or refurbished to various degrees. These two church buildings were to house the descendants of the original six parishes sanctioned by Alfonso VI. One of the Christian churches, Santa María de Alficén, served as the "principal church" of the community for a while, although it was not in a Christian neighborhood. This church was not a cathedral per se, though it seems to have functioned in a way similar to a cathedral.

Many Mozarabs of Toledo commingled and intermarried with the Arab, Berber, and Syrian invaders. During the eighth to the eleventh centuries they took on Arabic culture, acquiring both its traits and language. Nevertheless, although Arabic was the daily language of public communication and the vehicle for the transmission of a culture that came to dominate the Christians of Toledo, the community worked hard to maintain its ancient Visigothic script and Latin language.[70] This was the result of the community's efforts at conservation and self-affirmation. This intermingling was not devoid of conflict, persecution, and even martyrdom. The Mozarabs of Toledo suffered great losses at the onset of the Islamic invasion, when some of the more prominent citizens suffered crucifixion.[71] In 797 hundreds and perhaps thousands were executed and their bodies dumped in a ditch prepared to receive them as a result of a revolt against Hisham I (788–96), emir of Córdoba. The uprising began in 792 and was occasioned by the heavy financial burdens placed on the residents of Toledo. It involved not only Mozarabs but Jews and the *muwalladun*. This event was called *la jornada del Foso* (the day of the Foss).[72]

The most famous instance of persecution resulted in the ninth-century martyrdoms that took place in Córdoba.[73] Both religious and laity suffered for their faith. More than fifty Mozarabs were martyred at Córdoba between 850 and 859, including Saint Eulogius (d. 859), presbyter, and Saint Leocritia (d. 859), virgin, commemorated in the Mozarabic calendar on 1 June. Persecutions began in 852 under Emir Abd al-Rahman II (822–52) and continued until 859 under his successor Mohammed I (852–86). This occasioned some of the more extensive migrations of monks, nuns, and laity to the northern reaches of the Iberian Peninsula, where they contributed to a revival of monasticism and to the intellectual life in the Christian kingdoms.[74] There they settled among Christians who had slowly begun to reconquer territory from the invaders. Mozarabs in the north represented a conservative tradition that looked with nostalgia to a happier past in the formation of the northern Christian states.[75]

It appears that contact with Islam also influenced some Mozarab theological notions, resulting in their being accused of Adoptionism, originally a second-century heresy that taught that Jesus was adopted as God's Son at his baptism.[76] The intermingling of Christians and Muslims resulted in the Mozarabic church suffering some deterioration in terms of tenets and fervor as the Christian minority emphasized beliefs in agreement with Islam while ignoring those on which they differed.[77] The extent to which this contact influenced the liturgy is examined later on.

Mozarabs of Toledo by the latter half of the eleventh century numbered about 15–25 percent of the city's population.[78] They had enjoyed some autonomy in terms of religious practice and self-governance under their Islamic overlords but had begun to experience more persecution and growing conflict. Mozarabs were experiencing growing persecution as King Alfonso VI laid siege to the city in 1085. It is no wonder they cooperated with Alfonso in the reconquest of Toledo, providing him with a decisive victory over the Islamic overlords and welcoming him joyously at his formal entry into the city on 25 May 1085.

AFTER THE RECONQUEST OF TOLEDO

The reconquest of Toledo offered new freedom to the Mozarab Christian population. King Alfonso VI's *fuero* helped them consolidate their identity by means of the privileges it granted. It also afforded them opportunities to advance economically and politically under the new regime and after. For example, in the thirteenth century Mozarabs, along with bilingual Jewish and Muslim scholars, formed the core of King Alfonso X's (1252–84) School of Translators at Toledo. This school translated and helped transmit the works of Aristotle, among other important works from the ancient world, to the rest of Western Europe.[79] It was one of the shining examples of the *convivencia*, the period in Spanish history in which members of the three religions, Christian, Jewish, and Muslim, lived side by side in relative harmony.[80] The freedom offered by the reconquest, however, would be a mixed blessing in terms of the Mozarabic liturgy, for it meant another check on its development.

3

Factors Affecting the Development of the Hispanic Rite

Based on information gathered through interviews, reading Mozarab literature, and investigating other sources, I have come to the conclusion that three main factors contributed to checking the development of the Hispanic rite. The first factor was the Islamic invasion beginning in the eighth century; the second was the assault on the Old Spanish rite by agents of Rome in the late eleventh century; and the third was the successful imposition of the Roman rite in the Christian realms beginning in the eleventh century. On the other hand, there were also mitigating factors that contributed to the rite's preservation and continuous celebration. In this section I give an overview of both sets of factors as a way to examine cultural traits that mark the Hispano-Mozarabic rite. The reconquest of Toledo by Alfonso VI is particularly key to understanding these factors in relationship to Mozarabs and the rite.

ISLAMIC RESTRICTIONS

The first factor checking the development of the Hispano-Mozarabic rite was the Islamic invasion and conquest of the Iberian Peninsula in 711. Although a band of Christians from the north asserted its independence from the Islamic overlords and eventually led to the *reconquista*, the majority of the Christian population and the religious hierarchy were situated in the areas dominated by the adherents of Islam. This created difficulties in the first years of the conquest for communication with the Christian West, although it did not prevent it. Communication with the Christian East was also temporarily stymied because all of North Africa, much of the eastern Mediterranean, and the Middle East had also recently been conquered by Islamic forces.[1] Furthermore, the Islamic authorities,

27

though tolerant to a certain degree of Christianity, prohibited the construction of new churches, the public display of faith such as the ringing of church bells, and proselytism of non-Christians.

Clearly, these prohibitions limited the ability of the rite to develop naturally and perhaps even contributed to an attitude of conservatism intended to prevent any further losses. Nevertheless, as territories were taken back by Christians in the north, some Christians from the south fled to liberated areas and in certain cases contributed to efforts at repopulation of abandoned towns, particularly in the Kingdom of León. Some of the most striking examples of Mozarabic church and monastic architecture can still be found in places such as San Cebrián de Mazote (Valladolid) and San Miguel de Escalada (León).[2] There they continued to celebrate their liturgy and eventually to resume its development. Consequently, partially due to pressure from Rome, councils dedicated to the rite's reform and development took place at León (1020), Coyanza (1055), and Compostela (1056).

EFFORTS TO IMPOSE THE ROMAN RITE

The second factor checking the development of the rite was the effort of Christian authorities in the reconquered north as well as outside of Spain to impose the Roman rite in all of the western Christian realms.[3] The liturgy of the Christians in the north throughout the early years of the Islamic conquest was the Old Spanish rite. Nonetheless, Charlemagne's efforts to impose a uniform liturgy following the model of Rome in the Frankish realms at the end of the eighth century made headway into the Catalan regions first during the ninth century, then eventually in the eleventh century to the other reconquered northern realms.

A partial reason was the alliances made by Iberian rulers with Frankish rulers and monks. In particular, King Sancho III, *el mayor* of Navarre (1000–1035), gained ascendancy over León, Castilla, and Aragón and encouraged the introduction of the Cluniac observance into the monasteries of his realms.[4] His son, Fernando I, king of León-Castilla (1035–65), pledged an annual tribute to Cluny as a measure of his devotion. Both men developed and improved the pilgrimage route to Compostela, bringing in thousands of French and northern Europeans to Spain and, of course, their influence with them. The process of change accelerated tremendously during the reign of Alfonso VI (1065–1109), who, like his father and grandfather, was very open to French influence, as his several

French wives and his friendship with Abbot Hugh the Great of Cluny attest.[5]

In addition, Mozarab Christian bishops had attempted to explain the divinity of Christ in a way that would make sense to Muslim scholars and authorities. This led Elipandus, archbishop of Toledo (d. 805), and Felix, Bishop of Urgell (d. 818), in particular, to explain Christ's divinity as the result of "adoption" by the Father. In their efforts they relied on the teachings of Saint Isidore and Saint Julian of Toledo as well as the texts of the liturgy itself. A charge of Adoptionism led to the trial of Elipandus at the Council of Frankfurt (795), where he was condemned for his teachings. Bishops from the Frankish realms as well as some Anglo-Saxon and Italian bishops attended. Elipandus refused to accept the council's condemnation and continued to teach that Christ was indeed adopted by the Father. Though the other Mozarab bishops rejected this Christology, the specter of Adoptionism contributed to the assessment by Roman authorities and other church officials in the West that the Old Spanish rite was of dubious orthodoxy.[6]

Consequently, the Christian rulers and church authorities of northern Spain accommodated to the Roman model. They did so both voluntarily and in response to pressure from Roman legates sent by Pope Gregory VII (1061–85). In Gregory's attempts to assert his authority over the Christian rulers of the West, liturgy became the battleground and the Cluniac reform of monasticism became the agent. Cardinal Hugh Candidus, known as the White, was the first known papal legate in the peninsula from 1065–68 under Pope Alexander II (1061–73); he raised concerns about the Mozarabic liturgy with King Fernando I. Later, other legates were sent under Pope Gregory VII. The latter's efforts were most successful in terms of the replacement of the Mozarabic rite by the Roman rite in 1080.

King Alfonso VI was generally well disposed to the imposition of the Roman rite and the Cluniac reform. Yet, Alfonso rebuffed Gregory's attempts to claim the Spanish realms as the patrimony of Saint Peter, as Gregory maintained. However, Alfonso's attitude toward the Mozarabic liturgy is illustrated by the duel that he arranged between two knights, one representing the Roman rite and the other the Mozarabic rite. The winner would show which rite was superior. The knight representing the Mozarabic rite won! Unconvinced, Alfonso had a bonfire lit in which the Roman and Mozarabic rite books were thrown in to see which would survive. After the Mozarabic rite book "leapt" out of the fire, Alfonso in anger kicked it back in. Thus, he was determined to impose the Roman rite in his realms.[7] For this purpose he called a council of his bishops and court at Burgos in Castile near the border with Aragon in 1080. In fact, Alfonso had already decreed the adoption of the Roman rite in his realms at Burgos in council with his bishops and royal court in May or June 1076. Unfortunately, the canons of this council have not survived, and apparently action was not taken on them until 8 May 1080, when the preamble to a charter of immunity to the monastery of Sahagún Alfonso VI confirms the adoption of the Roman rite.[8] The principal outcome of the council was the official abandonment of the Mozarabic rite.

THE SUCCESSFUL IMPOSITION OF THE ROMAN RITE

The third factor is related to the second. As part of Alfonso's program, he installed Cluniac monks in the monasteries of Silos and San Miguel de la Cogolla and charged them with promoting the change from the Old Spanish liturgy to the Roman. After Toledo was taken in 1085, he installed his friend Bernard de Sedirac, former abbot of Sahagún, as the archbishop. This marked the entry of a series of French prelates who took over the administration of the church not only in Toledo but in other cities of Alfonso's realm.[9] Mozarab church officials in the meantime were relegated to secondary roles. Despite the official abandonment of the Mozarabic rite, they were permitted to continue celebrating it. However, they could not become canons of the cathedral or take on roles of authority, such as the episcopacy, unless they renounced the Mozarabic rite and began to celebrate the Roman rite exclusively.

This, of course, led to a diminishment in the ranks of Mozarabic rite clergy. Nonetheless, once in positions of authority, some, such as Archbishop Gonzalo García Gudiel (1280–99), used their position to promote the conservation of the Mozarabic rite.[10] Even though not all ceased to be ordained for Mozarabs, their ranks continued to wane so that by the mid-fifteenth century there were few priests to minister to the community and fewer who could read well the ancient Visigothic script or copy it into new liturgical books. This was paralleled among the Mozarab laity, who over time began to integrate with the "Latins," that is, the Christians following the Roman rite. In addition, many left Toledo for newly reconquered territories where they sought to advance socially and economically. With time, Mozarabs remaining in Toledo from the eleventh century on were numerically too small to sustain the six parishes allowed to continue the celebration of their ancient liturgy. This clearly contributed to a profound disruption in the development of the rite that could only be reined in by a conscious effort on the part of church officials and prominent members of the community.

FACTORS CONTRIBUTING TO THE RITE'S PRESERVATION

Despite the factors working against the survival of the rite, there were overriding factors that contributed to its preservation and ongoing celebration. These factors are linked to the same factors working against the rite.

Conservative Impulse

The Islamic invasion and domination contributed to a conservative stance on the part of those who remained Christian over and against the new religion. Efforts were made to celebrate the liturgy as authentically as possible, even using the Latin language, although the Hispano-Roman and Visigothic Mozarabs eventually became primarily Arabic-speaking. Despite difficulties, texts written in the Visigothic script were recopied by scribes trained by the community over the centuries in order to be able to hand on their liturgical heritage. Indeed, the oldest extant manuscripts for the rite come from the period just before the end of the Islamic era in Toledo.[11] Some of this appears in the liturgical texts as will be seen later.

Manuscript Compilations

In addition, efforts at imposing the Roman rite in the reconquered areas of Spain led Mozarabs to compile their manuscripts in a form that would be acceptable to Roman authorities. In particular, the papal legate, Cardinal Hugh Candidus the White, raised the issue of the rite's orthodoxy to King Fernando I between 1065 and 1068. This resulted in the compilation of manuscripts into books that were sent along with a commission of bishops to Pope Alexander II for his review. The manuscripts found by Dom Marius Férotin at Silos in the late 1800s were those compiled for the delegation to Alexander II. The pope approved them, and the Mozarabic rite was given a brief reprieve. Despite various moves by Roman authorities threatening to suppress the rite, Mozarab church authorities were able to stave off this event until the Council of Burgos in 1080.

Alfonso's *Fuero*

The third factor, King Alfonso VI's desire to impose the Roman rite in his realms, was mitigated by the *fuero* he made with the Mozarabs of

Toledo.[12] This agreement was a type of contract made between rulers and various client groups granting the latter certain privileges in exchange for specific obligations to the king. Often communities granted a *fuero* were able to maintain a measure of autonomy. The king also committed himself to certain obligations and to the suspension of various regulations on behalf of the particular group thus honored.

Alfonso VI entered into such a *fuero*, the *Fuero Juzgo*, on 20 March 1101 with the Mozarabs of Toledo in order to ensure their cooperation and aid in the reconquest of other territories.[13] The retention of the Mozarabic liturgy was an indirect benefit of the agreement. But how was this possible, given the suppression of the rite by Burgos in 1080? Recall that at this time papal supremacy over royal authority was not yet consolidated. Much of Alfonso's ability to do as he pleased in this regard was due to the difficulties inherent in communication between Rome and himself in that era because of distance, travel delays, a movable court, and the need to make practical decisions for the welfare of his political aims.[14] Furthermore, the change in liturgical system also created a change in the system of benefices and the status of the minor clergy who would have been opposed to any changes having an impact on their welfare. The resulting misunderstandings, mutual dismay, and frequent oppositions would create further breakdown. This gave Alfonso and other rulers much leeway in terms of interpretation and implementation of commitments made to the papacy. Furthermore, Pope Gregory VII died at Palermo on 25 May 1085, the day King Alfonso VI entered triumphantly into Toledo.[15] Thus, Gregory's program of liturgical uniformity evidently suffered from a lack of follow-through on the part of Alfonso and his bishops.

Though not specified in the *fuero* itself, it is apparent that Mozarabs asserted their privileges and extended these to the continued celebration of the liturgy. In the first place, the *fuero* as a juridical code dealt only with city life of a purely civil nature; second, it would have appeared imprudent to contradict a manifest policy of Rome; and finally, de facto toleration of the Mozarabic liturgy by overlooking it gave custom a chance to provide it legal sanction through its status as customary law *(lex consuetudinis)*.[16] Anecdotal evidence indicates that the community argued for the conservation of its rite based on the fact that it was this liturgy that sustained its Christian faith during 374 years of Islamic domination and suffering.[17] To claim that it was not an authentic and orthodox Christian liturgy was perceived as an affront to the community.

Already distinguished in dress, language, and culture, Mozarabs "seized upon their liturgy as a symbol of the values of the old Hispanic and Visigothic tradition and as a distinguishing mark of their social and religious community."[18] The six extant Mozarabic parishes were the sine qua non of a vital liturgy. At the time of the reconquest of Toledo, Alfonso VI reaffirmed their status, making Mozarabs and their descendants parishioners *in perpetuum* of them. As part of this reaffirmation, as we learned earlier, Mozarabs were to take responsibility for the parishes' sustenance and maintenance through the system of *tazmías* and *diezmos*.

These requirements were spelled out in the *Carta Mozarabum* and reaffirmed by King Alfonso VI's successors until the reign of King Fernando VII (1815).[19] Alfonso authorized the community to continue governing itself according to the ancient Visigothic code that it had been following prior to the reconquest of Toledo. As a result the community had its own *alcalde* (mayor), municipal officers, and magistrates. In regards to this, the 1999 *Constitutions* of the *Hermandad* declare: "In this way there emerged a historico-liturgical community, unique in the West, defined by its common Hispano-Visigothic origin and the personal subscription of its members to the parishes of their traditional rite, for whose splendor and conservation they were responsible and which they maintained by their tithes."[20]

SUBSEQUENT EVENTS AFFECTING THE RITE'S SURVIVAL

All of the above factors laid the groundwork for three key events in the history of the church of Toledo that have contributed to the rite's conservation for posterity. In particular, the reform of Cardinal Francisco Ximénez de Cisneros in the early sixteenth century in order to save the rite, the renewal of liturgical books by Cardinal Francisco Antonio de Lorenzana in the early nineteenth century, and the actualization of the rite by Cardinal Marcelo González Martín at the end of the twentieth century have served to keep the rite alive. Although these efforts are attributed to these distinguished churchmen,[21] in reality we have seen how very much the efforts of previous church leaders and the collaboration of select cathedral canons, of the Mozarabs of Toledo itself, and of the clergy assigned to them aided them in promoting the rite's survival.

Early Efforts to Save the Rite

Archbishop Gonzalo García Gudiel of Toledo (1280–99), a Mozarab by blood, was concerned enough about the grave circumstances of the rite at the end of the thirteenth century to entrust Joffré de Loaysa, archdean of Toledo, with the renewal of the Mozarabic clergy and the

copying of new liturgical books, giving new life to the Mozarab community and its rite.[22] Another humanist, Juan Vásquez de Cepeda, bishop
of Segovia (1398–1437), had attempted in the first half of the fifteenth
century to save the rite by leaving in his will benefices for the creation of
a chapel at Santa María de Aniago where the divine office could be celebrated.[23] He claimed that the rite was suffering from neglect and that
those charged with its celebration in Toledo had forgotten the chant and
even how to celebrate the rite correctly. The intended chapel was to be
staffed by Roman rite clergy and sacristans, as was the case in Toledo
later under Cisneros. Unfortunately, due to insufficient funds as well as
a lack of connection to any living Mozarab community, these efforts
failed. The continued deterioration of the rite was also a concern of
Archbishop Alonso Carrillo of Toledo at the Synod of Alcalá (1480).[24]
He decried the great decadence that had befallen the rite due to the fact
that the benefices destined for the celebration of the rite had been assigned to uninterested clerics. He attempted to correct this situation by
reforming the system of benefices. These actions, among others, laid the
groundwork for Cisneros's reform in 1500–1502.

Reform of 1500

Cisneros took over the see of Toledo in 1495. A Franciscan who had
begun his clerical life as a secular cleric for Toledo, he was imbued with
the humanist ideals being generated in the early Renaissance throughout
Europe at this time.[25] A trait of this era was the idealization of classical
culture, literature, and history. During a visit to the Capitular Library of
the cathedral in 1497, Cisneros was shown ancient Mozarabic liturgical
books and manuscripts in Visigothic script. He was so impressed that he
ordered these taken to his personal library in order to examine them
more closely. It is likely that this occasioned his decision to make known
and available to scholars and others the texts of the divine office and
Mass. To facilitate this he had them published by means of the printing
press, a newly available technology. The first Missal appeared in 1500
and the first Breviary in 1502. Such was Cisneros's interest in the advance-
ment of learning that three other literary monuments were published or
initiated under his direction, namely, the *Missale Mixtum* of Toledo
(1499), the first to be printed for the diocese rather than be hand copied;
the *Complutensian Polyglot Bible* (1503), considered the finest of its
time; and the *Misal Rico*, the last illuminated Missal of Toledo (1518).

The task of reform was spearheaded by canon Alfonso Ortiz (c. 1445–
1507), doctor in canon and civil law, and employed by Cisneros's predecessor, Cardinal Pedro González de Mendoza (d. 1495),[26] confessor to

Queen Isabel la Católica. Ortiz took pains to claim he was an Old Christian. Given the times and place, this implied both connection to Mozarabs, who had maintained Christianity over the centuries, as well as distinction from the newly converted Jews. It is not clear how he became interested in liturgical matters; however, it is clear that time spent in Rome at the onset of the vibrant Italian Renaissance inspired his interest in classical literary works.[27]

Apparently Ortiz had already begun work on Mozarabic codices under Cardinal Mendoza. When Cardinal Cisneros took over, it made sense that he be assigned the task not only of publishing the texts but also of reforming the rite according to the norms set out by Cisneros. Ortiz lays out the five general norms underlying the reform in the *Prefatio* to the Missal. These include the identification of extant codices, the license to edit and rewrite according to the original style, the excision of material deemed to be inauthentic or recent in source, the formatting of the text in a logical manner, and the printing of the liturgical books in an accessible form, namely, in Latin characters rather than Visigothic.[28] However, Ortiz had also been assigned by Cisneros the task of correcting and publishing the new Roman rite *Missale Mixtum* for the church of Toledo at the same time. This Missal was published in June 1499, about seven months before the new Mozarabic Missal. To accomplish the first task he relied heavily on the help of three Mozarab pastors, Antonio Rodríguez of Santas Justa y Rufina, Alfonso Martínez of Santa Eulalia, and Jerónimo Gutiérrez of San Lucas.

The resulting liturgical books reflected Cisneros's plan of reform including the selection of the texts and order of worship of Tradition B attributed to Saint Isidore. It seems this choice was made based on the status of Saint Isidore in the universal church as well as the interests of Cisneros and Ortiz to stress the antiquity of Spanish literary works: "The writers and patrons of the Iberian Peninsula, without diminishing their admiration for the authors born in the other Mediterranean peninsula, would respond by reclaiming the heritage of the great Visigothic Fathers as an example of their national patrimony."[29] For this reason Saint Isidore is given pride of place in the colophon to the titles of the Missal and Breviary, which reads *secundum regulam beati Isidori*. Cisneros desired to claim the recovery of the Mozarabic rite as a patrimony for Spain and save it for posterity; he saw the establishment of a chapel and corps of chaplains as a way to ensure this. Another Ortiz, Blas Ortiz, asserts that just as the Italians saw the Renaissance as the recovery of their Latin classical heritage, so Cisneros and his ilk, perhaps inspired by nationalism, sought the recuperation of the glories of Hispania, one of which was the ancient Hispano-Mozarabic liturgy.[30]

Renewal of 1775

Lorenzana became archbishop of Toledo in 1772 after serving as the twenty-fourth archbishop of Mexico City (1766–70). During his time in Mexico, Lorenzana showed an interest in things Mozarabic. This resulted in the publication of the *Missale Omnium Offerentium* in 1770. After his return to Spain he published a new edition of the Mozarabic Breviary in 1775.[31] It is significant that he was studying the Mozarabic rite while in Mexico, for I have heard of the existence at one time of a Mozarabic chapel in the cathedral of Mexico City. Although I have been unable to verify this after enquiry in Mexico and Toledo, it is plausible that Lorenzana established a chapel there during his brief term as archbishop, given his interest in things Mozarabic. During his regency in Toledo he published a new edition of the Mozarabic Breviary in 1775 and made improvements to the Mozarabic chapel.[32] After Lorenzana went to Rome at the request of Pope Pius II, he began a new edition of the Mozarabic Missal that was completed and published at his expense in 1804, the year of his death. Because of his death and various political difficulties of the era, the Missal did not get to the Mozarabic chapel in Toledo until around 1898. In fact, only through much effort by the Mozarabic chaplains did the Missal as revised by Lorenzana get there at all. Parts of the original 1804 edition were lost after 1936 and were only rediscovered in 1975 in a cabinet.

It appears that, like Cisneros, Lorenzana was motivated by the intellectual currents of his time, particularly the Enlightenment in Lorenzana's case. While the church in general rejected the propositions of the Enlightenment, some of its ideas exercised great influence on Spanish society, particularly under King Carlos III (d. 1788), until the French Revolution (1789) and its aftermath. The Enlightenment came to be called the Christian Enlightenment *(la Ilustración Cristiana)* in Spain.[33] This period, like the Renaissance of Cisneros's time, was another important era of intellectual curiosity and expanding of culture. In intellectual circles, rationalism and scientific methods were stressed, and greater emphasis was given to history and the uncovering of the sources of current cultural artifacts in all of their aspects. It was also a period of French cultural ascendency and eventual domination in Spain.[34] Lorenzana's motivation was to assert the Hispanic cultural heritage as encased in the Mozarabic liturgy as well as to replace the older Latin-Gothic typeset of the Cisneros edition, since it was no longer easily read by the users.[35] In addition, the work of Alexander Lesley, S.J. (d. 1758) in Rome (1755), with which Lorenzana was familiar, revealed grammatical and orthographic errors in the Latin, at least as then used. Lesley also raised questions as to the authenticity of some of the orations.

Like his predecessor, Lorenzana depended on the collaboration of others in order to renew the liturgical books and thereby effect changes in the celebration of the rite. In particular, he assigned Faustino Arévalo the task of re-editing the Breviary and Missal while incorporating Lesley's work.[36] Lesley's work was the result of scholarly study and not meant for celebration. Even so, it constituted an important basis for Lorenzana's program of renewal. As part of this effort, Arévalo was also assigned the task of examining the various texts and codices available in order to make corrections. A result of this was the identification and placement in the Appendix to the Missal of some of the prayer formulas devised by Ortiz. Overall the renewal effected by Lorenzana was not major in that he did not engage in extensive reform of the rite. Yet publication of new books facilitated and updated celebration in the Mozarabic chapel and parishes, thus happily making the rite available to hand on to future generations.

Actualization of 1988

González Martín came to the see of Toledo in 1972 after having served as archbishop of Barcelona (1967–72). Like Cisneros and Lorenzana before him, his efforts also reflect the intellectual and religious ambience of his time. For González Martín this means especially the influence of Vatican II, which he had attended as a council father while bishop of Astorga (1961–66).[37] Vatican II's openness to the modern world with its diversity of cultures provided the framework, and its openness to culture could be seen foremost in the liturgical renewal. González Martín took wholeheartedly to the implementation of the liturgical renewal.[38] Indeed, he saw himself as a liturgist, serving as chair of the Liturgical Commission of the Spanish Episcopal Conference.

As archbishop of Toledo (1972–95), González Martín not only became primate of Spain but also the ecclesiastical superior of the Mozarabic rite. Once in Toledo he was encouraged by Don Francisco de Sales Córdoba and other key Mozarabs together with their pastors, Don Jaime Colomina Torner and Don Balbino Gómez-Chacón, to work toward the actualization or updating of the ancient Spanish liturgy still alive in Toledo. Efforts toward its actualization had begun in the 1950s under the direction of Don Anastasio Granados García.[39] He was the pastor of San Marcos at the time; eventually he was made an auxiliary bishop of Toledo and then bishop of Palencia. Together with the pastor of Santas

Justa y Rufina, he published a small tract entitled "Los Mozárabes de Toledo" in 1955 that presented historical facts about the community. This apparently inspired members to work toward the reorganization of the community as well as the actualization of its rite.

González Martín, for his part, established the Instituto de Estudios Visigótico-Mozárabes de San Eugenio in 1977. The institute is dedicated to the study and publication of materials related to the Old Spanish rite. Don Jaime Colomina Torner was elected president of the institute.[40] Encouraged by the work of the institute, González Martín proposed the idea of revitalizing and updating of the rite to the Spanish Episcopal Conference. Colomina Torner reveals that Cardinal James Knox, former Prefect of the Congregation for Divine Worship, originally presented this idea at the First International Congress of the Institute in 1975.[41] The conference charged González Martín with accomplishing this task. Thus in 1982 he named a commission of twenty members to examine and revise the liturgical books for the Hispano-Mozarabic rite.

González Martín also inspired and promoted study days and international congresses dedicated to the Hispanic liturgy. The congresses were organized in 1975, 1985, and 1989. The First International Congress (1975) was dedicated to Mozarab history and addressed topics as diverse as the *convivencia*, the Mozarabic "cathedral" of Santa María de Alficén, and the work of Cisneros.[42] The Second International Conference (1985) addressed the role of King Alfonso VI and the reconquest of Toledo as well as its impact on the Mozarabic community and its rite.[43] The Third International Conference (1989) was linked to the fourteenth centenary of the Third Council of Toledo and examined the Visigothic conversion to Catholicism and its import for the Spanish church of the late twentieth century.[44] The most important action undertaken by González Martín on behalf of the Hispano-Mozarabic rite was the *Jornadas sobre Liturgia Hispánica*, a series of study days in March 1983. At this event Dom Jordi Pinell, president of the commission charged with the revision of the rite's liturgical books in 1982, presented his work on the *ordo missæ* and convinced those present of the merits of not only a restoration but a purification of the rite.[45]

González Martín clearly states that his reasons for the actualization of the Hispano-Mozarabic rite were linked to the liturgical-pastoral motives that led to the liturgical reform of Vatican II, "so that the faithful participate fully, actively and consciously in the liturgical celebrations."[46] He also states that he applied the principles of the reform to the Hispano-Mozarabic rite so that it would acquire new vigor and, therefore, "make it possible for a worthy celebration of the Mysteries of the Lord."[47] Also, it seems that González Martín's actualization was motivated by a resurgence in a sense of *lo nuestro* (that which is ours) inspired by *Sacrosanctum Concilium* and its express openness to "the genius and talents of the various races and peoples" (no. 37). Attention paid to the rite by study days, congresses, and the publication of new liturgical books is evidence of a great pride in the Spanish liturgical heritage.

González Martín's actualization has potentially more far-reaching effects for the rite than those wrought by Cisneros or Lorenzana. First, the modern means of communication and publication effected by an era of globalization have made it easier to make known the efforts toward its full restoration. Second, the permission granted for the rite's celebration throughout Spain and even elsewhere lays the groundwork for its celebration by a wider population. Third, the renewed cultural self-awareness of Mozarabs offers the possibility that people for whom the rite exists will take the celebration and give it the renewed vigor desired by González Martín.

FACTORS THAT HAVE AFFECTED
THE COMMUNITY'S SURVIVAL

There is much hope for the renewed vigor in the celebration of the rite. Nevertheless, the rite cannot continue without a viable community to celebrate it. There are certain factors that have made the Mozarab community's survival precarious even to this day. These include the history of integration of the community's members with the larger society, political turmoil resulting in the loss of privilege, and the recent suffering of the Spanish Civil War.

Blending into the Greater Population

The reconquest of Toledo provided for the intermingling of Mozarabs with coreligionists from the Kingdom of León-Castilla who had accompanied King Alfonso VI to Toledo. In addition, over the course of time many Mozarab families disappeared or forgot their origins. From the eleventh century on the Mozarab population of Toledo decreased in size to the extent that by the fifteenth century it could only sustain two parishes. The people who attended services in the other parishes were mostly from the surrounding neighborhoods and were generally Roman rite. Thus, in response to their needs, the Roman rite was also introduced into the Mozarab parishes sometime during the thirteenth century.[48] The Roman rite eventually replaced the Mozarabic rite in four of the six parishes. In the case of the other two parishes, the Roman rite was also introduced, but they had sufficient Mozarab parishioners so that the Mozarabic rite persisted in them.

Due to the continued shifting population and the need to close dilapidated buildings, in the mid to late 1800s the Archdiocese of Toledo engaged in a general reorganization of all the parishes in the *casco antiguo* (city core).[49] Those that had fewer members were combined with those that had more. It was at this time that the church building of Santa Eulalia was closed because it was deteriorated and there were not enough parishioners. The parish was combined with San Marcos and San Torcuato and eventually began to meet in the vacated parish church of the Calced Trinitarians. The original San Marcos was built in 634 but was in such bad repair that it had to be torn down at the beginning of the nineteenth century; the Trinitarians, whose church had been built in 1630, had been forced to leave Toledo, thus making their church available. The parish was popularly called San Marcos and was a combined Roman and Mozarabic rite locale. Only the parish of Santas Justa y Rufina was able to maintain its original site, although the church building, built around 554, underwent extensive renovations to accommodate the Roman rite and the increased number of parishioners. Thus a situation that had developed over time was formalized; in effect, all the Mozarab parishes became Roman rite.

Mozarabs, however, did not disappear. References in direct and indirect ways are made to them or to their parishes at various times. For instance, as noted above, the sixteenth-century reform by Cisneros relied on three pastors ministering in Mozarabic parishes. Also, Sixto Ramón Parro in his nineteenth-century guidebook on Toledo makes references to them as well.

We have seen Mozarabs' long history of acculturation to the dominant society. This is evident today in their having blended into contemporary Spanish society for the most part. They are justifiably concerned about their "invisibility." There is tension between their conservatism, which has helped them survive as a distinct ethnic group, and their history of blending in. This is not easy to resolve, given their status as a minority.

Political Turmoil in the 1800s

The nineteenth century was chaotic for Spain. It marked the end of the Old Regime with its privileged few and the introduction of Liberalism in government imbued with the ideals of the Enlightenment. Yet the forces of social and political development in the form of progressive government and a capitalist economy were held back by the forces of "enlightened despotism" and repression by the crown, which asserted its absolute sovereignty. The century included a series of competing governments, coup d'états, uprisings, riots, civil wars, and revolutions. It began with an invasion by Napoleon, led to the War of Independence from France, continued with the loss of the majority of Spain's overseas territories, and ended with the Spanish-American War. Spain fell from the heights of world power into the backwaters of history.[50]

The Spanish government confiscated church property because it claimed it was being held as unused wealth. In 1835–37 Juan Álvarez y Méndez (called Mendizábal), one of the prime ministers to hold office during the reign of Queen Isabel II (1833–68) while her mother Queen María Cristina (1833–40) was regent, engaged in this policy with great vigor. Many priceless art objects, liturgical implements, and ancient illuminated manuscripts were taken and placed in private or government collections. Religious orders of men and women suffered suppression. During Mendizábal's regime various religious orders, including the Jesuits and Trinitarians, were expelled from Spain.[51] The secular clergy and hierarchy lost their privileged status and became wards of the state. This action, called the *desamortización* (divestment),[52] created great difficulties for the church until a concordat was signed with the government in 1851. As part of this action, the system of sustenance of church properties and clergy was eliminated.

The long practice of recording the names of Mozarab families in the *tazmías* came to an end because they were no longer obligated to contribute to the parishes of their origin. Already after 1714, King Felipe V (1700–1724, 1724–46) began to curtail severely the system of privileges created by the *fueros*. Most of the nobles and hidalgos lost their rank as the Bourbon kings of Spain centralized their government and consolidated their power over the nobility and the church during the eighteenth and nineteenth centuries. Today most titles of nobility are honorary and carry no special privileges.[53] As a result of Mendizábal's *desamortización*, the one formal means of identifying the actual members of the Mozarab community ceased, although periodically Mozarabic pastors tried to keep records of their parishioners until the Civil War. Attempts to reconstruct these helped in the taking of the census of the community in 1958. The Mozarabs' privileged status ended too.

All these factors challenged the community's survival. The members are still recovering from the results of the *desamortización* since their numbers were reduced so drastically afterward, at least in terms of self-identification as Mozarabs. Only very slowly are those descended from Mozarabs reappropriating this identity.

The Spanish Civil War and Afterward

Another painful chapter in the Mozarabic community's history oc-curred during the Spanish Civil War (1936–39) when most of the churches in Toledo were closed either due to damage or to the disruption in the life of the church caused by the war. Thus, beginning with the end of the Old Regime in 1836 and culminating in the Civil War of 1936, Mozarabs suffered great degradation and alienation, including martyrdom. In To-ledo alone, 286 priests were killed, including all of the Mozarab chap-lains, and most of the contemplative nuns were exclaustrated.[54] The Span-ish Civil War still causes great disquiet for the people of Spain; in particular, those who were religious in nature were subject to great suf-fering and persecution. However, Santas Justa y Rufina stayed closed for only four months after war broke out in November 1936 and, as a re-sult, was able to house the parishioners of San Marcos and Santa Eulalia until around 1954. After repairs had been made, the San Marcos parish-ioners were able to return to their building. Nevertheless, the number of parishioners decreased as members continued to move out of the *casco antiguo* and fewer Mozarabs participated in Mozarabic rite liturgies other than on special occasions.

Because San Marcos was housed in the largest church building in the old city, and the parishioners were unable to sustain its maintenance, the Archdiocese of Toledo agreed to refurbish the old church building of Santa Eulalia for the Mozarab community. The name of the parish was changed to Santa Eulalia y San Marcos, and it began to celebrate the Mozarabic rite Mass on a more frequent basis once again in 1967. Years later, old San Marcos was taken over by the city of Toledo and officially reopened in 1999 as a new city arts facility.

It has taken a long time for the community to recover from the clos-ing of parishes and the suffering caused by the Spanish Civil War. Given the general secularization of Spanish culture since the Civil War, it re-mains to be seen whether or not Mozarabs will be able to maintain strong links to their parishes. I have celebrated with them at Santa Eulalia on various occasions throughout the years and have noted that very few participate in the Mass. The one exception is the Triduum, when more attend the services. Even then, those who participate in the Good Friday procession are greater in number than those who participate in the Good Friday services. This indicates to me that the liturgy is more important to them as a source of signification than as an opportunity to practice their "Mozarabic-Catholic" faith liturgically. The liturgy, in other words, is only a part of what it means to be Mozarab. Nonetheless, their par-ticipation in the liturgy, albeit periodically, is an important way they construct and foster their cultural identity, as we will see as we examine the ritual use of the Lignum Crucis.

Mozarabs of Toledo maintained a sense of identity as a distinct ethnic group not only through 374 years of Islamic domination but also through the over 900 years of marginalization caused by the imposition of the Roman rite after the reconquest. How were they able to do this? At first Mozarabs represented a conservative tradition that looked with nostalgia to a happier past for those forming the Christian states of the north. Mozarabs were seen as descendants of the Visigothic *imperium*, idealized by the northern rulers as they sought to establish a new empire. Though this ideal waned with the ascendancy of the Castilians in the tenth and eleventh centuries, Mozarabs held to the rule of law they had inherited from the Visigoths, the *lex iudiciorum*. King Alfonso VI's *fuero* reaffirmed this privilege. This provided Mozarabs with the necessary sanction to preserve their distinctiveness. Thus, the Islamic domination as well as the *reconquista* fostered conservatism among them, a value upheld by them still today. Their *conservadurismo* (strong conservatism) has contributed to their survival to this time.

In addition, the Mozarabic parishes of Toledo function as the source of their identity. Though the Mozarab population diminished in size in the ancient core of the city where the parishes were located, a sufficient number of members of the community, wherever they resided, continued to identify themselves with the six parishes. They also claimed political and ecclesiastical rights as members of the Mozarab community. Clearly the system of *tazmías* and *diezmos* helped them identify with the parishes. This was further enhanced by the handing on of family histories from generation to generation.

Nowadays Mozarabs are constructing contemporary Mozarab culture by stressing historical events with which they identify. Their work on genealogies, the *tazmías*, scholarly and popular articles, as well as *cabildo* meetings, *capítulos*, and periodic congresses help them find common meanings, directions, and growth. They are banding together and distinguishing themselves over and against their contemporaries in Spain by championing the Hispano-Mozarabic liturgy, by extending the influence of the *Hermandad Mozárabe* to those who identify themselves as Mozarabs, and by claiming their rights under church and civil law. They look to those in the past who acted similarly in the face of first Visigothic Arians, then Islam, and finally Roman rite Christians. This has inspired them to rally around the Hispano-Mozarabic liturgy, which they claim as theirs.

Cisneros's efforts clearly contributed to the preservation of the rite, at least a certain version of it. The edition of liturgical books and the establishment of the Mozarabic chapel in the cathedral with its corps of Roman rite priests designated for the celebration of the liturgy assured this. Nonetheless, although the books were also meant for use in the Mozarabic parishes, focus and responsibility for the rite shifted to the chapel and its chaplains, thereby effectively wresting control over the rite from the parishes and Mozarabs. This is still true today. This shift may have also contributed to a further turning away from the rite in the parishes as it came to be celebrated in only two of them and only on special occasions until recently.

It has been primarily by forming a proud, dedicated, and identifiable Mozarab community in Toledo that the leaders of the community and certain of its members have been able to inspire individual clerics assigned to it. Together they have turned to the rite as a way to construct who they are as Mozarabs, and this has helped the rite survive among them despite the ups and downs in the frequency of its celebration and periodic reformulations resulting from the work of scholars and religious elites. The efforts of Lorenzana and González Martín were primarily aimed at the Mozarabic chapel and perhaps motivated by the desire to assert Spanish nationalism. Even so, Mozarabs asserted themselves to ensure that they would not be excluded. Indeed, in terms of the latest restoration, individual Mozarabs have contributed greatly to the study, publication, and diffusion of the texts. These texts have meaning because of their relationship to the living, worshiping community for which they are destined.

4

The Hispano-Mozarabic Rite
and Its Evolution

On Good Friday the Mozarabic community is most visible, and through the rituals of this day it manifests and helps construct its identity. The contemporary celebration of Good Friday in the Hispano-Mozarabic rite represents a recovery of ancient rituals coupled with a development of the rite that has unfolded over time, a recovery and development that is particularly evident in the ritual use of the reliquary of the Lignum Crucis. So in this chapter I begin to present the liturgical context of the Hispano-Mozarabic Good Friday events in order to set the stage for analyzing the Lignum Crucis.[1] But first we look at the history of the liturgy in the West and the interrelationship between the Spanish liturgy and the two liturgies most closely related to it—the Roman and the Gallican.

LITURGIES OF THE LATIN WEST

As the historical survey of the previous chapter reminds us, there were nearly seven hundred years of continuous Roman involvement in the Iberian peninsula beginning in 264 BC and ceasing only when definitive Visigothic rule was established in AD 415. Romanization left its mark on many aspects of Iberian life, including governmental, social, and cultural institutions. Hispano-Roman civilization was a unique blend of the cultures of those already existing in the peninsula and the culture imposed from authority centered at Rome.

By the time Caracalla granted Roman citizenship to all residents of the empire in AD 212, the Romanization of the Hispanic peoples, and therefore also the citizens of Toledo, was completed in a legal sense. The adoption of Roman names, customs, and language took longer.

Nonetheless, a large number of Iberians considered themselves Roman in many ways by the time of the Visigothic triumph in the fifth century, not least of all in their Christianity. Thus, it is appropriate to refer to them as Hispano-Romans. The growth of the Hispano-Roman church was exemplified in many ways by the renown of the Council of Elvira (c. 314) and the influence of one of its bishops, Hosius of Córdoba (d. 357). Hosius not only was an advisor to the Emperor Constantine (d. 337) but presided in the emperor's name at the Council of Nicea (325).[2] Certainly, the *acta* of the Hispano-Roman and Visigothic councils of the fourth, fifth, and sixth centuries reveal a church in touch with the wider communion of Catholic churches while especially adhering to the Apostolic See.[3]

The third and fourth centuries witnessed great development in the celebration of the Eucharist among Christians, resulting in the formation of various liturgical families. So, for example, the Latin West saw the rise of various Latin-language liturgies between the fifth and seventh centuries.[4] Though this book concentrates on only one of these rites, the Hispano-Mozarabic, there are significant affinities between it and the other Latin liturgical families. This is particularly true of the Roman and Gallican rites in terms of common evolution, structure, memorial, and soteriology.

Hispano-Mozarabic Liturgy

The development of the Hispano-Mozarabic rite was a slow process that had its greatest unfolding during the Visigothic era in the sixth and seventh centuries.[5] The *acta* of the third and fourth councils of Toledo, conducted under the auspices of King Reccared (586–601) and King Sisenand (631–36), give clear evidence of this.[6] Three metropolitan sees had the greatest influence on the development of the rite: Seville, Tarragona, and Toledo.[7] Three bishops, Saint Leander (c. 540–600), Saint Isidore (c. 560–636), and Saint Ildephonse of Toledo (c. 610–67), especially contributed to its formation. Notably, Toledo III (589) was presided over by Saint Leander, whereas Toledo IV (633) was presided over by Isidore.

The *prenotanda* to the *Missale Hispano-Mozarabicum* of 1991 indicate that various sociocultural factors contributed to the evolution of the rite (no. 3). First of all, there was the overall synthesis of Roman cultural values and organization particularly maintained in the highly Latinized zones of the peninsula. By the time the Visigoths had triumphed in Spain, they had already absorbed many of the same Roman cultural values and patterns of organization. This helped form a solid cultural base of language and values that provided the Spanish church with the opportunity to develop its liturgy. Second, a relative religious peace was obtained through the official conversion of the Visigoths from the Arian to the Catholic faith.[8] Third, the Visigothic court generated a Latin humanism that flourished in the work of the Iberian fathers, such as Saint Braulio of Zaragoza (d. 631). A creative period resulted in terms of arts and letters as well as the composition of music that contributed greatly to the liturgy.[9] Fourth, the *acta* of several Visigothic councils reveal that great attention was paid to the celebration of the Eucharist during this period. These councils attempted to provide some semblance of liturgical unity emanating from Toledo, the capital of the Visigothic reign. This was accomplished in some measure under Saint Julian of Toledo (d. 690), who compiled the first liturgical texts into a format later ages would identify as a sacramentary.

Roman Liturgy

Liturgical development during the fifth to the seventh centuries was not limited to the Hispano-Mozarabic experience. Cyrille Vogel clearly demonstrates that the Roman liturgy also underwent an evolution influenced by "the ebb and flow of liturgical books across the face of Europe."[10] To grasp the development of the Roman liturgy, it helps to understand the cycles of exchange that took place between Rome and the Christian West, including the Spanish church. Exchanges took place with the East as well; for example, Sergius I (687–701), a Syrian and bishop of Rome, is credited with inserting the *Agnus Dei* into the Roman Mass and developing the feasts of the Assumption, the Annunciation, and the Nativity of the Virgin.[11]

In fact, the development of the Roman rite has been the most extensive and prolonged of all the liturgies in East or West, lasting even up to the present day. However, in terms of the Roman liturgy contemporaneous with the Old Spanish liturgy, evidence of its beginnings in the first five centuries of the church's history has not survived in textual form.[12] Nonetheless, the process of systematization of the liturgy of the City of Rome and of the papal court (the *Roman* liturgy in the strict sense) begins with Pope Gregory the Great (590–604).[13]

Gallican Liturgy

The Gallican rite, the style of worship prevalent in Gaul before the Carolingian reforms of the eighth and ninth centuries, also underwent continuous development. These shifts are linked to both the Hispano-

Visigothic church and the Roman church. Certain characteristics of the Gallican rite point to a possible Eastern Christian origin, though this has not been firmly established.[14]

A comparison of the Hispano-Mozarabic and Gallican liturgies reveals strong resemblances in terms of rites, liturgical books, prayers, and even vocabulary. This has led some to conclude the two liturgies are actually one, having come from the same source.[15] The bishops of both Septimania in southern Gaul and of Spain were under Visigothic rule from 418 to 711. This fact, combined with the lengthy period of time, would have been sufficient for liturgical practices in Spain and Gaul to be brought into conformity with one another either through the natural interaction of influential practitioners of these rites or through imposition by a central authority. The latter is very likely since the Visigoths favored religious uniformity in their realms to the extent possible.[16] A vestige of the Visigothic attempts at liturgical uniformity is the fact that the patrons of the Primatial Cathedral of Narbonne are the Spanish martyrs Justo and Pastor (d. 6 August 304). The *acta* of the Visigothic councils demonstrate in their lists of signatories that bishops from both regions sat together at these gatherings.[17] Bishops of Gaul are found among the signers of the *acta* of the Visigothic councils for over one hundred years beginning with Toledo III (589) until the last surviving documents of Toledo XVII (694). One of these councils was held at Narbonne in 589. Canon 2 of Toledo IV (633) particularly decreed that all were to worship following the same rites in the entire Visigothic realm in Spain and Gaul. This was reiterated by Toledo XI (675); it called for unity within metropolitan provinces but did not address variations among metropolitan provinces (canon 3). Therefore, it is reasonable to think that the two liturgies might have had a common origin. In regard to this issue Férotin writes, "The Mozarabic liturgy has in the Gallican liturgy a sister, which we have easily recognized as such by the particularities of her character and the general traits of her physiognomy. But, is she an older sister or a younger sister?"[18] Nonetheless, due to the notable variations in the eucharistic celebration within the Visigothic church of Spain, it is certain that important differences would have occurred in the various locales under Visigothic rule.

Certainly, after the definitive political separation of Septimania and Spain in 719, the Gallican rite evolved in different ways. This is especially true in terms of the opening part of the Eucharistic Liturgy and the Preparation for Communion.[19] Eventually, the Gallican rite would exercise great influence on the development of the Roman liturgy under Frankish rule.[20]

Undoubtedly the Gallican, Roman, and Hispano-Mozarabic rites influenced one another throughout this period of history. This can be seen in the fact that the three rites have important commonalities. One of these is variability.

The Principle of Variability

The Gallican, Roman, and Hispanic rites are marked by the principle of variability. The principle governs variations in the content of what otherwise are set euchological formulas. The *prenotanda* explain that this principle was first introduced in the fifth century into the Roman Preface (nos. 57–58). The presider could now choose from a variety of texts in order to link the otherwise set formula of the Eucharistic Prayer to a variety of celebrations by means of the Preface. This value was applied by the Hispano-Mozarabic and Gallican rites to the rest of the Eucharistic Prayer as well. Jungmann calls this a ruling principle of the Gallic liturgies, for "everywhere a majority of formularies was to be available either for particular feasts or for free choice."[21]

This principle of variability may be another factor pointing to a common origin for the three liturgies. Archdale A. King speculated that the three rites may have developed from an "original" liturgy of Rome.[22] Jungmann rejected this idea but acknowledged similarities among them.[23] Because of their great similarities I suspect the Mozarabic and Gallican rites emerged from the same root, though it is not clear what that root was. Jungmann lists the two liturgies under the general category of Gallic liturgy. Perhaps instead of Gallic, Visigothic would be a more appropriate category since the Visigoths ruled the region where both the Mozarabic and Gallican liturgies began to unfold. Nonetheless, Jungmann includes the Celtic and Ambrosian rites in this category. More extensive study of Gallican liturgical sources has been published than of Spanish sources because up to now they have been more available for study.[24] Consequently the *prenotanda* note that the Gallican sources have been indispensable for a greater understanding of the characteristics of the Hispano-Mozarabic rite (no. 84). And although the Gallican sources have had more attention in English and French-speaking scholarly circles, the texts for the Mozarabic rite from the period of the fifth through the seventh centuries are more complete than all the Western rites other than the Roman.[25]

TOLEDO AS THE CENTER OF THE HISPANO-MOZARABIC RITE

The commission established in Toledo by Cardinal González Martín in 1982 was charged with identifying and retrieving the structure of the

Eucharist and its subsequent reformulation into the *Missale Hispano-Mozarabicum*. The commission based its work on what can only be identified as the ideal of a "classical period" in the development of the rite. Pinell was particularly influential in this regard. Unfortunately, there has never been an ideal Roman or Hispano-Mozarabic period; the churches influenced one another on many levels and incorporated liturgical practices that suited their worship and held these as part of their treasure. Nonetheless, Pinell identified the classical period as the fifth to seventh centuries, when most of the euchological texts and musical compositions were formulated.[26] This was the period just prior to the Islamic invasions of 711. It was also the period in which the Visigothic kingdom centered in Toledo reached its apex. Pinell particularly points to the seventh century as the period of highest creativity. Obviously the commission agreed enough so that the updated rite as it appears in the *Missale Hispano-Mozarabicum* and the *Liber Commicus* reflects the texts of this period while excluding most of what was introduced between then and the Cisneros reform.

King Leovigild (569–86) made Toledo his usual royal residence. Geographically, this made sense because Toledo, at the epicenter of the Iberian peninsula and situated on the Tagus River, allowed him to control movement from east to west on this important waterway.[27] In the centuries that followed, Christian tradition remembered it as the *urbs regia*, the symbol of the Visigothic monarchy.

At the core of this "Golden Age" were the authorities of the Hispano-Roman Catholic church. Under the Visigoths, the church in their realm also became centered at Toledo. The church provided a confessional and political counterweight to the Arian Visigothic overlords. It also became a guiding moral force in Visigothic formulation of both civil and ecclesiastical laws once they converted to Catholicism. Church authority over the ruler was further strengthened by the introduction of the anointing of the king, a quasi-sacramental act that conferred on the king a quasi-sacerdotal quality.[28] This practice was soon imitated by the Franks and Anglo-Saxons, thus becoming common throughout Western Europe. Outstanding among the church figures increasing church power over the ruling authority were Saint Leander and Saint Isidore. The latter is credited with setting the groundwork for a more standardized liturgical discipline throughout the realm. This program was carried out by Saint Julian, whose compilation of texts served as the basis for installment of the liturgy according to the Toledan usage in the cathedral in Oviedo in northern Spain by Alfonso II, King of Asturias, known as the Chaste (791–842).[29]

On the part of the ruling authority, the strong link between king and church was introduced by King Reccared (586–601), who proclaimed Toledo the primatial see of his realm.[30] Understandably this was not accepted easily by other places that perhaps had more right to this title. In particular, Cartagena had more claim. It had been the capital of the Roman province of which Toledo was a part; but at this time Cartagena was in Byzantine hands. Once given primacy, however, the See of Toledo exercised great influence over the development and celebration of the liturgy throughout the realm.

The series of church councils held at Toledo served as a way to extend its influence. There were at least fifteen councils in the period between 587 and 688 under the auspices of the church of Toledo. Part of the church's influence was based on the weakness of the monarchy. During this period evidence points to a church in Visigothic Spain that is efficiently organized and served by highly trained and scholarly bishops of high moral character who exercise moral influence over the people, including the civil authorities.[31] Nonetheless, the church was also subject to the whims and dictates of the king, since he had authority to name bishops.

Once Toledo's ecclesiastical primacy was lost with the Islamic invasion of 711, a significant group of Christians remaining there continued to hold to their faith and to celebrate as well as develop their liturgy. With great difficulty they continued to recopy their texts and to add new prayer formulas that would help them interpret the experience of domination and marginalization. In the meantime the Christians who had managed to escape and form the core of resistance to the Islamic forces in Asturias and then León eventually came to idealize the Visigothic kingdom, and thus Toledo, as that time and place or "Golden Age" when "all of Hispania" was united under one faith and one king. These Asturian, Cantabrian, and Basque warlords, reinforced by the Hispano-Roman-Visigothic Mozarabs escaping the Islamic kingdoms, came to see themselves as the heirs to the Visigothic kingdom and church. Upon establishing his court in Oviedo, King Alfonso II the Chaste made a conscious effort to restore the civil and ecclesiastical order of the Visigothic monarchy. As part of his program he attempted to establish in Oviedo all as it had been in Toledo, including the liturgy. Is it possible that these two legitimate heirs to Toledan antiquity, Oviedo and Islamic-dominated Toledo, gave rise to the two Mozarabic liturgical traditions identified by Dom Jordi Pinell, O.S.B., in the texts?[32]

Once Toledo had been retaken in 1085 and the Roman rite imposed, the Mozarab community there continued to hold on to its rite. We have seen that the parishes of Santa Eulalia and Santas Justa y Rufina, in particular, had their own schools of scribes that recopied the liturgical texts for their use. Thanks to these two parishes and their efforts to preserve their liturgical heritage, canon Alfonso Ortiz was able to compile the necessary manuscripts that formed the core of the *Missale mixtum* published by Cardinal Cisneros in 1500.

Over several centuries numerous factors have kept Toledo at the forefront of efforts to maintain the rite, even though other places such as Salamanca and Plasencia have contributed to this effort as well.[33] Specifically, Toledo regained its position as the primatial see with the reconquest in 1085. Later, Cardinal Cisneros established a Mozarabic chapel in the cathedral of Toledo in 1502, assuring the ancient Spanish liturgy a home and a center where the rite could be conserved for posterity. Most recently, Cardinal Marcelo González Martín's role as former president of the Spanish Episcopal Liturgical Commission and his interest in the rite have contributed to the latest efforts to preserve it. The efforts of the Mozarab community itself to preserve and promote the rite since the reconquest have helped maintain Toledo's leadership as well.

These factors have borne fruit in the updating and reestablishment of the Hispano-Mozarabic rite in the contemporary era. The structure of the Mass as described below is a sign of this accomplishment. The efforts to update the Mass have also resulted in the updating of the Hispano-Mozarabic Triduum, the liturgical context for the ritual use of the Lignum Crucis.

STRUCTURE OF THE EUCHARIST IN THE HISPANO-MOZARABIC RITE

The Eucharistic Liturgy reflects a tripartite structure of Proclamation of the Word, Anaphora, and Communion.[34] These are elements common to other Western and Eastern rites.[35] In 1982, however, Cardinal Marcelo González Martín established a commission in Toledo to identify and retrieve the authentic texts and structure of the Hispano-Mozarabic *ordo missæ*. The commission's starting point was the *Missale mixtum* published by Cardinal Francisco Ximénez de Cisneros in 1500 and the *Missale Gothicum* published by Cardinal Francisco Antonio de Lorenzana in 1804. The texts of Tradition B (Seville) made up the bulk of both Cisneros's and Lorenzana's Missals and remained the core of the updating; however, texts from Tradition A and manuscripts from other sources were included as options or to fill in missing elements.[36] The commission was also charged with updating and reformulating the Eucharistic Liturgy, and this resulted in the subsequent publication of the *Missale Hispano-Mozarabicum* in 1991. In the following pages I provide an overview of the updated eucharistic celebration with special emphasis on its distinctiveness.[37]

INITIAL RITES

The two Hispano-Mozarabic traditions, A (Toledo) and B (Seville) as identified by Pinell, reveal an important difference in how the eucharistic celebration commenced. The *prenotanda* indicate that probably in the second half of the seventh century an introductory section was added to the structure of the Mass, apparently due to the influence of other rites. Tradition A kept this addition for Mass throughout the year.[38] Tradition B, however, omitted it on ferial days and on the Sundays of Lent. The updated rite follows the practice of Tradition B.

Prælegendum

When the Mass begins with the Introductory Rites, they consist of an antiphon called *Prælegendum*, the hymn *Gloria in Excelsis*, and an *oratio Post Gloriam*. In addition, on solemnities the *Trisagion* is sung between the *Gloria* and the Oration. The Gallican rite also named the opening antiphon *Prælegendum*,[39] while in the south of Spain it was designated *Officium*. This antiphon is analogous to the *Introitus* of the contemporaneous Roman rite. By its title it is evident that this was to be chanted before the readings. The Entrance Rites began to expand in the seventh century and continued in the tenth. With the insertion of devotional practices, especially in the sixteenth century, such as the Preparation of the Gifts at a side table, the chant became a processional song accompanying the ministers as they entered and approached the altar. Private devotional prayers and actions by the priest were added in the *Missale mixtum* (1500), probably due to Roman practice.[40] Most of these have been excised from the updated rite. The Preparation of the Gifts at this point of the Mass has been eliminated in the updated rite. The *Prælegendum* is only sung for liturgical feasts and solemnities during Ordinary Time.[41]

Gloria

The *Gloria* is a christological hymn that appears for use at Matins in some of the Eastern liturgies as early as the third century.[42] The hymn

praises the Trinity while especially focusing on Christ's unique role as
Mediator. This particular theological emphasis appears often in the
euchology of the Hispano-Mozarabic rite.

The *Gloria* entered the Spanish rite sometime in the seventh century
and provided a precedent for the incorporation of hymns in the Eucharistic Liturgy. Toledo IV (633) sanctioned the use of hymns, citing the
example of Jesus and his disciples, who sang a "hymn" before departing
for the Mount of Olives. Current English-language translations of the
Bible use either "hymn" or "psalm." The *New Jerusalem Bible* uses the
word "psalm," while the *Revised Standard Version* uses "hymn." Just
as there are modern examples of differences in English translations, surely
there were differences in the Latin recensions of the scriptures at use in
the West prior to the general acceptance of the Vulgate translation.[43]
Perhaps this is why the Spanish church accepted hymns as a regular
feature of the Mass while the Roman church rejected them until the
twelfth century.[44]

The Roman rite incorporated the *Gloria* as the opening of the Christmas Mass at Midnight in the sixth century.[45] It was sung at the Easter
Vigil and then extended to Sundays and feasts in the eighth century.[46]
The use of hymns is significant. Hymns often reflect the popular dimen-
sion of faith rather than the official, for they tend to offer a poetic and
less precise interpretation of scripture and doctrine. Apparently this is
why hymns in general were resisted by the Roman church, that is, due to
their history of questionable theological content. For example, hymns
with Gnostic overtones were eliminated in the third century; in the fourth
century songs with Arian leanings were banned; and in the sixteenth
century many medieval hymns were rejected.[47] However, the integration
of popular elements into the Old Spanish rite is a trait that appears in
the Good Friday services, as I will show.

Trisagion

This chant is only used on special solemnities outside of Lent. The
Trisagion entered into the Hispano-Mozarabic rite under Byzantine influence. The Council of Chalcedon (451) provides the earliest information about the chant by connecting it to the condemnation of the
Monophysites.[48] The chant was linked to the entrance of the bishop during the Opening Rites of the Eastern liturgies and served to solemnize
the celebration in the Hispano-Mozarabic liturgy. The Mozarabic texts
are more varied than in the Eastern liturgies and can be sung in Greek,
Latin, or both languages, according to the *prenotanda* (no. 30).

Oratio Post Gloriam

This prayer forms the last part of the Introductory Rites.[49] It roughly corresponds to the Roman Collect in that it is the first euchological text directed to God in the name of the assembly by the presider. Though the purpose of the Collect is debated in Roman circles, the *Missale Hispano-Mozarabicum* interprets the *oratio Post Gloriam* as a prayer that serves to gather together the aspirations of all present and, to some extent, declares that the community is now constituted as the assembly-celebrant.[50] A characteristic aspect of Hispano-Mozarabic prayers is that they tend to echo preceding texts. The *oratio Post Gloriam* does this by reiterating themes from the *Gloria*, the *Trisagion*, or both. Consequently, the *oratio Post Gloriam* completes the Introductory Rites rather than initiating the Liturgy of the Word.

The updated rite follows the practice of Tradition B (Seville) during ferial days and the Sundays of Lent, omitting on these occasions the *Prælegendum*, the *Gloria*, the *Trisagion*, and the *oratio Post Gloriam*. When this occurs, the priest enters, kisses the altar, goes to the chair, and greets the people with "Dominus sit semper vobiscum," to which they respond, "Et cum spiritu tuo." The Liturgy of the Word then commences.

LITURGY OF THE WORD

A feature common to both the Gallican and Hispano-Mozarabic rites during the sixth through eighth centuries is the regular use of three scripture pericopes during the Liturgy of the Word.[51] In contrast, the contemporaneous Roman rite usually used two pericopes. Notably there was great diversity in the arrangement of readings of the non-Roman churches during this era. In the Spanish rite the reader announces the source of the pericope, to which the congregation responds, "Deo gratias," or "Gloria tibi, Domine" if the pericope is from the Gospel. The congregational response to all three readings is "Amen" at their conclusion.

The Hispano-Mozarabic readings are contained in a lectionary called the *Liber Commicus* and are grouped according to the rite's distinctive liturgical calendar. The etymology of *commicus* is the Latin *comes* (companion) and refers to the readings as fragments or pericopes of scripture that accompany the celebration. Whereas the Roman and Gallican rites opted for *Lectionarius*, *Evangeliarius*, or *Epistolarius* to describe the books for the Liturgy of the Word, the Spanish church opted for *Liber Commicus*. This has been retained for the 1994 collection of readings.

In the past each see apparently had its own collection. In the updated rite there are two distinct distributions of readings and chants for most of the solemnities and some liturgical seasons.[52] Nevertheless, the *prenotanda* state that the readings may be chosen from either cycle during certain times of the year (nos. 151, 167). Some of the pericopes for the Eucharist are marked by centonization rather than the *lectio continua* of the Roman rite. Centonization is the practice of putting together into one reading a variety of passages drawn from different parts of the Bible, an especially notable feature of the Gallican liturgy.[53] This is especially evident in the Passion, begun at Holy Thursday and completed on Good Friday.

Readings and Chants

The first reading is titled *Prophetia* and is taken from the Prophets or the Law. It is replaced by a reading from the Wisdom books and an additional reading from the historical books during Lent, resulting in four readings during this season. During Eastertide the *Prophetia* reading may be replaced by a reading from Revelation.

After the first reading the *Psallendum* is sung. This is the name given to the repertoire of psalm texts used as a response to the reading. The *prenotanda* attribute the composition of some of the chants for these texts to Saint Leander (no. 35). The *Psallendum*'s function and structure are analogous to the Roman *Graduale*. On the Wednesdays and Fridays of the first five weeks of Lent in the Hispano-Mozarabic calendar, the *Threni* are chanted in place of the *Psallendum*. The *Threni* texts are penitential in character and dramatically express the church's repentance as well as recount the suffering of Christ. The texts are based on various passages from Lamentations, Job, and Isaiah.

The second reading is called *Apostolus* and refers to the readings from the epistles, both Pauline and Catholic. The *Apostolus* may be preceded by a reading from the Acts of the Martyrs on the feast day of a martyr according to the *prenotanda* (no. 37). Therefore, on these feast days, there are four readings. The incorporation of a nonscriptural reading in the Eucharist is significant, for it implies an openness to a canon of readings that goes beyond scripture. After the reading from the martyr's life, a portion of the *Bendictiones* or Canticle of the Three Children from the Book of Daniel (Dn 3:51–90) is sung and leads to the *Apostolus*. The *Evangelium*, a reading from the Gospel, completes the scriptural readings. The Gospel reading is distinguished from the other two readings by the greeting "Dominus sit semper vobiscum" as in the Roman rite. The Liturgy of the Word is concluded by the chanting of *Laudes*, an antiphon of praise that includes singing Alleluia, except in Lent. This antiphon is always sung after the Gospel, never before. In addition, if there is a homily, *Laudes* follows it.

Clearly much emphasis was placed on the reading of scripture and of passages from the martyrology. Perhaps this resulted from a need to reiterate an orthodox foundational narrative in the face of competing religious perspectives. In addition, it is not clear how rapidly the universal church's canonization process of scripture had advanced in the local Spanish church during the period of the rite's formation.

INTERMEDIARY RITUAL

The actions and prayers that take place between the Liturgy of the Word and the Anaphora are another distinctive feature of the Hispano-Mozarabic Eucharist. They consist of the Offering, Diptychs, and Sign of Peace, three elements that are linked by four variable prayers: The *oratio Admonitionis, Alia, oratio Post Nomina,* and *oratio Ad Pacem.* These prayers are divided among the presider, the deacon, and the assembly. The usual interjection of the assembly is "Amen," but also included are phrases that echo what has been said before. This intermediary ritual is also found in the Gallican rite's eucharistic celebration, though not in the Roman rite. From this point the Gallican and Old Spanish rites are almost identical in structure until Communion. At times this transitional unit is referred to as Diptychs or Solemn Intercessions, but this is only one portion of the ritual. Férotin gives the title *Preces* and indicates that it refers to a "solemn supplication and invitation to prayer."[54]

Offering

The first element of the Intermediary Ritual is the chanting of *Sacrificium,* an antiphon that recalls the sacrifices of Old Testament figures such as Abel, Abraham, Melchizedek, and so forth. The antiphon accompanies the offering that takes place at this point, which consists of the preparation of the bread and wine as well as their placement on the altar by the ministers. *Sacrificium,* with its theme of sacrificial offering, sets the tone for what follows. At the conclusion of the antiphon, the priest prays the *oratio Admonitionis,* a unique prayer in that it is addressed to the assembly. Much like an invitation to prayer, this prayer functions to prepare the assembly to exercise the gift of prayer in the Solemn Intercessions that are about to begin. Nonetheless, the doxology that completes this presidential prayer blesses God. In this way it changes from an admonition to a prayer.

Apparently this was the first presidential prayer before the *oratio Post Gloriam* was introduced.[55] As a variable prayer, the *oratio Admonitionis* reflects the motif of the feast or liturgical season being celebrated. It is followed by the monition "Oremus," to which the choir responds singing, "Hagios, Hagios, Hagios, Domine Deus, Rex æterne, tibi laudes et gratias." This is the first of two occasions in the celebration on which the presider says "Oremus."

Diptychs

The Diptychs or Solemn Intercessions are the next element in the celebration. The title refers to a litany of intercessions for the needs of the church and of humanity, in the course of which the names of the living and the dead are introduced. They assume the character of a solemn profession of unity in faith and love with the universal church, which encompasses the clergy, the faithful, the saints, and the faithful departed. They also include petitions for temporal needs, such as for the ill, prisoners, and travelers.

Diptychs are an ancient element found within the earliest Eucharistic Prayers.[56] They take their name from the hinged tablet used in Byzantine court ceremonial for the announcement of official proclamations and continue to form part of the Anaphora in Eastern liturgies. Their use in the Hispano-Mozarabic rite is an indication of Byzantine influence. However, the *prenotanda* (no. 50) note that some of the texts of these prayers reflect the teachings of Saint Cyprian of Carthage (d. 258). Thus, the North African church may have influenced the Spanish liturgy in this aspect. This would indicate the assimilation of Diptychs into the rite at an early date.

In the Hispano-Mozarabic Eucharist the Diptychs are separated from the Anaphora. General Intercessions were apparently an original component of the ancient Roman rite as well, though it is not clear what form these took.[57] Eventually, the intercessions incorporated into the Roman Canon overshadowed the General Intercessions. The early General Intercessions seem to have fulfilled a similar function as the Hispano-Mozarabic Diptychs, namely, uttering prayer for the needs of the church and expressing unity between the living and the dead. These intercessions also were linked to the offering of those present by means of a verbal referent to this action.

Variable Prayers

Two of the four variable prayers composing the Intermediary Ritual occur in the midst of this formal supplication: The *Alia* and the *oratio*

Post Nomina. The *Alia* echoes the earlier offering by asking God to accept the gifts of the church, the bread and wine, as well as what they signify, namely, the submission of the Christian community to God's saving action. The intercessions are joined to the bread and wine as part of the offering. The *oratio Post Nomina* concludes the Diptychs by reiterating their content. The text of the oration often requests that the names proclaimed be inscribed in the heavenly Book of Life. This notion reappears in the Good Friday afternoon service *Ad nonam* in the solemn intercessions.

Sign of Peace

The last phase of this Intermediary Ritual consists in the fourth variable prayer, the *oratio Ad Pacem*, as well as a trinitarian blessing, the Sign of Peace, and the antiphon *Pacem meam do vobis.* The placement of the Sign of Peace here seems to reiterate the ecclesial communion professed by means of the Diptychs, according to the *prenotanda* (no. 56). That is, the unity expressed in prayer is now actualized in the action of the assembly as the peace is shared among its members.

LITURGY OF THE EUCHARIST

Upon completion of the Intermediary Ritual, the Liturgy of the Eucharist commences with the Anaphora. The Anaphora follows a fixed structure consisting of Dialogue, *Illatio, Sanctus, oratio Post Sanctus,* Institution Narrative, *oratio Post Pridie,* doxology, and *Amen.* There is no set content to the prayers of the Anaphora per se in the Hispano-Mozarabic liturgy; they vary in content, length, and subject of address, seemingly according to the specific season or feast being celebrated. Prayers composed in the ninth and eleventh centuries tend to be longer than those of older vintage.[58] Perhaps writing prayers down eventually contributed to their lengthening. Nonetheless, the various parts of the Anaphora cannot be mixed and matched among Mass sets.

The underlying motive for the difference in length and content appears to be the principle of variability. This principle allows for the articulation of different themes by means of Mass sets or groups of prayer formulas destined for specific celebrations. Only the Dialogue, *Sanctus,* Institution Narrative, and *Amen* are invariable. Férotin discusses this variability and judges the number of formulas destined for the Anaphora to be "excessive."[59] On the other hand this trait reflects the tastes of the time. Moreover, the Spanish liturgy is marked by a catechetical and mystagogical character that is seen in the number of texts directed to the assembly. This variability of texts allows for an array of ways to instruct the congregation in the faith of the church. This variability for catechetical purposes served well during the Visigothic and Islamic eras, as will be noted below.

Dialogue

The Anaphora begins with a Dialogue between presider and assembly similar in structure to the Roman Preface Dialogue. However, the Hispano-Mozarabic Dialogue begins with "Introibo ad altare Dei." The incipit is identical to the antiphon from Psalm 43:4 at the beginning of the Tridentine usage of the Roman rite, which was prayed by the priest as he entered the sanctuary. In this position the incipit reiterates the sacrificial theme of the earlier chant and prayer that occurs during the Preparation of the Gifts.

Illatio

The next element in the Eucharistic Prayer is the *Illatio*.[60] It is equivalent to the Preface of the Roman rite and, like it, is variable in content, although its focus tends to be thanksgiving for salvation. The rhetorical principle behind the *Illatio* is the *oratio structurata*, a type of prose intended to provide a demonstrative exposition of some idea, according to the *prenotanda* (no. 65). Much of the time the *Illatio* is directed to both the Father and the Son, though this can vary according to the main idea expressed in the body of the prayer. In this way the prayers stress the coequality of the Father and the Son as well as the Son's full divinity. The need to do this will be examined in Chapter 8.

The incipit of the *Illatio* is not fixed, as it is in the Roman rite. Rather, various words or locutions are used. The *prenotanda* judge this as a demonstration of the function of the *Illatio*, which is not only to recognize and thank God but also to proclaim with praise and adoration God's saving work made known by God (no. 69). As a result, the exposition may be very lengthy or very brief. Its usual format is one in which the argument is developed through enumeration of qualities in symmetrical progressions, antitheses, or parallelisms that bring to mind one or more concepts. Enrique Carrillo Morales describes the *Illatio* as the most exuberant and exultant of the prayers of the Eucharist, a quality that leads the assembly to sing the *Sanctus*.[61] Thus, whichever small detail, attitude, assertion, or movement in thought found in the Gospel reading of the day becomes a motif for comment, admonition, confession, or contemplation and also typically provides the main theme of the celebration.

Often, if it is a saint's feast day, an exposition of the life of the saint comprises a large part of the content. The prayers for these days are largely expositions of the life of the saint. The majority of saint's feasts in the liturgical calendar are dedicated to martyrs. The "Proprium de Sanctis" lists 141 saint's days (*Missale* 1991). Of these, 85 are designated specifically as martyrs and another 13 are feast days of apostles, including Matthias and Timothy. The apostles are presumed to be martyrs. This totals 98 days dedicated to martyrs, or 70 percent of the total. Ortiz, in the *Missale mixtum* (1500), designated saints according to the Roman categories of his day, including designations such as virgins, confessors, and pontiffs.[62] Even so, the *Illatio* always concludes with some stereotyped though variable reference to the heavenly hymn of Isaiah.

Sanctus

Now follows the heavenly hymn as found in Isaiah 6:3 with its Christian modification. This element is invariable, but unlike the Roman *Sanctus*, the Spanish version adapts the conclusion of the second phrase from "full of your glory" to "full of your glorious majesty." This may have occurred in the Gallican liturgy as well.[63] As for the third, fourth, and fifth phrases, a unique feature of the Hispano-Mozarabic version is its dependence on the Vulgate Matthew 21:9, which says, "Hosanna filio David. Benedictus, qui venit in nomine Domini. Hosanna in altissimis." However, the Hispano-Mozarabic version replaces "in altissimis" with "in excelsis" in the last acclamation. Finally, the *Sanctus* concludes with the Greek version of the opening acclamation: "Hagios, Hagios, Hagios, Kyrie O Theos [*sic*]." This is the second time "Hagios" is used in the Spanish liturgy as a regular congregational response in the updated celebration; it also occurs in the midst of the Diptychs.

Oratio Post Sanctus

The next element in the Spanish liturgy is a prayer called the *oratio Post Sanctus*. It also varies in length and content according to the liturgical season or particular feast being celebrated. The prayer's main function is to form the transition from the *Sanctus* to the Institution Narrative. The *oratio Post Sanctus* ends with "Christ, both Lord and Redeemer," a *fórmula de enlace* or transitional phrase that leads to the first words of the Institution Narrative.

Institution Narrative

The Institution Narrative of the Hispano-Mozarabic liturgy is taken almost literally from 1 Corinthians 11:23–26, with minor adaptations to the incipit and the Pauline gloss at the conclusion.[64] The use of the Pauline version distinguishes the Institution Narrative from other Catholic rites in both East and West. Also distinctive is the use of "Amen" as the congregational response to two of the three sections of the Narrative. Originally there were three "Amens," but the third was replaced by a declaration of belief and hope in the coming of the Lord.

Oratio Post Pridie

Another variable prayer following the Institution Narrative is the *oratio Post Pridie*. Although the placement of this prayer corresponds to the anamnesis and epiclesis of the Roman rite, its content rarely elaborates remembrance or the invocation of the Spirit. Instead, the prayer tends to be addressed directly to Christ and makes explicit the object of memory, his saving work and life-giving power. This is another point in the Eucharist when the congregation responds "Amen."

Doxology

The Anaphora concludes with a doxology. The text is variable with only the first few words and the *sæcula sæculorum* leading to the "Amen" fixed. This means that the content of the doxology can vary greatly. While it is marked by awe and exuberance, honor and glory are proclaimed more in tone than in specific words, unlike the Roman doxology. It is interesting to note that in the midst of the doxology the presider makes the sign of the cross over the bread and wine, although rarely does the text ask God to bless the eucharistic elements. While attending the liturgy at the Corpus Christi chapel of the cathedral in Toledo, Spain, in May 1989, I observed the presider bless the eucharistic elements with his forefinger, middle finger, and ring finger extended, while the thumb and little finger were crossed under the palm. Presumably this was a ritualized trinitarian blessing. The rubric only requires that the elements be blessed at this time; it does not describe how.[65] Each presider seems to bless the elements using a gesture in accord with when he was trained.

Amen

As a congregational response, "Amen" is interspersed throughout the Spanish liturgy, and not only during the Anaphora. It is the usual response to the readings as well as to several prayers throughout the celebration, including the eight petitions of the Lord's Prayer. In effect, its appearance at the end of the Anaphora does not give it an acclamatory aspect as in the Roman rite.

It is not clear why the term *amen* is used in such diverse ways. Perhaps it not only means "so be it" but also "we believe" or "we hear" or some such idea of acknowledgment and response. The *prenotanda* assess the use of "Amen" as a response to the Institution Narrative, for instance, as akin to a response of obedience or willingness to fulfill the command of the Lord (nos. 93, 94).

COMMUNION RITE

From this point on the Spanish rite becomes more elaborate than its Gallican counterpart. Though it seems that Communion should immediately follow the Anaphora since one of its functions is similar to a solemn table blessing,[66] the ritual instead pays maximum attention to preparing for the distribution of the Eucharist. This is true of the Roman rite as well.

There are four distinct elements of preparation, including the Symbol of Faith, Fraction Rite, Lord's Prayer, and Blessing. The two Spanish traditions ordered these elements differently. Tradition A began with the Fraction Rite and then followed with the Symbol of Faith and the Lord's Prayer. Tradition B began with the Profession of Faith followed by the Fraction Rite and the Lord's Prayer. The updated rite follows the order of Tradition B.

Symbol of Faith

A sacerdotal monition, "Fidem, quam corde credimus, ore autem dicamus," initiates the communal recitation of the Symbol of Faith in unison by the community. In this way a link is made between the "Sic credimus" that follows the Institution Narrative and the reception of communion. The Spanish liturgy was the first in the West to introduce into the Eucharist a version of the Symbol of Faith following the form of Nicea I (325) as amended by Constantinople I (381).[67] This was done in 589, shortly after the conversion of the Visigoths to Catholicism, and was dictated for the churches under their jurisdiction, including those in Gaul.[68] The text used in the liturgy today is the version promulgated by Toledo III (589). The collective solemn profession of faith by the Arian King Reccared, accompanied by his court and bishops, must have been a powerful sign to the witnesses. The recitation of the Symbol very transparently conveyed the triumph of the Catholic faith over the Arian faith of the Visigothic church. Therefore, it stands to reason that the recitation of the Creed would be included in the ritual-sacramental program of the church. Thus, canon 2 of Toledo III establishes the recitation of the Creed before the Lord's Prayer as a way to stress clearly and precisely in the mind of all present the true notion of God, particularly in contrast to the Arian notion.

In contrast, the Nicean-Constantinopolitan Symbol of Faith was not introduced into the Roman Mass until the eighth century and was inserted at the end of the Liturgy of the Word.[69] In the Hispano-Mozarabic rite, the Toledan Symbol of Faith is recited at every Mass after the Anaphora and before the Fraction Rite, supposedly as a way to prepare and "purify" the faithful for communion. The Spanish church also incorporated the "filioque," seemingly without difficulty although the use of this term led to polemical discussions between East and West later.[70] The ritual action that follows it further serves to reinforce both the creedal and preparatory aspects of the Symbol.

Fraction Rite

The recitation of the Symbol of Faith is followed by the Fraction Rite, during which the host is broken into nine pieces, each with an assigned allegorical name. The Fraction Rite is accompanied by a very brief acclamation; the *ordo missæ* offers four choices for most of the year and one for Eastertide.[71] At one time the Fraction Rite took place while the Symbol of Faith was recited;[72] perhaps this implies that the reformed rite has opted for greater emphasis on the Fraction Rite. On rare occasions there is a special acclamation at this point, such as on Holy Thursday and Corpus Christi. Upon being broken, the pieces are arranged on the paten in the form of a cross. As the presider places them on the paten, he names the nine mysteries of Christ celebrated throughout the Hispano-Mozarabic liturgical year: *Corporatio, Nativitas, Circumcisio, Apparitio, Passio, Mors, Resurrectio, Gloria,* and *Regnum.*

Although this action was a practical operation that allowed for the distribution of the Eucharist to individuals, this ritual is given a symbolical sense by being performed in imitation of the Lord's action at the Last Supper when he took, blessed, broke, and gave the bread to those gathered with him. The Fraction Rite also has a symbolic value because it helps recall Christ's "brokenness" in his passion. Breaking the host into several pieces was directed by the Second Council of Tours (567); however, this practice must have arisen when the faithful generally did not receive communion at every Eucharist. The *prenotanda* state that there is evidence, nonetheless, that the practice was already in place in fourth-century Gaul (no. 125). In the updated Spanish Eucharist the entire host is consumed by the presider after the Fraction Rite. I suspect this is a leftover ritual from the time when communion by the faithful was rare. Today, a ciborium of hosts for the Communion of the Faithful is consecrated during the Anaphora along with the larger host.

Lord's Prayer

The recitation of the Lord's Prayer and its relation to Communion is an ancient element found in the eucharistic celebrations of both East and West. The prayer, though, is prayed in a unique way in the Hispano-Mozarabic rite. After a variable introduction, the presider begins the prayer with "Oremus" and then divides the Lord's Prayer into eight petitions. After each petition, the assembly responds, "Amen." This is the second and last time "Oremus" is used in the Eucharist. Furthermore, the Lord's Prayer and its responses are usually chanted. Evidently in the Gallican rite everyone vocalized the Lord's Prayer together.[73] Although the chanting and division into eight petitions by the presider serve to solemnize its recitation, the communal nature of the prayer is diminished in the sense that the assembly does not vocalize it. On the other hand, the Symbol of Faith is vocalized by all in the assembly in unison, even if sung.

An embolism, or prayer for deliverance from evil, similar to the current Roman version though lengthier, follows the Lord's Prayer. An important difference though is that the assembly responds to the embolism with "Amen" instead of with a doxology. At this point the presider elevates the paten and chalice declaring "Sancta sanctis." This is the only elevation in the ritual. Afterward the presider takes the ninth particle, *Regnum*, and deposits it into the chalice, saying a prayer that refers to the reconciliation wrought by the body and blood of Christ.[74] The use of "Sancta sanctis" and this prayer at this juncture seems to be an adaptation of the Eastern practice, especially since the mingling of the consecrated bread and wine are linked to the memory of the dead.

Blessing

Before the presider consumes the various particles, the deacon instructs those present to bow their heads for the blessing. The assembly responds "Deo gratias." The presider then invokes the blessing. It is a unique prayer in that it consists of three variable verses generally directed to those present; they respond "Amen" to each verse. A stereotyped formula referring to God in the third person follows. Toledo IV (633) fixed the position of the blessing, though it gives no reason why.[75]

The *Apostolic Constitutions* (c. 400) may have provided the precedent for the practice as it contains a blessing just prior to communion. It is interesting that the editor of the best manuscript preserved (Vat. gr. 1506) has been shown to have had Arian leanings. Could this have been an Arian practice that influenced the celebration of the Old Spanish rite?[76] The Eucharist found in this document has been judged to have been celebrated in fourth-century Syria. This church order was most likely known in Spain and so could suggest Eastern influence on the practice of blessing the assembly just prior to the Communion. Caesarius of Arles, on the other hand, "resorted to the expediency of dismissing noncommunicants before communion time, lest their presence disturb the devotion of those approaching the table."[77] This may be the reason the blessing was placed before the Communion in the Hispano-Mozarabic Eucharist as well. In practice, though, the blessing does not evince dismissal in the updated celebration. At the same time, a blessing at this point makes a blessing at the end redundant. Nonetheless, for one who has worshiped in the Roman rite, it is a bit odd to leave the celebration without a blessing. Perhaps the greatest blessing upon completion of the Eucharist is to have partaken of it and to take with one the blessing received in this action.[78]

Communion

After the blessing, the Communion itself takes place accompanied by an antiphon based on Psalm 33:6. The *prenotanda* note that apparently the use of this psalm at Communion was common to the liturgies of both East and West (no. 138). As for the Spanish rite, it is not clear how communion was distributed in the past or when exactly general participation in communion waned. Clearly the Middle Ages saw a general decline in the communion of the faithful in both West and East due to many factors.[79] Today communion is favored, though reception of both species is optional. After the distribution an antiphon expressing thanksgiving is chanted, titled *Post Communionem*. The antiphon is followed by a final oration titled *Completuria*. This oration was apparently introduced sometime later, since the most ancient sources do not provide any evidence for it.[80] Perhaps this insertion was due to Roman influence.

Dismissal

The celebration is finalized with a greeting by the presider and dismissal by the deacon. This is a very abrupt ending to a somewhat elaborate ritual about which the *Missale Hispano-Mozarabicum* does not speculate. The abruptness may point to the notion that the assembly is not to sit and contemplate what it has done but rather to go out and live what it has celebrated. The text used at the dismissal, however, does not give this idea. The text reads as follows: "Solemnia completa sunt. In nomine Domini nostri Iesu Christi votum nostrum sit acceptum cum pace."[81] The congregation responds, "Deo gratias."

The *ordo missæ* texts and structure of the Eucharist reflect a stress on the cross and Jesus Christ's role as the divine victim who redeems his followers through his sacrifice on the cross. The eucharistic celebration centers on this sacrifice while also relating to it other aspects of Christ's salvation found in his life, death, and resurrection. These themes are even further highlighted in the Sacred Triduum of the Hispano-Mozarabic rite, especially on Good Friday, and the build up to it, the preceeding forty days of Lent.

5

The Structure
of the Hispano-Mozarabic Lent

The immediate context of the Triduum liturgies is the liturgical season of Lent. Unlike the Roman rite, Lent in the Hispano-Mozarabic rite begins with the sixth Sunday before Easter. There is no Ash Wednesday, nor is the imposition of ashes a practice in the rite. The reform effected under Cardinal Cisneros by Ortiz introduced a Mass set for Ash Wednesday in addition to other changes in rubrics, order of prayers, and recompositions of some of these. This Mass was eliminated in the *Missale* (1991).[1]

Nonetheless, Ash Wednesday originates in Spain and Gaul, where it was connected with entrance into the order of penitents. The custom developed as practices reserved for serious public sinners became standard for all the faithful. Eventually, in 1091, Pope Urban II ordered the imposition of ashes on the heads of all the faithful, thus "the reception of ashes became mandatory and the Wednesday preceding the First Sunday of Lent became known as Ash Wednesday."[2]

In the Hispano-Mozarabic rite today, the forty days of Lent begin with what is the Sunday after Ash Wednesday in the Roman rite, that is, the First Sunday of Lent. As a result, the forty days are completed on Good Friday and include the six Sundays of Lent. Otherwise, the Hispano-Mozarabic Lent coincides with the Roman rite. This first Sunday is subtitled *de carnes tollendas* (the taking away of meat).[3] The Eucharist follows the same format of the rest of the year rather than the format of the other Sundays of Lent, which follow the Lenten structure. In addition, the assembly sings Alleluia at the *Laudes* after the homily on this Sunday. The Alleluia is also sung at Vespers in the Hispano-Mozarabic office on this day and, as if in anticipation of not singing it, the Alleluia is sung repeatedly "unto satiety," finally ending with *alleluia perenne, alleluia perenne* (Alleluia forevermore). In the Roman rite the church ceases singing Alleluia on Ash Wednesday. It is not sung again until the Easter Vigil Eucharist.

The other Sundays of the Hispano-Mozarabic Lent also carry subtitles that provide a clue to their focus. The subtitle indicates the topic of the Gospel pericope, which will be read from the version according to John. Thus, the second Sunday is *missa de muliere samaritana* (the Samaritan Woman),[4] the third is *missa de cæco nato dicenda* (the Man Born Blind),[5] the fourth is *missa in mediante die festo* (in the Midst of the Feast [of Passover]),[6] and the fifth is *missa de Lazaro dicenda* (Lazarus).[7] The Gospel texts are further glossed by means of the variable prayers for these days. This fosters sentiments and petitions in the congregation similar to those of the biblical characters. Furthermore, the Gospel passages have in common the theme of Christ's self-revelation.

The Sixth Sunday of Lent, *in ramis palmarum* (Palm Sunday),[8] is particularly significant for understanding the Triduum in the Hispanic rite. As in the Roman rite, the liturgy begins with a procession with branches, palms or olive branches in Spain and Latin America, to commemorate the Savior's triumphant entry into Jerusalem. This Sunday serves as the "portico" to the celebration of Christ's passion, death, and resurrection later in the week. However, while Palm Sunday in the Roman rite stresses the passion of Christ, in the Mozarabic rite it stresses the movement toward baptism and, therefore, has a catechumenal tone. It is the day catechumens participate in the *traditio symboli*, the giving of the Creed or Symbol of Faith. The version used on this day is the Toledan version of the Apostles' Creed. Those preparing for baptism are to learn the Creed by memory and to recite it from memory on Holy Thursday, according to Braga II (572).[9] The recitation is called the *redditio symboli* and is a manifestation of one's readiness for baptism. It also functions as part of one's preparation for baptism.

The instruction for the *traditio symboli* states that the recipients are to carve it on their heart and to say it daily to themselves before going to sleep and before leaving the house.[10] The Symbol is not written to be read but to be recited; therefore, one's mind is to be the codex upon which are written the words that one's lips repeat. In order to facilitate and encourage this memorization, the assembly is told to make the sign of the cross and then repeat the Symbol three times. Between the second and third repetitions a brief monition is made to begin the recitation. The third monition in particular elucidates the reason for three repetitions: "Let us recite again for a third time the text of the Symbol; for, since the Symbol contains within it the faith in the divine Trinity, the same number of repetitions will be in accord with the mystery of the Trinity."[11] The monition given after the third recitation is equally illuminating:

Keep with the utmost resoluteness of mind this rule of the holy faith, which Holy Mother Church transmits to you today, so that fearful doubt will not emerge one day in your heart. Because if, God forbid, in this you doubt even tenuously, the whole foundation of your faith will tumble down, and this generates danger to your soul. Furthermore, if one of you excludes a part of this Symbol, do not think you will be able to understand it. Believe rather, that all you have heard is true. May almighty God illumine your heart in such a way that understanding and believing what we have said, you will keep the faith correctly and you will shine in your holy works, so that in this way you may reach blessed life. Amen.[12]

THE STRUCTURE OF THE HISPANO-MOZARABIC TRIDUUM

Several liturgical services make up the three days of the Hispano-Mozarabic Triduum. The days are named *Feria V in Coena Domini* (Holy Thursday), *Feria VI in Parasceve* (Good Friday), and *Vigilia Gloriosæ Dominicæ Resurrectionis* (Holy Saturday). The common Spanish names for these days are *Jueves Santo*, *Viernes Santo*, and *Sábado de Gloria*. The liturgies for these days have been reworked to eliminate many of the ceremonies introduced from the pre-Tridentine Roman rite found in the *Missale mixtum* and repeated in the *Missale Gothicum*. The texts that had either been corrupted or simplified by Cisneros were restored using the *Liber Ordinum* as a starting point.[13]

Holy Thursday

The evolution of the Triduum in Spain, as in all the local churches, has its roots in the celebration of the primitive church. The primitive church commemorated the Paschal Mystery by celebrating the Pasch on the evening before the first day of the week. The church of Spain, like the others, eventually followed the model set out by the church of post-Constantinian Jerusalem. This included celebrating the events on the days they occurred, as in the Holy City, seeking to find similar sites at which to celebrate. The well-known travel diary of the fourth-century Spanish pilgrim Egeria reveals just how well developed the liturgical practices of Jerusalem were.[14] In Spain, as elsewhere, imitation of these eventually led to the construction of churches bearing the names of the holy sites or containing relics or images associated with them.[15] With time, individual church buildings themselves contained "stations" that served as reference points for the commemoration of the Paschal Mystery, particularly the passion, death, and resurrection.

The contemporary Holy Thursday liturgy in the Spanish rite takes place in the nave/apse of the church building in the evening. There are three main successive ritual units that make up the liturgical action of this night. The first, the Eucharist, follows the format for Lent. That is, to initiate the Eucharist there is only the brief greeting, "Dominus sit semper vobiscum," and response, "Et cum spiritu tuo." This is immediately followed by the first reading. As in the other Lenten Masses, there are four readings, two from the Old Testament and two from the New.[16] The first three are *Sapientia Salomonis* (Wis 1:13–16; 2:1, 6, 12–23; 3:9–10, 12–13; 4:6, 10, 14–15), *Lectio libri Ieremiæ Prophetæ* (Jer 11:15–23; 12:1–12; 17:1; 12:10–22), and *Sequentia epistolæ beati Pauli apostoli, ad Corinthios* (1 Cor 11:20–34). This last reading particularly exhorts the community to celebrate the Lord's Supper correctly; it is also found in the Roman rite Mass for this day.

The Gospel reading, on the other hand, is very different from the Roman rite. It is the beginning of the passion narrative formed by melding together the four Gospel versions into one. As noted, this is called centonization. The passion reading is completed during the afternoon liturgy of Good Friday. The proclamation of the reading begins with the usual "Dominus sit semper vobiscum" and response. Then the celebrant says, "Initio passio Domini nostri Iesu Christi" (beginning of the passion of our Lord Jesus Christ). The reading starts with the Lord's instruction to the disciples to go and prepare the Passover meal (Lk 22:7–11a) and ends with the fulfillment of Peter's denial (Lk 22:61–62). In between are sixty-one different pericopes for a total of sixty-three.[17]

Although there are references in the readings to the "sacrifice of the meal," "the body of our High Priest," and "the banquet of the New Testament," the principal theme is that of "the supper on the eve of his death." This initiates the solemn celebration of the Pasch. Nonetheless, the liturgy for Holy Thursday is dominated by the shadow of the passion. Thus, the Lord's patience with his traitor, his goodness to Peter, and especially his humility demonstrated in the washing of the feet, even of his traitor's, have particular meaning. As Don Enrique Carrillo Morales, pastor of Santa Eulalia y San Marcos, notes, it is a humility that is even more admirable due to the fact that Christ has become one of us and spilled his blood on the cross on our behalf.[18]

The second liturgical rite of the evening involves the Expoliation of the Altar. At the end of the Eucharist the ministers retire to the sacristy in order to form a new processional group, which will approach the altar. The group, in addition to the ministers, is composed of twelve men carrying lighted candles.[19] The celebrant, however, returns without chasuble. The men surround the altar while the ministers strip the altar of its linens and other ornaments. As the stripping of the altar takes place, they extinguish the candles one by one while the choir intones psalms and antiphons. At Santa Eulalia, where there currently is no choir, the entire congregation reads sequentially the verses and responses in unison. Carrillo Morales interprets this action as a gesture that recalls the expoliation undergone by Christ in three events recalled by the readings of the Holy Thursday Mass.[20] These include his incarnation, in which he put aside his glory as God in order to take on the form of a servant (Phil 2:6–11); taking off his cloak in order to wash the feet of his disciples (Jn 13:3–19); and, during the crucifixion, being stripped of his clothing (Jn 19:21–24) in order to expiate the sins of those who believe in him.

The verses and responses, actually a centonization of various psalm and Gospel verses, recalls Jesus' abandonment by his disciples.[21] For example, the first verse says: "O God of my praise, do not remain quiet. The impious mouth, the lying mouth, are opened against me." The response follows, "Have trust, I have conquered the world." Later the response includes a verse that recalls the Gospel of John and Jesus' words as the congregation says, "The hour has arrived in which you will be dispersed and you will leave me alone; but I am not alone, for the Father is with me. Have trust, I have conquered the world." The leader says, "And you, Lord, Lord, do unto me according to the grace of your name; because your love is good, free me!" The congregation responds, "Have trust, I have conquered the world."[22] At Santa Eulalia in 1999 the entire congregation recited the verses and responses together, which can have the effect of eliciting sentiments of one's own experience of abandonment and thus fostering an empathy and identification with Christ.

The last liturgical rite of the Holy Thursday celebration is the washing of feet.[23] According to the *Liber Ordinum*, the people leave the church at the conclusion of the Expoliation and the clergy retire to the atrium of the church.[24] After the doors have been secured, thus expressly excluding the laity, the clergy wash one another's feet while singing antiphonally another centonized text composed of psalm and Gospel verses recalling the washing of feet and keeping the Law of the Lord.

At Santa Eulalia in 1999, after the completion of the Expoliation, the twelve men left the sanctuary and took the candles back to the sacristy while the celebrant and ministers went to the foot of the altar. A large ceramic bowl, a matching ceramic pitcher with water, a slice of lemon, and a towel were brought forward and placed on a credence table that had been moved into place. Five members of the congregation came forward when the celebrant called for volunteers. These included two women and three men. Two of these were young people, Doña María Jesús Jurado Lozano and Óscar Urbiola Álvarez. María Jesús told me she has volunteered since she was a girl because she wants to be involved in the ministerial aspects of the liturgy in ways that present themselves because the pastor has not permitted her to read at the Eucharist despite her requests; Óscar supports her in this.[25] While the celebrant, assisted by the two lay ministers, washed one of the feet of each person, one of the concelebrating priests led the congregation in the recital of the antiphons.[26] At the conclusion of the washing of the feet, the congregation was invited to return the following day for both the morning and afternoon services. Then the ministers left the church in silence after reverencing the altar.

Two Good Friday Liturgies

The second day of the Hispano-Mozarabic Triduum provides the immediate ritual context for the ritual use of the Lignum Crucis. The day is comprised of two liturgies, neither of which involves a Communion of the Presanctified. The first service takes place in the morning and is titled *Ad tertiam*.[27] The second is titled *Ad nonam pro indulgentia* and, as the name suggests, takes place in the afternoon.[28] I describe in greater detail the ritual action and the texts for these days in Chapters 7 and 9. It is important to reiterate that these services in the contemporary rite represent a reappropriation of those found in the *Liber Ordinum* and the *Liber Misticus,* as well as a reform of the one Good Friday service found in the *Missale mixtum* and *Missale Gothicum.*

The Veneration of the Cross is central to the *Ad tertiam* liturgy. The reliquary of the true cross, the Lignum Crucis, begins to play a pivotal ritual role here.[29] Obviously not all the parish churches had a relic of the true cross; therefore, in Toledo the Veneration of the Cross rite would begin at the principal church. When this liturgical action took place there, it would follow the liturgy of Terce.[30] The deacon brought in the relic of the true cross on a paten and then elevated it, demonstrating it to those assembled. Then all left the church in procession to the Church of the Holy Cross, where the faithful approached to kiss the relic while the choir intoned hymns. Once the Veneration of the Cross was completed, all formed the procession anew and returned to the principal church. The clergy remained in the church praying and waiting for the afternoon liturgy at Nones. The people could leave at this point but were to return for the afternoon liturgy.

The *Ad nonam pro indulgentia* liturgy also involves the Lignum Crucis.[31] This time, instead of Veneration of the Cross, a long string or litany of intercessions asking pardon in front of the cross takes place. The litany is interrupted three times with acclamations of "Indulgentia!" The word as a congregational response or a diaconal acclamation is interspersed throughout the intercessions as well. The Visigothic church had three classes of public prayer.[32] One form, of course, was eucharistic prayer, in which the assembly united itself to the prayers of the priest and responded "Amen" at the many points in the liturgy indicated, as is done today. The second form was collective prayer, in which the presider invited the assembly to pray. Those gathered would pray in silence, usually with their arms outstretched in the form of a cross. After a period the presider would express a prayer that can be called a Collect, for it collected and expressed in a summary fashion the prayers of the community. The third form was litanic prayer, in which the presider invited the participants to pray for the intentions he would express. After each intention the assembled would answer with a supplicatory formula. This is the form of the Intercessions for Pardon as well as the Solemn Intercessions or Diptychs of the Mass.

A principal feature of the afternoon service is the completion of the centonized passion narrative. The parts are divided between the presider and two readers, as was the case at the Holy Thursday liturgy the evening before. The proclamation of the reading this time does not begin with the usual "Dominus sit semper vobiscum" and response. Rather, the celebrant says, "Sequitur passio Domini nostri Iesu Christi" (continuation of the passion of our Lord Jesus Christ). The reading starts with the meeting of the Sanhedrin and its decision to send Jesus to Pilate (Mt 27:1). It ends with the Pharisees asking Pilate for a guard at the tomb (Mt 26:62–66). A total of fifteen pericopes constitute the reading.[33]

The afternoon service has a decidedly penitential overtone. Sancho Andreu describes the Intercessions for Pardon particularly as a "collective penitential act that affects the entire community."[34] In effect, the Toledo IV (633) in canon 7 linked participation in this liturgy to the possibility of participating in Communion on the feast of the Resurrection.[35] Canon 7 also requires the mystery of the cross be preached on Good Friday so that the need for pardon can be elicited in those gathered. Pinell notes that Tradition A included a text for this, while Tradition B did not. Today, the *Sermo* is in the *Liber Commicus* for the presider to read at the *Ad nonam* liturgy.[36]

It is possible that at one time this was the public, communal penance service for the early Spanish church since private confession and penance were discouraged, though not prohibited, by the Toledo III (589).[37]

Also, unlike the rest of the Western churches, this council rejected leniency in regard to the repetition of penance, in addition to discouraging private confession. Unlike the private form of confession, the dramatic expressiveness of the Intercessions for Pardon, with its connection to the passion and the human need of divine forgiveness, transforms this litanic prayer into a solemn, collective penitential act.[38] Thus, those completing public penances as members of the order of penitents were reconciled at this liturgy not only to God but to the community. Nonetheless, it was a severe process, for Toledo III prescribed tonsure and penitential garb for penitents (canon 12) while the order of penitents and their reconciliation was prescribed by Toledo IV (633) (canon 55). Once in this order, one could not return to secular life, although Toledo VI (638) permitted some "adolescents" to return to the married state, at least temporarily, until they could live without concupiscence (canon 7).[39] This way they were admitted once again to the church's sacramental life. Toledo IV (633) particularly formalized the norms related to the order of penitents and their reconciliation (canon 7).[40]

Holy Saturday

The final day of the Easter Triduum begins with the Vigil liturgy on Saturday evening, as in the Roman rite. Like the latter, the Vigil is divided into four main sections: lighting of the fire and service of the light (Lucernarium), Liturgy of the Word, Baptism, and Eucharist.[41] Unlike the Roman rite, the Hispano-Mozarabic Vigil liturgy organizes these differently and stresses some things over others.[42]

The Lucernarium is particularly noteworthy in that the lighting of the fire takes place with only the ministers present on the patio of the church.[43] In addition to lighting the Paschal candle, a torch is lit first, from which the Paschal candle is lit. Then both are brought into the darkened church to the acclamation "Deo gratias." As the Paschal candle enters, those in the assembly light their tapers. Eventually the torch and candle are brought to the space before the entry to the narthex and the narthex itself, where they are placed in stands. Then a type of Easter Proclamation takes place that involves singing the praise of Christ the Light of the World as symbolized both by the torch and by the candle. Thus, a lengthy blessing, divided into two sections, takes place: one of the torch and the other of the candle. These blessings are justified by Toledo IV explaining that both are blessed because of the glorious mystery of that night. The text says this is done so that sanctified by the blessing of light, we may perceive the sacramental grace of Christ's resurrection, celebrated during that sacred Vigil.[44] The torch is extinguished and removed after the blessing.

The liturgy then moves into the readings from the Old Testament. As in other Easter Vigil liturgies, the church in this rite contemplates the history of salvation as found in the scriptures in order to come to see God's design and fulfillment of it in the Paschal Mystery. The Spanish rite has twelve readings for this purpose, with interspersed responses, canticles, and a series of intercessory prayers that can only be described as analogous to the Good Friday Intercessions of the Roman rite.[45] For example, the readings in Tradition A for this part of the liturgy are grouped according to themes rather than the biblical order. They come mostly from Genesis, Exodus, and the Prophets. It is noteworthy that after the third reading (Gn 22:1–19) and its corresponding oration, the rubrics call for the baptism of the catechumens. In the updated rite, baptism is placed after the last reading of the Old Testament and before the *Apostolus* reading.[46] Although there are no baptisms performed this night in the present era, at Santa Eulalia we moved to the baptismal fount for the blessing of the water. After the twelfth reading from the Old Testament, a reading from Romans (Rom 6:1–11) takes place. This is followed by a reading from the Gospel of Matthew (Mt 28:1–20) and a homily. The *Alleluia* closes the Liturgy of the Word for the first time since the First Sunday of Lent.

The remainder of the Mass follows the usual format, as described earlier. As can be seen, the structure is quite different from the Roman rite, and there are certain elements, such as the singing of the *Gloria* and the renewal of baptismal promises, which do not take place in the Hispanic rite. Moreover, the Symbol of Faith proclaimed in preparation for Communion is the Toledan version of the Nicene-Constantinopolitan Creed rather than the Apostles' Creed. Yet the same themes of light, water, blessing, baptism, thanksgiving, Eucharist, and resurrection are present. Even so, much of the euchological text makes a strong link to the cross, albeit to its victory rather than to the glory of the resurrection. For example, the monition directed to the assembly at the onset of the Diptychs clearly makes reference to the cross, declaring at one point:

That body carried, not the death of those who die, but rather love. In that belly was not contained weakness, rather mercy. Hung [on the cross], it is the body of mankind; rising, it is God's. . . . You nailed your sins [*sic*] on those hands. My death and your salvation you stitched together with those nails that trespassed those feet, which must be kissed, if it were possible . . . in order that creatures, rescued, might know their Maker whom mankind, if not rescued, would never have known perdition. Amen.[47]

GOOD FRIDAY PROCESSIONS IN TOLEDO

The Lignum Crucis is taken from the parish Church of Santa Eulalia to the other Mozarabic parish of Santas Justa y Rufina, located very near to the central plaza of the Old City of Toledo. Once there the Lignum Crucis is attached to a platform that has a canopy or *palio* above it. The Good Friday processions begin in the evening, around 8:30 p.m., and last until about midnight. They are the most elaborate of all the processions that take place throughout the week and involve not only six confraternities but also civic, military, and ecclesiastical officials, including the archbishop, who processes at the end of the cortege. Near the rear is the *Hermandad Mozárabe* with its *damas* in black, heads covered with *peineta y mantilla,* and its *caballeros* in their blue mantles and birettas.

The oldest confraternity in Toledo was formed after the reconquest of Toledo by King Alfonso VI in 1085 in order to help bury the dead from the battles with the Islamic forces.[48] This group still exists and is housed at Santas Justa y Rufina. There was apparently also a brotherhood *(hermandad)* of priests under the advocation of *Jesús Nazareno* based at Santa Eulalia until c. 1850.[49]

One informant told me that the processions may have had their origin in the fact that on these special days not all could fit into the main church for the services. Thus, the ecclesiastical authorities deemed it worthy to take the venerated object, like the relic of the true cross, out in procession. In this way those who could not get into the church building could still celebrate the occasion.[50] Whether or not this is true, some scholars believe that the processions are indeed extensions of the liturgy that convert the city into liturgical space.[51] In some places since Vatican II processions have been dissociated from the liturgy and have been relegated to the realm of popular religious practice.[52] Thus, in certain areas of the Catholic world processions have all but disappeared, but not yet in Spain or Latin America.

The process of recovery of the Hispano-Mozarabic rite for celebration in the contemporary era has involved the identification of authentic texts and structures. Those compiled into the new liturgical books for the rite's celebration reflect a type of "classical period" in the development of the rite. This period, mostly identified by Jordi Pinell, occurred just before the Islamic invasion, that is, the fifth to the seventh centuries. This was the apex of the Visigothic kingdom and church centered at Toledo whence have come the majority of the texts used as a basis for the construction of the *Missale Hispano-Mozarabicum* and of the *Liber*

Commicus. Nonetheless, there are aspects, such as the Institution Narrative and the prayers *Post Gloriam* and *Completuria*, which have been retained despite entering into the rite after the classical period.

The retrieval of ancient texts, rituals, and liturgies has also contributed to the retrieval of the structure of the Triduum. This has led to a reappropriation of the *Ad tertiam* liturgy of Good Friday, including the procession with the Lignum Crucis. Popular religious practices, such as the processions on Good Friday evening, have served to reinforce this reappropriation as well.

The recovery of both texts and structures for the Eucharist and Triduum provides the basic liturgical context for accessing the significance of the Lignum Crucis in the contemporary era. The Hispano-Mozarabic rite is closely related to the Latin liturgies of the West, particularly the Roman rite. The Eucharist reflects the core fourfold structure of Word, Intercessions, Anaphora, and Communion. Great stress is placed on the Word and on catechesis-mystagogia.

In the Triduum, emphasis is placed on the passion, and consequently on the cross, even when it is linked to the victory of the resurrection. The passion is upheld in all liturgical celebrations of the Triduum. It is the focus as well in the processions that extend the liturgical into the popular realm.

The stress on the passion is reflected in the liturgical calendar, with its emphasis on the martyrs and their relics and on the relic of the true cross, the Lignum Crucis. These factors point to a sense that martyrs and the Lignum Crucis mediate the aura of Christ's presence for the Mozarabic community. Thus, using Valenziano's notion that a rite is an institution based on a theme, or culturally directed values, and a model, or the repetition of these values in a cultural exemplar,[53] the theme of the cross, expressed as the values of suffering, of witnessing to one's faith, and of martyrdom, comes through most clearly. This allows the Mozarabs who celebrate this liturgy to experience God-with-them and confirms them as a people. The Good Friday events, in particular, provide a model, since they repeat these values for the participants to affirm and to appropriate through their participation. In the following two chapters we will examine the ritual setting and actions of the Good Friday events in order to see how these values are affirmed and appropriated.

6

The Lignum Crucis and Its Ritual Setting

That the cross appears as an important element in the spirituality of the Mozarab community of Toledo is most evident on Good Friday, when the community gathers for two liturgical services and then participates in the evening processions that wend their way through the streets of Toledo. It is the cross in the form of the seventeenth-century reliquary that contains a relic of the "wood of the true cross," the Lignum Crucis, that is particularly venerated that evening. By examining its ritual use in the Good Friday liturgies and the evening processions we can come to a deeper understanding of its significance as a symbol of the cross for Mozarabs in particular and for Hispanic spirituality in general.[1]

Religious ritual is a unity of conscious action and social being that not only constructs meaning but actualizes that meaning through texts, symbols, beliefs, gestures, and so forth. In this way a given culture is constructed, manifested, and made available as a source for further action. In addition, identity, social relations, and values at the core of a culture are ordered and given their power. However, because part of the social relationship being constructed through religious ritual involves God, what is being revealed about God has to be identified as well. Ritual as an activity at the core of human existence that constructs and manifests culture can be distinguished from other activities, and therefore it can be examined and analyzed. In an effort to interpret the theological meaning of the Mozarab's ritual use of the cross, I rely on the theory of ritual scholars as well as that of liturgical theologians. Let us begin by mapping the ritual field.[2]

THE CITY OF TOLEDO

The city that inspired the painter El Greco in the sixteenth century has remained relatively unchanged since then in parts of the city's core, the *casco antiguo*. Toledo sits atop a rugged promontory surrounded on three sides by a meander of the Río Tajo (Tagus River). Over millennia the river has carved a steep, sloping canyon in the granite, making the Old City a natural fortress overlooking the arid plains of Castilla-La Mancha, Toledo's region. The steep, crooked streets in the *casco antiguo* are narrow and often impassible by car. Public buildings and private residences seem to be piled on top of one another, and are partially surrounded by what remains of the medieval turreted walls.

Geographically, Toledo is near the center of the Iberian Peninsula; it was because of this setting and location that the Visigoths chose it to be their capital.[3] After the *reconquista* of 1085, Toledo became the capital of the Kingdom of León-Castilla, and under Emperor Charles V (1519–56), the capital of his Spanish empire. It lost its status to Madrid in 1560. Though no longer the capital of Spain, it is the capital of the Province of Toledo and serves as a reminder of Imperial Spain. The city is forty-two miles southwest of Madrid and has a population of about sixty-two thousand. In addition to Catholics, Toledo has been home to Jews and Muslims, vestiges of whom are seen in the two remaining medieval synagogues and one medieval mosque. They were built between the eleventh and fourteenth centuries and taken over by Christians and converted into churches in the fifteenth century. Eventually they were abandoned and used as garrisons and warehouses. Today they serve as historical sites. One of the synagogues, El Tránsito (the synagogue of Samuel Ha-Levi) became the Sephardi Museum in 1971.[4]

As the seat of the primate of Spain, Toledo is the country's Roman Catholic religious center. Locals say that the city is built on seven hills. Because of this feature and because of its religious importance, several of my informants, both Mozarab and non-Mozarab, call it the Rome of Spain. Others have described it as the "Jerusalem of the West."[5] Certainly, the Gothic cathedral is ranked among the greatest in the world and dominates the center of the city as well as the skyline. It reflects a variety of styles, having been constructed between 1226 and 1493.[6] Cardinal Cisneros converted the Corpus Christi chapel in the cathedral's southeast corner in 1502 for use by the Mozarabic rite chaplains.[7]

THE PARISH CHURCH OF SANTA EULALIA

On the southwest side of the *casco antiguo* the parish church of Santa Eulalia sits ensconced in an out-of-the-way barrio. This barrio once abutted the northwestern part of the medieval *judería* (Jewish quarter). It is precariously set on a steep, narrow, cobblestoned street and adjoins the retaining wall of a school perched on the hill above it. The street falls away below it into what seems an impassible path between two neighboring buildings.[8] The church is set off on two sides by this path and on the third by another precipitous street. Both feed into a narrow opening leading down the hill toward the Puerta de Cambrón, one of the ancient gates leading out of the Old City.

The church itself has the aura of antiquity. It is constructed of the same drab, dusty, beige stone and bricks common to the buildings of Toledo. Its tile roof is faded from the lichen that grows on it. The building would blend into its surroundings if it did not jut out so from the hill following the outline traced by the gully-*cum*-street. There are some gnarled trees just to the south side of the building in Santa Eulalia Plaza, really a widening in the street where several spaces for cars have been recently painted. The huge double door to the church is of heavy wood and reaches almost to the roof line. It is near the west end of the wall facing the plaza. The axis of the church is slightly off east-west.

Santa Eulalia was built in 559 during the reign of King Athanagild (554–67).[9] It has suffered reforms, rebuilding, abandonment, and reconstruction over the last fourteen hundred plus years. The building was abandoned in 1842 due to the *desamortización*. The last major repair was in the late 1960s, when the government prepared the building for use by the parishioners of San Marcos y Santa Eulalia. Electricity was installed and lights strategically placed throughout the building. The church was reconsecrated for worship on 14 October 1973.[10]

Upon entering the building one can be overcome with the simple grandeur and spaciousness of the interior; one almost feels transported back in time. One is immediately struck by the Mudéjar-style horseshoe arches. The church is dimly lit by light entering through the three widely spaced windows placed high in the western wall. These windows are covered with impressive, dark, wooden lattice work. The middle window, the largest of the three, is divided into four quadrants by thin, wooden slats. This feature makes it appear as if a cross has been superimposed on the window. Little natural light enters into the building, so until the lights are turned on, the effect is one of quiet somberness.

Architecturally, the building is in a modified Visigothic and Mozarabic style with Mudéjar elements.[11] The floor plan is that of the Roman basilica as adapted by the Visigoths. The main body of the church is divided into three sections, the nave and two lateral aisles. The nave is spacious and has a higher elevation than the two aisles. It is distinguished by a series of ten blind clerestory windows in Mudéjar style on each side and a series of six thin, marble columns with Corinthian capitals, also on each side. The columns sustain the horseshoe arches, an element common to Visigothic and Mozarabic architecture. The walls are not stuccoed and are unpainted, which gives the space a sense of antiquity. The stone floor is mostly bare.

The presbyterium is the recessed, curved apse at the east end of the nave. Between it and the nave is a tall, rectangular chancel separated from the apse by a wide and high arch. Here stands the altar. The altar area is separated from the nave by wide masonry-work columns topped by a horseshoe arch; each column has two smaller openings on either side. They too have modified horseshoe arches. Together, the masonry work gives the impression of a massive, brick screen or iconostasis, without icons, that separates the chancel from the nave. The only decoration is the design built into the masonry and a statue in the opening at the right. More masonry work separates the altar area from two side chapels. These chapels complete the lateral aisles. The Blessed Sacrament chapel is at the end of the left aisle. Large horseshoe arches sustained by masonry work separate the side chapels from the lateral aisles. Three masonry risers covered with a thin carpet form the floor of the presbyterium. A large rectangular red carpet lies on the floor in the nave at the entrance to the chancel creating ample room for ritual activity in front of the altar. An uneven, scissor-legged, wood lectern stands directly behind the altar at the first riser under the inside arch.

The Iconography
of the Church

The exterior walls are made of *mampostería* (rubble work) and masonry. They have been left unfinished inside the church. There are four paintings of scant artistic merit hung along the back and side walls of the building. One painting of note is that of Saint Mark painted in 1987 hanging near the baptismal font. Recall that the parish community of San Marcos moved to this site in 1973; the painting was made as a reminder of the origins of the community. Under the high window in the western wall is a deep-blue velvet hanging decorated with the Mozarabic cross of King Alfonso VI and the words *Ylustre Comunidad Mozárabe* (Illustrious Mozarab Community) in large letters.

A large stone plaque hangs on the back wall of the apse with the putative Creed of Toledo incised in Latin.[12] Above this is a large, wooden crucifix placed in 1987; presiding over the entire church is Christ crucified."[13] Together, the creed and the crucifix draw one's attention to the presbyterium. A metal chrismon, a cross composed of the Greek letters Chi-Rho, sits below the altar in front; it is in Visigothic style with the letters Alpha and Omega hanging from each arm of the crossbeam. The right wall separating the chancel from the nave contains a niche that encases a neo-Gothic imitation image of Our Lady of Hope, seated with the Child Jesus on her lap. She holds an anchor, a symbol of hope. The statue is reminiscent of the image venerated by the *Hermandad Mozárabe* at the Mozarabic rite Church of San Lucas.[14] The top of the anchor traditionally has a crossbeam, so that it appears to be a cross. Many Hispanics throughout the world wear this symbol with a corpus on it making clear its relationship to the cross of Christ.

The most striking image in the building is the figure of a woman hanging on a cross. She is Santa Eulalia, the patroness of the parish. Dated to the sixteenth century, the exquisitely carved and painted figure hangs in the chapel at the end of the right nave. Santa Eulalia is important in the Spanish church. She was a virgin martyr who died during the persecution of Diocletian in the third century. There is controversy, however; there may have been two Eulalias. One is venerated in Mérida in the Western part of Spain, where a young girl of twelve was burnt at the stake. On the other hand, the city of Barcelona claims Eulalia as its patroness and recounts her martyrdom by crucifixion in that city. Even so, there was probably only one Eulalia, who was from Mérida. Nonetheless, both Eulalias are named in the Diptychs of the Hispano-Mozarabic Mass.[15] Ferrer Grenesche justifies this anomaly by saying that just as there is scant evidence that there were two Eulalias, there is scant evidence that there were not.[16]

The Blessed Sacrament chapel contains a large, stone baptismal font. Nearby hangs a brass imitation of a seventh-century Visigothic votive crown with letters suspended from its circular rim that spell out SANTA EULALIA. A Visigothic-style cross hangs down in the middle from the crown past the bottom rim and letters. Above the top of the rim is a lighted sanctuary lamp. The most famous of these liturgical objects is the votive "crown" of King Reccesvinth (649–72), found buried in a field at Guarrazar near Toledo. Members of the aristocracy gave these crowns as votive offerings to the Catholic church during the Visigothic period.[17] The chapel also contains an altar attached to the back wall with a baroque-style *retablo* in the midst of which is the tabernacle. Here one encounters the Lignum Crucis affixed to the top of the tabernacle except when it is taken down for the Good Friday events.

THE LIGNUM CRUCIS RELIQUARY

The principal ritual object under consideration is a relic of "the wood of the true cross," the Lignum Crucis. It is encased in a gold-plated, silver reliquary in the shape of a Latin cross, also referred to as the Lignum Crucis. Relics have played an important role in Catholic faith from at least the fourth century. The word *relic* comes from the Latin *reliquiæ* (remains), and though Catholics are not the only ones who honor relics, the practice is most often associated with them.[18] At times their use has been controversial in some circles because of their association with the abuses that led to the Reformation.

Origin of the Relic

The wood of the true cross is one of the oldest relics honored by Christians. Legend has it that Saint Helena, the mother of the emperor Constantine, found the true cross. Constantine then ordered construction of the Church of the Holy Sepulcher (c. 326) over the place where it was thought Jesus had been buried. The church was dedicated c. 334. There are four legends about the finding of the true cross. In three of them Helena figures as the main protagonist. The most widely known is that she found three crosses and that the true cross was identified after a dead man was raised when touched by it. Dates for the finding of the true cross vary from 318 to 334. However, the first written reference to the true cross is made by Cyril of Jerusalem in a Lenten catechetical instruction c. 350.[19]

Helena and Constantine soon distributed pieces of the true cross as gifts in the fourth century and placed them in different reliquaries. They also placed a piece of the true cross in a statue of Constantine in the Forum of Constantinople. A large portion of the true cross was placed in Rome's Basilica of Santa Croce in Gerusalemme, erected for this purpose by Constantine. This portion has been divided into three pieces, about six inches in length each, and placed into a cross-shaped reliquary located in the reliquary chapel of the basilica.[20]

The remaining wood of the cross was placed in a silver reliquary and venerated in Jerusalem until 614, when it was captured by Persian forces led by Chosroes II.[21] Egeria in her diary describes vividly the Veneration of the True Cross in the Holy Week services of Jerusalem sometime around 393–96.[22] The Byzantine emperor Heraclius (610–41) recovered the reliquary around 629. It was returned on 14 September 629 or 630; this date became the origin of the feast of the Triumph of the Cross.[23] In order to protect the true cross from being taken again, Heraclius broke the remaining wood into pieces. He gave fragments as gifts to various Christian secular and religious leaders in both East and West. Quickly bits of the wood of the true cross, the Lignum Crucis, were distributed throughout the Christian world and placed in various types of reliquaries.

It is unknown how the Mozarabic parish of Santa Eulalia acquired a relic of the true cross. It is known, however, that the Byzantine emperor Alexius I Comnenus (1081–1118) gave a relic of the true cross to King Alfonso VI around 1101.[24] Alfonso, in turn, gave the relic as a gift to the abbey of Sahagún. It is possible that a piece was taken and given to someone else, perhaps Bernard de Sedirac, Alfonso's friend and the archbishop of Toledo who had previously been the abbot of Sahagún. A piece could have been given to the Mozarab community as a peace offering, considering the animosity between them and the newly installed Roman rite hierarchy. Recall that Alfonso needed the help of the Mozarabs to hold onto Toledo, for there was still danger that it would be lost again to the Islamic forces. Bernard Reilly suggests that this fear was part of the reason behind the *fuero* signed by Alfonso in 1101 to the benefit of the Mozarabs.[25]

Information on the existence of relics of the true cross in Toledo is sketchy. For example, in the twelfth century Ruy Díaz de Vivar (El Cid) founded the *Cofradía de la Vera Cruz* (Confraternity of the True Cross) in Toledo; this *cofradía* acquired in the fifteenth century a Lignum Crucis that was taken out in procession on Holy Thursday.[26] In addition, Cisneros's Mozarabic missal of the sixteenth century gives evidence that there was a church built in honor of the cross in Toledo, at which the veneration of a relic of the cross took place after having been taken there in procession. This liturgy, a combination of Mozarab and Roman elements, was presided over by the bishop of Toledo.[27] A Mozarabic chaplain from the early seventeenth century noted that the *Cofradía de Santa Elena*, linked to the parish of Santa Eulalia, took out a Lignum Crucis in procession on Holy Wednesday. Finally, Lynette Bosch in her study of the Toledo cathedral reports that at one time the cathedral was endowed with three small relics of the true cross that were part of a larger collection of relics.[28]

The relic of the true cross currently owned by the Mozarabs was discovered in a small coffer when repairs were being made to the Church of

Santa Eulalia in the mid-fifteenth century. It was among other relics in a wall of the church.[29] Shortly after this discovery Cardinal Pedro González de Mendoza (d. 1495) took a small piece of the relic to place in his *guión* (processional cross).[30]

Apparently the relic was once larger than it is today. Don Mario Arellano García discovered in his work on the genealogy of a Mozarab nobleman buried in the nave of Santa Eulalia that this nobleman owned a portion of the Lignum Crucis that had been encrusted in a gold pendant with twenty-four emeralds.[31] Don Tomás Bernardo Zorrilla Loaisa (1670–1740) in his will made shortly before his death in 1740 declared that he and an unnamed pastor of Santa Eulalia took the Lignum Crucis from its crystal container, which was kept in the tabernacle. They took a slice, and then Don Tomás had the pendant made so that it could be worn by the pastor and be available for veneration by the faithful. However, he left the pendant to the parish of San Martín of Aldeamayor (Valladolid), along with instructions that it be made available to the public for veneration, for making oaths, and for the feast of the Holy Cross on 3 May. Today at Santa Eulalia the only relic of the Lignum Crucis is the one in a small crystal container set in the transept of the arms of the cross reliquary. It is barely visible to the beholder. Because the reliquary already existed at the time of Don Tomás, there must have been a larger relic contained in another crystal case from which the segment given to San Martín was taken.[32]

Given the above reports, and the fact that the crystal in the transept of the Lignum Crucis reliquary is sealed and cannot be opened, we can establish, first, that there was obviously more than one relic of the true cross in Toledo and at Santa Eulalia. Second, at least two *cofradías* took a relic of the true cross in procession, albeit on different days. Third, Cisneros's Missal gives no information about where the Lignum Crucis used by the bishop was kept; the rubrics only say it is taken in procession to the Church of the Holy Cross. It is possible the Good Friday services in the Mozarabic parishes were supplanted at the time by the ritual created by Cisneros. In that case the services may have been suppressed in the parishes and the relic taken to the cathedral. However, this does not explain how Santa Eulalia eventually acquired or reacquired its relic.

Because the true cross was found three hundred years after the death of Christ, any claims to the authenticity of relics of the cross are suspect; if all the so-called pieces of the true cross were gathered they would far exceed the one on which Jesus died. Nonetheless, Mozarabs do not question the authenticity of their relic. In interviews they expressed complete confidence in the relic as the wood on which their Savior died and, therefore, its worthiness of veneration. That the relics of Santa Eulalia are also in the reliquary make it even more worthy of veneration in their eyes. Carrillo Morales declares there is an important symbolism created by "the fact that in one and the same reliquary there is both a piece of the cross and at its feet the relics of the titular patroness of this parish. At the cusp is the cross and at its feet is the martyr."[33]

Origin of the Reliquary

The reliquary of the relic of the true cross was made in 1636, as indicated by the inscription at its base.[34] At the foot of the cross is a neoclassical-style rectangular box placed lengthwise that contains the relics of Santa Eulalia. Carrillo Morales, the Mozarabic rite pastor of Santa Eulalia y San Marcos, identified a small cartouche in the base of the Lignum Crucis reliquary on 7 October 1987 with an inscription that says the contents are ashes and pieces of bones of Santa Eulalia.[35] The reliquary also has four blue, semi-precious stones encrusted on each side of the box. A bar separating the box from the base has two levels. At the second level an inscription indicates that the donor was a former rector of the parish who contributed the money for the reliquary after having wondrously recovered his health. Thus, Hurtado's reason for giving the money for the reliquary, the recovery of his health, makes it a type of *ex voto* given in thanksgiving for a favor received. This is a popular religious practice among Hispanics all over the world. I estimate the reliquary stands approximately three feet from base to top. The crossbeam forming the arms is about two feet in length and about three inches from the top. The base measures about twenty-four square inches.

The reliquary is quite contemporary in appearance with its clean lines, minimal detail, and lack of a corpus. It gives very little indication that it was made over three hundred years ago. One wonders if the design reflected the tastes of the donor. In any case, the reliquary stands in contrast to the typical Spanish baroque style of art and architecture of the era.[36] The seventeenth century saw the flowering of exuberance and great detail in the crosses and figures of Christ upon them; they tended to present Christ's agony in his features and twisted body as well as in the copious blood flowing from his wounds. The baroque style is very evident in the other crosses, figures, and *pasos* that go in procession on Good Friday in Toledo.

There is no record as to what was done with the cross after an inventory of 1921 indicated the reliquary was kept at the parish of La Magdalena. Sometime after this it came back into the possession of the Mozarabs at Santa Eulalia. In an interview with Don Enrique Carrillo

Morales, I learned that just prior to 1987 it was on its *anda* (a platform used by carriers on which images are placed for processions) and kept in a corner of the sacristy.[37] In any case, the reliquary owned by Santa Eulalia is the one given by Hurtado in 1636. The *Hermandad Mozárabe* takes it out in procession on Good Friday. After the rehabilitation of the church building in 1987, Don Enrique decided to "return" the Lignum Crucis to its "rightful place" above the tabernacle.[38]

Carrillo Morales affixed the Lignum Crucis reliquary to the tabernacle in the Blessed Sacrament chapel in 1987.[39] His reasoning is partially based on descriptions by witnesses who note the placement of the relic on top of a tabernacle or inside it. The main reason Carrillo Morales gives for this arrangement, however, is liturgical. The Lignum Crucis is placed over the tabernacle "so that, due to the singular veneration that is given to it [the tabernacle] by the Catholic liturgy, it is assimilated to and is united to that which the church gives to the presence of Jesus in the Blessed Sacrament."[40] Thus, he deliberately wants to associate the Lignum Crucis with the Blessed Sacrament. As we will see later, the reliquary is treated as if it were a monstrance containing a particle of the sacramental presence of Christ.

The overview of Mozarab history and culture given earlier reveals the community's tortuous history. Theological controversy, conquest, martyrdom, and loss of status have all marked it, yet it has managed to survive. Therefore, it is significant that the emblem of the community is a certain adaptation of the cross. Unique amid the usual iconography of the cross found in contemporary Spain, with its depictions of the bloody and suffering Christ, the Mozarabic cross carries no corpus.[41] The cross is based on a Visigothic cross in the shape of a slender Greek cross with flared ends. An Alpha and Omega hang from the crossbeam arms of the Visigothic cross. The oldest example of the Mozarabic cross can be found in a frieze on the seventh-century Visigothic Church of San Pedro de la Nave (Zamora) as well as on Mozarabic coins minted at Toledo in the twelfth century.[42] The cross has appeared in the community's iconography in various ways over the centuries.

The *Constituciones* of the *Hermandad Mozárabe* state that as a symbol of the antiquity of the Mozarab community, the *Hermandad* has chosen as its emblem and coat of arms the cross of Alfonso VI.[43] It is to be worn as a pendant on a gold link with a blue ribbon containing a narrow band of yellow along the center; the women wear the emblem on a folded ribbon over their breast, while the men wear it around their neck. This is yet another form of the cross held dear by Mozarabs of today. It is enameled in white and plated in gold, with twelve points, three on each arm. Each arm of the cross is divided into four segments by three gold bars. In the center is a circle containing the golden imperial crown of King Alfonso VI in a field of azure, the ancient emblem of Toledo. The emblem is worn on formal social and religious occasions. It appears on official documents, letterhead, and other paraphernalia used by Mozarabs such as church furnishings and liturgical books. The emblem is highly honored and has come to symbolize the community. It is easily recognizable and only available to members of the community who have joined the *Hermandad* as well as to selected honorary members.[44]

The cross in these three forms—the Lignum Crucis reliquary, the Mozarabic cross, and the cross of Alfonso VI—stands out as an important symbol for the community. It is a paradoxical symbol, for how could such an ignominious instrument of death be a sign of life and reveal the divinity of a human being, Jesus of Nazareth, the Christ? Yet both testaments of scripture provide the theological precedence for this meaning. Moses takes up the serpent, an instrument of death for the Hebrews in the desert, and converts it into an instrument of healing upon lifting it up (Nm 21:4–9). The serpent lifted up by Moses is often seen as an archetype of the cross of Jesus.[45] Early Christians proclaimed that salvation comes through the cross of Jesus (1 Cor 1:17; Eph 2:16; Col 1:20; Gal 6:14). Belief in the cross as an instrument of healing "allows a Christian to face the cross with a certain equanimity and trust in the power of God."[46] The scriptures also indicate that the cross is the means to model Jesus for the world (Gal 5:24) by taking up one's cross daily (Lk 9:23; 14:27; Mk 8:34; Mt 16:24).

These references form part of the underlying significance of the cross for Mozarabs and the reason it has become their emblem. Yet, when asked why the cross of Alfonso VI is their emblem, neither religious elites nor members of the Mozarab community were able to articulate its significance beyond typical interpretations such as that it is the sign of Christianity and the like. I suspect that part of the reason is that it is one of those taken-for-granted symbols whose meaning is so deep-seated that only by seeing how and when it is used can its depth of meaning be plumbed. For this reason let us now examine the ritual use of the Lignum Crucis in the two Good Friday liturgies at Santa Eulalia y San Marcos.

7

The Ritual Use of the Lignum Crucis on Good Friday

The first liturgical service of Good Friday is the *Ad tertiam* service, literally "at the third hour." This service has been celebrated anew at Santa Eulalia y San Marcos only since 1996. It represents a recovery of a service found in the *Liber Ordinum* that was altered and combined with the *Ad nonam* service under Cardinal Cisneros in the 1500 Missal. In the liturgy of the hours Terce, the third hour, is usually 9:00 a.m. At Santa Eulalia the service on Good Friday, 2 April 1999, was scheduled for 11:00 a.m. in the parish church. Don Enrique explained that *Ad tertiam* means the period between 9:00 a.m. and noon, and he has maintained this practice over the years. I was a participant-observer in this liturgy as one of two visiting priests. The liturgy consists of ten ritual units. What follows is a description of the service with particular attention to the ritual use of the Lignum Crucis reliquary.[1] I use the present tense to help the reader enter into the event, although clearly it was a contingent historical event put together by the actors.

DESCRIPTION OF THE *AD TERTIAM* SERVICE

The people begin to gather quietly in the parish church at about 10:45 a.m. Only a few lights are on. A small credence table covered with a white linen cloth has been placed in the nave in front of the altar but outside the chancel. A tall, floral arrangement of white and yellow daisies sits on the raised floor between the credence table and the altar. A red cushion has been placed at the foot of the credence table for kneeling. In the space between the pews and the credence table are three wooden chairs, two on the left side and one on the right facing each other. They form a frame on either side of the space just before the credence table.

These are for the presider and attending priests. Another red cushion lies on the floor before the presider's chair on the right side of the credence table. These furnishings are on the large red carpet that separates the pews from the chancel.

Twelve unlit tall red votive candles are on the altar. The same candles were placed on the altar the evening before toward the end of the Holy Thursday liturgy. Don Enrique told me the rubrics say twelve men are to take candles and surround the altar. He thinks the candles represent the twelve apostles. He puts them on the altar the next day so that the Lignum Crucis will "look nicer."[2] I asked the Jurado Lozano family what the twelve candles mean to them; they said that they symbolized the light of God. The altar top and front has been completely covered by a red cloth, while a white cloth covers the lectern; on the front is the Mozarab emblem, the cross of Alfonso VI, embroidered in silver thread.

The ministers consist of the presider, Don Enrique, two visiting priests, and two laymen who serve as acolytes during the service. The latter wear black suits, white shirts, and black ties. They gather in the sacristy where Don Enrique, dressed in an alb and cincture, dons a seventeenth-century red brocade Roman-style cope and stole. The two assisting priests also wear albs, cinctures, and matching red stoles. These are part of the set of vestments worn by the presider. Before the service begins, Don Enrique turns on all the church lights. Then, just prior to assembling for the procession, he dons the humeral veil of the set and takes up the Lignum Crucis. He covers his hands and the base of the reliquary with the veil.

Entrance of the Liturgical Ministers

The ministers process into the church from the sacristy to the foot of the altar, led by Don Antonio Perea Muñoz as thurifer. He is followed by the two assisting priests; the second lay minister, Don Mario Arellano García; and Don Enrique. As they approach the front of the altar while still in the nave, Don Enrique goes to the center of the group. All face the congregation. Don Enrique lifts high the Lignum Crucis, while Don Mario holds the service booklet for him.

From this beginning the social drama unfolds in which the reliquary becomes the focus of attention for those present.[3] Here we see the hierarchical structure of the church and community at play. Both Don Mario and Don Antonio are officers of the *Hermandad Mozárabe*. Don Enrique is not only the pastor but the beloved chaplain of the *Hermandad*. The two visiting priests take positions of honor, while the congregants participate from the pews. In this way social relationships are exalted and reinforced. Also reinforced is the idea that the relic is worthy of exaltation as a symbol of the presence of Christ in the midst of the assembly. Further legitimacy is provided by the antiquity of the setting and vestments, giving a sense of rootedness to the service, although it lay dormant for centuries.

Procession with Lignum Crucis

Don Enrique greets those gathered, inviting them to participate in the service with their attention and prayers. He addresses a prayer to the Father in which he mentions that this fraction of the wood of the cross is the sign of salvation; therefore, it is carried in procession so that as "we cross the sea [of this life]" we pray for the salvation that comes through it. Then he instructs the assembly to leave the church in procession. The people go out the main doors of the church into Santa Eulalia plaza. Don Enrique starts a hymn to the cross, "¡Victoria! ¡Tú reinarás!"[4] This is an idiosyncratic introduction; the *Missale* and the *Liber Ordinum* offer the text of a Latin hymn, but due to the lack of notation, Don Enrique has substituted this hymn of recent vintage. The people sing the hymn *a capella* as they go out of the building into the plaza, down the hill and up around the building, and back into the church through the Santo Domingo doors. At the back of the procession Don Antonio continues to swing the thurible filled with incense. The two visiting priests, walking side by side, follow him. Don Enrique is at the very end of the procession, still elevating the Lignum Crucis, with Don Mario at his side. A parishioner shuts the patio doors, the Santo Domingo doors, and the curtains once all have gone back into the church.

Back in the church the members of the congregation return to their pews, while the ministers go back to the front of the altar, still remaining in the nave. They stand and face the congregants as they complete the processional hymn. Don Enrique continues to hold high the Lignum Crucis for all to see. The visiting priests stand at each end of the row while the lay ministers flank Don Enrique. At the completion of the hymn he reads a monition calling on all to adore the wood on which hung Christ the Savior.

Once again the social drama unfolds as the assembly takes to the streets to manifest itself and its faith, even in an isolated and depopulated barrio. The strenuousness of the return up the steep street to the Santo Domingo doors fosters a sense of climbing Calvary. Participating in the procession reveals particular values. The first prayer makes evident the conflation of Christ and the Father common to Mozarabic liturgy. The procession helps the participants make public their faith. As the group climbs the back street to the Santo Domingo doors, a young mother and child climbing the street are enthralled by the procession and join at the end, entering the church after the presider. The *communitas*[5] fostered by emptying the church of those present and engaging them in the procession is not exclusive, for it takes in people on the street. In this way others are brought to see and worship Christ present by means of the reliquary held high in the church. The sacredness of the Lignum Crucis is constructed by means of the humeral veil that "protects" the presider's hands as he holds it.

First Veneration of the Lignum Crucis

At the completion of the monition, Don Enrique takes the Lignum Crucis reliquary to the altar. He places it in the middle of the twelve votive candles, with six on either side. Don Mario takes the humeral veil off Don Enrique and puts it on a table in the right-hand chapel. Afterward, Don Enrique returns to the foot of the altar in front of the credence table. The visiting priests have moved to either side of the space. Don Antonio brings the thurible for Don Enrique who spoons incense into it. Taking the thurible, Don Enrique kneels on the red carpet in front of the credence table, but not on the cushion, and begins incensing the reliquary in silence. While the entire assembly kneels, he swings the thurible, following the Roman rite practice of three doubles, called *triplici ductu*; this practice was reserved for incensing seven different objects or dignitaries, including the Blessed Sacrament and a "relic of the Sacred Passion."[6]

By means of this ritual action the importance of the Lignum Crucis is further stressed. The top of the hierarchy of relationships is revealed to be Christ, symbolized by the Lignum Crucis. The community's identity as the humble people of Christ is also constructed in this action by means of their adoration and the incensing by Don Enrique. The incense represents the church's prayer rising up like smoke to engulf the reliquary as well as being a symbol of adoration and sacrifice. In the Tridentine usage of the Roman rite the cross is incensed as a mark of respect, for it, like the altar, "represents Christ and recalls in a very special way the identity of the Sacrifice of the Cross and that of the Mass."[7] A relic of the passion of Christ especially symbolized this.

Homily-Instruction

After the incensing of the Lignum Crucis the two visiting priests take their seats on the left side of the credence table. The two lay ministers stand on the first gradient in the chancel in front of the altar, partially hidden by the walls that separate the chancel-altar area from the nave. Don Enrique begins a homily-instruction in which he explains the origin of the *Ad tertiam* service. He attributes it to the texts of the *Liber Ordinum* found by Marius Férotin and to the prayer book of the monastery of Einsiedeln. In his research he discovered that Férotin in the *Liber Ordinum* and the *Ordo Einsidelns* describes the use of the Lignum Crucis for both the morning and afternoon services, as well as for procession.[8] He explains that the service is related to one experienced by Egeria in Jerusalem, to the service at the Church of the Holy Cross in Rome, and to the Visigothic service celebrated in the Church of the Holy Cross at Toledo. He says he has attempted to be faithful to "our Catholic-Spanish tradition."[9] It is for this reason, he claims, that we are gathered for the *Ad tertiam* liturgy.

Don Enrique continues by extolling the attitudes of reverence and humility necessary for the veneration of the tree on which Christ hung. He links the service to the *Illatio* of the Christmas liturgy in the Hispano-Mozarabic rite, which speaks of Christ, the church's spouse, who spilled his blood on its behalf, clothing it in a mantle of holiness. This is especially reflected in the virtues of martyrdom, virginity, and repentance. In this regard Don Enrique declares that "Christ offers martyrs as roses; virgins as lilies; and penitents as violets."[10] He explains that these flowers will be offered as part of the service today. The red represents martyrdom, and the roses will be offered by some laymen. The white represents virginity, and the lilies will be offered by two women, one single and another a religious. The purple represents repentance, and two priests will offer violets (but see the account of the actual service below). He then instructs the people to stand.

Don Enrique makes explicit more values that reinforce the identity of the Mozarab community. These are its antiquity, the continuity of its worship from earliest Christianity, its need to continue acknowledging Christ's presence and to repent of one's sins in light of this reality. It also sets the *Ad tertiam* liturgy within the larger framework of the Hispano-Mozarabic rite by linking it to the Christmas liturgy. The homily, in addition, serves to construct and reinforce the identity of the community as comprised of martyrs, virgins, and penitents.

Flower Offering

All stand, and two ladies of the parish, Doña María Jesús Lozano Duran and Doña María Victoria Hernández, distribute the flowers, placed on a credence table near the entrance to the church. Both ladies are leaders of the *Damas Mozárabes*. Doña María Jesús and Doña María Victoria determine the order and who will take up the flowers as this ritual unit unfolds. An unmarried young woman of the parish and a visiting religious woman lead off the offering with bouquets of lilies. Six men, each bearing a rose, immediately follow; they include three young men of the parish and three visitors, one of whom is a visiting priest not ministering in the service. Two married women (not two priests) of the parish bring up two small pots of African violets to complete the offering. The lilies and roses go in the vases on either side of the credence table but behind it; the violets go on the altar at each end. Prior to the beginning of the liturgy I observed Don Enrique ask members of the congregation to participate by taking these flowers to vases near the Lignum Crucis reliquary before the first veneration of the cross. He informed Doña María Jesús about this while we were in the sacristy. Those who brought forward the flowers were slightly different from those he named in the homily-instruction. The flower offering ritual unit is idiosyncratic and does not appear in any liturgical book. He told me he uses flowers because of the Christmas reference as well as the custom of using these flowers at the popular celebration of the feast of the Cross on 3 May.[11]

Two of the young Mozarab men participants, one of the male visitors, and one of the Mozarab women make a slight bow of their head as they approach the altar. They are quietly directed by Don Mario to place the flowers in the vases and then go through the chancel to the left entrance and back into the nave. They are to make a wide arc from the back credence table to the altar, around the wall separating the altar area from the nave, and down the left aisle back to their pews. The males comply, but the women decide to return the way they came. One woman makes the sign of the cross as she backs away.

Don Enrique's idiosyncratic introduction of the flower offering reveals that the ritual is developing, neither static nor conservative. Those with whom I later talked found this introduction pleasing and see in it a way to take a more active part in the liturgy. The negotiation taking place in the ritual is also made evident by the differences in the homily indicating the order of the offering, who would do it, and its actual execution. The contention for the appropriation of symbols is seen when the women leaders of the parish take command of the flower offering. Some women with whom I spoke told me that they seek to have a more active role. At times they feel they have to remind Don Enrique of what comes next in the ritual. Doña María Jesús declared, "I make sure that Don Enrique doesn't forget anything, since he tends to forget."[12] She revealed there is a group of women who do what they can because they have not been allowed to participate as ministers in the services. Doña

Justa cares for the linens, for instance, and she makes sure the liturgies are done correctly. She tells me that as a result of such work, some women have ministered as readers at this and other liturgies.

The contention for the appropriation of symbols was also evidenced by signals being given to the participants by Doña María Jesús about what was to happen next as the ritual unit unfolded. One could notice it also in the instructions Don Mario gave to the participants as they approached the altar. The participants also made decisions for themselves as to how to approach or proceed by bowing their heads in veneration of the Lignum Crucis, signing themselves, or backing out of the altar area rather than going through it. In this way they contribute to the development of the ritual and construct meanings for themselves.

Second Veneration and Collection

Once the flowers are in place, the two lay ministers move away to prepare for the Veneration of the Cross. They light tall tapers in their holders, two each at side tables in the right and left chapels. They then light the twelve votive candles on the altar. Meanwhile, Don Enrique asks the people that as they come to venerate the Lignum Crucis they make a donation for the Holy Land. This is a yearly collection following the example of Saint Paul in behalf of the Jerusalem Christian community (see Acts 24:17; Rom 15:26ff.; 1 Cor 16:1–4; 2 Cor 8:1–9, 15; Gal 2:10) and requested by the Holy See. He says that after the clergy at the altar make their veneration, the congregants may come forward to venerate the reliquary and deposit their gift in a basket placed near it.

Don Enrique goes to the altar and takes the reliquary to the credence table. He does so without donning the humeral veil or making any special obeisance. Don Mario brings him a breviary from a side table. Then Don Enrique goes out to the space in front of the credence table, genuflects, bows his head, then rises. He goes forward to the reliquary and kisses the crystal containing the relic. Don Mario wipes it afterward with a purificator. Don Enrique goes to his chair and stands while the two visiting priests follow suit. They are followed by Don Antonio and then Don Mario.

The congregants approach one by one to do the same. As they do, Don Enrique sits, places the red cushion at his feet, wraps himself in the cope, and begins to sing "Vexilla Regis" from the Roman rite Breviary. Though he uses this text, he sings it to what he claims to be a Mozarabic melody.[13] During the course of the veneration the people come up and make various forms of reverence. Some approach and bow their head, then kiss the reliquary, attempting to kiss the crystal as best they can.

Others come and kneel briefly, rise, and kiss the reliquary. Still others genuflect and then kiss. All do their reverence from a slight distance before nearing the reliquary to kiss it. None uses the red cushion, which remains at the foot of the credence table; it becomes a sort of barrier to the reliquary, since all have to get past the pillow in order to approach the reliquary. Almost all deposit money, either coins or small bills, in the basket next to the reliquary on the credence table. During the course of the veneration rite, lasting about twenty minutes, Don Enrique completes the "Vexilla Regis" and then begins to sing the processional hymn, "¡Victoria! ¡Tú reinarás!" The congregants join in.

In this ritual component we see the appropriation of the Lignum Crucis symbol by most of the congregants. They approach, make a reverence in their own manner, and attempt to get as close as possible to the relic. This action is "costly," for it requires effort to approach the reliquary. The placement of the collection basket next to the reliquary seems to put pressure on the people to make a monetary contribution. When asked about this, my informants told me they were not offended by this. They see it as just part of the ceremony.

Don Enrique's use of "Vexilla Regis" and the repetition of the earlier processional hymn is idiosyncratic; it represents another instance in which the ritual is developing. Don Enrique claims that while he uses the text of the "Vexilla Regis," he applies "authentic Mozarabic music" to it, although he cannot recall where he acquired it.[14] In this way a negotiation and contention for the appropriation of the *Ad tertiam* liturgy has been set up between those who fashioned the *Missale* and those charged with its celebration. It also generates the possibility for further development, as it signals the introduction of novelties, meaningful as they might be.

The fact that the "Vexilla Regis" is a Roman rite hymn also forges a link between it and the Hispano-Mozarabic rite. Blending the two rites in this way can indicate that the latter is somehow within the former's aegis, or at least in its ambit. The vestments and the way Don Enrique incensed the Lignum Crucis also construct this link. The veneration he models for the congregation stresses this further. The approach to the Lignum Crucis reliquary from a distance, bowing one's head while kneeling in front of it, and then nearing it to kiss the relic is similar to the practice of venerating the exposed Blessed Sacrament in its monstrance. The practice of adoring the eucharistic species is a Roman rite ritual introduced in the thirteenth century in Western Europe after the Mozarabic rite was no longer extensively celebrated in Spain. Nonetheless, John McKenna notes that the earliest form of exposing the Blessed Sacrament was just before Communion with the expression "Holy things for the holy" *(Sancta sanctis)* in the Hispano-Mozarabic eucharistic liturgy.[15]

Acclamation of the Cross

After the last person has venerated the reliquary and the people are finishing the hymn, Don Enrique takes the reliquary back to its previous position on the altar. He returns to the credence table, instructs the people to stand, turns to face the Lignum Crucis, and makes a brief monition inviting all to acclaim the cross with him in a litany of praise. Don Enrique begins the litany extolling the blessed cross on which Christ hung and whose blood washed our wounds. The people repeat the first verse as an acclamation after each of the following five verses. After the litany all kneel and Don Enrique prays a closing prayer; he kneels on the cushion in front of the credence table. At the conclusion the congregants respond "Amen."

In this ritual unit the people are encouraged to continue appropriating the meaning being generated by the ritual, that is, that this is a symbol of the presence of Christ on the cross. By means of the litany the participants are invited to enter into a type of liminality; that is, they enter a realm beyond the here and now so that the crucifixion of Jesus becomes present to them symbolically and they can join themselves to it in order to be transformed or undergo conversion. Moreover, just as at one time penitents were reconciled with the community by means of this ritual, now those present are invited to be reconciled with one another and with Christ. The meanings proclaimed by the litany in relation to this will be examined in Chapter 9.

Dismissal and Exit

All stand. Don Enrique faces the congregants and invites them to return to the church at 5:00 p.m. for the *Ad nonam* liturgy. He and the ministers line up, turn and face the reliquary, genuflect, and retire to the sacristy. They leave in silence in single file led by Don Antonio, followed by the two visiting priests, Don Mario, and finally Don Enrique. The people disperse in silence as well.

The ending is somewhat abrupt and feels like an interruption. This signals that the ritual process is not complete. Don Enrique reinforces this notion by inviting the participants to return later in the day for the next liturgical service. In this way the processual nature of the Good Friday rituals stands out.[16]

The Ritual Use of the Lignum Crucis

The description above makes obvious that the main ritual object and center of attention is the reliquary. The presider brings it in with honor. Those present give it several physical and oral acts of reverence throughout the service. The Lignum Crucis also focuses the purpose of the service. The main purpose is the Veneration of the Cross. In the updated Hispano-Mozarabic rite this takes place in the morning at the *Ad tertiam* service.

It is obvious that the reliquary is treated as more than just a reminder of the cross on which Jesus died. Indeed, it is treated as if it were the actual cross because of the relic of the true cross it contains. When asked about this, several Mozarabs reported that it makes Christ present to them because it is the wood on which he died. To them it has the same importance as the monstrance with the Blessed Sacrament in it. For example, Doña María Jesús Lozano Duran said, "The way the Lignum Crucis is brought in by Don Enrique with cope and veil signifies that it is a very important act."[17] She continued, "I realize that the way the reliquary is treated means that the Blessed Sacrament and the Lignum Crucis have the same importance."[18] She said further, regarding her husband's attitude toward the reliquary, that "there are two events Felipe will not miss—processing first of all *con su custodia* (with his monstrance, that is, the Blessed Sacrament on Corpus Christi); and second, processing in the Good Friday procession with his Lignum Crucis, which is like his *santísimo* (Blessed Sacrament)."[19]

THE *AD NONAM PRO INDULGENTIAM* SERVICE

The second liturgy of the day at Santa Eulalia y San Marcos is scheduled at 5:00 p.m. The title in English is "At the ninth hour for mercy." This service is the longer of the two, lasting approximately ninety minutes. In a sense it is a continuation of the morning service. Like the *Ad tertiam* service, Don Enrique broadens *Ad nonam* to mean the period of the day between 3:00 and 6:00 p.m.[20] In 2002 all the Mozarabic rite chaplains were made canons of the cathedral and required to attend major services there. As a result the *Ad nonam* liturgy now begins at 4:00 p.m.

A feature of this service is the Litany for Mercy or Indulgence *(Indulgentiam)* instituted by Toledo IV (633).[21] *Indulgentiam* can be translated "indulgence," "pardon," "tenderness," or "mercy." I use *mercy* for the most part because it best conveys to me the request for mercy implied by the congregation's plea for forgiveness throughout the liturgy. Because penance and reconciliation of penitents was public in the Visigothic church, this service was designed to be the sacramental reconciliation liturgy. The litany played a major role in the completion of the penance, as well as incorporating the rest of those attending into a communal penance service.

There were actually two principal ways of reconciling penitents in the Visigothic church. The first could take place at any time of the year and usually occurred at Eucharist after the period specified by the bishop— and later by the priest—was completed. In the case of the very ill, both penance and reconciliation could take place in the same ceremony. Both could be for a single penitent or many penitents. The second was the Good Friday service described here, at which the whole congregation participated in a type of communal penance service.[22]

It appears that the elements of this liturgy became the core of the Good Friday service in Cisneros's *Missale mixtum* of 1500.[23] The format of the service is very similar to the contemporary Roman rite Good Friday service consisting of the Liturgy of the Word, Universal Prayers, Veneration of the Cross, and Communion. However, the readings are those indicated for the Mozarabic rite, the Universal Prayers are composed of the Litany for Mercy *(Indulgentiam)*, and the object of veneration is a Lignum Crucis. Furthermore, only a designated priest receives communion. Also, the service begins with a procession with the Lignum Crucis from the principal church *(ecclesia maior)* to the Church of the Holy Cross. Clearly this is one of the services reformed by Ortiz under Cisneros that incorporated Roman rite elements. The Mozarabic service is also found in the *Liber Ordinum*,[24] even though, unlike the *Ad tertiam* service, the way it was celebrated on 2 April 1999 included few elements not found in the *Liber Ordinum*, the *Missale mixtum*, or the *Missale Hispano-Mozarabicus*. The ritual Don Enrique used, however, comes from a book prepared for the University of Salamanca[25] and its celebration of the Triduum in the Mozarabic rite prior to the updating undertaken by González Martín. Following is a description of the service consisting of nine ritual units; again we will pay particular attention to the ritual use of the Lignum Crucis reliquary.

DESCRIPTION OF THE SERVICE

The people begin to gather in the semi-lighted church about ten minutes prior to the scheduled hour. Even so, some will arrive after the service has begun and others will leave in the course of it. The ministers have gathered in the sacristy to await the beginning of the liturgy. They are the same ministers as in the morning service and are vested in the same red vestments as before. Prior to the arrival of the two visiting priests, assistants to Don Enrique removed the Lignum Crucis to the sacristy, stripped the altar of the twelve votive candles and cloth, and placed on it four tall tapers in their brass holders, two on each end of the altar. The cloth on the lectern was replaced by a red one. The floral arrangement was also removed from the front of the altar, exposing the chrismon underneath it.

Entrance of Ministers

The ministers file in from the sacristy in silence. They are led by Don Antonio, followed by Don Mario, the two visiting priests, and Don Enrique. Don Enrique is carrying the Lignum Crucis, as in the morning, with a humeral veil covering his hands and the base of the reliquary. They all go directly into the chancel without pausing. As the assisting ministers go to their places in the apse, Don Enrique sets the Lignum Crucis in the middle of the altar between the tapers. He takes off the humeral veil with the help of Don Mario and then makes his way to the presider's chair. All sit, and the congregants follow suit in the nave. There is no ritual or informal greeting. Throughout the liturgy the ministers remain in the apse, facing the congregation; the congregants remain in their pews, facing the ministers. The altar with the Lignum Crucis upon it is in between the ministers and the congregants.

The fact that the ministers enter once again in the same fashion as in the morning service stresses the continuity between the two liturgies. As noted earlier, the *Ad tertiam* service seemed to end abruptly, as if interrupted. Now the same entrance ritual helps to resume the liturgy. This is further evident in that there is no greeting; instead, the next component is initiated as if all know what comes next. In this way the process nature of the ritual becomes overt. The hierarchical nature of the social relationships emphasized in the morning are once again made obvious by the ritual. The participants are reminded again of the symbolic presence of Christ in the assembly. This is done by means of the Lignum Crucis, that is, by the manner in which it is carried in and by its placement on the altar.

Scripture Reading

The liturgy continues with three scripture readings; these precede the Gospel reading. Don Mario rises and goes to the lectern to read the first reading, Proverbs 3:24–26. In response to the reading, Don Enrique, while remaining seated, begins a litany based on Micah 6:1–8; the response makes specific references to the cross. The congregants respond to the seven invocations as appropriate while remaining seated. All have worship aids with which to follow the service.

At the completion of the litany Don Antonio rises and goes to the lectern for the second reading, Isaiah 52:13—53:1–12. At its completion and after a brief pause, Don Enrique, still seated, makes a statement about the significance of the reading. He then invites the people to respond with Psalm 21 (22):2–3, 7–23. He reads a verse, and the congregation responds with the next verse, resulting in eighteen strophes read in a call-and-response format. All remain seated. One of the visiting priests rises after the responsorial psalm in order to do the third reading, 1 Corinthians 5:6; 6:1–12.

The readings serve to help all present appropriate the meanings that the designers of the liturgy wished to convey, namely, that the liturgical celebration of Christ's passion is scripturally based. Also, the number of readings and responses stresses the importance of scripture for the Hispano-Mozarabic rite. It helps to catechize and elicit meanings from the liturgy under way. The values constructed in the morning service now receive a scriptural foundation and thus acquire more authority. Furthermore, the participants in the liturgy are not just to sit and listen passively to the readings but are to appropriate them by actively responding. In this way they, too, are engaged in the construction of the social relationships and values being highlighted by the liturgy; that is, they are to engage one another in the construction of a community that places itself in the presence of God and responds to God's call to repentance. As evidenced by those present, this community is to include the young and aged, the ordained and non-ordained, males and females, natives and visitors alike. Thus, responsibility to live out these values and relationships is not limited to the clergy or Mozarab leaders in the apse but to all in the assembly.

The Passion

After the third reading Don Enrique, Don Antonio, and Don Mario rise from their seats and go to the lectern while the two visiting priests stand at their seats. The congregants also rise. Don Enrique then announces the centonized Gospel reading, which was begun the evening before at the Holy Thursday liturgy. Don Mario reads the narrator's words, Don Antonio reads the characters' words, and Don Enrique reads Christ's words. The rest of the assembly listens. After the first three minutes of the reading, Don Enrique instructs the congregants to be seated and the reading continues. The rubrics say this is to take place after the verse from John 18:37, when Pilate asks Jesus if he is the king of the Jews.[26] Only the three readers remain standing.

At the point in the reading when the good thief asks Jesus to remember him when he comes into his kingdom, and Jesus tells him that this day he will be in paradise with him (Lk 23:42–43), Don Enrique instructs all to rise.[27] This is followed by the verse in which the narrator says that from the sixth hour until the ninth hour the skies were clouded in shadows (Mt 27:45). At the ninth hour, Jesus calls out, "Eli, Eli, lama sabachthani?" (My God, my God! Why have you abandoned me?) (Mt 27:46). All remain standing, including at the point when Jesus expires; unlike the Roman rite the congregants do not pause and kneel in silence after the expiration of Jesus on the cross is read. The reading ends with the verses from Matthew in which the chief priests request that a seal and a guard be placed at the tomb (Mt 27:62–66).

As with the earlier readings, the reading of the passion helps link the liturgy under way to Christ's death on the cross. My informants have indicated that the Lignum Crucis reliquary helps bring this to their consciousness as they participate in the ritual. In addition, all are engaged in this activity not only in their hearing but bodily by having to rise, sit, and rise once again. *Communitas* is also apt to occur because all are engaged as one body experiencing the same event, albeit interpreting it and appropriating it idiosyncratically.

Homily

When the reading is completed, Don Enrique instructs all to sit. Don Enrique then begins a homily from the lectern reflecting on the death of the Lord. He makes brief reference to the fact that Jesus has voluntarily and generously offered himself as a host of salvation for all. This is how he introduces a text found in *Triduo Sacro* which he reads.[28] The homily probably comes from the seventh century, because Toledo IV (633) ordered that a homily be given on the mystery of the cross on Good Friday.[29] It speaks of Christ's redeeming work, accomplished by his death, a death that conveys God's mercy *(indulgencia)*. It also includes a list of defects that Christ's death has redeemed, such as impiety, lack of wisdom, dishonesty, injustice, evil-doing, and death. Reference is made to the thief who requested forgiveness of Christ on the cross. At this point Don Enrique, following the text, invites the congregants to repeat the words of the thief if they too want to share in paradise: "acuérdate de mí Señor, cuando entres en tu reino" (Lord, remember me when you come into your kingdom). They do so enthusiastically while remaining seated. Don Enrique continues with the text, asking the congregants to take to heart the confession they have just made and to be truly converted, "for the Lord will truly hear our prayers if he sees the conversion in our hearts."[30] The homily is completed by repeating the thief's words. This is followed by Don Enrique's instructions in preparation for the next ritual unit, Prayers Imploring Pardon.

The value of appropriating the themes and meanings of the liturgy generated by the readings is furthered by Don Enrique's homily. Also, the fact that it is read and represents an ancient text links the present service to the past. This encourages a sense of antiquity and continuity. Once again the participants' identity as an ancient Christian people, faithful to Christ from earliest times, emerges. Part of that identity is linked to the good thief, who acknowledges his sinfulness and dependence on God's grace to be able to share in paradise. This also encourages those present to identify the sins that prevent greater dependence on God's grace when they repeat the good thief's words to Christ on the cross. The reliquary's placement on the altar additionally serves to make this foremost in the consciousness of those present.

The Litany for Indulgence

All rise at the invitation of the presider, who tells the congregants where to find the *Preces Para Implorar Perdón* (Prayers Imploring Pardon). He instructs them to kneel. They briefly pause in silence and, while kneeling, Don Enrique recites the prayer requesting mercy *(indulgencia)*. The congregants respond with the text in their worship aid. Then they all stand at his invitation for the acclamation "¡Indulgencia!" The rubric says this is to be repeated no more than three hundred times. The congregation, led by Don Enrique, does it ten times. This is followed by an antiphon proclaiming the Lord to be the Good Shepherd, who gave his life for his sheep, repeated by the congregants. A brief verse follows requesting the Lord to hear and have mercy, followed by the antiphon proclaimed by all.

The presider invites all to kneel for the second time. As before, Don Enrique recites the indicated instruction inviting all to plead for the Lord's pardon of our sins and for peace. There ensues a litany of nine verses that state that those present are sorrowful and are in need of God's help; the response to each verse is "¡Indulgencia!" At the completion of the litany, all rise, following Don Enrique's instructions.

Don Enrique offers a prayer in the *orans* position directed to Christ. It restates Christ's death on the cross and refers to the flowing of water from his side. The prayer ends with a request that as Jesus experienced human death, he might give to those present a share of his victory over the enemy.

The prayer is followed by the second set of acclamations of "¡Indulgencia!" The rubric says this is to be repeated no more than two hundred times; the assembly, led by Don Enrique, does it eleven times. The worship aid indicates that all are to kneel once again for the proclamation of the same antiphon as earlier regarding the Good Shepherd. This time there is a different verse proclaiming our weakness and God's pardon and mercy *(clemencia)*. Don Enrique remains standing until he gives the instruction "Orad, arrodillaos ante Dios" (Pray, kneel before God). The prayer is offered while kneeling and follows the same format as earlier: a litany of nine verses followed by the response "¡Indulgencia!"

At the completion of the litany all stand and a prayer is offered by Don Enrique in the *orans* position. Addressed to the Son, it makes explicit reference to the extension of his hands on the cross, now the tree of life that revives all who taste of it. The prayer ends with a request for God to forget our sins. It also requests that God give us the "coming blessings," abhorrence of the false light of this world, and the interest to search the inextinguishable light of eternity.

Don Enrique in his own words tells those present that this section now concludes with Psalm 50 (51) in responsorial fashion. The congregants recite the antiphon after the presider, who does nine strophes beginning with "Have mercy on me, O God, in your kindness" (verses 3–4). It ends with verses 20–21, asking God to favor Zion by rebuilding the walls of Jerusalem, after which he will accept ritual sacrifices. At the conclusion of the psalm all recite the *Gloria*.

The third set of "¡Indulgencia!" acclamations now takes place while all remain standing. The rubric says these are to be repeated no more than one hundred times. The assembly, led by Don Enrique, does it ten times. This is followed by the Good Shepherd antiphon for the third time, recited now without a verse. All are invited to kneel again, and a third litany takes place. The seven verses request that the gates of paradise be opened and that we be freed of condemnation. They also request eternal rest for the dead. The response to each verse is "¡Indulgencia!" All rise for the prayer, once again done by Don Enrique in *orans* position. The prayer, addressed to the Son, proclaims that he is recognized not only by two animals, "as the prophet says," but also as he hangs on the cross "between two thieves or between two testaments."[31] It ends by requesting Christ's mercy so that we may understand just how much benefit we will receive in his kingdom from his death and resurrection from hell to glory.

By means of the kneeling and rising as well as the litanies, orations, and acclamations, participants in this ritual unit begin physically to integrate their earlier words of asking Christ to remember them when he comes into his kingdom. The repetitious aspect of this unit is engaging and freeing. Thus, the reconciliation sought by those present can begin to take hold physically if not consciously. Once again, social relations are constructed in which human beings are bonded together into a community of sinners in need of God's forgiveness as the participants engage in collective actions and exclamations revealing this need. At the same time, an attitude of penitence is experienced physically by the ritual movement, and one hopes also consciously by the cries of "¡Indulgencia!" This is reinforced by the orations and the progression of themes they contain assuring those present of God's mercy and pardon as the ritual unfolds.

Lord's Prayer

The service is completed by reciting the Lord's Prayer in the Mozarabic format, as at Mass. All stand facing the Lignum Crucis upon the altar while the presider says eight verses, to each of which the congregation responds "Amen." The presider assumes the *orans* position for a very brief final embolism (specially inserted prayer text for the occasion) asking God to free us from evil and to confirm us in our good works. It is completed by praising God.

The sense of need for forgiveness is extended by the Lord's Prayer, for it reminds all present of this need. It also links the liturgy to the Eucharist, accepted by Mozarabic Catholics as the greatest sign of Christ's reconciliation. Furthermore, although they may feel physically that they have demonstrated their remorse and repentance, the prayer acknowledges that only God can forgive sins, and that takes place when God is ready.

Dismissal and Exit

Afterward Don Enrique dismisses the assembly to go in peace. He then invites all to return to the Easter Vigil at 9:00 p.m. the following day. The ministers leave the apse, go through the chancel, past the altar, and to the nave. At the foot of the gradient into the altar area, they line up facing the Lignum Crucis, genuflect, and process out in single file to the sacristy. They are led by Don Antonio, followed by the two visiting priests, then Don Mario and Don Enrique. The people leave in silence. The Lignum Crucis remains on the altar until all have left except for

Don Enrique, some of the officers of the *Hermandad Mozárabe*, and the two priests.

Thus, the *Ad nonam* liturgy constructs and reinforces the social relationship between human beings and God. It also affirms the human need to help one another surrender to God and live a life that witnesses to the centrality of Christ in our lives. This witness must be public, not only in the liturgy but on the streets. This is seen in the evening when many of the Mozarab members in the congregation take part in the Good Friday processions as penitents.

The Lignum Crucis in the Service

Although ritually very little is done with the reliquary during the afternoon service, it is prominent throughout the liturgy. Its distinction is evident as the presider processes in with the reliquary as if it were the Blessed Sacrament in a monstrance. Its placement on the altar makes it a focus throughout the service. The prayers and readings, with their frequent references to the wood of the cross and to Christ's salvation through the cross, also serve to make the reliquary a symbol of that salvation present in the midst of those gathered. It is as if all are asking for mercy from Christ symbolically present in the reliquary, for it seems that the litanies and prayers are addressed to it. This is further made explicit, because the orations are addressed to Christ, and not to the Father as in the Roman rite. Thus, the veneration of the Lignum Crucis in the morning liturgy is now completed by addressing it as if it were Christ present, asking him for forgiveness. The authenticity of this request will be demonstrated by means of a penitential act in the evening when Mozarabs take the Lignum Crucis in procession.

THE GOOD FRIDAY EVENING PROCESSIONS

In Christian circles processions began to come into use once persecution waned in the fourth century. As John Baldovin notes, "The relaxation of persecution meant that Christians were free to take to the streets, and after the first decade of the fourth century such public manifestations were permanently legitimized."[32] Consequently processions became a regular feature in Christian religious expression. In Jerusalem particularly, processions at Holy Week became a way to recall and reenact to a certain extent the events of Christ's passion. Egeria describes these in her diary and takes note of their novelty as well as pointing to some similarities between what takes place in Jerusalem during Holy Week and practices back home in Spain.[33] The religious practices there captured the imagination of Christians throughout Christendom and had a great impact on their religious practices.

Ronald Grimes defines procession as a "linearly ordered, solemn movement of a group through chartered space to a known destination."[34] Its main purpose is "to give witness, bear an esteemed object, perform a rite, fulfill a vow, gain merit, or visit a shrine."[35] He further states that participation in processions is usually more restricted than in parades. Even so, they have a tendency to relax their exclusivity and become a parade that bystanders can join. Though this distinction is not precise enough, since both involve bystanders and ritual actors that move through the city, I suggest a key distinction can be found in the religious or sacred nature of processions. Grimes notes that processions are oriented toward a destination rather than a "center."[36] He says processants carry their center with them rather than occupying centralized sacred space, such as a church building.

In a procession the ritual space is created as the processants make their way through the city or countryside. Grimes says the ritual space of a procession is linear; even if it is completed by returning to its starting point, making it "bi-linear," its circuit is not generally continuous.[37] This is not an adequate definition to distinguish processions from parades. Both are linear in movement, and both can have a destination where they end or return to their starting point. Also, the use of the word *procession* is problematic because it is used for those events of Holy Week and other times when certain people go through the streets, carrying their venerated ritual object for religious purposes, and then return to their point of origin. In Toledo the continuity of the Good Friday processions is broken only by slow-downs and the incorporation of other groups. The destination in this case is the point where six confraternities join together to form one long procession and then at a given point separate to return to their starting point.

ORIGIN OF THE HOLY WEEK PROCESSIONS

It is reasonable to expect the language and practices of pre-Christian religions to have had some impact on Christian worship in Iberia. For instance, Keay describes various mystery-religion festivals that took place during the second to the fourth centuries AD in Iberia. They included shrines, processions, and confraternities carrying sacred images that resemble current Catholic practices in Spain. For example, the great spring festival in honor of Cybele and Attis occurring between 15 March and

27 March involved various ritual processions.[38] The cult of Cybele and Attis reached Hispania in the first century AD. The cult made its way to towns throughout the provinces by the second century. Cybele, the great Earth Mother, personified the regenerative forces of nature, whereas Attis, an attractive youth, personified death and resurrection. On 15 March reed-bearers processed through the town; the reeds symbolized Attis's birthplace in the Gallus River. The procession ended with the sacrifice of a bull. This initiated a period of mourning for Attis as well as preparation for the grand celebration. On 22 March a sacred pine tree was carried in procession to the temple of Cybele; this anticipated Attis's death. The 24th was called the day of blood: "It started out with fasting and mourning, and culminated in self-laceration by the *galli*."[39] The *galli*, a college of eunuch priests, painted their faces and eye sockets so as to bring out the brightness of their eyes; they also wore miter-shaped headdresses, saffron-colored chasubles, and silk surplices, girdles, and yellow shoes. The 25th, the festival of joy, commemorated Attis's rebirth; it was a day of sacrifices and celebrations in honor of the victory of life over death. Other non-Christian religions in Iberia also had similar activities marked by pomp and excitement.

It is reasonable to expect that these activities would have appealed to the populace, thus influencing later practices. Certainly the descriptions of these practices and costumes call to mind the Holy Week processions conducted by various confraternities throughout Spain even to this day. In fact, modern-day processions in Spain appear to be growing in popularity and new *cofradías* and *hermandades* for this purpose have been established since the 1960s.

Thus, there appears to be a link between the modern-day Spanish practices of Holy Week and the earlier pagan practices.[40] Indeed some scholars have noted that Christians in the late antique world of the Mediterranean took over many pagan practices as a way of supplanting them and exerting Christianity's triumph over them.[41] "In supplanting the cults that preceded them, the Christians saw themselves as a triumphant army overpowering the idols of paganism, but by the very form of their victory they were adopting the idiom of those they had conquered."[42] I propose that the earlier practices provided a way of commemorating death and resurrection that appealed to the early Iberian Christians. They were adapted and transmitted to later generations and made their way into Holy Week celebrations.

Pagan practices were not the only influences on the religious practices of Christians in Spain. Christian practices in the major centers of Christian life also played a role in the development of Holy Week in Spain. This is especially true of Jerusalem, Rome, and Constantinople. One of the more outstanding practices in these centers was the procession. Although it too may have had its origin in pagan practices, the fact that Christians in these places engaged in it would have legitimized it for Christians elsewhere—so much so that "the late antique world of the Mediterranean was a world of processions."[43]

Processions became a means to proclaim faith publicly and to take the liturgy hidden in church buildings into the street. In this way the city became liturgical space. Baldovin asserts that the processions themselves were liturgical in nature. He names certain characteristics of them that reflect current Spanish practice in general and the processions in Toledo in particular: "Processions of all sorts are, of course, public in nature, but popular liturgical processions differ in that they are much larger in scale and succeed in bringing together people of diverse backgrounds and status. Thus, as a kind of democratic form in a very undemocratic world, they succeeded in bringing liturgy onto the streets."[44]

Christians in Spain, including Toledo, would have begun to incorporate these practices only later, certainly after the fourth century. The reasons for this are varied. First, Christians in Spain had explicitly rejected pagan practices, as evidenced by the Council of Elvira (c. 305);[45] non-Christian religions continued to hold sway on a large scale into the fifth century. Second, Byzantine influence on the Spanish liturgy apparently occurred in the fifth century; in this period processions had taken hold in Constantinople. Third, Roman influence played a key role in the development of Hispanic liturgy, and processions did not take hold in Rome until the sixth century. There is clear evidence of processions in Spain in the sixth century, however, but these tended to be penitential in character.[46] This is a characteristic that continues to mark Holy Week in Toledo today. More dramatic elements entered the celebration of Holy Week in the ninth century.[47] Indeed, liturgical drama in Holy Week celebrations occurred throughout Western Europe in the same era. Processions at times formed part of the liturgical dramatization of the events of the Lord's passion, for example, when placing the cross and/or Blessed Sacrament into a *monumentum*, a type of tomb structure, for a type of "burial" called the *Depositio;* for their removal, called the *Elevatio;* and for the ceremony of the empty tomb, called the *Visitatio.*[48] Vestiges of these practices are still seen in Latin America and Spain today in the use of *monumentos* on Holy Thursday, the removal of the corpus from the cross on Good Friday, and the procession of the *Santo Encuentro* (holy meeting) of the risen Jesus and his mother early Easter Sunday morning.

It is not clear when the Holy Week processions began in Toledo. However, given the Islamic conquest and domination until the eleventh century, Holy Week practices could not have fully developed there before the Christian domination of Toledo was consolidated in the twelfth century. There is clear evidence of Holy Week processions in the fourteenth century in reference to the *Cofradía de la Santa Cruz*. The current Holy Week processions, nonetheless, have their firmest foundation in the sixteenth century, when many confraternities were established and sculpted processional images were introduced.[49] It is important to note that in 2001 the *Directory on Popular Piety and the Liturgy* affirmed processions as worthy liturgical and pious acts meriting renewal and participation by all the faithful.[50]

Processions are organized hierarchically, according to Grimes. The usual places of honor are either at the head of the line or at the end. Because part of the purpose of the procession of the Lignum Crucis is to "bear the sacred," it fits within Grimes's definition of procession and of liturgy. For him, liturgy declares "this is the way things are" and it does so by focusing all things through a few things. Liturgy does this by "re-presenting" events and "event-ualizing" structures.[51] These traits appear in the case of the Lignum Crucis as the Mozarabs take their *paso* out in procession.

MOZARABS AND THEIR *PASO*

After all the people have left Santa Eulalia at the completion of the *Ad nonam pro indulgentiam* liturgy, Don Mario and Don Antonio go to the altar. After extinguishing the four tapers on the altar, they take the reliquary and cover it with a purple velvet sack, being careful to wrap it snugly and tie the ends of the drawstrings. In the meantime Don Enrique and the two visiting priests make sure the vestments are put away and the lights are off. Outside, a group of members of the *Hermandad Mozárabe* waits for those inside to emerge. The group will take the Lignum Crucis to the Church of Santas Justa y Rufina where it will be prepared for the Good Friday Processions that will go through the central sector of the *casco antiguo*. What follows is a description of the processions, with special focus on the use of the Lignum Crucis. This ritual activity consists of nine ritual components.

Transporting the Reliquary

It is about 6:45 p.m., Friday, 2 April 1999. The ministers exit the church and Don Enrique locks the plaza doors. He takes his leave and an informal procession now begins, with Don Mario leading the way carrying the covered Lignum Crucis. The group of about twenty people is happy; its members chat cheerfully and amicably among themselves. Some accompany Don Mario, while most trail behind. There is no purpose or formal arrangement to the movement other than to get the reliquary to the Church of Santas Justa y Rufina. They take the most direct route possible over the crest of the hill above Santa Eulalia, past the Museum of the Councils and Visigothic Culture, and down narrow streets far from those usually traversed by tourists. The few people we meet along the route only glance to see what we are carrying with us; otherwise they continue on their way. The group makes no attempt to draw attention to itself or to its ritual object, the Lignum Crucis. Along the way Don Mario tells me about the procedures that will take place at the church, as well as how the processions are to unfold later. We arrive at the church about ten minutes after having left Santa Eulalia. It is set off from one of the main streets of the city core's business district.

Placement on the *Anda*

The group enters Santas Justa y Rufina through an outside door to the left of the main entrance of the church. The entry gives access to storerooms and other parts of the building abutting the church; it also gives access to a door placed directly across the room from the apse of the church. The church has undergone various renovations, including a reorientation of the building and the recent placement of a facade of plasterboard on all the walls. The board is painted white and marked as if it were composed of blocks. The candle sconces on the walls and liturgical furnishings carry the Mozarab emblem, making it clear that this is a Mozarabic rite parish.

Others in the building are assembling and putting the final touches on their *pasos*, which will go out in procession this evening. Santas Justa y Rufina is the base for three non-Mozarab groups.[52] The *Hermandad y Cofradía del Santísimo Cristo del Descendimiento* (the Brotherhood and Confraternity of the Most Holy Christ of the Descent from the Cross) takes in procession a seventeenth-century tableau of Christ being taken down from the cross.[53] The penitent members wear a black habit with a bone-colored pointed hood and girdle. A drum-and-bugle corps accompanies this group, dressed in the same costume. The second group, the *Venerable, Real e Ilustre Hermandad de Nuestra Madre María Inmaculada en su Mayor Angustia, Piedad y Desamparo* (the Venerable, Royal and Illustrious Brotherhood of Our Mother Mary Immaculate in her Great Anguish, Pity, and Helplessness), popularly known as *Angustias* (Agonies) takes a Pietà in procession. The image of the Virgin was made in 1999; the image of Christ laid over her lap was made in the seventeenth century. The penitent members wear a navy velvet cape, stiff pointed hood with face mask *(capirote)*, and cincture over a white habit. The *capirote* and habit or *Sambenito* (literally, "Saint Benedict") of the penitents was instituted by the Inquisition in the fifteenth century. In the eighteenth century this costume was taken over by the *cofradías* and *gremios* (guilds) for Holy Week processions. People from the United States seeing this costume for the first time are shocked, because the Ku Klux Klan has taken it as its own.[54] The third group is the *Real e Ilustre Cofradía de Nuestra Señora de la Soledad* (the Royal and Illustrious Confraternity of Our Lady of Sorrows). It takes a nineteenth-century image of the Sorrowful Mother. The female penitents wear a black dress and mantilla along with the group's emblem. The male penitents wear an ivory cape and habit with a black hood and girdle; they also wear the group's emblem around their neck. Twenty-seven members of this group dress in armor dating from 1686; some of them escort the *Hermandad Mozárabe* in the procession.[55] Most of these are youths, because the armor is for people of smaller physical stature; they include girls as well as boys. The armor is fairly heavy and requires much stamina to wear in procession.

In addition to the above groups, the Knights of the Holy Sepulcher begin and end their participation in the Good Friday evening procession from Santas Justa y Rufina. They accompany a cart *(carroza)* carrying an eighteenth-century sculpted image of Christ in a glass coffin, called the *Santo Sepulcro* (the Holy Sepulcher). The members wear a heavy, white mantle with a large, red Jerusalem cross on their left arm. They also wear white gloves and biretta topped by a red pom-pom.

As soon as the group accompanying the Lignum Crucis enters the church, individuals set about finding the tools and materials needed to prepare the *paso*. The platform on which the Lignum Crucis will be placed has been previously assembled in one of the side chapels in anticipation of our arrival. Don Mario and Don Antonio with two other Mozarab men climb a stepladder so that they can bolt the Lignum Crucis onto the *anda*, designed to be carried by four people. The three-inch thick platform measures five feet by four feet and sits on two six-foot beams that are the "arms" for carrying the *anda* and a set of four-foot cross beams on either end spaced about four and one-half feet apart. Four metal, removable legs about four and one-half feet tall complete the structure. The *anda* is covered by a red cloth that hangs over its sides about three feet. The Lignum Crucis is attached to the center of the platform on a one-foot riser. It faces forward toward one of the ends.

Once the reliquary is bolted in place, a lamp is attached at the front of the *anda*. It has a battery, and in the evening it will be lit so as to focus on the reliquary. When this is in place, the four posts of the canopy that go over the *anda* are set in position. The brass posts are thin but sturdy enough to sustain a white, fringed, satin canopy *(palio)*. They rise about six feet above the platform. The Mozarab emblem, the cross of Alfonso VI, is embroidered on the inside of the canopy. The entire structure is referred to as a *paso* (step or tempo), since it is to be carried rhythmically. The *paso* stands about twelve feet tall.

Other members place flowers including white and yellow daisies all around the base of the reliquary and the floor of the *anda* until it is carpeted with them. Doña María Jesús Lozano Durán told me this was the first year they put flowers on the *paso* despite objections from the men. Afterward all said that it made it lovelier and made the Lignum Crucis stand out more.[56] Every year since then flowers of various kinds have been placed on the *paso*. Often the same types of flowers used in a particular year are found near the altar at the Holy Saturday Vigil Mass, thus linking the two events.

The assembly of the *paso* takes about an hour to complete. As the individuals charged with preparing the *paso* finish, they retire to nearby homes or to the nearby *sede* (seat or meeting place) of the *Hermandad* to get dressed for the evening. In the meantime, others who are already dressed arrive to keep the Lignum Crucis company.

Gathering of the *Hermandad*

The members of the Mozarab community of Toledo who will be processing have slowly been arriving at Santas Justa y Rufina since 7:30 p.m. In addition to members who live in Toledo, others from Madrid and other parts of Spain have come to take part in the processions. The processants include men and women, boys and girls. The males come dressed in the distinctive royal-blue, voluminous, round-cut mantles of the *Hermandad*; a large Mozarab emblem adorns the left arm of the mantle. They wear their *venera* (Mozarab emblem) around their neck on a blue and gold ribbon under the open collar of the mantle. They carry in their white gloved hands a three-foot taper and the blue biretta of the *Hermandad*. The front of the biretta carries a Mozarab cross emblem patch. The females arrive dressed in black dresses, white or black lace gloves, and *peineta* (Spanish comb) with black mantilla. Their emblem, attached to a blue and gold ribbon in the form of a bow *(lazo)*, is pinned over their heart. Many wear pearls and carry rosaries in one hand and three-foot tapers capped with a protective cup in the other. Once they are all gathered, thirty *damas* and an equal number of *caballeros* will line up in two parallel files according to their ranks: females first, followed by males; younger followed by older; and officers of each branch at the end of each section. Some arrive at the church as the group begins to exit to the street. Don Enrique arrives dressed in the distinctive costume of the Mozarabic chaplains, consisting of a black cassock, white surplice, black cope, and ruffled collar. The Mozarab cross emblem on a blue and gold band hangs around his neck.

Only processants are allowed to be in the church at this time. Also arriving and lining up are the members of the four other groups named earlier. Their priest-chaplains, dressed in alb or cassock and surplice topped by a cope, accompany them. The current Mozarabic rite pastor of Santas Justa y Rufina, Don Julio, goes with the *Cofradía de Nuestra Señora de la Soledad*; two seminarians from the theologate of Toledo, dressed in black cassocks and white surplices, escort him. The archdiocese authorizes and assigns a chaplain to each group. In this way the popular religious practice of Holy Week processions is legitimized and integrated into the ecclesial life of Toledo.

The first group to leave is the one that accompanies the *Descendimiento paso*. It is followed by the group accompanying the *paso* of the *Virgen de las Angustias*. About half of those dressed in the seventeenth-century armor are next. The next to line up are the members of the Knights of the Holy Sepulcher, who accompany the *Santo Sepulcro* image. A young man in armor drags behind him a black pennant attached to a spear before the dead Christ. Then comes the *Hermandad Mozárabe* with the Lignum Crucis. Cardinal González Martín in 1976 decreed the participation of the *Hermandad* in the Good Friday processions and indicated their placement behind the *Santo Sepulcro paso*.[57] They are followed by the rest of the armored processants. The group accompanying the *paso* of *Nuestra Señora de la Soledad* follows. In this order a living tableau is set up in which Jesus is taken down from the cross, placed on the lap of his weeping mother, escorted by soldiers, followed by Christ laid out in a coffin, leaving an empty cross (the Lignum Crucis reliquary), and leaving the mother weeping. Thus, the Gospel narratives describing the last moments of Jesus' passion are set up to be "sacramentally" reenacted for all who observe the procession go by.

Elsewhere in the *casco antiguo*, two other processions are being prepared. The first, scheduled to go out at 8:15 p.m., is the *Procesión del Cristo de la Misericordia* (the Procession of Christ of Mercy). It is comprised of the *Real e Ilustre Cofradía del Santísimo Cristo de la Misericordia y María Santísima de la Caridad* (the Royal and Illustrious Confraternity of the Most Holy Christ of Mercy and Most Holy Mary of Charity), originally founded before 1671 and refounded in 1989 by a group of youths.[58] It takes two images in procession from and to the

Church of Santa Leocadia on the northwest side of the city core; the images are Christ on the Cross, dating from the seventeenth century, and a recently made image of the Sorrowful Virgin. The penitents wear maroon tunics with black piping and maroon *capirotes*.

The second procession is scheduled to begin at 8:30 p.m. It is called the *Procesión del Santísimo Cristo de la Fe* (the Procession of the Most Holy Christ of the Faith). The *Antigua, Venerable e Ilustre Cofradía de Penitencia del Santísimo Cristo de la Fe y Nuestra Señora del Rosario* (The Ancient, Venerable, and Illustrious Penitential Confraternity of the Most Holy Christ of the Faith and Our Lady of the Rosary), popularly known as *Calvario* (Calvary), takes three images in procession: a sixteenth-century image of Christ on the cross leaning toward the right *(Calvario)*, an image of Our Lady of the Rosary dating from the nineteenth century, and a contemporary image of *Nuestro Padre Jesús Divino Cautivo* (Our Father Divine Jesus Prisoner or Christ Tied to the Column). The penitents wear red-buttoned, maroon tunics, burgundy *capirotes*, burgundy waist sashes, and white gloves. The procession begins at the Church of El Salvador on the south-central side of the city core not far from the cathedral.

Onset of the Procession

By 8:30 p.m. locals and visitors have lined the route of the Good Friday processions. Thousands of observers excitedly wait for the procession to come their way. They have been gathering since 7:30 p.m. Along Comercio (the main business street) and in Zocodover, the main plaza, seats have been set up for paying customers. In the plaza, seats are several rows deep; this is where the largest group of observers has gathered. On Comercio observers are two rows deep on either side. Some of the streets feeding the route are roped off so that people may not easily cross the path of the processions.

The ringing of a bell inside Santas Justa y Rufina calls the participants in the *Procesión de la Virgen de la Soledad y del Santo Entierro* (Procession of the Virgin of Sorrows and of the Holy Burial) to order. About 8:40 p.m. the drum-and-bugle corps that will accompany the *Descendimiento* group approaches the main entrance of the church on Santa Justa Street. As it does, the rhythmic beating of the drums announces its approach. The sound echoes along the high walls lining the narrow street, filling it until the beating finally overcomes those waiting outside with its loudness. Abruptly the drumming stops. Those in the street are silenced and patiently await the first group.

The door opens about 8:50 p.m. and a hush comes over the crowd in the street. The first to emerge are male and female penitents in their habits. They are led out by a beautiful processional cross with a sculpted wood Jesus whose right arm hangs down as if reaching toward the earth. They walk up to the mouth of Santa Justa Street to await the signal from their marshall to continue. Instructions are given in a low voice. Slowly the anonymous processants start to move along the route. About 9:15 the first *paso* emerges. The crowd stands transfixed. The *Descendimiento paso* is about twelve feet tall. The porters must squat to take it out of the main door. As they do, they very slowly turn to avoid getting stuck in the narrow street. Once they are out and are given the signal by their marshall to rise, they do so in unison, eliciting loud applause from the observers. The combination of the standing porters and the height of the *paso* adds up to almost eighteen feet in stature. Once the *paso* is facing the correct direction and climbs up the street a few feet, the porters are allowed to put legs under the *paso* so that they can rest a moment. A short time later, a marshall calls out a command and the porters lift up the *paso* in unison and start to move. The combined width of the *paso* and the penitents escorting it fills the narrow street, causing those lining the street to squeeze up against the walls as it passes. As the *paso* moves, drummers begin to beat out a death-march rhythm.

More penitents come out until the *paso* of the *Virgen de las Angustias* emerges. At this point the drum-and-bugle corps plays a fanfare to the Virgin, and the observers in the street applaud. Along the route observers call out the *piropo* (unsolicited compliment)—"¡guapa!" (Beautiful!)— and then a cheer spontaneously begins of "¡guapa!, ¡guapa!, y ¡más guapa!" (Beautiful! Beautiful! And most beautiful!). The *paso* of the Virgin moves to the rhythmic beat of the music as it goes along the route. Behind it is the priest-chaplain with his seminarian escort, followed by the drum-and-bugle corps.

The next group to emerge is the Knights of the Holy Sepulcher followed by the first half of the armored escort. The people in the street can still hear the now-distant music of the drum-and-bugle corps. Slowly the processants move up the street guided by their marshall. The leader of the armored group is a little blond girl, ten or eleven years old, looking a bit insecure as she takes in the eyes looking at her. The marshall reassures her and gives her some instructions. As the group moves, people in the street whisper to one another.

About 9:45 p.m. the first members of the *Hermandad Mozárabe* emerge. They are led by Don Felipe Jurado Puñal bearing the banner of the *Hermandad*. It is attached to a twelve-foot pole. The banner is in the royal blue of the *Hermandad* with an appliqued Mozarab cross emblem on it. Because the flag's dimensions are twelve feet by five feet, in order to be transported along the route Don Felipe must gather a corner in his arms while allowing the bulk to hang down toward the street. Don Felipe is accompanied by four young boys dressed in Mozarab mantles. As the Mozarab women line up along the route up to the mouth of Santa Justa Street, Don Mario emerges from the church, giving instructions to the participants to move, go slower, or stop when needed. He is the marshall, and thus he moves up and down the space between the processants, guiding the group quietly as he does so. At the end of the women's group are three of the four officers of the *Brazo de Damas* (women's branch). They are lined up three abreast in between the two rows of processants on either side of the street. Two of the officers are Doña María Victoria Hernández, president, and Doña María Jesús Lozano, secretary; earlier they were involved in the Good Friday liturgies, making sure that the ritual was carried out correctly. As they move along the street the women acknowledge people they recognize with a smile and a slight nod of the head. Eventually the Mozarab women move and the men emerge. They, too, move slowly up the street. As they move along they, like the women before them, acknowledge people they know.

At 10:00 p.m. or thereabouts the Lignum Crucis emerges from the church. The *paso* is guided by Don Antonio and is carried by four Mozarab young men. Along the route they will trade off with others. Doña María Jesús Jurado Lozano told me later that some of the Mozarab women would also like to be able to carry the *paso*, but the *paso*'s arms would have to be extended, since more women would be needed to carry it due to its weight.[59] The *paso* is led by two boys dressed as altar boys; one swings a thurible. It is more flimsy than the earlier ones, and so any movement is immediately seen in the canopy. These carriers seem to be less adept at carrying the *paso* than those in the other groups. The viewer is immediately struck by the *paso*'s simplicity and starkness. The spotlight on the front of the *paso* is focused on the reliquary, making it shine underneath the canopy. A respectful hush comes over the crowd as the Lignum Crucis moves rhythmically up the street. Officers of the *Hermandad* line up behind the *paso* three abreast. They include Don José Miranda Calvo, *Hermano Mayor* (lead brother), and Don Enrique, the *Prior–Capellán Mayor* (prior–head chaplain).

While the *Hermandad* was emerging from the church, the civic and military officials approached the church from the lower part of Santa Justa Street. They are the final people to line up. These include members of the city council, the provincial government president and representatives, military officers from the nearby military academy and garrison, and officers of the *Guardia Civil* (government police). They are led by the mayor, who wears a black suit, white shirt, and black tie; around his shoulders he wears the Mozarab cross emblem on a gold chain as a symbol of the city government's role as civil protector of the *Hermandad Mozárabe*.[60] A drum-and-bugle corps of the *Guardia Civil* accompanies them. The civic and military officials follow at the back of the *paso* of Our Lady of Sorrows.

Along the route I overhear observers saying, "Those are the Mozarabs!" Some bless themselves as the Lignum Crucis passes by. Others ask who this group is. Yet others note the simplicity of the Lignum Crucis *paso* and are not very taken by it. For Mozarabs, though, to go in procession on Good Friday is to engage in "an act of recollection. It means to accompany the Lignum Crucis. It is to do penance."[61] Don Mario asserts that taking the Lignum Crucis in procession is very important: "It is the most important element in the procession of Good Friday since it is the authentic relic of the cross. The rest are just statues."[62]

Integration into One Large Procession

At two points along the route the other two processions integrate themselves into the larger *Santo Entierro* procession. The first to do so is the *Procesión del Santísimo Cristo de la Fe* at Hombre de Palo Street near the cathedral. It takes the head of the procession since it has the image of Christ Tied to the Column as its first *paso*. The *pasos* of *Calvario* (Christ suffering on the Cross) and of Our Lady of the Rosary complete this group, ahead of the *Descendimiento* group. A drum-and-bugle corps accompanies this group behind the *paso* of the Virgin.

The officials of the Archdiocese of Toledo wait at Hombre de Palo Street for the approach of the *paso* of Our Lady of Sorrows. Once the group with its chaplain passes by, they insert themselves before the civic and military officials. The center of the church group is taken by Archbishop Francisco Álvarez Martínez. He wears the typical bishop's black cassock with maroon piping, buttons, and sash, as well as maroon *solideo* (zucchetto) on his head and a maroon cape. Around his shoulders he wears the Mozarab cross emblem on a gold chain, a sign of his role as the ecclesiastical superior of the Hispano-Mozarabic rite and titular head of the *Hermandad Mozárabe*.[63] He is accompanied by, among others, the rector of the archdiocesan theologate, Don Juan-Miguel Ferrer Grenesche, also a Mozarabic rite chaplain, and Don Juan Pedro Gamero Sánchez, chief archivist for the archdiocese and also a Mozarabic rite chaplain.

When the procession gets to the intersection of Comercio and Tendillas Streets, the second procession integrates itself. This procession of *Cristo de la Misericordia* inserts itself after the procession that integrated itself at Hombre de Palo Street. The reason is that its image of Christ is Jesus expired on the cross. This *paso* is followed by the image of the weeping Our Lady of Charity *paso*.

The end result is a huge, blocks-long procession that comprises hundreds of men, women, and children dressed as penitents or in formal attire. Three drum-and-bugle corps and ten *pasos* are interspersed among them. The *pasos* are very elaborate and bedecked with colorful fresh floral arrangements. The *pasos* are sizeable, except for one small Lignum Crucis under a *palio* (canopy). It elicits attention and quiet respect, which is only surpassed by the reverence paid to Christ laid out in the coffin. Taken together, the various parts of the procession form a living tableau of the passion of Jesus Christ. Those in the procession and those observing it are temporarily suspended in time as they return to the moments of Jesus' suffering and death. They are moved to pity for the Virgin as she weeps at her beloved Son's death. The ritual process allows the related scriptures to come to life before all who have eyes to see. The social drama allows the ugliness of Christ's ignominious death to be transformed into a beautiful and majestic pageant of victory. As a result, the participants are inserted into a liminal state; they are betwixt and between the events of the past made present to them. For the participants, a sense of connection and bondedness is fostered by the processions, which are physically demanding on the penitents, carriers, and other processants due to the winding and steep cobblestone streets they traverse over a period of three to four hours. This experience extends *communitas* among the participants and deepens their identity as people of faith, willing to undergo arduous effort to manifest their faith publicly.

Separation and Return

The three components separate again when the procession arrives at Plata Street. The *Procesión del Santo Entierro y de Nuestra Señora de la Soledad* now only has to climb Santa Justa Street to the church where the processants will enter and complete their penance. It is close to midnight on Good Friday. Fewer people await the processants' return to Santas Justa y Rufina than awaited their emergence from the church. The same ordeal is now repeated as they take the *pasos* back into the church. The carriers and processants are tired and weary. Shoulders, backs, and feet are sore from the long hours of walking, carrying, and standing. When the civil and military officials get to the church, they disperse informally.

The *Salve*

As each group enters the church and returns its *pasos* to the chapels, the members of the *cofradías* gather to await the entry of the last *paso* and the persons bringing up the rear. Once all are in the church, someone initiates singing the *Salve* of Toledo. All sing with enthusiasm and fervor. Each group repeats the same process, including the *Hermandad Mozárabe*.

Informal Dispersal

The *Salve* sung, the members of the *Hermandad* go their separate ways. The Lignum Crucis is left on its *anda* in the secured church. Next morning a small group will quietly return to take the Lignum Crucis off the *anda,* disassemble the *paso,* and take it to the *Hermandad*'s *sede* for storage. A couple of members will wrap the Lignum Crucis in its purple velvet sack. As on the day before, a small group will return the reliquary to Santa Eulalia, taking the same route it took to get to Santas Justa y Rufina. At Santa Eulalia the Lignum Crucis will be affixed to the top of the tabernacle in the Blessed Sacrament chapel and left there until the next Holy Week. Afterward, only passing reference will be made to the wood of the cross in the orations and readings of the Holy Saturday Vigil.

THE RITUAL SIGNIFICANCE OF THE LIGNUM CRUCIS

The ritual theory of Victor Turner, Ronald Grimes, and Catherine Bell help us examine the ritual use of the Lignum Crucis. Turner's notions of liminality, ritual process, social drama, and *communitas* aid in showing how the rituals surrounding the use of the Lignum Crucis help Mozarabs enter into an experience of Christ present in their midst. The rituals also help them reveal, exalt, and reaffirm values that bind them together. Through them they affirm themselves as Mozarabs, followers of Christ, willing to proclaim their faith even if the consequences might be dire.

The antiquity of the setting and of the objects and vestments used ground the Mozarab community in its history. Although the contemporary *Ad tertiam* service is a recovery of a liturgy long out of use, its origins are in the Mozarabic liturgical heritage; therefore, it links Mozarabs to the past. The focus on the Lignum Crucis as the main ritual object of the two liturgies and the processions converts it into a pivotal symbol. Grimes's category of liturgy helps reveal the Lignum Crucis as a symbol of a specific frame of reference decisive to Mozarab faith and identity, Christ's death on the cross.

Bell's notion of ritual as praxis helps to identify the ways in which the rituals surrounding the use of the Lignum Crucis construct and order the social relations and identity that mark Mozarabs of Toledo. From my interviews and observations I have been able to see how the rituals are also subversive. They provide an opportunity for the members of the community to bring to and take away meanings from the rituals that are not always foreseen. They provide the members of the community a catalyst by which they engage in the contention and negotiation involved in the appropriation of their symbols. This is particularly seen in the relationships between their priest and themselves as laypeople, as well as between the men and women as they vie for roles in the activities of the community. The subversiveness of their rituals is apparent as they participate in the Good Friday processions in a position of honor, manifesting their identity as distinct from their compatriots, yet asserting themselves as part of the greater Catholic Church and Spanish society, even in their diversity. The liturgies, processions, orations, readings, homilies, and their symbols serve to legitimate their local identity and the culture they are constructing.

As a liturgical theologian I have plumbed the work of these ritual theorists in order to help me analyze and understand the power and meaning encased in liturgy. One area of agreement is in the attention paid to symbols. As Turner, Grimes, and Bell, among others, have noted, actions are symbolic. They evoke feelings, reveal values, and embody what is meaningful.

As a result, symbols have a role in the incarnation of meaning. Bernard Lonergan describes a symbol as "an image of a real or imaginary object that evokes a feeling or is evoked by a feeling."[64] That is to say, symbols are primarily related to the affective capacity of people. For him, the affect is the power of conscious living in that feelings orient one's being and involve intentional responses. These constitute one's world of meaning or culture. Also, according to Lonergan, feelings respond to value and do so according to a scale of preference. Religious values are at the summit because they are at the heart of living.[65] Values are embedded in human culture, and symbols help apprehend them.

The Lignum Crucis fills this role perfectly. Mozarabs' use of it incarnates meanings that support their identity and uniqueness. The liturgical services and processions help make Christ's suffering and death present to them, for it is their own death. The Lignum Crucis is treated as a monstrance carried by the priest wearing a cope and humeral veil. It goes out in public under a canopy, as if it were the Blessed Sacrament, drawing those on the street to itself. The fact that it is plain, that there is no corpus on it, is a stark reminder to all who see it that the cross is the central symbol of the events of Good Friday. They are thus invited to appropriate it along with Mozarabs, who hold it dear.

Clearly, the Lignum Crucis serves as a symbol of Mozarab history and experience. In terms of this, the other visiting priest in Toledo with me asked:

> I wonder if their privileged status sustained them during the long, historical period of Islamic domination and the subsequent imposition of the Roman rite? Now, is it possible that the Lignum Crucis serves as a symbol of the crucifixion, both of Christ and of the Mozarabs? Do they find new strength and identity as a people linked to the wood of the cross? Certainly their emblem, the Cross of Alfonso VI, not just the Lignum Crucis, and their liturgy point in that direction.[66]

I agree. It is evident that among Mozarabs of Toledo today, the Lignum Crucis serves as a reminder of their struggle to recover and assert their identity as the people who embraced Christ in the earliest times of the arrival of the faith in Spain. They celebrated that faith in a beautiful liturgy that communicated to them the meaning of that faith. They held on to both despite many vicissitudes, including the marginalization symbolized by Santa Eulalia on the cross. Thus, their rituals have functioned as the actions needed to help them integrate themselves into their society and to constitute their culture.

It is no wonder, then, that the reliquary and the emblem are core symbols for them. The Lignum Crucis is a symbol of holding to a liturgy that has sustained them over the centuries, even when it was only celebrated on occasion. It is now reinforced by the updating of that rite and the recovery of two Good Friday liturgies. It is also reinforced by their efforts to integrate the faith expressed in that liturgy into their everyday lives. This is seen in the formation of the *Hermandad*, processing with the reliquary, and wearing their unique emblem. Perhaps they are not now being called upon to give their blood, but they do have a renewed consciousness of the real presence of Christ in their midst and a sense of being faithful people to that presence. It is a consciousness that has invested the Lignum Crucis with a sacrality only equaled by the Blessed Sacrament.

The Lignum Crucis is also a mediating symbol. As a blessed liturgical implement, it is a sacramental meant to be used in the liturgy. By taking it out in public, the liturgical events at which the Lignum Crucis is used are extended into the popular realm. Thus, it mediates between the liturgy, the official prayer of the church, and the procession, an activity linked today with popular religion. In the former the priest plays the role of the ritual authority; in the latter the laity plays that role by taking responsibility for the events. That the Archdiocese of Toledo legitimates the Holy Week processions by sponsoring cofradías and hermandades only serves to stress that it is laymen and laywomen who have infused the processions with meaning. As a result, church authorities must participate, that is, they cannot ignore or absent themselves from the processions if they are to draw people to the church's understanding of the passion of Christ, even by arranging services to accommodate the processions, as in Toledo.[67] Enthusiasm for the processions is a sign that people have appropriated the scriptures and have attempted to make them come alive by means of the pasos, even if their motives are mixed. It is a sign they are trying to integrate what is celebrated in the liturgy into their lives outside of the liturgy. The Lignum Crucis does this for Mozarabs too. Don Mario declares: "To take the Lignum Crucis in procession is homage done publicly, even if there is a service in church. In church it is more intimate, since it is only those there who are venerating the relic. But when we go in procession it becomes a public expression of faith."[68]

I examine next how the texts related to the ritual use of the Lignum Crucis reveal who this Christ is who accompanies them. The texts also say how he saves them. This will help to understand further the Lignum Crucis and the cross in Mozarab culture.

8

Christological Controversy
and Orthodoxy

We can see from the description of the Good Friday rite's enactment and the participants' responses to it that the texts used ritually in relation to the Lignum Crucis are carriers of theological meaning. It is therefore interesting that a primary reason given for the substitution of the Hispano-Mozarabic rite with the Roman rite in the eleventh century was the questionable theological orthodoxy of its texts. Particularly troubling for Pope Gregory VII (1061–85) was the supposed image of Christ and his salvific work, the Christology and soteriology, cultivated by the rite.[1] To give this debate some context, it is well to recall that three major christological controversies were especially dominant in Spain during the rite's development. Pricillianism, Arianism, and Adoptionism had their adherents in Spain, and Roman authorities interested in suppressing the Mozarabic rite suspected these heretical christological perspectives could be found in the rite's texts. Since the texts used today in the actualized Good Friday liturgies are reputed to be the original texts of the liturgy, it is illuminating to examine the Christology and the implied soteriology presented by the use of these texts in relation to the Lignum Crucis. Examining the few texts used in relation to the processions likewise makes important connections. How, particularly, does the ritual use of the Lignum Crucis carry and/or modify the Christology and soteriology presented in the texts? How does this indicate the pivotal symbolism of the Lignum Crucis?

We turn first to the questionable orthodoxy of the rite's texts. Pope Gregory VII's correspondence to King Alfonso VI (1065–1109) demanded the suppression of the Mozarabic liturgy due to its heretical content.[2] The rite had already come under suspicion in the seventh century after Pope Leo II (682–83) requested that the Spanish bishops affirm the decrees of the Third Council of Constantinople (680–81) against Monothelitism;

Julian of Toledo (d. 690) responded with his *Confessione fidei*.[3] This response by the archbishop of Toledo elicited questions of clarification from Pope Benedict II (684–85), to which the bishops at Toledo XV (688) responded defensively, feeling their orthodoxy had been questioned unjustly.[4] The rite's orthodoxy was once again questioned at the Council of Frankfurt (795) which condemned Bishop Elipandus (717–c. 805, archbishop of Toledo, from c. 754), and Bishop Felix of Urgel (d. 818).[5] A key figure in the controversy was the monk Alcuin of York, Charlemagne's chief advisor. The two Spanish bishops had been sanctioned for their Adoptionist theology, with Elipandus citing the texts of the liturgy to support his position. Although most of the bishops of the Spanish church rejected the teachings of Elipandus and Felix, the latter were unwilling to change their teaching. No liturgical texts generated by Elipandus and Felix have survived.[6] Nonetheless, under pressure from Rome, the Council of Burgos (1080) officially suppressed the ancient Spanish liturgy and substituted the Roman rite in the reconquered Christian realms of Iberia.

Yet the Mozarabic rite continued to be celebrated in the non-reconquered realms until c. 1492, and in Toledo until this day. The rite's practitioners survived the onslaught of rejection and substitution that resulted in their marginalization and the deterioration of the rite's status. Indeed, during the course of its development, the rite faced not only the Adoptionist conflict but two other major christological controversies, Priscillianism and Arianism. The impact of these controversies can be discerned to some extent in the rite's changing liturgical texts. So we turn here to examine Priscillianism, Arianism, and Adoptionism and their impact on the rite.

PRISCILLIANISM

The Hispano-Roman church in the fourth century faced theological conflict and schism from a popular movement led by the nobleman Priscillian (c. 340–86).[7] After his conversion to Christianity, Priscillian became part of an ascetic group of lay preachers who went about seeking the reform of the clergy. Under his leadership the movement gained popularity in the old Roman provinces of Lusitania and Galicia in western and northwestern Iberia respectively. The movement especially attracted women devotees.[8] Priscillian was supported by Bishop Instantius and Bishop Salvian, but Bishop Hyginus of Córdoba denounced the movement. The controversy was addressed by the First Council of Zaragoza (380), at which the twelve bishops present prohibited the participation of women with men in religious gatherings, lay preaching, and absence from church during Lent,[9] three activities particularly associated with the movement. Despite this, Priscillian was elected bishop of Avila that same year.

Priscillianism was marked by mysticism and a call for disdain of the world by ordinary Christians. It was a movement similar to Manicheism in that it taught a dualism of two supreme principles of good and evil associated with light and darkness; it denied the humanity of Christ; it stressed the liberation of the soul from the corrupt human body; and it scorned marriage.[10] Strangely enough, fertility rituals associated with the control of nature were prominent in the movement's practices and indeed were common among the Celts of Galicia generally. Joyce Salisbury suggests that this may have been one reason women were especially attracted to Priscillianism.[11]

Priscillian's opponents, especially Bishop Hydacius of Mérida and Bishop Ithacius of Ossonoba, appealed to the secular authorities, accusing Priscillian of Manicheism and magic. As a result, Priscillian and his supporters, Instantius and Salvian, were exiled from their province. They traveled to Rome, where Salvian died, to seek the support of Pope Damasus I (d. 384), and then to Milan, seeking the support of Ambrose (c. 340–97). Although they failed to win over these two prominent church figures, they were reinstated by the civil authorities. However, Maximus usurped the throne in 383, becoming Roman emperor of the West; under his auspices the Council of Bordeaux (384–85) deposed Instantius. Priscillian appealed to Maximus but was rebuffed and instead charged with Manicheism; together with six supporters, he was executed at Trier in Germany.[12] His body was taken to Galicia, where it was buried near present-day Santiago de Compostela; his tomb was a popular pilgrimage site until the eleventh century. Interestingly, Salisbury speculates that the tomb of Saint James in Compostela is actually the tomb of Priscillian.[13]

Priscillian's execution made him a martyr in the eyes of his followers. His movement dominated almost all of Galicia, and its adepts successfully elected their leaders as bishops there and in Lusitania. The movement extended into southern France where there was a Priscillianist bishop as late as 417.[14] Juan Manuel Sierra remarks that much of the teaching attributed to Priscillian developed after he died.[15]

Priscillianism allegedly comprised various heretical stances including the use of apocryphal writings and excessive moral rigor expressed in hostility to marriage, wine, and meat. It emphasized prophecy based on a theory of inspiration, raising the specter of Gnosticism and Montanism. J. N. Hillgarth claims that the extreme asceticism of Priscillian has parallels in the practice of his contemporary Eastern ascetics whose orthodoxy was not questioned.[16] Priscillian's real heresy seems to have been that he and his followers attacked the practices of certain powerful clergymen and that he and his lay followers, mostly women, threatened the growing importance of the male clerical elite. Nonetheless, the accusations of Gnosticism and Manicheism stuck. Later works by Priscillianists contained a mixture of Sabellianism, Gnosticism, Marcionism, and Modalism, adding to the sect's reprobation. Occasionally, individuals were accused of Priscillianism *qua* Manicheism, among them Elipandus of Toledo in the eighth century.[17]

The Priscillianist bishops of Galicia were reconciled to the Catholic church in Iberia at Toledo I (c. 397–400) where eighteen Priscillianist teachings were anathematized.[18] Among these teachings were the notion of Christ as a mutable and lesser divinity than the God of the New Testament, the denial of Christ's two natures, and a rejection of the incarnation. Despite this, Priscillianism survived in Galicia for almost two hundred years after Toledo I, even though it was condemned by various important church leaders such as Orosius (c. 414),[19] Bishop Turibius (Toribio) of Astorga (c. 445), and Bishop Montanus of Toledo (c. 530).[20] The First Council of Braga (561) anathematized another seventeen errors attributed to Priscillianists.[21] Most of these were the same as those condemned earlier but nuanced to reflect better the church's rejection of Gnosticism, Sabellianism, and Manicheism.

Because what is known of Priscillian's teaching comes from his detractors, it is difficult to assess the accuracy of the charges against him. Nonetheless, abhorrence of procreation, the incarnation, and bodily resurrection, as well as esteem of virgins and hermits, astrology, and fertility rituals seem to have been some of the views most strongly held by his followers and attributed to Priscillian. Texts attributed to him containing these notions have not survived. Neither have liturgical texts attributed to Priscillianists survived as such, but Salisbury contends that Priscillian tapped into a Galician religiosity that slowly came to be incorporated into orthodox Christian ritual. This was formalized by the ancient Spanish liturgy in certain rituals related to fertility and the control of nature.[22] Pagan practices of this sort continued well into the Visigothic and Islamic eras. These practices included the exaltation of virgins who were popularly thought to bring fertility to the land. Offerings were made to "living water," such as natural springs. Fertility rituals also played a role at planting and harvest time. It appears these pagan practices were modified and incorporated into the liturgy by means of blessings of virgins, water, and agricultural products; these can be found in the *Liber Ordinum*.[23] Vestiges of these practices can still be seen today in Don Enrique's incorporation of the three types of flowers—lilies, roses, and violets—as an offering during the *Ad tertiam* service on Good Friday.

The principal christological features of Priscillianism had to do with a concept of Christ as a spiritual being who only appeared to be human yet was not fully God either. The Spanish church rejected this notion, instead stressing Christ as the God-Man who redeems human flesh and life by being truly God and truly human. Thus the suffering of Christ became a focus of Hispanic spirituality as evidenced by the carved images taken in procession on Good Friday of Jesus' agony in the garden, his stripping and scourging at the pillar, his dejection as he is being judged by Pilate, his cruel crucifixion, and even the painful extraction of his body from the cross in the *descendimiento paso* described earlier.

ARIANISM

The most important christological influence on the Mozarabic rite was Arianism because the rite had its greatest development during the Visigothic era.[24] The Visigoth overlords were Arian Christians who at times sought to impose Arianism on the Catholic populace. In opposition to the Arians, the Catholics stressed orthodoxy, particularly regarding the doctrine of Christ. The liturgical texts reflect this, as we will see later. Thus, to some degree the euchology of the Hispanic rite makes anti-Arian points.

Arianism appeared in the church of Alexandria in the early fourth century. The priest Arius (d. 336) raised the question of the preexistence of Christ.[25] He was perplexed by John 1:14, which indicates that the Logos was begotten of the Father. If this was the case, then was there a time when the Son did not exist? Arius was not satisfied with Bishop Alexander's (d. 328) response that the Son is co-eternal with the Father. Instead Arius emphasized the notions of "sonship" and "begotten" as indicative that the Logos was posterior to the Father and therefore created, not eternal. Furthermore, since the Father is eternal and the Son is not, the Son could not be of the substance of the Father. This raised the issue of Christ's divinity. As a created being, even as the *ktisma teleion*, the "perfect creature" through whom all things were made, he was not worthy of divine worship as the Father is. Jesus, in the Arian scheme, was not divine *by nature*; rather, he developed into divinity by virtue of his evolving moral union with God.[26] Arians considered Jesus the Savior in that he taught divine truth and furnished the perfect example of commitment to the good. This soteriology presented by Arianism stressed learning from Jesus and imitating his example.

Harold Brown assesses Arianism as a "doctrinal innovation," for no one had ventured to teach up to then that the Logos was "radically distinct from the Father, of a different substance."[27] The Council of Nicea (325) condemned Arius's teachings. Even so, Arianism attracted many adherents, including bishops and emperors. Even Constantine the Great was influenced by the Arian Bishop Eusebius of Cæsarea. Later, Constantine's adviser, Bishop Hosius of Córdoba, went over to the Arian side. Constantine's immediate heirs were Arian and gave Arianism sufficient status and liberty to survive Nicea. But the Arian bishops failed to consolidate their position with the masses and the Western bishops, who resisted the perceived efforts to diminish the deity and majesty of Christ. The maneuvering of the Emperor Julian (361–63) allowed the exiled orthodox bishops to return to their sees; he hoped the conflict between Arians and Catholics would result in the repudiation of Christianity by society and, therefore, occasion the return to pre-Christian religion. Instead, Julian's action allowed the orthodox position to come to the fore and eventually triumph at Constantinople I (381).

Arianism was suppressed by Emperor Theodosius I that same year.[28] It continued to compete with the Catholic position well into the fourth century within the lands of the late Roman Empire. It was overcome by the orthodox declaration that Christ was indeed co-eternal with the Father, "God from God, light from light, true God from true God, begotten not made, one in being with the Father *(homoousios)*," as reiterated by Constantinople I (381). Emperor Theodosius I enacted the necessary laws making Christianity the state religion and the Catholic affirmation of Christ the official doctrine.[29] Brown notes that, as a result, Theodosius established "not simply early catholicism—embracing a moderate diversity of opinion—but an explicit, Nicene orthodoxy."[30] As a consequence, Arians who had previously continued to be part of the one church of Christ, were defined out of it after Theodosius.

Arianism, however, lived on outside the empire among the Goths. They converted to Christianity in the fourth century as a result of the evangelizing efforts of the Arian Bishop Ulfilas (d. c. 383), a participant at the Council of Nicea.[31] His deathbed creed was probably emblematic of the Visigothic faith: "There is one eternal, unbegotten, and invisible God, who before time existed alone. Within time he created the Son, the only-begotten God. He is the creator of all things, the Lord of the Holy Spirit whom the Father created through the Son before all things. The Holy Spirit is obedient and subject to the Son like the Son to the Father."[32] When the Visigoths overran the Late Roman Empire and eventually established themselves in Iberia, they kept their Arian faith even though they had taken on other aspects of Roman culture.[33] Until their acceptance of the Catholic faith in 589 under King Reccared, the Visigoth overlords made several attempts to impose their Arian faith on the general populace.

It is not known what the Arian eucharistic liturgy was like. Perhaps the situation of rival churches of that era was very similar to that of today, in which mainline Christian churches have similar worship structures but different theological orientations. Thus, one who attends a Catholic Mass and a Presbyterian communion service may be struck by the similarity in structure and even to some extent euchological content. Yet the eucharistic elements are seen by one as the real presence of Christ while the other takes them to be symbols of an event from long ago now memorialized. It is possible that the Old Spanish liturgy was a mirror of Arian liturgy in structure; however, the former stressed orthodox christological themes over and against the latter.

The *acta* of Toledo III give evidence of the differences in christological orientation. For example, the council decreed that the doxology was to be said in such a way that the Father, Son, and Holy Spirit were to receive the same honor and dignity. Therefore the formula to be used is "Gloria et honor Patri et Filio et Spiritu Sancto."[34] The Arian doxology used an older formula, "Gloria Patri per filium in Spiritu Sancto."[35]

Furthermore, the Hispano-Mozarabic prayers composed in the Visigothic era are often addressed to Christ rather than to the Father through Christ. It is reasonable to conclude, therefore, that the contributors to the Old Spanish rite's development in this period sought to stress clearly an orthodox Christology in terms of the full divinity of Christ. The most important evidence of this is the incorporation of the Niceno-Constantinopolitan Symbol of Faith into the liturgy at Toledo III (589).[36] The Toledo version of the creed introduced the concept of *filioque* (and of the Son) in relation to the procession of the Holy Spirit, although the *acta* of Toledo III make no comment as to why.[37] The liturgical use of the Symbol with the *filioque* antedated its use in other Western churches by two hundred years. The Symbol with the *filioque* first spread to Gaul from Spain, where it was recited before the Preface. The Roman church resisted the use of the creed at liturgy until 810 and allowed for inclusion of the *filioque* only in 1014; it was declared licit by the Council of Florence (1439). Kelly attributes the introduction of the *filioque* in Spain to the Priscillian controversy and its condemnation by Zaragoza I (380). However, the extant *acta* give no evidence of this. Furthermore, Kelly indicates that the *filioque* doctrine clinched the case against Arianism and allowed King Reccared to affirm enthusiastically that the Spirit proceeds from the Father and from the Son in his declaration of faith at Toledo III (589).[38] Brown remarks that the addition of the *filioque* took place in the West because of a second round of confrontation on the Arian issue, this time with the Visigoths, and speculates the question of the *filioque* arose "in order to make it abundantly clear to the newly converted Arians of Spain that the Son is equal to the Father."[39] Because the concept of *filioque* was introduced at Toledo and was eventually incorporated into the Niceno-Constantinopolitan Creed throughout the West, perhaps the correct name ought to be the Niceno-Constantinopolitan-Toledan Creed.

It appears, then, that Arianism influenced the development of the Mozarabic rite by impelling it to stress the divinity of Christ. This is clearly seen in the prayers addressed to him throughout the liturgies of the Mozarabic Triduum, particularly on Good Friday. Nonetheless, this potentially incipient Monophysitism did not attract attention from the rite's detractors. Instead, it was the notion of Christ's adoption, emerging during the eighth century in the Islamic-dominated regions of Iberia, that raised questions about the Old Spanish rite's orthodoxy, and to this we now turn.

ADOPTIONISM

The enemies of the Mozarabic rite focused on a Christology that taught that the historical person Jesus at his baptism was "adopted" by the Father. The term *Adoptionism* actually refers to various strands of this teaching, which began to appear at the end of the second century, only some of which are related.[40] Early Adoptionism had more currency in the Eastern Roman Empire than in the West. The affirmation of Christ as both true God and true man by Chalcedon (451) virtually eliminated the notion of Jesus' adoption by the Father throughout most of the Catholic world. For that reason Brown identifies the Adoptionism of Iberia in the eighth century as Spanish Adoptionism in contrast to earlier forms of the second and third centuries.[41]

There was no question that the Word had become flesh or that Jesus Christ was truly God and truly man. This doctrine had been affirmed and reaffirmed by the Visigothic church in its councils ever since Toledo III (589). In particular, it had been emphatically restated at Toledo XI (675).[42] The preamble to the *acta* of Toledo XI elaborates on each statement of the Symbol of Faith, which was developed from the creeds of Nicea (325), Constantinople (381), Ephesus (431), and Chalcedon (451). The preamble reads almost like a long, litanic profession of faith in Catholic orthodoxy. Rather, the Spanish strand of Adoptionism centered on the question of how Jesus the human being figured in salvation. Both sides of the controversy in Spain focused on the *homo* Jesus and his status as Son insofar as he was truly a human being.[43]

Elipandus was accused of teaching that Jesus, considered solely from his human nature, was an "adoptive" Son of God.[44] Elipandus had written a tract against Migetius, the leader of a Spanish sect with Sabellian, Priscillian, and Donatist leanings. Elipandus claimed that Migetius taught that the three Persons of the Trinity had all been incarnated: the Father in David, the Son in Jesus, and the Holy Spirit in Paul. It is in his tract against Migetius that Elipandus lays out his nascent Adoptionist Christology, though he does not specifically use the term *adopted* in relation to Christ.[45] Nonetheless, his response to Migetius and the subsequent declaration of the Council of Seville (c. 782) against Migetius under Elipandus's presidency drew the attention, first of other Spanish church officials, and eventually of Roman and Frankish authorities. The anti-Adoptionist party in Spain was led by Beatus of Liébana (d. 798)[46] and Etherius, the bishop of Osma.[47] Etherius had found refuge in the monastery of San Martín, later Santo Toribio, in Liébana, after fleeing the Islamic forces that captured his city. Beatus was the abbot of the monastery.

In actuality what Elipandus was teaching was that the Son, the Second Person of the Trinity, emptied himself to take up or assume "adoption." Jesus the man is not adopted; rather the *Unigenitus* Son, in order to become the *Primogenitus*, assumes adoption so that we too may become adopted sons and daughters of the Father and so be saved. In this way Jesus is the first of many adopted sons and daughters. John Cavadini calls this "*Primogenitus* Christology" and observes that it is related to Elipandus's soteriology of "likeness" and "conformation," which appears in his *Symbolus*.[48] Elipandus, in his various defenses, made reference to the teachings of Augustine, Isidore, Pope Leo I, Philippians 2:6–11, and John 14:28 to support his position.[49]

In Elipandus's scheme Jesus, the Son of Mary, is the total self-emptying of the Word, the perfect and complete human being through which salvation comes to the world because he is the "first born."[50] Insofar as he is God, he is the *Unigenitus*, but insofar as he is *homo*, he has become *Primogenitus* by adoption. Cavadini sums up Elipandus's Christology:

> His status as Unigenitus is not impeached or removed; rather, the self-emptying of the Word has permitted this unique relation to be exhibited in the terms which respect the limitation of another nature. That is why this self-emptying is salvific. It is the same *persona* who is at once Unigenitus by nature and Primogenitus by adoption.[51]

By conforming ourselves to Jesus, we share in his status. Thus, Elipandus does not stress the salvific role of Jesus as Mediator in the manner favored by his opponents.

Elipandus enlisted the aid of Felix, bishop of Urgel. Cavadini speculates that Elipandus did so to refute the charges made by Beatus and his colleague Etherius that Elipandus had been influenced by Islam.[52] This was due to the fact that Toledo was in Islamic-dominated territory and Elipandus was seeking support for his perspective from bishops in territories not dominated by Islam. Liébana, Beatus's city, on the other hand was in the independent kingdom of Asturias. Like Liébana, Urgel was in territory free of Islamic domination. Unlike Liébana, however, it was in Frankish-ruled territory.

Felix, on the other hand, may have been motivated by a desire to ally himself with the prestigious church of Toledo.[53] He also may have hoped to seek autonomy from the Frankish court and the movement toward the Roman rite taking place under Charlemagne. Felix initially submitted to the requirements of the Council of Frankfurt to abjure his Adoptionism. Afterward, Felix fled to Toledo but shortly thereafter returned to Urgel. Once again he was deposed by Charlemagne and forced to go to Rome, where he abjured anew to Pope Hadrian I. He was exiled to Lyon, where he died, apparently unconvinced of his errors regarding the person and nature of Christ.

Part of the problem may have been political, cultural, and linguistic differences difficult to overcome. Much of the controversy centered on the interpretation of *adoptio* in relation to the concepts *persona* and *natura*; the failure to distinguish clearly between the latter two concepts was an issue that had led to the Nestorian schism in the fifth century.[54] The terms as used by Elipandus and Felix created consternation for Alcuin and Hadrian. As a result of their particular reading of Philippians 2:6–11, Elipandus and Felix stressed the concept of the *persona* of the Word who "emptied *himself*." As Cavadini explains, the act of self-emptying serves both to define this *persona* and to provide the basis for continuity in the subject who is Christ. Therefore, "all of the actions of Christ, from the point of view of either of his natures, are moments in this one definitive act of the *persona* of the Word."[55] The use of "self-emptying" implied to Alcuin and Hadrian that Christ's human nature was somehow diminished. As a result, Elipandus and Felix were accused of Nestorianism as well as Adoptionism. However, it is possible that, at least in Spain, the exactness of meaning that the terms *persona* and *natura* had acquired as a result of the early ecumenical councils was diminished by this time, almost four hundred years after Chalcedon.

There is an analogous situation today among Spanish-speakers in the use of terms taken for granted in everyday speech that, when analyzed, have very different meanings. On a very prosaic level, the example of how different Hispanic groups use the word *almuerzo* (lunch) comes to mind. Though a common Spanish word, it has its origin in rural life where it meant a heavy mid-morning meal taken by farmers. Today some use it to refer to a hearty breakfast, others use it for the midday meal, while still others view it as an archaism. This can result in a fairly in-nocuous breakdown in communication; more loaded terms can have greater consequences. Consider the terms *priest* and *priestly*, for example. Depending on the context, they can refer to baptismal or ordained reali-ties, describing unique or common characteristics. If the context is un-clear or influenced by political considerations centered on power, mis-understanding can lead to controversy.

Did the Latin word *adoptio* as used by those linked to Rome and those in Spain suffer a similar fate? Brown speculates that much of what was painted as heresy and led to theological divisions in the early church was due to such a problem.[56] Cavadini also suggests that political fac-tors, such as the attempts of Charlemagne to extend his realms further into Spain as well as Hadrian's desire to bring the autonomous church of Toledo under his control, may have added to the controversy.[57] Elipandus in his defense cites texts of the liturgy that he claimed used the word *adoptio*.[58] Specifically, he refers to *missa de Coena Domini,* and others from the Easter Season, including *tertia feria Paschæ*, *quinta feria Paschæ*, and *missa de Ascensione Domini*. He also refers to *missa sancti Sperati, missa defunctorum,* and *vigilia Paschæ* to fortify and substantiate his claims. As a consequence, Alcuin responded that the liturgy then was full of heresy.[59] Joseph O'Callaghan judges both Elipandus and Alcuin incorrect,[60] while Walker observes that the accusation of heresy was per-petuated by Charlemagne's *Epistola ad Elipandum* and other tracts such as Paulinus of Aquileia's *Libellus Sacro syllabus contra Elipandum et ceteros episcopos*.[61] Nonetheless, the use of the word *adoption* by Elipandus and Felix was unfortunate. Their attempts to forge a theo-logical perspective centered on it only alienated them from their col-leagues and from the greater Catholic church. Their obstinacy in using the concept over and against their enemies, moreover, only served to taint the Old Spanish liturgy with heresy.

Beatus offered an alternative Christology to that of Elipandus. Beatus's response to Elipandus, in which he lays out his Christology, is known as the *Apologeticus*.[62] Both men focused on the *homo* Jesus as the locus of salvation. Beatus, like Elipandus, began with the concept of the Son's self-emptying. Instead of emptying himself to become an adoptive son in order to become one like us and thus the first of God's adopted sons and daughters, Beatus declared that the Son emptied himself in order to become a servant. This status is especially evident in his sacrifice on the cross. As a result, the soteriology offered by Beatus is one in which we are saved by Christ's self-emptying love for the Father and for human beings in order to make himself the servant of God, even unto death. By conforming to and imitating the Son's service and total surrender to God, we also are elevated to a share in divine life, salvation. However, Christ is not the first of many but the unique Savior of the world who mediates salvation to those who become like him.

Cavadini observes that both Elipandus and Beatus evince a theological tradition that operated independently of most of the Catholic world.[63] This tradition built on some of the same sources as the rest of the Catholic church, including Tertullian, Augustine, and the church of North Africa, but also with particular emphasis on Isidore of Seville and on the councils of the Spanish church. Consequently, in their remonstrations and fulminations on the person of Christ, Beatus and Elipandus rarely referred to Chalcedon or to the Eastern disputes that defined Christology for the larger Catholic church. Not did they evidence much knowledge of the heresy of Nestorius, of which Elipandus is accused by Alcuin. Rather, Cavadini suggests that the theological tradition from which Elipandus, Felix, and Beatus emerge was unique: "One could almost say that when North African theology began to fall silent in the seventh century and beyond, it was in Spain that the voice of its traditions continued most clearly to be heard."[64] This perspective fits in well with a theme that Sierra identifies as running through Spanish theology since the second century.[65] It appears in Potamius's "Theology of the Flesh" and the writings of Gregory of Elvira and is still at play in the time of Elipandus and Beatus, that is, the stress on the humanity of Christ balanced by his divinity. This is expressed by the christological category of Christ as the *Verbo-Carne* (Word-Flesh). Thus the focus on the bodily suffering of Christ in his humanity is reflected in the images of agonized bloodiness in the modern-day Good Friday processions. Yet his divine nature is demonstrated in every image of him by means of the three rays, the *potencias*, emanating through the crown of thorns from his head.

To sum up: Because of cultural, linguistic, and theological differences, the orthodoxy of the Spanish church and its ancient liturgy came to be questioned. The two most famous incidences of this occurred in the eighth century under Charlemagne and in the eleventh under Pope Gregory VII. Many scholars have attributed the rite's questionable orthodoxy to the influence of Islam.[66] Cavadini calls this into question by giving evidence that these were charges leveled by rivals to Elipandus as well as to the Spanish church in order to bring them into conformity with an agenda that went beyond theological clarity.[67] It is reasonable to expect that as an autonomous church it would have developed its own Christology, which on the surface could be seen as contrary or a challenge to Catholic orthodoxy.

THE IMPACT OF HERESIES
ON THE HISPANO-MOZARABIC RITE

The rituals of Good Friday seen previously reflect the strong emphasis on the central salvific role of Christ, especially in terms of the cross and his bodily suffering. Through Christ, the *Verbo-Carne*, and through his suffering, his followers become sons and daughters of God. Some of the texts of the liturgy that have come down to us give evidence of this unique Christology as it was affected by these controversies. For that reason the commission established by Cardinal González Martín to actualize the Hispano-Mozarabic rite was charged with examining the texts of the liturgy and eliminating what could be construed to be unorthodox. I have not had access to all the extant texts used for the new *Missale*, but I have been assured by members of the commission that nothing was altered from the ancient texts save for the shortening of a few prayers in order to eliminate unnecessary repetitions. In interviews I was informed by Don Jaime Colomina Torner, member of the commission, and by Don Cleofé Sánchez Montealegre, secretary of the commission and general editor of the *Missale*, that only editorial changes were made.[68] In fact, efforts were made to include the texts from Tradition A, that is, texts from Toledo and the north, used in the parish of Santa Eulalia, that had been left out of the Missals developed by Cardinals Cisneros in 1500 and Lorenzana in 1775.[69] Therefore, the judgment of this commission seems clearly to be that the ancient texts were not in need of doctrinal revision.

Nonetheless, the christological controversies unmistakably left their mark on the texts and ritual. The accusation of Priscillianism diminished the egalitarianism it promoted in terms of men and women, lay and cleric, and led to a strong emphasis on hierarchy and limited lay participation in the celebration of the liturgy. The emphasis on popular religious practices emerging from the local culture was sacramentalized as rites and blessings. The challenge to the Catholic understanding of Christ was met by a strong adherence to the teachings of Nicea and Constantinople as seen in the *acta* of Zaragoza I (380) and Toledo I (c. 400).

Clearly, the need to combat Arianism resulted in an overemphasis on the divinity of Christ evident in the prayers addressed to him. However, the Visigothic and Hispano-Roman councils articulate a conspicuous adherence to and reiteration of the orthodox view of Christ and the Trinity. As a result, the Old Spanish rite became the first Western liturgy to require the use of a version of the Niceno-Constantinopolitan Creed at every Sunday Eucharistic Liturgy. The stress on Christ's mediation of salvation by being a servant unto death emerged as a reaction to Adoptionism. As a result, emphasis on the cross and sacrifice came to the fore. This is evident in the texts used in relation to the Lignum Crucis, to which we now turn.

9

The Christology and Soteriology of the Texts

The principal image of Christ presented in the texts used during the Good Friday events is that of the divine Savior who suffers death on the cross for his people. Who is this Christ, and how are people saved by his suffering and death? In order to answer these questions a hermeneutical analysis will help us by examining the actual texts used on 2 April 1999 in relation to the Lignum Crucis during the *Ad tertiam* liturgy, *Ad nonam pro indulgentiam* liturgy, and the evening processions in Toledo. The liturgical texts have their origin in the seventh century and have been translated from Latin into Spanish.[1] They are recorded in two worship aids prepared by Don Enrique Carrillo Morales, the pastor of Santa Eulalia y San Marcos parish, for use at the liturgies on Good Friday,[2] and a booklet prepared by him titled "Sagrados Oficios de Semana Santa según el antiguo Rito Hispano o Mozárabe." Further material to consider is found in the two programs prepared by the *Junta de Cofradías y Hermandades de Semana Santa de Toledo* describing the confraternities and the images they carry in procession[3] and other official texts related to the liturgies.[4]

AD TERTIAM

The title of the morning service is *A la hora de tercia: exaltación y adoración de la cruz* (at the hour of Terce: exaltation and adoration of the cross).[5] The cross on which Jesus died is clearly the focus of the service. This is stressed in the phrases at the onset of the service:

Poseyendo la señal de la salvación para conmemorar el mandato de tu ley, creemos que por este trozo del madero, al cruzar nuestras almas el mar, seremos liberados por tí [*sic*] Salvador de todos.	Possessing the sign of salvation in order to commemorate the command of your law, we believe that by this piece of the tree, our souls upon crossing the sea, we will be freed by you Savior of all.
Marchamos portando tu leño, nosotros que te invocamos, Padre, para que al surcar el mar seamos liberados por este leño.	We go carrying your wood, we who invoke you, Father, so that plowing through the sea, we may be freed by this wood.
Bendito el leño por el que se restablece la justificación.	Blessed is the wood by which is reestablished justification.
En el manifestaste, Señor, a nuestros enemigos que tú eres quien libras de todo mal.	On it you manifested, Lord, to our enemies that you are the one who frees us from all evil.[6]

The way Don Enrique performed this opening portion of the *Ad tertiam* liturgy made it sound like one unit, as if it were one prayer, despite the fact that it is composed of three separate antiphons. They appear as one unit in the worship aid as well. Nonetheless, the theme of justification through the cross is explicitly declared in this opening. The text seems to be addressed to both the Father and the Son because of the use of *Salvador* (Savior) in the first phrase. This title is equally applicable to both the Father and the Son. The use of *tu leño* (your wood [of the cross]) in the second phrase is confusing. The second phrase explicitly names the Father, but by saying "your wood," the Son is implied. The use of *Señor* (Lord) in the last phrase can also refer to either God the Father or God the Son. The combination of the three antiphons into one prayer conveys the message that the Son and the Father are co-equal in divinity and eternity. However, it also puts emphasis on Christ and thus effectively rejects the Arian position.

The text also declares that the Lord, implicitly Jesus Christ, is the Savior of all. The sign of his salvation is the *madero*, the wood/tree or cross on which Jesus manifests the reestablishment of justification; he is the one who frees from all evil. The notion of *madero* echoes the metaphor of Christ's cross as a tree found in various New Testament passages such as Acts 5:30, Acts 10:39, Galatians 3:13, and Revelation 22:14. The notion of "freedom from evil" echoes the Lord's Prayer. In this way a link to scripture and the liturgical use of the Lord's Prayer is forged.

Furthermore, the piece of wood being carried, the Lignum Crucis relic, is declared by the text to free those who believe and who carry it. Freedom from what is not clear; however, the context implies freedom from evil, namely, lack of justification. Thus, the opening text declares that salvation won by Jesus on the cross is actualized in the liturgy now under way. The liturgy allows for those present to take part in Jesus' victory over evil. In this way they are saved. The liturgy also helps those present to cross "the sea [of life]" that is marked by danger and enemies who can keep believers from salvation. That is because they possess the sign of salvation, the cross. As a result, Beatus's perspective on the mediating role of Christ as the God-man is affirmed against that of Elipandus.

The source for this text can be found in the *Liber Ordinum* (LXXXIIII) and the *Missale* (1:345). The texts in these two sources clearly indicate that the three phrases of the worship aid are actually three antiphons to be sung while the relic of the cross is carried in procession. At Santa Eulalia the presider, Don Enrique, proclaimed the three antiphons in a loud voice as if they were a prayer before initiating the processional hymn, "¡Victoria! ¡Tú reinarás!"[7]

Hymn

The processional hymn reiterates the themes of the antiphons.[8] The refrain declares "¡Victoria! ¡Tú reinarás! ¡Oh Cruz! ¡Tú nos salvarás!" (Victory! You will reign, O Cross! You will save us!). The verses round out the theme of salvation presented in the antiphons as well as add ideas about what that means. For example, the first verse adds the notion that the Word was nailed on the cross and that by his dying we were rescued. This is linked to the wood of the cross, the *santo madero* (holy tree), from which comes redemption. The following three verses ask an unnamed subject, understood to be the cross, to extend throughout the world the reign of salvation, to rule over hate, and to increase in our souls the reign of holiness. These verses also declare the cross to be the life-giving fount of blessing, unity, and the river of grace that extinguishes iniquity. The final verse ties all these ideas together by making explicit that by the cross Christ takes believers to heaven, the promised land.[9] For this he is worthy of praise as the believers sing, "La gloria por los siglos a Cristo libertador" (Glory to Christ the liberator forever).

Showing of the Cross

Once the people have returned to their places in the church at the conclusion of the procession, the presider shows the reliquary of the Lignum Crucis to those gathered. He commands them to look on the glorious wood from which not long ago hung the members of Christ the Savior.[10] These members are "the redeemers of the world" *(redentores del mundo)*. Therefore, those present are to go forward, prostrate themselves, and present their petitions with tears.

Flower Offering

Although this activity is an idiosyncratic interpolation by Don Enrique, he bases it on the texts of the Christmas liturgy, in particular the *Illatio*.[11] Don Enrique orally explains that roses, lilies, and violets will be offered. This he gets from the antepenultimate verse of the *Illatio*, which reads: *Dedit illi tamquam rosas mártyres, velut lília vírgines, quasi víolas continéntes*.[12] The *Illatio* sets up in the first part a contrast between Mary and the church, laying out what Mary has given and the church received through the birth of Christ. The prayer moves to an exposition of what Christ gives to the church, his spouse, in terms of sacramental signs: *Dedit sponsus sponsæ suæ múnera aquas vivas; Dedit óleum lætítiæ; Iustítiæ impósuit oranméntum; Se ipsum illi in cibo ac potu indumentóque concéssit;* and so forth. The final section recounts what the church returns to Christ, including martyrs as roses, virgins as lilies, and the pure as violets.

Christ, in this reference, appears as the bridegroom who takes the church as his spouse. He offers the gift of salvation through various means, including his incarnation and birth through Mary, the sacramental signs of baptism and Eucharist, as well as right living or justice. By participating in these the church returns to Christ a "bouquet of flowers" seen in martyrs, virgins, the pure, and ministerial service.[13] With this as a backdrop, the Veneration of the Cross follows. This implies that those participating in the service are invited to appropriate the spirit of this text. They are to become Christ's spouse and to enter into his life, including taking up the cross. In this way Christ mediates salvation to them.

Veneration of the Cross

The *Missale* offers a long Latin text to be sung while the people come forward to venerate the cross.[14] Instead, Don Enrique used the text of a hymn from the Tridentine usage of the Roman rite, "Vexilla Regis."[15] He told me he sang the hymn using Mozarabic chant because the text in the *Missale* provides no music and the text of the "Vexilla Regis" is easily adapted to the Mozarabic music of the liturgy.[16] The text of the hymn fits well with the purpose of the service, that is, the exaltation and adoration of the cross. Indeed, its purpose is precisely for such a liturgical setting.

The hymn exalts the victory of the cross and of the victim who hung on it, Christ. Joseph Connelly observes that the hymn loses sight neither of the divinity nor of the humanity of the victim.[17] The text of the hymn as found in the *Liber Usualis* ends with praise to the Trinity as the fountain of salvation that has bestowed the reward of victory on the cross.[18] The first verse of the original hymn clearly states Christ took on human flesh, while verse three says "Regnavit a ligno Deus."[19] This gloss, found in Justin Martyr's *Apologia*,[20] appears to have had some impact on the development of the *Antifonario de León*, for several antiphons reflect this usage. The antiphonary of the Old Spanish liturgy was developed for use at the cathedral in León in the tenth century. Many of the Leonese antiphons appear in the contemporary Hispano-Mozarabic *Missale*.[21] Maybe the concept of "God reigning on the tree" of the cross has contributed to the sense that the Lignum Crucis acts as a symbol of the presence of Christ in the contemporary Good Friday liturgies in Toledo.

The image presented of Christ by the "Vexilla Regis" hymn is one of a king who rules from his throne, the cross. Salvation comes through the cross which brings life out of death. This is accomplished by the water and blood that flows from the lanced wound of Christ. In this way he washes away the stains of people's "crimes."[22] Given the Adoptionist controversy over Christ's role as self-emptying servant who dies on the cross advocated by Beatus or the *Primogenitus* who is the first of many advocated by Elipandus, the hymn serves to stress the former. Jaroslav Pelikan refers to the metaphor of *Christus Victor* that portrays the cross as the sign of God's invasion of enemy territory and of the *mirabile duellum* by which Christ accomplishes salvation.[23] He remarks that the metaphor describes the most typical image of Christ and the cross emerging during the Middle Ages. In this sense the cross becomes a sign of the divine power to overcome the enemies of God and of humankind, who strive to keep them apart.

Acclamations

After the Veneration of the Cross has taken place, Don Enrique and the congregation knelt for the next part of the liturgy. He used the Spanish-language translation of the second hymn offered in the *Missale* for the Veneration of the Cross.[24] The title in the *Missale* is "Hymnum de

Cruce Domini."[25] The six verses are divided between a leader and the congregation. Instead of singing the hymn, it was recited.

Once again, the cross is praised as the shining example of salvation. Especially striking is the notion that salvation is equated with new life. Verse four states this in terms of new fruit (Fierce and powerful, for us, O sacred tree, that carries in your branches fruit so new), and verse five in terms of new flowers (You extend your branches adorned with new flowers).[26] Christ is presented in verse two as the humble one who loves mercifully. The same verse also indicates he has been made a victim for us, the sacred lamb who has saved the sheep from the jaws of the wolf.[27] By his pierced hands he has redeemed the calamity of the world, closing the road to death by what has been stripped away from him.[28] Furthermore, his bloody hand has forged the key that took away Paul's guilt and Peter's death.[29] Finally, from his arms hang the vines from which flow delicious purple wines like blood.[30]

The image of Christ presented in this text is the victorious victim who loves and gives his life for his sheep. In this way salvation is presented as sacrifice and humility that brings new life to the world. This reflects Beatus's perspective. One participates in that salvation by linking oneself to the church, represented by Peter and Paul and the image of sheep, as well as by the liturgy, partaking of the wine that "flows like blood."

Closing Prayer

The morning liturgy concludes with a prayer in praise of Jesus Christ as the creator of the world.[31] He shares in the same splendor of glory with the Father and the Holy Spirit. Thus, the stress on Christ's divinity over against Arianism emerges. Also, he has deigned to *assume* immaculate flesh, allowing himself to be nailed to the executioner's cross.[32] In this way, the Adoptionist perspective is rejected by using the word *assumptio* instead of *adoptio*. At this liturgy the people come before Christ aware of the stains of their oppressive sins and asking his mercy.[33] They ask him not to abandon them but to grant them full pardon *(plena indulgencia)* for the wrong they have committed.

The Christ presented is one who sits in glory but who can be approached with reverence and deference. The salvation of his cross is available to those who come before it. His freedom from sin can be conveyed to them by means of these sacred solemnities, understood to be the liturgies of the Triduum, so that they may deserve to be immaculate before him.[34]

Interpretation

Christ is presented in this morning service as the incarnated Spouse of the church who is Lord, Savior, and Creator of the world. Though born of Mary, he lives in glory with the Father and the Spirit. He saves the world primarily by his death on the cross, and that salvation is made available to those who believe (1) by the wood of the cross, symbolized for Mozarabs in the relic of the true cross, the Lignum Crucis; (2) by the river of grace that flows from that cross in Christ's blood; (3) by freeing people from their enemies and from their iniquity; (4) by putting all creation right with God through justification; and (5) by allowing his glorious hands to be nailed to the cross and so conveying to his people pardon for their sins. They participate in that salvation by (1) worshiping him in the liturgy, (2) coming before the cross upon which he died, (3) recognizing their sinfulness and need for his mercy *(indulgencia),* (4) presenting their needs in tears before the one who has power to forgive and save then and now, and (5) living a virtuous life that reflects a return to Christ—a fragrant bouquet of the gifts of witness, service, and surrender to him.

AD NONAM

The afternoon liturgy picks up where the morning service leaves off.[35] The texts also present Christ as the Savior of the world who conveys salvation through his death. As the readings and euchology are quite extensive, I cite only examples of them to show how Christ and salvation are presented in the texts. However, there is no specific mention of the Lignum Crucis other than in the rubrics, which state that it is to be carried in silence to the altar at the onset of the liturgy.[36]

Readings

Like the other Lenten eucharistic celebrations in the Hispano-Mozarabic rite, the *Ad nonam* liturgy has three readings before the Gospel. They include Proverbs 3:24–26,[37] Isaiah 52:13—53:1–12, and 1 Corinthians 5:6; 6:1–12. The first two readings are each followed by responses involving the presider and congregation. The Gospel is a centonized continuation of the passion narrative begun the evening before at the Mass of the Lord's Supper *(Feria V in Cena Domini).* Let us examine all the readings before considering the two responses.

The reading from Proverbs proclaims that the faithful one need not fear, for when the Lord comes he will be that one's source of security and freedom. As a result the faithful one may go to bed and sleep sweetly (Prv 3:24). The last verse says "The Lord will be your confidence and will keep your foot from being caught" (Prv 3:26).[38] The reading calls to mind the third temptation in the desert, in which Satan tells Jesus that God will not allow his foot to be dashed upon a stone; rather angels will support him (Mt 4:6; Lk 4:10–11). This reference to Psalm 91:11–12 alludes to Christ's privileged relationship to God, who protects him from danger, even changing evil (the cross) to good (the sign of salvation). The reading also encourages the listener to remember that freedom will come from God's salvation in Christ's return, if one turns to Christ now. The popular saying, *No hay mal que por bien no venga* (there is no evil that does not come for some good), captures this sense as well. If one experiences evil, with God's indulgence it can be turned to good. In the context of this liturgy, if one acknowledges one's sin, the evil in which one has participated, and turns to God asking for mercy, God will grant freedom from the consequences of that evil.

The second reading is Isaiah's fourth servant song, Isaiah 52:13—53:12.[39] It speaks of God's servant who undergoes trial and punishment, carrying the people's sins humbly like a lamb being shorn (Is 52:13). Traditionally it has been seen as a foreshadowing of Christ's passion. The penultimate verse reads: "The just one, my servant, will justify many and will carry their iniquities" (Is 53:11).[40] The last verse goes on to say that as a result of having surrendered himself to death, taking away the sins of many and interceding on their behalf, he will share in greatness (Is 53:12). Thus the reading serves to point to Christ as the victim and the servant who empties himself in order to carry the people's sins *(kenosis)*. As a result he becomes the glorious one who makes salvation available to those who turn to him. The Spanish saying, *No hay gloria sin la cruz* (there is no glory without the cross), points to this concept as well.

The third reading from 1 Corinthians 5:6—6:11[41] also serves to reinforce the notion that one's sins keep one from possessing the reign of God. Paul exhorts the Corinthians to do away with the old leaven, understood to be sin of all sorts including pride, avarice, fornication, idolatry, drunkenness, and so forth (1 Cor 5:6; 6:9–10). Instead, they are to be pure and avoid mixing with evildoers (1 Cor 6:9). It is best to avoid conflict in the community, Paul counsels; it is better to suffer injustice and to be stripped than to fight with one another and so give a bad example to unbelievers (1 Cor 6:5, 6–7).[42] The passage ends with Paul's declaration that some were evildoers, but now you "were washed, you were sanctified, you were justified in the name of the Lord Jesus Christ and in the Spirit of our God" (1 Cor 6:11).[43] Thus along with the previous readings the listener is told where salvation as freedom, peace, and justification can be found: in the Lord. The third reading tells salvation from what: sinfulness, that is, whatever separates us from the love of the Lord. It does so in terms of concrete actions that mark human life and, therefore, indicts the hearers who share that life. In this way one is prodded to acknowledge that God is the source of freedom from sin that marks one's life.

The Gospel narrative then tells the hearer how Christ comes to bear people's sinfulness and makes salvation available to them. The passage is comprised of fifteen pericopes.[44] It begins with the gathering of the priests and elders of the community who, having judged Jesus guilty of blasphemy, decide to take Jesus to Pilate so that he may be put to death (Mt 27:1). In between, Jesus is questioned by Pilate, rejected by the crowd, scourged, taken to be crucified, and ridiculed. On the cross Jesus forgives the repentant thief, cries out to God in pain, and then surrenders to God. The centurion declares that this was truly the Son of God (Mt 27:54). Jesus' side is pierced, and water and blood gush forth. This passage follows: "The one who saw gives witness, and his testimony is true. And we do believe this is true, and believing, we will have life in his name" (Jn 20:30–31).[45] The passage ends with the priests and elders returning to Pilate after Jesus has died on the cross asking him to put a guard at Jesus' tomb in case his disciples come and take him away and so further the fraud they claim he has committed (Mt 27:62–66). The hearers come to see that Jesus bears people's sins and provides them his salvation through his rejection, condemnation, crucifixion, death, and burial. If the hearers believe, like the witness in the Gospel narrative, then they will have life in his name. The implication is that if hearers take it to be fraud, then they will not be washed by the water and blood flowing from Jesus' side and, as a consequence, will not have access to salvation.

Responses

The responses after the first and second readings also help to draw out the meanings identified. The first response is based on Micah 6:1–8.[46] It is read antiphonally between the presider and the congregation. The presider reads each verse, to which the people respond, "Y me preparaste la Cruz" (and you prepared for me the cross). It declares that despite the salvation provided by God, such as taking the people out of the slavery of Egypt (Mi 6:4), and their desire to perform liturgical actions, such as offering holocausts and oil (Mi 6:6–7), they have caused God to cry out against them. They have sinned against God. They have prepared for him a cross. The response ends with the declaration of what God wants as a sign of repentance: "hacer justicia, amar el bien y caminar en la presencia de tu Dios" (to do justice, to love good, and to walk in the presence of your God). Thus, God's lament against his people on the lips of the worshipers at Santa Eulalia helps them identify with God's experience of their sins. It also reminds them of what it will take to overcome those sins.

The second response is Psalm 22.[47] It is read by the presider and con-gregation who alternate each verse. Both priest and congregation start their first verses with "Dios mío" (my God). The presider asks, "¿Por qué me has abandonado?" (Why have you abandoned me?), and the people declare, "De día te grito y no respondes; de noche, y no me haces caso" (I cry by day but you do not answer; by night, but you pay no attention to me). The presider ends by crying out, "Sálvame de las fauces del león" (Save me from the mouth of the lion), and the people promise, "Contaré tu fama a mis hermanos; en medio de la asamblea te alabaré" (I will tell of your name to my brothers; in the midst of the assembly I will praise you). This psalm is traditionally understood to express Christ's agony on the cross. The first verse is heard on Jesus' lips in Mark 15:34 and Matthew 27:46. But recited on the lips of the people, especially after the reading of the suffering servant of Isaiah, it urges them to identify themselves with Christ's agony. It invites them to see that they too die on the cross with Christ and so have a share in his salvation. Yet this sense comes before they have been challenged by the reading from 1 Corinthians to see that their sins have nailed Jesus to the cross and that they must repent of them in order to share in the salvation he has suffered to attain for them.

Homily

Toledo IV (633) decreed that on Good Friday a sermon be given ex-plaining the mystery of the cross.[48] Sometime after this a text was com-posed and handed on to later generations. The text appears in the *Liber Ordinum* as well as in the *Liber Commicus* (1991).[49] During the service Don Enrique made some spontaneous comments on the readings before proceeding to read the text of the sermon. The sermon seeks to elicit from the hearers identification with the good thief, who, after confess-ing his guilt, asks Christ on the cross that he be remembered when Jesus comes into his kingdom. Toward the end of the sermon the homilist invites those present to repeat the words of the good thief so that they may ask pardon for their sins: "Si queremos imitar al ladrón, clamemos gimiendo como él, y digamos: 'Acuérdate de mí, Señor, cuando llegues a tu reino'" (If we desire to imitate the thief, let us cry out like him and say: "Remember me Lord, when you arrive at your kingdom").[50] The sermon resumes briefly and ends with the congregation repeating these words once again.

Certain images of Christ and his salvation emerge in the sermon. The first is that of the God who, in his human death, put the price of salvation in the balance "on this day," thereby redeeming the entire world.[51] In this way he who was the creator also became the restorer of humankind. Even so, the price he paid did not cover the cost incurred; rather, his death represents the mercy or pardon *(indulgencia)* of the redeemer for the redeemed. The spilling of his innocent blood redeemed the human being weighed down with sin; the one without sin carried with dignity the sins of others.[52] Christ alone is the victim for all in order to raise all up; in this way the only one who owed no debt paid in justice the price of his blood for the debtors. The text notes that this reveals the fulfillment of Isaiah's prophecy, which states, "I gave my back to those who struck me,/ I did not hide my face from insult and spitting" (Is 50:6).[53] The text calls upon the hearers to recognize how much they are worth and how much they owe, for Christ "received our evils, in order to give us his goods."[54] That is, Christ took evil away that he might give his blessings, that is, salvation.

A series of contrasts follows, using attributes of Christ to raise the consciousness of the hearers, who presumably manifest the opposite attributes: piety is tormented because of the impious one, wisdom is laughed at by the fool, truth is denied by the liar, justice is condemned by the sinner, innocence is tortured by the guilty one, and life is put to death by the one who is dead. The series ends with a question posed to the hearers: "What should I say of the mercy of him who, so that no one despairs, receives in his paradise the thief, who upon dying, confesses him?"[55] This leads the homilist to invite those present to repeat the thief's words asking admittance to paradise.

The last part of the sermon admonishes the hearers, as the homilist's beloved brothers and sisters *(hermanos amadísimos)*, to feel deeply the confession they have just recited. They are to proclaim loudly their confession so that they may be heard and saved. They are to say it with faith and wholeheartedly. "For our Lord will surely hear the voice of our petition if he sees the sincere devotion of our soul."[56] A series of petitions follows asking that the one who shattered the gates of hell may open the gates of paradise to us; the one who took us out of the lake of sorrow may take us to the tree of life; the one who consented to be arrested by Pontius Pilate may free his people from punishment, taking to his kingdom those who confess the one who agreed to suffer for sinners, despite his own innocence. The last repetition of the thief's words then follows.

Christ appears as the one who takes on our sins in order to open the gates of paradise and of his reign to us. In contrast to the Christ of Priscillianism, who only *appeared* to be human, the Christ of the sermon is the one who in his fully human flesh saves humankind. In contrast to the Christ portrayed by Arianism, who was not fully divine, the Christ of the sermon is the God who takes on our human life in order to redeem us so that we may share in his divinity. In contrast to the Christ of Adoptionism, who was the first of the children of God adopted to share in his glory, the Christ of the sermon is the suffering servant who surrenders unto death so that God's people may be saved. It is this Christ the people are invited to confess and acknowledge. In this way they recognize their need for pardon and, thus, salvation from their sins.

Petitions for Pardon

Toledo IV (633) decreed that in response to the sermon on the cross, the people were to ask aloud for pardon for their sins, so that once having completed their penance, they could receive the sacrament of the Lord's Body and Blood at the celebration of the resurrection.[57] By means of these texts the entire assembly fulfills the invitation of the sermon to acknowledge the sin that marks the lives of those present and to ask Christ to demonstrate his mercy once again. The congregation follows the text provided in Worship Aid II.[58]

The petitions are broken into three principal segments. Each segment presents a slight variation on the image of Christ as the Good Shepherd who lays down his life for his sheep (Jn 10:11). Furthermore, Christ is clearly presented as the God who forgives our sins. The instruction at the onset of the petitions reads, "Let us implore the Lord our God to deign to grant us mercy for our crimes and pardon for our sins."[59] This same God is asked to extend a hand to the fallen and to protect those who request divine protection. The people are instructed to ask the same God to help them recognize the evil they have committed and avoid from now on the temptations of the enemy, so that those who have been separated from the altar of God may return to it with tears of repentance.

The first segment of the petitions now ensues. It begins with repeated cries of "¡Indulgencia!" (mercy, pardon, indulgence), which they are to cry out no more than three hundred times.[60] It is followed by ten petitions in which the presider asks the Lord to descend from on high, help us who suffer, cleanse us of our sins, have pity on the penitents, come to the aid of those who cry, straighten out those who have gone astray from the faith, and raise up those who have fallen into sin.[61] A prayer addressed to "the Only Begotten Son of the Father" follows. It is a gloss that reiterates the themes of the petitions as well as the homily and Gospel reading. For example, to stress the Son's suffering and rejection the prayer notes that his "precious flesh was tortured by the Jews, ridiculed by the ungrateful and crucified like that of the thieves."[62] Given the context, one is to reject torturing and mocking Jesus by recognizing one's sin and begging pardon *(indulgencia)*. The main focus, however, is on the blood and water that flowed from Christ's side, noting that it is not strange that blood flowed. Rather, the prayer asks, "Is it not strange that water would also flow?"[63] It goes on to declare, "This is certainly the water that, flowing from his body, serves to regenerate and give new life to those who have died in Adam."[64] For this reason those present now ask that he who deigned to suffer our death give us victory over the enemy defeated by his resurrection from the dead. The doxology at the end of the prayer proclaims the Trinity, although it is addressed to Christ as *Dios nuestro* (our God).[65] This doxology is repeated after each of the three orations closing the three segments of petitions.

The second segment of petitions imploring mercy commences. It is initiated by the cries of "¡Indulgencia!," although fewer in number according to the rubric. The ten petitions once again reiterate that Christ is the Good Shepherd who lays down his life for his sheep. The prayers, however, change focus and address the Trinity. The first petition asks the Lord to grant the appropriate pardon and peace for our sins. The second petition asks the Father to reconcile us. The third asks that the grace of Christ reform us. The fourth asks that we be strengthened by the Holy Spirit. The others are vague in subject, but they ask for freedom from hunger, pestilence, illness, for the return of captives, and for good weather. The image of Christ as Lord of Creation and the giver of life emerges from this segment of petitions. The closing prayer reveals this in the contrast between the tree of life "of which Adam did not deserve to eat" and the cross, which is now the tree of life that gives life to those who taste of it.[66]

The flow of the petitions imploring mercy is interrupted by the antiphonal recitation of Psalm 50.[67] The psalm is initiated by the presider, who asks God for pardon for having rejected his commandments, the God who despite our sin grants pardon. The psalm is broken into nine pairs of strophes. It is completed by the recitation of the *Gloria* by all.[68] The form of the *Gloria*, which begins *Gloria y honor al Padre* (Glory and honor to the Father), was specifically formulated over and against the Arian version in order to emphasize adherence to the orthodox Catholic notion of Christ as equal to the Father and to the Spirit in glory and honor.

The last segment of petitions is initiated by cries of "¡Indulgencia!" The segment begins the eight petitions reiterating that Christ is the Good Shepherd who lays his life down for his sheep. This time the petitions ask that we be returned to paradise, that the doors of heaven be opened to us, that we be freed from condemnation, that the fire of hell be extinguished, that eternal rest be given to the dead, and that the dead be associated with the blessed of heaven. The closing oration presents Christ on the cross as if he hung between the two testaments as he hung between the two thieves. He is the one who has gone into the depths of hell, thereby opening the graves of the just. It ends with a request that we may, in his mercy and resurrection, understand just how much he will give us in his kingdom, for he is the one who raised us from hell unto glory by his death.[69] In this way Christ is presented as the Lord of revelation, represented by the two testaments, who out of death on the cross brings life and who through his descent into hell brings glory to those who recognize him.

Closing

The final portion of the *Ad nonam* liturgy comprises the recitation of the Lord's Prayer in typical Mozarabic fashion.[70] This includes the recitation of an embolism for this day that asks the Lord to free us from sin as well as to confirm us in our fear of God and in our good works. The people are then dismissed to go in peace. The use of this prayer links the service to the entire liturgical system of the Hispano-Mozarabic rite. It also serves to stress that although the greater portion of the euchology of the service is directed to Christ, it is also addressed to the Father.

Interpretation

Christ appears as the Good Shepherd, the voluntary victim who dies for his sheep so that they may be saved. Thus, the notion of the suffering servant is key to understanding the Christology of the *Ad nonam* liturgy. The trinitarian doxologies at the end of the prayers addressed to Christ serve to reiterate that all three divine Persons merit honor and glory through the worship of God's people, especially as they ask pardon for their sins. They are invited to encounter God's salvation wrought through Christ by his voluntary death on the cross and the outpouring of the

Holy Spirit in the water that emanates from Christ's side. The cross as the instrument of salvation emerges as the most obvious soteriological symbol presented in these texts. The Lignum Crucis on the altar throughout the liturgy serves to link it to Christ's cross and his death upon it. By imitating Christ and adhering to him on that cross, God's people are provided with salvation. They are saved when they acknowledge Christ as their savior and repent of their sins. The Lignum Crucis is clearly the key liturgical symbol for helping the people do this and the texts help make this connection for them.

PROCESSIONS

The texts available for understanding the christological and soteriological meaning of the Good Friday processions are very limited. Nonetheless, the programs published for the processions of Holy Week in Toledo and the decree by the archbishop of Toledo for the placement of the Lignum Crucis in those processions provide important clues. Employing both a hermeneutic of retrieval and of suspicion will help us understand and interpret those clues.[71]

Booklet

The *Semana Santa '99* booklet provided details of the ceremonies and liturgies that formed the basis for the processions throughout Holy Week in 1999. It encompassed the events that began on Monday, 15 March 1999, and ended on Easter Sunday, 4 April 1999. The booklet was meant for visitors and local people alike though it was apparently geared particularly to outsiders, since it was made available through the Province of Toledo's tourist offices. In addition to giving a calendar of events, including speakers, topics, liturgies, and processions, it gave a detailed description of the *Hermandades* and *Cofradías* and the images they take in procession. Particularly significant, however, was the "Introduction" by the president of the *Junta de Cofradías y Hermandades de Semana Santa de Toledo*, Manuel Lanza Alandi:

> We of the Council of Confraternities and Brotherhoods of Toledo invite all you of good will to share with us, in our churches, in the great temple, in our cathedral, the liturgy of the Love of the Father of Mercy and of the Sacrifice of the Son. Afterward, in the streets, accompany us or simply contemplate the passing of the processions in which each brotherhood or confraternity will offer its prayer,

its silence, its devotion. They are very conscious that what motivates them has been left behind in the celebration of the sacred liturgies or of a Holy Hour celebrated in the silence of a quiet convent, in peaceful meditation on the supreme act of redemption, accompanying the sorrow of the Mother and always confident in the message of the beloved disciple: *Deus Cáritas est*, God is Love.[72]

Clearly this stresses the centrality of God as a God of mercy, of pardon, and of redemption. That redemption is found in Jesus Christ, the Son of God, who has sacrificed himself for humankind out of his great love. The people participate in that salvation to the extent that they participate in the liturgy and the devotional practices organized by the church as well as by the *Hermandades* and *Cofradías*. In this way one can see an integration of the centrality of Jesus the God-man found in the liturgical life of the church into daily human life. This notion is reinforced by the mayor's letter at the front of the booklet:

Toledo and Holy Week have attained in the last few years a point of encounter of which we are all very pleased. The city, with its alleys, plazas, and covered walkways, offers a spectacular stage to draw out the magnificence of the processional groups, which permit us to enjoy the best pieces of Toledan religious art. They are days in which beauty and the most sincere sentiments take hold of the Toledan ambience. The best of our tradition returns to the street. . . . I encourage all the people of Toledo to participate in these festivities and I express my respect for those who live these days in intense religious intimacy.[73]

The booklet is very circumspect about the Lignum Crucis. It simply remarks that the reliquary appeared in the Mozarabic parish of Santa Eulalia toward the end of the Middle Ages. It also indicates that it began to be taken in procession in the fifteenth century on Holy Wednesday from the parish to the Church of Santa María la Mayor, today the cathedral. The booklet also observes that the *Hermandades* and *Cofradías* of Toledo have their origin in the Mozarab community in the reign of King Alfonso VI after 1085. It is reasonable to conclude that the integration of faith into life and life into faith that the processions represent is a value held in great esteem by Mozarabs of Toledo and is attached to the relic of the cross they take in procession. This faith is clearly centered on Jesus and his death on the cross for the salvation of humankind. It is celebrated liturgically in the services held earlier in the day and extended in the streets by means of the processions.

Pamphlet

The *Semana Santa '99* pamphlet is less explicit on the doctrine of Christ and salvation emerging from the Good Friday services. It gives the schedule of liturgical and devotional events from Sunday, 21 March 1999, to Easter Sunday, 4 April 1999. The pamphlet also gives a basic description of the *Hermandades* and *Cofradías* of Toledo. Its description of the Lignum Crucis and *Hermandad Mozárabe* is the same as that of the booklet. Like the booklet, it conveys the message that the devotional activity represented by the processions is solidly linked to the liturgical life of the church.

Decree

The decree of González Martín placing the Lignum Crucis toward the end of the processions indicates that the relic is linked to Jesus on the cross and his burial.[74] That is because the decree requires it to be placed between the *pasos* of Jesus laid out for burial *(Santo Sepulcro)* and just before the image of the Sorrowful Mother *(Nuestra Señora de la Soledad)*. Furthermore, the archbishop desires to foster greater piety and devotion on the part of the faithful; to aid in this he decrees that the Lignum Crucis be carried on an *anda* and under a *palio* (canopy).[75] He also orders that specific liturgical norms in relation to the Lignum Crucis be followed.[76] This serves to give it more honor and importance. Surely this is due to its symbolism as a sign of the presence of Christ among the people.

The meaning of the ritual use of the Lignum Crucis in the liturgy and the processions is not confined to the texts but emerges from the combination of texts and practice. What implications can be drawn from this? First, a hermeneutical analysis of the placement of the Lignum Crucis in the processions and its scheduled time of departure as indicated in the booklet, pamphlet, and decree reveals that it is clearly linked to Jesus' death on the cross as celebrated on Good Friday. For instance, the procession in which the Lignum Crucis is carried is scheduled to begin at dusk; for those familiar with the scriptural references (Mt 27:45, Mk 15:33, Lk 23:44–45), this hour symbolizes nicely the darkness that comes over the world at Jesus' death. Second, the fact that the processions of Good Friday are the most elaborate of Holy Week and draw the most observers indicates that the people who participate in them put great stress on the centrality of Jesus Christ and his sacrifice. That the processions draw so many observers also helps the participants announce publicly their faith in Christ and his salvation through the cross to the world.

CHRISTOLOGICAL AND SOTERIOLOGICAL MEANING

The doctrine of Christ emerging from the Good Friday services is that of the God-man who suffers for his people in order to save them from their sins. In this way the loving Good Shepherd protects his sheep from the enemy and conveys to them his mercy. Jesus Christ is central to the economy of salvation and to the relationship between humankind and God. The death of Christ is the principal means of salvation presented in the texts of Good Friday. God turns evil to good in Jesus' case.

IMPLICATIONS FOR THE RITUAL USE
OF THE LIGNUM CRUCIS

Our examination toward the beginning of Chapter 8 of the three christological controversies that tainted the Hispano-Mozarabic rite has helped to reveal that the texts present a clear rejection of the Christ presented by those heresies. This is especially the case in relation to Arianism. The texts used in the contemporary era reveal a stress on the divine Christ who dies for his people. But it is not just any death. Rather, it is a death on the cross, the sign of great rejection, marginalization, and suffering. Nonetheless, this evil is not the end. Rather it leads to salvation; evil is turned to good and one understands the foundational meaning of the saying *No hay gloria sin la cruz* (there is no glory without the cross). Furthermore, it is not through Adoption that Christ saves. Christ saves because he is the God-man who empties himself to be the servant who gives his life on the cross. By entering into and joining that suffering and death, those who are faithful to Christ, their spouse, are saved. Christ is not divorced from human life, as proposed by Priscillianism. Instead, he is the incarnate one who shares human life that human beings may share divine life with him.

How then does the ritual use of the Lignum Crucis reliquary support or modify this Christology and soteriology? The relic of the wood of Christ's cross is crucial, for it conveys a sense of the "real presence" of Christ; thus, it functions as a particularly powerful vehicle of salvation. It does so by inviting those who approach it to take on the life of Christ in their own time and place, especially by seeing the cross as a source of life and salvation. This is integrated into life by taking up one's cross. The emphasis on Christ as the God-man found in the texts and in the ritual use of the Lignum Crucis at liturgy and in the processions reveals that Christ is to be the universal model of what it is to be authentically human. As Sierra summarizes, humankind is realized to the degree it nears its model.[77]

The Good Friday liturgies and processions reveal the centrality of the person of Jesus Christ and of trust in him despite awareness of one's sinfulness. The texts for the most part emphasize the Lignum Crucis's role and value in this regard. Ritually, it is the focal point of the prayers and actions. The starkness of the reliquary, its simple lines, and the lack of corpus stress the centrality of the cross in salvation. The ritual use of the reliquary draws out these meanings. At the same time, the texts impose these meanings on the ritual use of the reliquary because there is a dynamic of exchange that occurs between the ritual action and the texts. The Lignum Crucis draws these out by serving as a pivotal symbol in that it mediates between both the texts and the ritual.

10

The Spirituality
of the Cross

That Mozarabs of Toledo highly honor the cross as a symbol of their Christianity and as an emblem of their community we have seen borne out by the important role it plays in Mozarabic liturgy and spirituality. The ritual use of the Lignum Crucis in the liturgical and popular religious realms contributes to the construction of meanings shared by both realms. This is particularly evident in the liturgies and events of Good Friday. The use of the relic of the true cross, the Lignum Crucis, as a special object of veneration and identification has theological meanings that signify a certain way of viewing Christ, his cross, and his saving action at the heart of the Paschal Mystery. The liturgy in particular is the foundation for the Christology and soteriology that mark the ritual use of the Lignum Crucis both as a liturgical article and as an object of popular devotion. The liturgy is also the foundation for Mozarab identity. Several questions are raised by the links among Mozarabic liturgy, spirituality, and identity: How is this link forged through ritual and texts? What are liturgy and popular religion, and how are they linked? What theological meanings emerge from the use of the cross as a symbol? Finally, what are some parallels between Mozarabs and the cross in relation to Hispanic spirituality in general?

LITURGY AND POPULAR RELIGION

Part of the meaning generated by the ritual use of the Lignum Crucis occurs at the intersection of liturgy and popular religion. The fact that the Lignum Crucis reliquary stands out as a principal symbol in the liturgies and in the evening processions of Good Friday raises three basic but important questions. What is liturgy? What is popular religion? And

158

what is the relationship between liturgy and popular religion? By answering these questions one can come to see how the Lignum Crucis is a pivotal symbol for Mozarabs' liturgy, spirituality, and identity.

WHAT IS LITURGY?

A major result of Vatican II was the reform of the Roman liturgy. Inspired by Vatican II, Cardinal James Knox in 1975, at the First International Congress on Mozarabic Studies, encouraged the Mozarabic community to renew and update the ancient Spanish liturgy. Those present at the Congress convinced Cardinal González Martín to work toward the actualization of the Mozarabic rite. He did so following the principles of the *Constitution on the Sacred Liturgy (Sacrosanctum Concilium)*, which recognizes the liturgy as central to the life of the church as its "fount and summit" and delineates the program for reform (*SC*, no. 10). It also describes liturgy by presenting its characteristics. In particular, the church teaches that liturgy is a participation in the Paschal Mystery of Christ as well as a human activity "whereby the faithful may express in their lives and manifest to others the mystery of Christ and the real nature of the true Church" (SC, no. 2).

Motivated by *Sacrosanctum Concilium*, liturgical theologians have been examining the question of how the liturgy is both the fount and summit of the church's life. Several have demonstrated how the liturgy is not only a *locus theologicus* but also *theologia prima*. *Locus theologicus* refers to something that serves as a point of departure for theological reflection; *theologia prima*, theology in the first instance, refers to that which is theological in and of itself, causing one to reflect or engage in *theologia secunda*, theology in the second instance, or theological reflection.[1] This is not a new idea, but one that has come more to the forefront since Vatican II. For instance, Justin Martyr, Tertullian, Cyprian of Carthage, Augustine, Cyril of Jerusalem, Isidore of Seville, and others during the so-called Patristic Era of the church made explicit references to liturgical rites as a point of departure for their theological reflection, especially in terms of Christian initiation.[2]

The liturgy is what I call enacted theology. It is theology in action that calls forth *theologia secunda* or reflection on the experience of God taking place through word, song, ritual, and so forth. By reflecting on what takes place at a specific liturgical event, one can identify, among other things, how God is present, what the church understands God to be saying, and what the church is saying about God. Because liturgy is more than texts and involves God's action as well as that of the worshipers,

Alexander Schmemann notes that the task of liturgical theology is to examine what is done in worship.[3] In this way the theologian is able to identify the real nature of worship and thus attain correct comprehension or true interpretation of a liturgical event.[4] This is why I have focused on the ritual use of the Lignum Crucis.

I identify five major characteristics of liturgy. Four of these are based on *Sacrosanctum Concilium*. The fifth, the concept of liturgy as *ecclesial ritual praxis*, is articulated by Margaret Mary Kelleher.[5] I see these characteristics in the Good Friday events in Toledo and the ritual use of the Lignum Crucis. The principal characteristics of liturgy presented in the documents of Vatican II are the following: liturgy is Christo-centric, anamnetic, epicletic, and ecclesial. Clearly the two Good Friday services at Santa Eulalia exhibit these traits. The procession in the evening with the Lignum Crucis also exhibits them.

Christo-centric

Sacrosanctum Concilium portrays liturgy as the exercise of the priestly office of Christ; that is, it is Christ's offering of self in worship to God (*SC*, no. 7). Furthermore, "Christ is always present in his Church, especially in its liturgical celebrations" (*SC*, no. 7). He is present in many ways: in the person of the minister, in the scriptures that are read, in the sacraments, in the eucharistic species, and in those gathered in his name (*SC*, no. 7). Thus, liturgy is Christo-centric.

The two Good Friday liturgies are clearly Christo-centric. First, the assembly is convoked in Christ's name through two official liturgical celebrations. Second, Christ's passion and death as a sacrifice in worshipful obedience to the Father provide the main focus of the prayers and scriptural readings for both services. Third, the services are presided over by the church's minister, Don Enrique Carrillo Morales, pastor of Santa Eulalia; other liturgical ministries in the form of readers and acolytes also appear in service to the worshiping assembly. Fourth, most of the prayers are addressed to the Father in Christ's name; some are addressed directly to Christ as the mediator between God and humankind because of his death on the cross. Fifth, the liturgies invite the assembly to recognize its need for Christ's reconciliation through veneration of his cross in the morning *Ad tertiam* liturgy and in the afternoon *Ad nonam* penitential service.

The penitential aspect of surrender to Christ is extended into the Good Friday processions. These too are Christo-centric: the events of the final day of Jesus' life are presented in sculpted tableaux carried by the faithful. The processions are sanctioned by church authorities and accompanied by its ministers. The participants engage in prayer and penances, self-imposed or assigned by their confessors. The processions act as an invitation to onlookers to appropriate faith in the salvific sacrifice of Christ on the cross that the participants are proclaiming publicly by their actions. The plain, spare Lignum Crucis carried at the end also serves to focus on Christ as the source and summit of Christian worship. As Doña María Jesús Lozano Durán states, taking the Lignum Crucis in procession is more important than the images "because it is a sliver of the cross of Jesus; it's like taking Christ in procession, that's why it is under the *palio*. It is the only one under *palio* like the Blessed Sacrament. The rest are only images and they do not have much spiritual value despite their beauty."[6] Thus Christ, hanging between two thieves as between two testaments, is like the hinge of the diptych tablets: he mediates between the God who humbles himself to share in our humanity that we might share in his divinity, between human sinfulness and divine indulgence, and between official worship and the popular devotion that make up Hispano-Mozarabic liturgy and spirituality.

Anamnetic

Sacrosanctum Concilium also declares that in Christ the perfect achievement of our reconciliation was attained and "the fullness of divine worship was given to us" (*SC*, no. 5). This has been accomplished by his incarnation and the offering of his life, death, and resurrection for our salvation. This sacrifice is his ongoing Paschal Mystery, which not only offers worship to God but also actualizes his redemption of the world. Liturgy, then, is centered on Christ's Paschal Mystery and is built on it. In other words, liturgy is anamnetic. It memorializes and actualizes the Paschal Mystery. As a result, liturgy is also an eschatological event, for it helps move the worshipers toward the fullness of the kingdom made present sacramentally.

Although the passion and death of Christ provide the central focus of the two Good Friday liturgies and the evening processions, it is only part of the total Paschal Mystery celebrated that day. By introducing the Offering of Flowers before the Veneration of the Cross during the *Ad tertiam* service in the morning, Don Enrique makes a link to the Christmas liturgy, at which the birth of Christ is celebrated by means of the flowers chosen—roses, lilies, and violets. They represent the ongoing redemption of the Lord after his glorification found in martyrs (roses), virgins (lilies), and the pure (violets). These are signs of Christ's kingdom in the world. In this way the totality of the Paschal Mystery found in the incarnation, life, passion, death, resurrection, glory, and continuous presence of Christ in the church is celebrated. As such, not only do the Good Friday liturgies memorialize Christ's redemption, but they actualize it in the primary sign of the church gathered in his name.

Within the context of the entire Triduum this is most clearly seen in the Eucharist celebrated on Holy Thursday and at the Easter Vigil, especially during the Fraction Rite, where the entire Paschal Mystery is represented by the nine pieces of the broken host used by the presider. As the presider breaks the host, he names the pieces according to the feasts in the Hispano-Mozarabic liturgical calendar that encompass the totality of Christ's redemption. The anamnetic character of Hispano-Mozarabic liturgy is also stressed at the Institution Narrative based on 1 Corinthians 11:23–26. Here, one is reminded that what is taking place is done in memory of Christ, since this is stressed after each of the three divisions of the narrative. The priest says after the consecration of both bread and wine, "Whenever you do this, do it in memory of me"; at the third part the presider says, "Whenever you eat this bread and drink this cup, you proclaim the death of the Lord until he comes in glory."[7]

The Good Friday evening processions extend the anamnetic quality of the liturgies into the streets. By taking the Lignum Crucis in procession, the honor accorded to the relic of Christ's cross serves to bring to mind Christ's redemption and to raise consciousness of Christ's presence in the midst of those gathered for the processions. Don Enrique identifies this task like this: "We are following the example of the Jerusalem Church, doing what is described by Egeria."[8] For this reason I judge the processions to be quasi-liturgical. They are Christo-centric and anamnetic.

Epicletic

Another characteristic of liturgy is the presence of the Holy Spirit. The first gift Christ gives to his followers is the Spirit (Jn 20:22; Acts 2). Since Pentecost, the church has "come together to celebrate the Paschal Mystery: reading [scripture] . . . celebrating the Eucharist . . . and at the same time giving thanks . . . in Christ Jesus . . . through the power of the Holy Spirit" (SC, no. 6). Through the Spirit those gathered in liturgy are transformed into the Mystical Body of Christ and are empowered to offer perfect worship to God in union with Christ (see 1 Cor 12:3). In this way liturgy is epicletic, for it conveys the Spirit to those gathered, that is, the Spirit is poured out on those open to it.

The Holy Spirit's role has been integral to the economy of salvation for the Spanish church since earliest times, and this is reflected in its liturgy. Recall that the concept of the *filioque* was introduced at Toledo III (589) as part of the Symbol of Faith that was to be recited by the faithful at every eucharistic celebration. Furthermore, the orations of the Hispano-Mozarabic rite regularly end with a doxology in praise of the Trinity. For example, the *Ad tertiam* liturgy ends with the doxology: "Who with God the Father and the Holy Spirit lives and reigns, one God, forever and ever. Amen."[9] The doxology for the three presidential prayers in the midst of the Litany for Mercy says: "By your mercy, our God, who lives with God the Father and reigns with the Holy Spirit forever and ever. Amen."[10] These convey the sense that the Holy Spirit is present in the gathering of the people as they worship God. In my estimation the doxologies convey a sense of being convoked by the Spirit. Consequently, through their worship Mozarabs are strengthened and shaped into the body of Christ; they reveal this reality in their lives of submission to God by following Christ's example. I submit it is the same Spirit that impels them to proclaim their faith publicly by going into the streets in procession.

Ecclesial

A fourth characteristic of liturgy is its ecclesial aspect. Those who participate in liturgy are transformed by Christ into his body. At the same time, Christ's body, the church, is his temple: "The liturgy daily builds up those who are within into a holy temple of the Lord" (*SC*, no. 2). *The Dogmatic Constitution on the Church (Lumen Gentium)* teaches that the transformation into the body of Christ makes his followers the church, and this occurs in every legitimate gathering of the faithful: "This Church of Christ is truly present in all lawful, local congregations of the faithful, which, united with their pastors, are themselves called Churches in the New Testament" (*LG*, no. 26). Because the bishop cannot preside over his whole flock in person, the door is open to the gathering of smaller groupings of the faithful for liturgy which "in some manner . . . represent the visible Church established throughout the world" (*SC*, no. 42). Liturgy constitutes the church; at the same time it is an action of the church. Therefore, liturgy is ecclesial.

One way to approach the ecclesial nature of the ritual use of the Lignum Crucis is from the legal aspect. The Hispano-Mozarabic rite is an official liturgical system, sanctioned by the Roman Catholic Church; its ecclesiastical superior is the archbishop of Toledo.[11] In this way the rite becomes a particular expression of the ecclesial nature of the body of Christ. The archbishop, as a sign of the ecclesial nature of worship,[12] regulates the liturgical life of the Mozarab community by assigning it parishes and ministers, as well as by publishing liturgical books in accord with regulations set forth by the Holy See.[13] He guides the community's religious life by being the official *Hermano Mayor* (major brother or leader) of the *Hermandad Mozárabe*. He approves the *Hermandad*'s *Constituciones* and presides at the annual ceremony incorporating new members. He also influences the community by means of the official chaplain assigned to the *Hermandad*.

Cardinal González Martín officially sanctioned the use of the Lignum Crucis in the two Good Friday liturgies by the publication of new liturgical books as well as by its use in the evening processions. When the community gathers in worship in its different forms with the archbishop, or his designated agents, the pastors and chaplains of the Mozarabic rite, they make visible to the world the body of Christ encompassed in a particular gathering of the faithful. Because the archbishop also participates in the evening processions the question might be posed: Does this make them liturgical given the characteristics above?

Ecclesial Ritual Praxis

To explore further the liturgical nature of the ritual use of the Lignum Crucis, it is necessary to see how the church is being constituted by the Good Friday events. Bernard Lonergan's theory of symbol and incarnate meaning as well as Margaret Mary Kelleher's theory of liturgy as an act of meaning are helpful here. Earlier I developed the notion of ritual as action constitutive of culture; it makes meanings and values real. I also noted that liturgy is the action of the church at prayer. This means liturgy is ritual that actualizes the church and its share in Christ's redemption. That is, liturgy is ecclesial ritual praxis, action that incarnates meaning and constitutes the church.

Actions are symbolic; they evoke feelings, reveal values, and embody what is meaningful. As a result, symbols have a role in the incarnation of meaning. Bernard Lonergan describes symbol as an image of a real or imaginary object capable of evoking a feeling or of being evoked by a feeling.[14] As a consequence, symbols are primarily related to the affect. The affect is not to be dismissed as nonrational, for it is the power of conscious living. Feelings orient one's being and involve intentional responses that constitute one's world of meaning or culture. According to Lonergan, feelings respond to value following a scale of preference. Religious values are at the top of the scale, because they are at the heart of living.[15] Human culture is partially composed of values; symbols help us apprehend them. Conscious acts and intended contents give rise to meanings that become incarnate when all carriers of meaning are combined into a world of meaning and are lived out through intentional responses.[16]

Margaret Mary Kelleher takes the notion of symbol and incarnate meaning and applies it to liturgy as an act of meaning. She calls liturgy "an act of ecclesial performative meaning in which the church symbolically mediates itself."[17] Kelleher identifies the subject of liturgy as "any legitimate local assembly."[18] At the heart of this notion is human subjectivity; a human person is "one who comes to be in and through acts of meaning."[19] The assembly, made up of individual subjects, becomes a collective subject, "a community, a group of persons who have achieved a certain degree of common meaning."[20]

Through its use of symbols originating in the community's shared experience and common knowledge, meaning is created and communicated. It is evident that, since symbols carry a community's meanings, they will vary from community to community because the composition, history, and culture of the assembly set the initial context for any celebration. The term of meaning, that is, what is "meant" in liturgical praxis, is the mediation of the church itself. As *church*, the assembly "discloses a horizon, a corporate vision of what it means to live as a Christian."[21]

The Good Friday events disclose that the Mozarab liturgy makes evident the sense of being a particular community accompanied by the presence of Christ as it interacts with the larger church and culture that surrounds it. A scriptural underpinning for this notion is Matthew 18:20. The Lord says to the disciples that where two or three are gathered in his name, he is there among them. Because the Mozarab community gathers on Good Friday at two liturgies and for the evening processions in Christ's name, it chooses to respond to the Spirit that convokes it to give witness to Christ's centrality in the lives of the members as a community.

The community also brings its faith to bear on worship by actively participating in the liturgies and the processions. The Lignum Crucis serves to help focus this worship and to bind the members together as the body of Christ. As several of my informants stated, the Lignum Crucis makes them aware of the presence of Christ among them, as if it were the Blessed Sacrament. Don José Miranda Calvo further explains that the reliquary "is a symbol of our Catholic faith; there is nothing better since it is a little piece of the Lignum Crucis; nothing else can represent the sacrifice of our Redeemer."[22] In terms of the procession with the Lignum Crucis, Don Miguel Pantoja declares they display it publicly because "it is a sign of faith which we manifest in the streets."[23]

The faith being demonstrated is not only individual but communal and helps the community integrate and manifest what it means to be a Mozarab Catholic Christian. The Mozarabic rite arises from the cultural milieu of Spain and for Mozarabs is a way to mediate symbolically a "Mozarabic church" marked by the integration of faith and culture in a culturally congenial manner. By means of the rite, the community constructs its identity and constitutes itself. The symbols it uses, including the Lignum Crucis, help individual members appropriate Mozarab identity through the ritual use of the reliquary both in the Good Friday liturgies and the evening processions. The number of Mozarabs participating in the evening procession is larger than those participating in the two Good Friday liturgies. Part of the reason is that members come to Toledo from Madrid and elsewhere later in the day for the express purpose of participating in the processions. The shared history, experience, and values these encompass help shape them into a distinctive church and community. They gather as individuals into the community for communal participation in the official worship of the church as well as in the processions. Both activities are obviously valued by the community, and participation in them facilitates what Turner calls *communitas*. The penitential character of the evening processions, a practice linked to popular religion, particularly contributes to this sense.

WHAT IS POPULAR RELIGION'S ROLE IN MOZARAB IDENTITY AND SPIRITUALITY?

A tremendous amount of sociological, ethnographic, and theological research has taken place on the topic of popular religion both as a Christian and non-Christian phenomenon. A cursory review of resources indicates that there are studies available for different historical eras as well. I limit my frame of reference to Catholic Hispanic popular religion as it is currently addressed by Catholic theologians as well as other scholars of religion who provide useful insights into the phenomenon.

Many terms strive to describe the religious practices of common people or those who are not the elites of a religion. Some of the terms used include *little tradition, folk religion, common religion, popular piety,* and variations thereof. All are attempts at describing a very complex reality: the experience of, or faith in, a transcendent reality and its incorporation into everyday life, especially by common people. It is noteworthy that the US bishops recognize that "popular devotions arise in the encounter between the Catholic faith and culture."[24] The Holy See's 2001 *Directory on Popular Piety and the Liturgy* recognizes that there is no uniform definition for this phenomenon and uses the term "popular piety." The nomenclature used points to the dominant notion of religion comprising two opposite poles: the religion of elites, such as clergy, theologians, and religious professionals; and, the religion of the people.

Peter Williams argues that popular religion comes from and belongs to the *people* rather than to "the 'elite' specialists specifically trained in religious functions."[25] Charles Lippy also addresses religion from this perspective. He views the religious elite as "concerned with matters of right belief and practice, offering rational arguments to support them, providing guidance in their appropriation by the people at large, and transmitting them as part of a formal religious tradition to subsequent generations."[26] Williams and Lippy reflect a common sociological perspective that sees popular religion as something distinct from official, institutional, or formal religion. At the same time, they reveal a functionalist approach to their study. This approach is greatly influenced by the theories of Emile Durkheim (1859–1917), who saw religion as the recapitulation of society itself and God as a metaphor for society. That is, religion, whatever form it takes, is a way for a culture to facilitate social integration, convey meaning, and provide identity to its constituents.

On the other hand, in terms of the dichotomous relationship between popular and official religion, Williams and Lippy seem to be unaware that many religious elites may themselves also practice some form of popular religion. Perhaps this is due to their emphasis on official Protestant Christianity, which seems to deny its practice within its ranks. In my experience, though, religious professionals, whether Protestant or Catholic, also apply religious tenets to everyday life in some form, whether as informal personal devotions or religious activities not necessarily recognized as worship but seen as necessary for a full integration of religion into life and vice versa. In other words, popular religion may also occur under the aegis of official religion. Moreover, the theorists seem to downplay the interconnectedness and symbiotic relationship that marks popular and official religion. Instead, I see that popular religion gets many of its themes and notions from official religion, and the latter gets many of its notions and insights into God's action in the world through the lived experience of people applying their faith, even when this involves incorporating meanings and practices outside of the belief and liturgical system of official religion.

Ann Taves indicates that, in the Catholic context, the Catholic hierarchy in the nineteenth century across the board made a concerted effort to promote and guide some popular practices while permitting others to develop on their own. She claims this was done in order to promote those practices that could more easily bind the laity to the institutional church.[27] Through the late 1960s, novenas, rosaries, Forty Hours, processions, and other forms of popular religion were still practiced by clergy and laity on a regular basis. Some were built into the liturgical calendar, while others were more spontaneous and informal. In some areas of the Catholic world these practices are still encouraged by church officials, particularly in Spain and Latin America. In fact, the *Directory on Popular Piety and the Liturgy* is a modern-day effort to promote and recover pious practices after a waning of these since Vatican II. The *Directory* declares that history shows that in certain eras the life of faith has been sustained by pious exercises and devotional practices, that is, by popular religious practices, "which the faithful have often felt more deeply and actively than the liturgical celebrations" (no. 11). It goes on to say that the liturgical renewal willed by Vatican II also must "inspire a correct evaluation and renewal of pious exercises and devotional practices" (no. 12). Finally, it names four aspects that should permeate popular piety: a biblical spirit (direct or indirect reference to scripture), a liturgical spirit (it should dispose one toward or echo liturgical celebrations), an ecumenical spirit (it should consider sensibilities and traditions of other Christians), and an anthropological spirit that "both conserves symbols and expressions of importance or significance for a given nation" (no. 12).

Indeed, after Vatican Council II, the Catholic church of Latin America actively sought to understand and promote popular religion as a form of evangelization.[28] Luis Maldonado, in his assessment of the Latin American Episcopal Conference's teachings emerging from its gathering in Medellín, Colombia, in 1968, notes that the Latin American bishops actively sought to open the way for popular religion as a form of pastoral practice for and by the masses.[29] Much of the theoretical basis for the promotion of Latin American popular religion has greatly influenced Hispanic Ministry efforts in the United States.[30] It seems that Latin American efforts may have also encouraged a recovery of religious practices in Spain.[31]

Hispanic scholars of popular religion tend to see popular and official religion in a symbiotic relationship, though they too are greatly influenced by the dominant sociological perspective. Virgilio Elizondo claims that since the beginning, Christianity was able to present a unique way of universalizing peoples without destroying their identities so they would not have to disappear either through assimilation or marginalization.[32] One way it was able to accomplish this was through the interweaving of the Christian message with the local religious traditions. Certainly this has been the case with the Hispano-Mozarabic rite. From Elizondo's perspective, the religious symbolism of a people, expressed through the ensemble of beliefs, rituals, ceremonies, devotions, and prayers, is a key factor in group identity. In other words, the meaning system created through popular religion is linked to a group's self-understanding. The use of the Lignum Crucis obviously participates in this realm.

Orlando Espín also examines popular and official religion.[33] He points to the intimate link between popular and official religion saying that "every major religion, to the degree that it has a well-defined normative core of beliefs and liturgy, has aided in the development of a popular version of itself."[34] Arturo Pérez examines Hispanic popular religion as a source for the inculturation of Catholic liturgy.[35] In his study he notes that the forms of popular religion among Hispanics vary, but they demonstrate a basic characteristic common to all. This entails a complex of underlying beliefs rooted in God expressed in a profound sense of the sacred and transcendent, openness to God's word, prayerfulness, an ability to endure, and detachment from the material world.[36] Pérez observes that among Hispanics in general, "liturgy is the expression of the spiritual life of the Church. . . . Popular religiosity is the ritual expression of the spiritual life of Hispanic people."[37] Consequently, popular religiosity seems to be pervasive at all levels of Hispanic society. Certainly Mozarabs share this characteristic with other Hispanics.

Taves, Elizondo, Espín, and Pérez suggest that popular religion is not necessarily in opposition to official, doctrinal, or formal religion but rather can be intimately linked to it. It is from this viewpoint that I see the Lignum Crucis as a pivotal symbol. It connects official and popular religion by serving as a point of reference for the liturgies of Good Friday as well as the devotional character of the evening processions. The link is further strengthened by the official sanction and participation of the church hierarchy in the evening processions and by the participation of those who carry the Lignum Crucis in procession in the official liturgies of Good Friday. Let us now examine this link in greater depth.

WHAT IS THE RELATIONSHIP
BETWEEN LITURGY AND POPULAR RELIGION?

The relationship between liturgy and popular religion is best seen in the concept of sacramentals. *Sacrosanctum Concilium* sees sacramentals as sacred signs instituted by the church to signify spiritual effects that dispose the faithful for the graces of the sacraments (*SC*, no. 60). Sacramentals include blessings, exorcisms, and blessed objects for use in liturgical events and popular devotion. The *Catechism of the Catholic Church (CCC)* places the use of sacramentals and popular piety in its discussion "Other Liturgical Celebrations."[38] In terms of popular religious practices it states, "The religious sense of the Christian people has always found expression in various forms of piety surrounding the church's sacramental life, such as the veneration of relics, visits to sanctuaries, pilgrimages, processions, the stations of the cross, religious dances, the rosary, medals, etc." (CCC, no. 1674). It goes on to say "these expressions of piety extend the liturgical life of the church, but do not replace it" (CCC, no. 1675). Indeed this perspective is repeated in the *Directory on Popular Piety and the Liturgy* (nos. 12, 13).

Taking the Lignum Crucis in procession extends the penitential character of the *Ad tertiam* and *Ad nonam* liturgies into the realm of popular religion. This occurs on Good Friday evening. In fact, on each of the three nights of the Triduum the *Hermandad* sponsors activities that extend the liturgy into the popular realm. One way popular religion extends the liturgy into the popular realm is by means of symbols. In this sense, foods can be symbolic,[39] as seen in certain practices that occur on the three nights of the Triduum. After the Holy Thursday liturgy, any ministers and parishioners who wish to do so traditionally share bits of Spanish pastries in the sacristy. These are sweets made of cake topped with whipped cream and/or fruit glazes. The pastries seem to represent the bread and wine of the Eucharist, which can be said to be the new "milk and honey" of the kingdom, the "land," established by Christ. On Good Friday the community abstains from the eucharistic food at its liturgies but later engages in a sort of "spiritual communion" with Christ symbolized by the Lignum Crucis as it carries the relic in procession. Another yearly tradition occurs after the Easter Vigil, when Don Enrique and the members of the *cabildo* (governing council) of the *Hermandad*, along with members of their families and invited guests, go to a local restaurant for a roasted lamb dinner. This seems to indicate that the banquet of the Paschal Lamb, Christ, begun at the Great Passover of his passion, death, and resurrection, must find its expression in the earthly life of his disciples. In both cases the foods themselves acquire a "catechetical" sense in that they link the liturgy to the everyday lives of the minister, parishioners, and members of the *Hermandad* who partake of them. I believe the link must be made in order for people to find their lives celebrated in the liturgy and the liturgy celebrated in their lives.[40] Popular religion is one way this is done; these Mozarab customs are indicators of that.

THE LIGNUM CRUCIS AS A PIVOTAL SYMBOL

Clearly the Lignum Crucis reliquary is a pivotal symbol. It is used both in the two services marking the Good Friday liturgy in the contemporary Hispano-Mozarabic rite and in the evening processions emerging from popular religion. One of the reasons for its symbolic significance is its shape. The cross is venerated by Christians as the sign of their faith. Another reason is because of the relic of the true cross it contains. This connects the reliquary directly to the object of faith, Jesus Christ. However, I also believe the reliquary is pivotal because it is a symbol of the Mozarabs themselves.

In the Mozarabic liturgical system, the Lignum Crucis is at the center of the two Good Friday liturgies. In the form of the cross, it is the focus for the community as it recognizes its sinfulness and need for God's mercy and pardon *(indulgentia)*. The Lignum Crucis is a sacramental, a liturgical implement blessed for use at liturgy. Since it contains a relic of the true cross, it enjoys the status of other symbols directly related to Christ, such as the consecrated bread and wine, the body and blood of the Lord. The reliquary also helps the community experience Christ's presence in its midst.

At the same time the Lignum Crucis is an object of popular devotion. People kneel before it in prayer outside of its liturgical use, and the *Hermandad* carries it in procession. The reliquary becomes an implement of popular religion when it is taken out in the "non-liturgical" activity of the Good Friday processions. Nonetheless, because it is taken out as if it were the Blessed Sacrament—under *palio,* accompanied by a priest, and surrounded by other liturgical symbols such as incense and candles—the Lignum Crucis extends the liturgy into the popular religious realm. In this way it blurs the line between liturgy and popular religion. Indeed, it reveals the nexus between the two. As a result, the Lignum Crucis is a pivotal symbol for the construction of the relationship between liturgy and popular religion. It is also pivotal in the integration of faith into life and life into faith. Mozarabs are renewed in their faith in Christ through its ritual use in the liturgy, and they proclaim that faith publicly through the processions. The experience of faith in Christ in their everyday lives draws them to the liturgy, especially to venerate the Lignum Crucis on Good Friday.

The ritual use of the Lignum Crucis helps Mozarabs enter into an experience of Christ present in their midst. The use of the Lignum Crucis also helps them reveal, exalt, and reaffirm values that bind them together as a community. The Lignum Crucis helps them remember they are the people who kept their Catholic faith, followers of Christ who have been willing to proclaim that faith even in dire circumstances. The antiquity of the implements and setting as well as the recovery of the *Ad tertiam* liturgy and updating of the *Ad nonam* liturgy ground Mozarabs in their history. In addition, they present themselves as distinct from their Spanish compatriots while still part of the greater Catholic church. As a pivotal symbol between Mozarab faith and life, the Lignum Crucis symbolizes the crucifixion of both Christ and Mozarabs themselves as they struggle to integrate themselves into their society and constitute their culture. It also provides them hope and strength as they assert themselves and negotiate for control of their symbols and for influence on the celebration of their liturgy.

THEOLOGICAL MEANINGS

There are two central theological meanings that emerge from the ritual use of the Lignum Crucis by Mozarabs regarding Christ and his salvation. I suggest those who composed the euchological texts for the rite stressed the cross, martyrdom, and sacrifice because of these central theological meanings. The veneration afforded today by Mozarabs to the relic of the true cross they possess and their use of a particular design of the cross as an emblem of their community have led me to identify five additional theological meanings related to Christ and his salvation. These meanings emerge from the Triduum events and say something about Mozarabs and their cross. I present all seven meanings in this section. They are related to Mozarab history, culture, and liturgy.

Christ's Death Saves

The Christology emerging from the texts and the Good Friday events focuses on a Christ who saves us by means of his suffering death on the cross. This Christ is both God and Man, the *unigenitus*, the unique Son of God, yet the *primogenitus*, the son of Mary,[41] who by sharing in our humanity in every way but sin is able to give us a share in his divinity by being the source of salvation for all. Becoming one of us has meant sharing in the totality of human life, best seen in the experience of suffering, particularly death. He offers his death as a sacrifice on behalf of all human beings so that they can have a share in his victory over sin and the enemies of humans: Satan and all sorts of evils. Because Christ has embraced death, he has been exalted and is the unique mediator between God and humankind. As such he is able to convey God's mercy *(indulgentia)* and present our needs to the Father.

The Holy Thursday Mass explicitly links the Eucharist to the cross. For example the *Illatio*, the first variable prayer of the Anaphora, declares that "the Cross of Christ saves, his Blood purifies, his Body nourishes."[42] Throughout the liturgical year the Hispano-Mozarabic rite alludes to Jesus' saving death. Thus at Christmas the *Illatio* proclaims that Christ has given his soul for the church to possess,[43] the *Post Nomina* for the Fifth Sunday of Easter invites those present to truly glory in Christ's cross,[44] and the *Post Gloriam* for the feast of the Finding of the Holy Cross declares that by the mystery of the cross, every knee will bend at Jesus' name.[45]

When asked the difference between the Roman and Mozarabic view of Christ in the liturgy, my answer relates to the way each portrays Christ's unique role as the mediator of salvation to the world. While in the Roman liturgy prayers are usually offered to the Father *through the Son* in the Holy Spirit, in the Mozarabic liturgy prayers are often directed *to* Christ or to the Son and the Father *together*. I suggest this is due to the fact that, in an anti-Arian emphasis, they want to stress Christ is the God-man who encompasses both humanity and divinity as the only begotten Son, one in being with the Father. He is the only one who can relate us to God, who is totally other, by sharing in our humanity. Furthermore, by his sacrifice on the cross, he conveys God's reconciliation to those who take up their cross and follow him. This requires believers to imitate Christ. By being at the center of the liturgy, the fount and summit of the church's life, to use Vatican II language, believers are integrated into his life and empowered to follow him more closely.

Salvation Is Found in Obedience like Christ's

The soteriology emerging from the Good Friday texts and events reveals that salvation is found in being obedient like Christ, even unto death, and death on a cross. One takes up one's cross by means of self-sacrifice. In Spanish, we say we must sacrifice ourselves in order to attain some good *(hay que sacrificarse)*. This means practicing humility and stripping oneself of one's self-centeredness *(hay que despojarse)*. This means on occasion one must give public witness to one's faith *(hay que practicar su fe)*. In this way we experience Christ's salvation as he accompanies us in our own suffering and as we allow him to transform that suffering into a source of new life by means of faith. The signs of Christ's continuing presence and salvation are found both in and outside the liturgy. For the Mozarab community of Toledo, Christ's presence in the liturgy is especially symbolized by martyrs, who have been obedient even unto death, like Christ, but also by the Lignum Crucis, as we will discuss shortly. One witnesses to one's faith publicly by venerating the relic of the true cross and by participating in the Good Friday processions. The following five theological implications flow from the Christology and soteriology presented by the rituals and texts of the Hispano-Mozarabic Triduum, particularly on Good Friday.

The Cross Is Central to Understanding Christ's Saving Action

The death of Jesus had been a traumatic event in the life of the primitive church, and certainly its memory was still somewhat "fresh" in the mind set of the Christians of the first centuries. Evidence for this are the New Testament scriptures themselves, especially the fact that there are four versions of the passion and that in all four Gospels the authors describe the last days of Jesus in greater detail than all the other events of his life. In addition, Paul's stress on the cross points to the centrality of Christ's death for the spreading of the Gospel. Clearly, the cross in relation to the resurrection is most important, not the cross alone. The Book of Revelation indicates that the death on the cross and the new life that flows from it are relived in the liturgy to a large extent. For this reason the most dramatic pages of the New Testament are those that recount the passion as well as the experience of Christ's resurrection. This indicates that a key to understanding Christianity is not so much the Great Commandment, as important as that is, but the experience of the cross, which gives meaning to that commandment as a sign of the resurrection.

In terms of the Mozarab community and the Mozarabic liturgy, the passion is celebrated in not one but two services on Good Friday. The significance of Christ's death on the cross is seen in that the four versions of the passion are combined into one long reading, divided between the Holy Thursday evening Mass and the *Ad nonam* liturgy of Good Friday afternoon. This is then integrated into the spirituality of the community by taking the Lignum Crucis out in procession during the Good Friday evening event, an event that invites Mozarabs to proclaim their faith publicly and the onlookers to recognize the simple cross as the meaning behind the elaborate *pasos* with all their magnificence that go before and after the Lignum Crucis. Those who embrace the cross are promised a share in the resurrection by Jesus himself; faith in this promise seems to motivate Mozarabs as they participate in all the events of the Triduum.

The Cross Is a Sign of Victory

The composers of the prayers and developers of the Old Spanish rite from the fifth century on had experienced persecution under the Arian Visigothic regime. They kept the memory of persecution alive as evidenced by the *acta* of the Hispano-Roman and Visigothic councils. The experience of persecution was vivid in their minds, and they remembered it by means of their legislation and euchological texts. Yet due to their tenaciousness and commitment to their faith, the Catholic Hispano-Romans experienced victory over the "death" of persecution and oppression, particularly at the conversion of their Visigothic overlords. This experience in all its aspects was to be lived out by Mozarabs once again under Islam and at their validation by King Alfonso VI. Though his agents who had embraced the Roman rite attempted to suppress their liturgy, Mozarabs asserted their faithfulness to Christianity and their links to the earliest Christians and were victorious. It was a victory symbolized by the cross, for out of suffering and death came new life and renewed status. Perhaps that is why early on the community began to use the Visigothic cross, with its Alpha and Omega hanging from the arms of the crossbeam, as a central symbol and emblem: it represented both the acceptance of the Catholic doctrine by the Arian Visigoths as well as the firm establishment of the church that had embraced the cross of Christ in its struggles to adhere to its faith despite the obstacles put in its way by Islam and even Roman rite Christianity. Thus, they potentially saw parallels in their experience to Christ's salvific death and victory.

The Lignum Crucis reliquary is used only on Good Friday, although references to "the wood of the cross" are made throughout the Lenten liturgies as well as the other liturgical celebrations of the Triduum. For example, the third paragraph of the *Illatio* for *Feria IV* of *II Hebdomada Quadragesimæ* reads:

> Through him then may the inadequate offering of our fast be pleasing to you who has reconciled us to you by the offering of the sacrifice of his body, so that by the wood of his cross we may be carried in the stormy passage of this world, and, having conquered sin and full of virtues, we may come to him.[46]

Similarly, the *Illatio* for the Easter Vigil, while praising the salvation wrought by Jesus, makes reference to his "sacrifice on the wood," saying, " . . . and having lifted up his hands on the cross both the evening sacrifice hung on the wood and the morning benefit rising up, he brought himself forth from the tomb."[47] References to the wood of the cross are also made at other times of the year, including the feast of the Holy Cross[48] and the Easter season,[49] among others.

Emphasizing the Cross Leads to the Transformation of Suffering

The Mozarabic euchological texts in general, instead of giving in to the hubris of success over enemies by extolling the glory of the resurrection, extol the victory of the cross and martyrdom. They are a reminder that all victory comes from God. I propose that the composers of these texts did not want us to forget that all are in need of God's grace. It was their way to recall that in embracing suffering and linking it to the discipline of the cross and even martyrdom, they were able to overcome the vicissitudes they had suffered. Otherwise, emphasizing the glory of the resurrection might lead them to pride, complacency, and overconfidence in the good times. Good times for Mozarabs over the centuries have not lasted, and even during them they have had their own share of suffering to face. The cross surely must have given hope to Mozarabs as they held tenaciously to faith and liturgy. This attitude and commitment are seen in the selection of readings for the entire Triduum. They can also be seen in the Mozarab devotion to Our Lady of Hope. She is a symbol of clinging to hope in the midst of uncertainty and suffering.[50]

The Martyr Functions as an *Alter Christus*

The vast majority of saints' days celebrated over the course of the Mozarabic liturgical year commemorate martyrs. This points to a particular theological anthropology in which martyrs are seen as signs of Christ's continued presence and salvation in the midst of the faithful, showing them the way to a faith that embraced the will of the Father, even to obedience unto death. Obedience unto death does not represent a morbid exaltation of death but rather a wisdom that recognizes intuitively that the denial of death, or attempts to escape suffering through whatever means, only worsens suffering. Instead, one has to embrace suffering, to face it in order to confront it, work with it, and move through it in order for one to improve life. Without faith this is extremely difficult. This is expressed theologically in terms of "wrestling with the devil," "gaining the crown of martyrdom," and "acquiring the palm of victory" found in the martyrologies and the iconography of the martyrs. Furthermore, the Hispano-Mozarabic liturgical texts give clear evidence that martyrs were *alteri Christi* for the composers of the texts. Juan Miguel Ferrer Grenesche remarks that Masses composed for the saints provide "a narrative of the life or the martyrdom of a saint, emphasizing the most marvelous facts which manifest the Kingdom brought about by Jesus Christ and his victory over the world."[51] Even the Anaphora tends to indicate that Christ is present in the saint, for "the saint receives the gift of God in Christ and with his or her life converts it into praise of God's glory."[52]

A case in point is the virgin martyr. The *Illatio* for the feast of Santa Eulalia of Mérida on 10 December contrasts her with Mary, the Mother of Jesus denoting that Eulalia exemplifies Christ's victory over evil through her martyrdom, which resulted from her refusal to give up her virginity.[53] The other Santa Eulalia, of Barcelona, is further linked to Christ as an image of his continued victory over evil through her martyrdom by burning spread-eagled on a cross. Notably, her iconography explicitly links her to Christ as a sign of his victory: she is shown crucified. This image appears in the parish church of Santa Eulalia in Toledo. The *oratio Post Gloriam* for her feast day on 12 February indicates that through her martyrdom, she shares in Christ's intercessory power.[54]

The stress on martyrdom and embracing the suffering it implies can also be seen in the sayings *no hay mal que por bien no venga* and *no hay gloria sin la cruz*. Not only did the Old Christians experience this in Roman, Visigothic, and Islamic times, but also in neo-Christian times under those who embraced the Roman rite. The descendants of these Old Christians experienced it during the *desamortización*, when church properties and institutions were confiscated by the state; this also led to the loss of status for Mozarabs as they lost their ancient privileges conceded by King Alfonso VI and his successors. Most recently, during the Spanish Civil War, all the Mozarabic rite chaplains and many other Mozarabs died in defense of their faith. Today Mozarabs defend their rite and their culture in the face of people who think they are descendants of the Moors or who are not even aware of their existence.

It is interesting that the Lignum Crucis has no corpus on it. I suggest this is because the body that goes on the empty cross is that of the one who embraces Christ's salvation through the cross as a faithful witness, even unto death. For Mozarabs under Islam during peaceful times, martyrdom meant remaining faithful to Christianity when opportunities for betterment were afforded to those who denied their faith. Under Roman Christianity it has meant asserting their privileges when the celebration of their rite has been seen as a historical curiosity. As a consequence, the martyr is an appropriate role model for those who put their trust in God's grace to overcome evil, even the seeming finality of death, whatever its source.

The Liturgical Use of the Lignum Crucis
Links the People to Christ

Liturgy is both a faith expression and a cultural activity. Thus, the liturgical use of the Lignum Crucis serves as a reminder of the continued presence of Christ in the midst of the Mozarab community as it struggles to recover and assert its identity as the people who embraced Christ in the earliest times of the arrival of the faith in Spain. They celebrate this faith in a liturgy that communicates to them the meaning of their faith.

They have retained both this faith and this liturgy despite many vicissitudes. It is no wonder that the cross in the form of the reliquary of the true cross and their emblems are core symbols for them. Clearly, the Lignum Crucis can be seen as a symbol of holding to the liturgy that sustained them over the centuries, even when it was only celebrated occasionally. The importance of the liturgy for them is now reinforced by the updating of the rite and the restoration of the two Good Friday liturgies. The connection between the liturgy and their identity is seen in their efforts to integrate the faith expressed in that liturgy into their everyday lives as evidenced by the formation of the *Hermandad*, the Good Friday procession with the Lignum Crucis, the regular wearing of the distinctive cross pin on the lapel, and so forth. They are not being called upon to give their blood as martyrs, but they do have a renewed consciousness of the real presence of Christ in their midst. It is a consciousness that has invested the Lignum Crucis with a sacrality only equaled by the Blessed Sacrament. Thus, the liturgy, by encompassing a liturgical implement that represents both the presence of Christ and the identity of the people celebrating the liturgy, shows that the liturgy is an expression of faith as well as a cultural event. In terms of the former, faith in Christ as the Savior of the world is celebrated and strengthened; in terms of the latter, the identity of a particular people as followers of Christ whose history has been marked by the cross is lifted up and affirmed. Both faith and cultural identity are thereby offered for appropriation by those who participate in the Hispano-Mozarabic liturgy.

PARALLELS BETWEEN MOZARABIC
AND HISPANIC SPIRITUALITY

Because Mozarabs and their rite reflect the liturgy and spirituality of the earliest Hispanics, they and their liturgy are an apt source for examining the roots of much contemporary Hispanic spirituality throughout the world, especially as expressed in popular religion. Many of the practices of popular devotion to Christ, Mary, and the saints as well as devotional practices found throughout Latin America, among Latinos/as in the United States, and even among Filipinos, can find their origins in the rituals, liturgy, and devotions emerging in the Mozarabic rite. Here are some of the more salient examples.

The Mozarab view of Christ as the God-man who is exalted above all others because of his sacrifice on the cross parallels the approach toward Christ found in Hispanic devotional practices throughout the world. The images of Jesus favored by Hispanics tend to be Jesus in his infancy, as the *Santo Niño* (Holy Child), or at the end of his life, as the *Nazareno* (the Nazarene).[55] These represent the vulnerable, dependent Jesus who not only reflects human weakness and vulnerability but also requires human solidarity in suffering. This reveals to Hispanics that Jesus accompanies them in their lives and inspires them to accompany him in his suffering and death, his resurrection and exaltation.

For Hispanics, the cross and resurrection are intimately interrelated. Roberto Goizueta notes that in the *Via Crucis* processions of Good Friday, for example, Hispanics engage in a praxis that, as an act of "accompaniment," constitutes and empowers them as persons and as a community of faith: "It is precisely the intrinsically *communal* character of our *confrontation* with and *struggle against* death that already embodies the victory of life—of love—over death."[56] The Good Friday events thus provide a way for Hispanics in general and Mozarabs in particular to stress the passion as an active, communal undertaking over against suffering passively endured by a solitary individual: "Suffering shared is suffering already in retreat."[57] The source of hope is not the resurrection of a solitary individual but "the ultimate indestructibility of the community that accompanies Jesus on the *Via Crucis* and is reconciled with him in the Resurrection."[58]

It appears that the stress on Christ's exaltation entered the Old Spanish liturgy because of the need to emphasize this in light of the Arian perspective at the time of the rite's greatest unfolding. This liturgical emphasis eventually influenced the spirituality of the faithful to the extent that by the time the Roman rite became predominant among the Spanish, the exaltation of Christ had led to an overemphasis on his divinity. As a result, the need for mediators who could approach the "throne of mercy" developed among Hispanics in general. In my opinion, that is why today Hispanics tend to approach Mary and the saints for help in asking Christ for his grace rather than approaching Christ directly.

A particularly telling devotion is that of *Nuestro Padre Jesús del Gran Poder* (Our Father Jesus of Great Power). Jesus is called Father based on an interpretation of scriptural passages that either are taken as prefigurations of Jesus or are applied to him. For example, Luis de León (1527–91) interprets Isaiah 9:6 to indicate that one of the names of Jesus is "father"; the verse says of the child "born for us," "we shall call him the everlasting father."[59] He goes on to say that God "has made another man, who is the Christ man, in order to engender us a second time. . . . He truly is understood to be our new Father and we also understand the manner by which He engenders us."[60] Consequently, Christ is understood to be the new Adam, who engenders the new creation.

The notion of "great power" comes from Revelation 11:17. This verse is commonly prayed at Thursday evening prayer as part of the psalmody. There are confraternities and parish churches dedicated to *Nuestro Padre Jesús del Gran Poder* in Spain and the Americas. I visited one such church in Ronda (Málaga) in southern Spain in 1996; I am also aware of a confraternity with this name in Sevilla.[61] Christ has great power, symbolized by three rays emanating from his head, which is crowned with thorns. The rays are called *potencias* (powers). They originated from the Greek cross commonly placed within the halo surrounding Christ's head in Byzantine and medieval iconography as a way to designate his divinity. St. Ignatius of Loyola assigned to them the "three faculties of the soul," namely, memory, understanding, and will.[62] Christ's power is linked to his suffering, by which he has been exalted at God's right hand (Rv 22:3–4; Col 3:1; Heb 12:2). This view is paralleled in the Hispano-Mozarabic liturgy in that the prayers of the Mass can be equally offered to Christ and to the Father, placing Christ in an exalted realm. The priest in this case becomes the mediator between the people and Christ.

There are other parallels. The Mozarab sense that one must embrace the cross, even to the extent of being an *alter Christus* as a martyr, has its parallel, among other ways, in the Good Friday processions found among Hispanics all over the world where individuals perform penitential acts of self-sacrifice. *Mandas* and *promesas* (penitential vows and promises) made to God, Mary, and the saints by individuals are another way. The carrying of the cross in everyday life is expressed by such concepts as *hay que sacrificarse por sus hijos* (one must sacrifice oneself for one's children) or *no hay mal que por bien no venga* (there is no evil that does not come for some good). These are common ways of speaking among Hispanics as they face difficulties and attempt to make sense of them in light of their faith in Christ and his sacrifice on the cross.

The Mozarab sense that the celebration of the liturgy is not to be confined to the church building but must be taken out in the streets parallels the general Hispanic desire to manifest faith publicly. This is seen, for example, in the appearance of great numbers of Hispanics at Ash Wednesday services seeking the imposition of ashes on their foreheads in the shape of a cross to be worn publicly. It also is seen in the Hispanic attitude toward processions and other devotional practices; they are seen as being as important as official liturgical celebrations, if not more so and thus attract much participation. In a sense Hispanic processions and some devotional practices are extensions of the liturgy because they often engage groups of members of the church who gather in the name of Christ to worship God, albeit unofficially.

Mozarabs bring elements of everyday life into the liturgy and transport liturgical elements into everyday life, as seen in the Flower Offering at the *Ad tertiam* liturgy and in the Good Friday procession of the Lignum Crucis under *palio*, described earlier. These find a parallel in Hispanic practices of celebrating important life events in church. Such is the case with the presentation of the three year old, the *Quince Años* celebration for the fifteen-year-old young woman, and the use of the *arras* and *lazo* (coins and yoke) at Hispanic weddings. In fact, all three have clear parallels in liturgical celebrations found in the ancient Hispano-Mozarabic sources.[63] Church elements are likewise transported into everyday life as seen in the creation of altars in homes and at grave sites, the use of holy water at home for various purposes, and the imparting of blessings by parents on their children, for instance, when the children take their leave from their parents.

The Mozarab history and sense of identity have parallels with the experiences of other Hispanics, especially in the United States. These experiences tend to be common to any subaltern culture. The Catholic Hispano-Romans experienced being a minority, even if they outnumbered the Visigoth overlords of yesteryear. They experienced being second-class citizens, of having less access to power and resources, and needing to assert their identity in dress, speech, customs, and even in their prayers. This experience was relived under the Islamic overlords, and then again when their coreligionists deserted their ancient liturgy for a foreign liturgy brought by new French and Roman overlords during the *reconquista*. This reminds me of the experience of Catholic Hispanics in Texas who were displaced and marginalized, even by the church, after the annexation of their homelands by the United States during the mid-1800s. They continued to cling to their culture and to stress their popular devotions at home in order to foster their dignity as a people with an identity and a history worthy of respect.[64] It reminds me also of the experience of those Hispanics today who continue to keep their Catholicism despite the embrace of Protestant and evangelical Christianity by many of their brothers and sisters as well as the rejection they often experience from dominant Euro-American Catholics. Often the experience of marginalization and the need to reassert one's faithfulness have been translated into popular devotional practices and into the liturgy as outlined above.

The turn to liturgy as the source of identity made by Mozarabs finds its parallel in the US context as well. People want to make themselves known and so they choose strategies, rituals, and artifacts to assert themselves. In the United States, liturgy is quickly becoming a source of identity. This is partly due to the fact that there are no large public displays of faith such as those that occur in Latin America and Spain during the most important liturgical seasons of Christmas and Lent/Holy Week, or during patronal feast days. These events sustain faith. In the United States the void is somewhat filled by Guadalupe tattoos, wearing religious jewelry including rosaries as necklaces, and massive participation in the Ash Wednesday services. Those who wish to maintain their Catholic identity, however, must become actively involved in their parish, especially in the liturgy as lectors, communion ministers, and other liturgical roles. As a result, the parish becomes the locus for developing, manifesting, and sustaining one's Hispano-Catholic identity. Consequently, we see parishes with large Latino/a memberships beginning to sponsor Good Friday processions and engage in the incorporation into liturgy of other devotional practices emerging from Hispanic popular religion.

Hispanic popular religion and celebration of the liturgy throughout the world have commonalities with the Good Friday celebrations of the Hispano-Mozarabic Triduum as performed in Toledo as well as other elements of Mozarabic liturgy and spirituality. Processions, beginning from the local parish and going through the streets, comprised of *pasos* and images of Christ in the various aspects of his passion as well as Mary as the Sorrowful Mother, are commonplace. In the United States the carved images are being replaced by actors who role-play Christ's passion by carrying the cross or by taking roles such as Mary or the Roman soldiers who crucify Christ. For Hispanics in general, to accept the cross is to accept that suffering is part and parcel of life, whether the suffering is caused by someone or something else or by the effort to make a difference in the world. By accepting the fact that suffering is inevitable, one can identify the causes of suffering, strategize ways to convert it to good, and thus make life better for oneself and others.

In terms of Mozarabs and the cross, the saying *No hay gloria sin la cruz* (There is no glory without the cross) aptly describes their liturgy, spirituality, and identity. Over the course of history Mozarabs have experienced much suffering, marginalization, martyrdom, and exclusion. But they have retained their Catholic faith, and their liturgy has provided them with much solace and meaning. They have also experienced long periods of honor and status because of their faithfulness and embrace of the cross of Christ. The latest restoration and updating of their liturgy are testimony to that fact, for without a Mozarab community there cannot be a Hispano-Mozarabic rite. Like the simple, barren reliquary taken in procession on Good Friday, Mozarabs stand out as examples of what it means to accompany Jesus on the way toward the fullness of the kingdom.

Today, the use of the Visigothic cross in Mozarabic iconography, the use of the cross of Alfonso VI as the community's emblem, and the veneration of the Lignum Crucis serve as reminders of Mozarabs' faithfulness to Christ and to the community's history. The importance of the cross also serves to encourage the members of the community to unite their continuing struggles to Christ's own passion as they attempt to restore their liturgy fully. This can be seen in the fact that the updated liturgy still carries their name in the title—Hispano-*Mozarabic* rite. As I was told by members of the community and of the commission charged with the task of renewal, the fact that there still exists a people that has clung to the Old Spanish liturgy as central to its identity and has helped the liturgy survive centuries of marginalization reveals that the conservation and actualization of the liturgy made no sense without recognizing the link between liturgy and community. Consequently, the liturgy continues to carry the Mozarab name despite efforts by some experts to elevate the developments of the Visigothic era above those of the Islamic era in the history of the rite. That Mozarabs were able to remind the experts that this is *their* liturgy reveals that for them there is indeed victory in the cross.

Notes

INTRODUCTION

1. Juan Francisco Rivera Recio, "Formas de convivencia y heterodoxias en el primer siglo mozárabe," *Historia Mozárabe: Ponencias y Comunicaciones presentadas al Primer Congreso Internacional de Estudios Mozárabes, Toledo, 1975,* serie C, no. 1 (Toledo: Instituto de Estudios Visigótico-Mozárabes de San Eugenio, 1978), 6; Thomas E. Burman, *Religious Polemic and the Intellectual History of the Mozarabs, c. 1050–1200,* Brill's Studies in Intellectual History 52 (Leiden: E. J. Brill, 1994), 7–9.

2. Burman, 7–8.

3. I am indebted in this regard to Jorge J. E. Gracia, *Hispanic/Latino Identity: A Philosophical Perspective* (Malden, MA: Blackwell, 2000).

4. See *Misa Mozárabe del Corpus Christi,* trans. and ed. Jaime Colomina Torner (Toledo: self-published worship booklet, 1974), 6.

5. Among others, Don José Miranda Calvo, Hermano Mayor, and Don Francisco de Sales Córdoba Bravo, chancellor, *Hermandad Mozárabe,* interview by author, Toledo, 23 March 2000.

6. Among others, Doña María Victoria Hernández de Pantoja, President, Brazo de Damas, and Don Miguel Pantoja, councillor, *Hermandad Mozárabe,* interview by author, Toledo, 21 March 2000.

7. I am especially indebted to the work of Catherine Bell, Victor Turner, and Ronald Grimes, among others whose works I cite in the text.

8. Catherine M. Bell, *Ritual Theory, Ritual Practice* (New York: Oxford University Press, 1992).

1. REDISCOVERING THE MOZARABS OF TOLEDO

1. My translation of "algunos en Toledo ni saben nada de nosotros ni que existimos. Algunos piensan que somos los moros. No somos los moros, somos los viejos cristianos." Doña Justa Margarita Córdoba Sánchez-Bretaño, interview by author, Toledo, 26 May 1999.

2. *Constituciones de la Ilustre y Antiquísima Hermandad de Caballeros Mozárabes de Nuestra Señora de la Esperanza, de la Imperial Ciudad de Toledo,*

Capítulo de Toledo (Toledo: Arzobispado de Toledo, parroquias Mozárabes de San Marcos y de Santas Justa y Rufina, 1966), 13. Revised 1984 and 1999. Hereafter *Constituciones* followed by date of publication.

3. See Burman, 13–14, 192–99. See also, José Miranda Calvo, "La continuidad cultural Nacional a través de la Mozarabía entre los siglos VIII al XI," *CM* 16 (1986): 2.

4. Burman, 23–30, 199–200.

5. Burman, 14. Some may use identifiable Mozarabic speech patterns, expressions, and grammatical forms, but I did not perceive this in their speech.

6. "Se siente orgullo porque indica ser descendiente de viejos cristianos; de ser herederos (y llevar) una tradición que es tan antigua (y que ha sido trasmitida por tantas generaciones)." My translation and combination of diverse statements made during the interview of Ildefonso (11), Juan (17), and Salvador (18), sons of Don Antonio Muñoz Perea and Doña Isabel Piñar Gutiérrez, three youngest of seven children; interview by author, Toledo, 26 May 1999.

7. See *Constituciones* (1999), 13. The note cites J. A. Dávila y García-Miranda, "La Nobleza e Hidalguía de las familias Mozárabes de Toledo," *Revista Hidalguía* 75 (March-April 1966), 257f.

8. These are two different ranks of nobility; the latter is a type of minor nobility while the other implies a higher status. The official organization of Mozarab families, *La Ilustre y Antiquísima Hermandad de Caballeros y Damas Mozárabes de Nuestra Señora de la Esperanza, de la Imperial Ciudad de Toledo*, is recognized as an "institution of nobility" in Francisco Manuel de las Heras y Borrero, *Apuntes Sobre Instituciones Nobiliarias en España*, Colección Persevante Heráldica Borgoña (Madrid: Prensa y Ediciones Iberoaméricas, 1994), 65–66.

9. Sixto Ramón Parro, *Toledo en la mano*, 2 vols., serie 4, Clásicos Toledanos 6 (Toledo: Instituto Provincial de Investigaciones y Estudios Toledanos, 1978), 1:256n1; José Antonio Dávila García-Miranda (Dávila), "Una nueva etapa en la comunidad mozárabe toledana," *CM* 30 (1991): 63.

10. *Conservadurismo* is a play on words combining the word for "conservative" and the adjectival ending indicating "hard"; a rough translation is "strong conservatism." See José Miranda Calvo, "Los Mozárabes: Su significado histórico (3)," *CM* 40 (1981): 6.

11. See Dávila, "Una nueva etapa," 64.

12. *Webster's New Universal Unabridged Dictionary* (rev. ed., 1989) defines *community* first as "a social group of any size whose members reside in a specific locality, share government, and have a common cultural and historical heritage." Second, "a social group sharing common characteristics or interests and perceived or perceiving itself as distinct in some respect from the larger society within which it exists (usually prec. by *the*)." Both definitions apply to the Mozarabs of Toledo, as we see in this chapter.

13. Don Mario also served from May 2000 to May 2003 as *Hermano Mayor* (Grand Brother or president) of the *Hermandad*.

14. See Edward P. Colbert, *The Martyrs of Córdoba (850–859): A Study of the Sources*, The Catholic University of America Studies in Mediaeval History, New Series 17 (Washington DC: CUA Press, 1962), 33.

15. See Balbino Gómez-Chacón, "Editorial," *CM* 4 (1981): 1. For the index of authors and their articles up through the last trimester of 1989, see Mario Arellano García, "Indice alfabético de autores," *CM* 26 (1989): 16–20.

16. *Constituciones* (1999), art. 14, 2–4.

17. Dávila, "Una nueva etapa," 64; Colomina Torner, interview by author, Toledo, 25 September 1999, and "Actualización del Rito Hispano-Mozárabe—Datos y fechas," a manuscript provided by interviewee describing the activities leading to the actualization of the rite.

18. For a report on the *tazmías* found, see "Sobre los Diezmos de las Parroquias Mozárabes de Toledo," *CM* 6 (1982): 3–4.

19. Dávila, "Una nueva etapa," 73.

20. I use *Hermandad Mozárabe* or simply *Hermandad*. Cf. *Constituciones* (1984) and *Constituciones* (1999), 16–17, and art. 1, 19.

21. My translation of "para continuar la piedad y tradiciones de los mozárabes." *Constituciones* (1999), 16.

22. *Constituciones* (1999), 16–17.

23. Dávila, "Una nueva etapa," 73.

24. The complete title is *Padrón de las Nobles Familias de Caballeros Mozárabes de Toledo según la parroquia de origen por "ius familiæ" de este rito de Santas Justa y Rufina y Santa Eulalia y San Marcos* (Toledo: Instituto de Estudios Visigótico-Mozárabes de San Eugenio, 1982).

25. The first appendix appeared in 1987, the second in 1991, and the third in 1995 as an extraordinary issue of the *Crónica Mozárabe*. See Mario Arellano García, "Introducción," Apéndice 3, *Padrón de las Nobles Familias de Caballeros Mozárabes de Toledo* (Toledo: CM, 1995), 1. A new edition of the *Padrón* is set to appear at the end of 2007; it will update the original and three appendices.

26. Cf. *Constituciones* (1986) arts. 9 and 10; *Constituciones* (1999), arts. 9 and 10; *Padrón* (1982), 10–11.

27. Don Mario Arellano García, interview by author, Toledo, 20 May 1999.

28. *Constituciones* (1984, 1999), 15.

29. See José Antonio Dávila, "La calidad Mozárabe en la Descendencia," *CM* 3 (1970): 3.

30. See *Constituciones* (1984, 1999), 15.

31. Arellano García, interview by author, Toledo, 25 September 1999.

32. See *Code of Canon Law* (1983), canons 111–12, 301, 312–20.

33. Cf. *Constituciones* (1984), art. 2 (19); *Constituciones* (1999), art. 6 (20).

34. *Constituciones* (1984), art. 16 (21).

35. See Alicia Arellano, "¿Quiénes somos?" *CM* 34 (1993): 10.

36. My translation of "No hay diferencia en cuanto a religiosidad ni a cultura; la diferencia es la liturgia y el hecho que las parroquias mozárabes son personales y no territoriales como las latinas" (Córdoba Sánchez-Bretaño, interview by author, Toledo, 20 May 1999).

37. My translation of "Ser mozárabe es ser descendiente de un pueblo que mantuvo su rito; el vínculo es el rito" (Don Felipe Jurado Puñal, Officer, *Hermandad Mozárabe, Brazo de Caballeros*, interview by author, Toledo, 2 June 1999).

38. José Miranda Calvo, "Los mozárabes: Su significado histórico (4)," *CM* 41 (1996): 14; my translation of "conscientes del tesoro histórico-litúrgico que encierra el simbolismo del mozarabismo."

39. Antonio Muñoz Perea, "Escrito de nuestro Hermano Mayor," *CM* 62 (2005): 9. My translation of "La defensa y pervivencia de la mozarabía, depende básicamente de nosotros, mientras haya fieles habrá culto y parroquias si un día se acaban los fieles será el fin del rito hispano mozárabe."

40. Muñoz Perea, 10. My translation of "llenando nuestros templos podremos pedir que se aprueben los sacramentales para practicar los Sacramentos en nuestro rito propio, al que tenemos derecho en especial los del bautismo, la confirmación, el matrimonio y la unción de los enfermos."

41. *Constituciones* (1984), art. 1 (19); my translation of "la conservación de las tradiciones de la comunidad histórico-litúrgica mozárabe."

42. It also celebrates using the new *ordo missæ*. Since Roman rite parishioners outnumber the Mozarab membership, the Eucharist in the Roman rite is the usual liturgical usage (Don Julio Gómez-Jacinto, Mozarabic rite pastor, Santas Justa y Rufina, interview by author, Toledo, 30 May 1999).

43. See, e.g., Cleofé Sánchez Montealegre, "El lenguaje es la liturgia mozárabe," *CM* 23 (1988): 1–3; Francisco de Sales Córdoba, "La cultura mozárabe y su difícil supervivencia," *CM* 24 (1989): 7–9.

44. Córdoba, "La cultura mozárabe," 9. My translation of "la expresión literaria más universal de la cultura mozárabe, la mejor dispensada a todas las clases sociales y fuente y origen de vida colectiva, centro viviente de la resistencia de las comunidades a todas las fuerzas centrífugas y diversas de asimilación."

45. Colbert, 402–3.

46. Cleofé Sánchez, "La Liturgia, razón de ser de la Mozarabía," *CM* 18 (1986): 1; my translation of "En la Mozarabía hay un hilo conductor que tiene su melodía en los altibajos propios de la vida y las dificultades inherentes a la cultura que atraviesa y este hilo es la Liturgia."

47. Don Juan-Miguel Ferrer Grenesche, a commissioner, says it is unlikely the rite of penance will be revived due to its public and communal nature. Also, the Spanish Episcopal Conference has not authorized the blessing of new Mozarabic churches or ordinations in the rite (Ferrer Grenesche, interview by author, Toledo, 26 June 1996).

48. See Cleofé Sánchez, "Celebración del Matrimonio en rito Mozárabe en Toledo," *CM* 29 (1990): 43–44.

2. THE ORIGINS OF THE MOZARAB COMMUNITY
AND ITS LITURGY

1. See S. Sobrequés Vidal, *Hispania: Síntesis de Historia de España*, 9th ed., rev. Joaquim Nadal Carreras (Barcelona: Editorial Vicens-Vives, 1979), 8–11, 13; Jaime Vicens Vives, *Approaches to the History of Spain*, 2nd ed., trans. and ed. Joan Connelly Ullman (Berkeley and Los Angeles: University of California Press, 1970), 1–2, 5–6, 8.

2. Roger Collins, *Early Medieval Spain: Unity in Diversity, 400–1000* (New York: St. Martin's Press, 1983), 7; José Terrero, *Geografía de España* (Barcelona: Editorial Ramón Sopena, 1956), 13, 278–79.

3. Cf. Collins, *Early Medieval Spain*, 7; S. J. Keay, *Roman Spain*, Exploring the Roman World 2 (Berkeley and Los Angeles: University of California Press/British Museum, 1988), 21; Joyce E. Salisbury, *Iberian Popular Religion 600 B.C. to 700 A.D.: Celts, Romans and Visigoths*, Texts and Studies in Religion 20 (Lewiston, NY: Edwin Mellen Press, 1985), 12.

4. Keay, 12, 18; also J. A. Thompson, "Tarshish,"in *Illustrated Bible Dictionary*, rev. ed., ed. N. Hillyer (Wheaton, IL: Tyndale House, 1980), 3:1517–8.

5. Collins, *Early Medieval Spain*, 8; Keay, 12; Sobrequés Vidal, 19–20; Vicens Vives, 11.

6. Keay, 18.

7. Keay, 22–23.

8. Keay, 25; Sobrequés Vidal, chap. 6 passim; Vicens Vives, 14–16.

9. See Susan Skomal, "World History: Great Empires Unite the Civilized World: 400 B.C.-A.D. 400," in *World Almanac and Book of Facts 2000* (New York: World Almanac Books, 1999), 578.

10. See Keay, 44–47.

11. At various times afterward, these initial provinces were further reconfigured. The last Roman administrative division of the peninsula occurred under Emperor Diocletian (AD 284–305) in AD 298. See Keay chap. 3 passim, and 179.

12. Cited by Keay, 63: Pliny, *Nat. Hist.* 37, 203.

13. Keay, 84, 85, 86: Lucius Annæus Seneca the Elder was one of the more famous Roman rhetors. His son, Lucius Annæus Seneca the Younger (4 BC–AD 65) became Nero's tutor and his principal advisor (AD 49, AD 54). Marcus Fabius Quintilianus, the most famous Roman writer on education, taught Pliny the Younger and the nephews of Emperor Domitian (AD 81–96).

14. See Keay, 84.

15. Keay, 199–200.

16. Manuel Sotomayor y Muro (Sotomayor), "La Iglesia y la España romana," BAC 1:12–14.

17. Keay, 169; Domingo Plácido Suárez, "El Bajo Imperio," *La España romana y visigoda (siglos III a.C.-VII d.C.)*, vol. 2, *Historia de España* (Barcelona: Editorial Planeta, 1988; 3rd ed. 1989), chap. 3 passim.

18. Sotomayor, "La Iglesia y la España romana," 12.

19. Cf. Sotomayor, "El concilio de Granada (Iliberri)," BAC 1:100; Elena Romero Castelló and Uriel Macías Kapón, *The Jews and Europe: 2,000 Years of History* (New York: A Henry Holt Reference Book, Henry Holt and Co., 1994), 16; Cecil Roth, *The Spanish Inquisition* (New York: W. W. Norton, 1964, reissued 1996), 18, 24; Hayim Halevy Donin, *To Pray as a Jew: A Guide to the Prayer Book and the Synagogue Service* (n.p.: Basic Books, 1980), 64.

20. See Rom 15:28; also, Collins, *Early Medieval Spain*, 5; Richard Fletcher, *Moorish Spain* (Berkeley and Los Angeles: University of California Press, 1992), 24.

21. Plácido Suárez, 381–82.

22. For the VII Gemina legion, see Keay, 169, and Manuel Sotomayor, "Sobre los orígenes del cristianismo en Hispania," BAC 1:134. For Marcellus and the VII Gemina's role in spreading Christianity to Iberia from North Africa, see Plácido Suárez, 382. For the liturgical feast of Marcellus, see Juan-Miguel Ferrer Grenesche, *Los Santos del Nuevo Misal Hispano-Mozárabe* (Toledo: Estudio Teológico de San Ildefonso, seminario conciliar, 1995), 115–16.

23. See Sotomayor, "Los testimonios históricos más antiguos del cristianismo hispano," BAC 1:39.

24. Plácido Suárez, 381–82.

25. Keay, 168–69.

26. Sotomayor, "La Iglesia y la España romana," 13–14.

27. *Adv. Iud*. VII 4–5, as cited by Sotomayor, "Los testimonios," 41.

28. Plácido Suárez, 383–84.

29. Keay, 169–70.

30. Collins, *Early Medieval Spain*, 5–6; Sotomayor, "El concilio de Granada (Iliberri)," 102.

31. Keay, 170; Jordi Pinell, O.S.B., *Liturgia hispánica*, ed. José Aldazábal, Biblioteca Litúrgica 9 (Barcelona: Centre de Pastoral Litúrgica, 1998), 58–59; Sotomayor, "Los testimonios," 49–58; Ferrer Grenesche, *Los Santos*, 47–48.

32. Keay, 182.

33. Diocletian ruled from 284 to 305. Sotomayor, "Los testimonios," 58–60.

34. Keay, 183; Sotomayor, "Los testimonios," 62–80.

35. Sotomayor, "La Iglesia hispana en el imperio romano del siglo IV," BAC 1:168; A. H. M. Jones, *Constantine and the Conversion of Europe*, Medieval Academy Reprints for Teaching 4 (Toronto: University of Toronto Press, 1978, repr. 1989), 80, 83.

36. Herwig Wolfram, *History of the Goths*, trans. Thomas J. Dunlap (Berkeley and Los Angeles: University of California Press, 1990), 7–9, 12–13, 19–24, 24–26. The Gothic name first appears in Latin and Greek sources c. 16 AD.

37. Wolfram, 23, 117–19.

38. Wolfram, 170–71.

39. Wolfram, 172, 181–90, 205, 211–22; Francisco de Sales Córdoba Sánchez-Bretaño (Córdoba), "La civilización del reino visigodo español," *CM* 5 (1981): 3.

40. Wolfram, 194.

41. Córdoba, "La civilización del reino visigodo español," 3.

42. Wolfram, 243–46.

43. Wolfram, 75–85.

44. Collins, *Early Medieval Spain*, 50–53.

45. Cf. Keay, 208; Collins, *Early Medieval Spain*, 53–58; Sobrequés Vidal, 48–49.

46. Dom Jordi Pinell, O.S.B. (d. 1997) was the first to identify these two main traditions. See J. Mª. Pinell, "Los textos de la antigua liturgia hispánica. Fuentes para su estudio," *Estudios sobre la liturgia mozárabe* (Toledo, 1965), 109–64.

47. Keay, 208.

48. Cf. Keay, 208 (Keay says they were expelled in 621); Collins, *Early Medieval Spain*, 38. Collins claims that the Byzantines were finally expelled in 624 and that their authority did not extend very far. He says their main purpose was to defend their territories in North Africa rather than to pursue substantial conquest inside the peninsula.

49. J. N. Hillgarth, "El Concilio III de Toledo y Bizancio," in *Concilio III de Toledo: XIV Centenario 589–1989*, 297–306 (Toledo: Arzobispado de Toledo, 1991).

50. See, among others, Josef A. Jungmann, S.J., *The Early Liturgy to the Time of Gregory the Great* (Notre Dame, IN: University of Notre Dame Press, 1980), 228; Henri Leclercq and Fernand Cabrol, "Mozarabe (La Liturgie)," in *Dictionnaire d'Archéologie Chrétienne et de Liturgie* (DACL), Tome Deuxième-A (Paris: Librairie Letouzey et Ané, 1935), 392.

51. Collins, *Early Medieval Spain*, 61.

52. Keay, 108.

53. Wolfram, 245.

54. Cf. Norman Roth, *Jews, Visigoths, and Muslims in Medieval Spain: Cooperation and Conflict* (New York: E. J. Brill, 1994), 45; W. Montgomery Watt, *A History of Islamic Spain* (Edinburgh: University Press, 1967), 7–9.

55. Joseph F. O'Callaghan, *A History of Medieval Spain* (Ithaca, NY: Cornell University Press, 1994), 91.

56. Collins, *Early Medieval Spain*, 228–30; J. Fernández Conde, "La Iglesia en el reino astur-leonés," BAC II-1:64.

57. O'Callaghan, *A History of Medieval Spain*, 91.

58. Watt, 17–21, 29–30.

59. Watt, 91–94; O'Callaghan, *A History of Medieval Spain*, 133, 194.

60. Watt, 7, 18–19.

61. O'Callaghan, *A History of Medieval Spain*, 151.

62. Watt, 20.

63. Colbert, 25; note 10 cites Francisco Javier Simonet, *Historia de los mozárabes de España, deducida de los mejores y más auténticos testimonios de los escritores cristianos y árabes* (Madrid, 1903), 771–95.

64. L. P. Harvey, *Islamic Spain, 1250 to 1500* (Chicago: University of Chicago Press, 1992), 13–14.

65. See Fletcher, 40; O'Callaghan, *A History of Medieval Spain*, 104, 176–77.

66. Colbert, 385–86; note 8 cites the work on Recemundus's *calendarium* by the German scholar Pius Bonifacius Gams, *Die Kirchengeschichte von Spanien*, vol. 2/2 (Regensburg, 1862–79), 455f.

67. Bernard F. Reilly, *The Contest of Christian and Muslim Spain 1031–1157* (Cambridge, MA: Blackwell, 1995), 17–21.

68. See Reilly, *Contest of Christian and Muslim Spain*, 2, 19–20. In note 15 he cites Bernard F. Reilly, *The Kingdom of León-Castilla under King Alfonso VI, 1065–1109* (Princeton, NJ: Princeton University Press, 1988), 11; *The Kingdom of León-Castilla under Queen Urraca, 1109–1126* (Princeton, NJ: Princeton University Press, 1982), 115; *Series Episcoporum Ecclesiæ Catholicæ* (Ratisbon, 1873); *Diccionario de historia eclesiástica de España*, 4 vols. (Madrid, 1972–75); *Dictionnaire d'histoire et de géographie ecclésiastique* (DHGE), 21 vols. (Paris, 1912–).

69. Parro, 2:171–72; Juan Francisco Rivera Recio, "La iglesia mozárabe," BAC II-1:22–24.

70. M. C. Díaz y Díaz, "Breves notas sobre los mozárabes de Toledo," in *Estudios Sobre Alfonso VI y la Reconquista de Toledo, Actas del II Congreso Internacional de Estudios Mozárabes (Toledo, 20–26 Mayo 1985)*, Serie Histórica 5 (Toledo: Instituto de Estudios Visigótico-Mozárabes, 1989), 3:13.

71. See Fletcher, 19–20, 49; Rivera Recio, "La iglesia mozárabe," 25. Rivera Recio cites the CM of 754 regarding the rapidity and violence of the invasion.

72. Francisco de Sales Córdoba, "Jornada del Foso (807)," CM 8 (1982): 8; O'Callaghan, *A History of Medieval Spain*, 103–4.

73. Rivera Recio, "La iglesia mozárabe," 21–60; O'Callaghan, *A History of Medieval Spain*, 107–11; Fletcher, 38–40.

74. O'Callaghan, *A History of Medieval Spain*, 176, 189–90; A. Linage Conde, "Introducción de la regla benedictina," BAC II-1:149–51, 164–67.

75. O'Callaghan, *A History of Medieval Spain*, 177.

76. Leclercq and Cabrol, 394; Rivera Recio, "La iglesia mozárabe," 37–46.

77. C. R. Haines, *Christianity and Islam in Spain: AD 756–1031* (New York: AMS Press, 1972), 33.

78. Reilly, *The Kingdom of León-Castilla under King Alfonso VI, 1065–1109*, 172.

79. O'Callaghan, *A History of Medieval Spain*, 305–6, 313–14, 321, 326–30; Colbert, 394; Fletcher, 8, 133–34, 147; Reilly, *Contest of Christian and Muslim Spain*, 21–42.

80. Cf. Luis Suárez Fernández, "Toledo, 1085: Un cambio para la convivencia," in *Estudios Sobre Alfonso VI*, 1:157–64.

3. FACTORS AFFECTING THE DEVELOPMENT
OF THE HISPANIC RITE

1. Fletcher, 19–20; Collins, *Early Medieval Spain*, 207–13.

2. See Javier Sainz Saiz, *Arte Prerrománico en Castilla y León* (León: Ediciones Lancia, 1996).

3. Joseph F. O'Callaghan, "The Integration of Christian Spain into Europe: The Role of Alfonso VI of León-Castile," in *Santiago, Saint-Denis, and Saint Peter: The Reception of the Roman Liturgy in León-Castile in 1080*, ed. Bernard F. Reilly, 105–13 (New York: Fordham University Press, 1985).

4. O'Callaghan, "The Integration of Christian Spain into Europe," 101.

5. Bernard F. Reilly, "Alfonso VI: Conqueror, Politician, Europeanizer," *Estudios Sobre Alfonso VI*, 1:25–30. Regarding Alfonso VI's five wives and two paramours, see Clemente Palencia, "Historia y leyendas de las mujeres de Alfonso VI," *Estudios Sobre Alfonso VI*, 2:281–304.

6. Reilly, *The Kingdom of León-Castile under King Alfonso VI, 1065–1109*, 96–97.

7. O'Callaghan, "Integration of Spain," 106–7.

8. Teófilo F. Ruiz, "Burgos and the Council of 1080," *Santiago, Saint-Denis, and Saint Peter*, 121–30.

9. Collins, *Early Medieval Spain*, 268.

10. Ramón Gonzálvez, "The Persistence of the Mozarabic Liturgy in Toledo after A.D. 1080," *Santiago, Saint-Denis, and Saint Peter*, 178–79; idem, "El arcediano de Toledo Joffré de Loaysa y las parroquias urbanas de Toledo en 1300," *Historia Mozárabe, Primer Congreso Internacional de Estudios Mozárabes: Toledo, 1975*, Serie C, no. 1 (Toledo: Instituto de Estudios Visigótico-Mozárabes de San Eugenio, 1978), 100, 141–44.

11. Marius Férotin, *LO*, ix, xxxviii; José Janini and Ramón Gonzálvez, *Catálogo de los Manuscritos Litúrgicos de la Catedral de Toledo*, Patronato "José María Quadrado," del Consejo Superior de Investigaciones Científicas 11 (Toledo: Diputación Provincial, 1977), 99–100; Rose Walker, *Views of Transition: Liturgy and Illumination in Medieval Spain* (Toronto: University of Toronto Press, 1998), 32–33.

12. On Alfonso VI's use of *fueros* as political instruments, see Ana María Barrero García, "La política foral de Alfonso VI," *Estudios Sobre Alfonso VI*, 1:115–56.

13. See "Documentos Mozárabes," *CM* 3 (1970): 13–16; Reilly, *The Kingdom of León-Castile under King Alfonso VI, 1065–1109*, 305, 308.

14. Reilly, *The Kingdom of León-Castilla under King Alfonso VI, 1065–1109*, 97, 101–2.

15. See Juan Francisco Rivera Recio, "La supresión del rito mozárabe y la introducción del romano," *BAC* II-1:282.

16. Gonzálvez, "Persistence of the Mozarabic Liturgy," 174–75.

17. Ramón Gonzálvez, "Cisneros y la Reforma del Rito Hispano-Mozárabe," a talk presented at the International Colloquium on the Bible and the Spanish Renaissance: Cardinal Ximénez de Cisneros (1436–1517) and the Complutensian Polyglot, Loyola University Chicago, 10–13 June 1999 (text provided by author), 6.

18. Gonzálvez, "Persistence of the Mozarabic Liturgy," 165.

19. The text of the *fuero* of Alfonso VII (1118) reaffirming his grandfather's *fuero* with the Mozarabs of 1101 is reproduced in "Documentos Mozárabes," *CM* 3 (1970): 13–16.

20. My translation of "De este modo surgió una comunidad histórico-litúrgica, única en Occidente, definida por el común origen hispano-visigótico y por la adscripción personal de sus miembros a las parroquias del rito tradicional, cuyo esplendor y conservación les correspondía y a las que mantenían con sus diezmos." *Constituciones* (1999), 14.

21. Dávila, "Una nueva etapa," 75.

22. Gonzálvez, "El arcediano de Toledo Joffré de Loaysa," 142–44.

23. Juan Meseguer Fernández, O.F.M., "El cardenal Jiménez de Cisneros, fundador de la Capilla Mozárabe," in *Historia Mozárabe*, 1:183–88.

24. Meseguer Fernández, 154.

25. Gonzálvez, "Cisneros y la Reforma," 11.

26. Gonzálvez, "Cisneros y la Reforma," 28.

27. Gonzálvez, "Cisneros y la Reforma," 20; Roth, *The Spanish Inquisition*, 160.

28. See Alfonso Ortiz, "Prefatio," in *Missale mixtum secundum regulam beati Isidori dictum Mozarabes*, Museo del Hospital de la Santa Cruz, Toledo, Inventorio General número 1324 (Toledo: Petri Hagembach impensis Melchioris Gorricii, 1500).

29. My translation of "Los escritores y mecenas de la Península Ibérica, sin menoscabo de la admiración que sentían por los autores nacidos en la otra Península mediterránea, darían la réplica reivindicando la herencia de los grandes Padres visigodos como un patrimonio nacional." Gonzálvez, "Cisneros y la Reforma," 34.

30. *La Catedral de Toledo 1549, según el doctor Blas Ortiz en su obra "descripción Gráfica de la catedral de Toledo"* (Toledo, 1999), 241, as cited by Gonzálvez, "Cisneros y la Reforma," 39–40n73.

31. See José Janini, "Appendix," in *Liber Missarum de Toledo* (Toledo: Instituto de Estudias Visigótico-Mozárabes, 1983), 1:554–79: *Missæ Gothicæ et Officii muzarabici dilucida expositio*, a D.D. Francisco Antonio Lorenzana, Archiepiscopo Mexicano, et a D.D. Francisco Fabian et Fuero, Episcopo Angelopolitano, Ad usum percelebris Sacelli Muzarabum, in alma Ecclesia Toletana Hispaniarum Primate ab Emmo. Cardinali Ximenez de Cisnersos erecti, Editio novissima jussu et aprobatione Illmi. D.D. Santos ab Arciniega, Vicarii Capitularis, huius Archidiæceseos Gubernatoris, et Archipresbyteri dignaitate in hac Ecclesia Primate præditi, facta (Toledo: Typis Severiani Lopez Fando et filii, anno domini MDCCCLXXV).

32. Mario Arellano García, *La Capilla Mozárabe o del Corpus Christi* (Toledo: Instituto de Estudios Visigótico-Mozárabes de San Eugenio, 1980), 39–43.

33. *1998 Grolier Multimedia Encyclopedia*, Grolier Interactive (1997), s.v. "Enlightenment" and "Spain, history of."

34. Lluís Roura Aulinas, "La guerra de la Independencia," in *La transición del Antiguo al Nuevo régimen (1789–1874)*, vol. 9 of *Historia de España*, 3rd ed., ed. Antonio Domínguez Ortiz (Barcelona: Editorial Planeta, 1989), 151.

35. Leandro Higueruela Del Pino, "Don Francisco Antonio de Lorenzana, Cardenal Ilustrado," *Toletum* 23 (1989), 169–73, 189. Also, Faustino Arévalo (Faustinus Arevalus), "Notæ ad Missale Gothicum," cols. 1295–96. He states that the new lettering is "Matrite" (of Madrid) and gives both the Breviary and Missal "new form and a greater elegance" (my translation of "novum robur, majoremque elegantiam addidit").

36. Arévalo, cols. 1295–96.

37. "Nuestro Sr. Arzobispo," *BOAT* 128 (1972): 4.

38. A review of González Martín's (d. 2004) efforts toward liturgical renewal and implementation appears in Andrés Pardo, "Don Marcelo y la liturgia," *BOAT* 142 (1986): 253–58.

39. See "Noticias Mozárabes," *CM* 3 (1970): 11; and Dávila, "Una nueva etapa," 64.

40. Colomina Torner, interview by author, Toledo, 27 September 1999; Colomina Torner, "Actualización del Rito Hispano-Mozárabe—Datos y fechas." Regarding his work and the work of Don Balbino Gómez-Chacón on behalf of the reorganization of the Mozarab community and actualization of its liturgy, see Dávila, "Una nueva etapa," 65.

41. Colomina Torner, "1992: Toledo Mozárabe en Roma," *Toletum* 28 (1992): 154.

42. Found in *Historia Mozárabe*.

43. Found in *Estudios sobre Alfonso VI*.

44. The acta and documents are found in *Concilio III de Toledo: XIV Centenario 589–1989*.

45. See José Aldazábal, "Presentación," in *Liturgia hispánica*, ed. José Aldazábal, Biblioteca litúrgica 9 (Barcelona: Centre de Pastoral Litúrgica, 1998), 11.

46. My translation of "a fin de que los fieles participen plena, activa y conscientemente en las celebraciones litúrgicas." Marcelo González Martín, "Presentación," in *Missale*, 1:11, citing *Sacrosanctum Concilium*, no. 14.

47. My translation of "que hicieran posible una digna celebración de los Misterios del Señor." González Martín, "Presentación," *Missale*, 1:11.

48. Parro, 2:253–54 (including notes).

49. Ángel Fernández Collado, "Situación económica de las parroquias mozárabes de Toledo en 1822," *CM* 17 (1986): 6–7.

50. For more on this era and information, see *La transición del Antiguo al Nuevo régimen (1789–1874)*, vol. 9 of *Historia de España Ilustrada*, gen. ed. Juan Reglá (Barcelona: Editorial Ramón Sopena, 1972).

51. Juan Reglá, "Isabel II," *(15) El siglo XVIII, (16) el siglo XIX, y (17) el siglo XX, Historia de España Ilustrada*, 2:793–94.

52. There were six *desamortizaciones* from the end of the eighteenth century through the nineteenth century, beginning with King Carlos III in 1764. The

last took place in 1859–67 during the Provisional Government of Gen. Francisco Serrano (1868–71). See, among others, Pedro Ruiz Torres, "Economía y sociedad en la crisis del Antiguo régimen," in Domínguez Ortiz, *Historia de España*, 9:417; Victoria López Cordón, "De la crisis de la monarquía a la Primera República," in Domínguez Ortiz, *Historia de España*, 9:561; Reglá, 793–94.

53. See de las Heras y Borrero, 8.

54. See Arellano García, *La Capilla Mozárabe*, 80; Ángel Fernández Collado, "Canonización de D. Ricardo Plá Espí," *CM* 33 (1992): 155–56.

4. THE HISPANO-MOZARABIC RITE AND ITS EVOLUTION

1. Much of this chapter has been published in the *New Catholic Encyclopedia*, 2nd ed. (New York: The Gale Group, 2003), s.v., "Mozarabic Rite" (10:42–47).

2. Teodoro González, "Paganismo, judaísmo, herejías y relaciones con el exterior," BAC 1:697–98.

3. For the extant *acta*, see Vives. For relations with Rome, see Sotomayor, "Sobre los orígenes," 135; O'Callaghan, *A History of Medieval Spain*, 21.

4. Jungmann, *Early Liturgy*, 229.

5. Leclercq and Cabrol, 391.

6. Vives, 107–45, 186–225.

7. "Prenotandos," no. 2, *Missale*, vol. 1 (referred to as *prenotanda* in the text).

8. See *acta* of Toledo III, in Vives, 107–45.

9. See Ursicino Domínguez del Val, O.S.A., "Características de la Patrística hispana en el siglo VII," in *La Patrología Toledano-visigoda, XXVII Semana Española de Teología (Toledo, 25–29 Sept. 1967)* (Madrid: Consejo Superior de Investigaciones Científicas, Patronato "Menéndez Pelayo," Instituto "Francisco Suárez," 1970), 5–36.

10. Cyrille Vogel, *Medieval Liturgy: An Introduction to the Sources*, rev. and trans. by William G. Storey and Niels Krogh Rasmussen, O.P. (Washington DC: Pastoral Press, 1986), 1.

11. P. M. Gy, "History of the Liturgy in the West to the Council of Trent," in Martimort, 1:50; Vogel, *Medieval Liturgy*, 95.

12. Vogel, *Medieval Liturgy*, 37.

13. Vogel, *Medieval Liturgy*, 61.

14. R. C. D. Jasper and G. J. Cuming, *Prayers of the Eucharist: Early and Reformed*, 3rd ed., rev. (Collegeville, MN: Liturgical Press, 1990), 147.

15. Leclercq and Cabrol, 464; "Prenotandos" speculates the possible origin of the Gallican and Hispano-Mozarabic rites may have been the liturgy of third century Carthage (no. 91).

16. O'Callaghan, *A History of Medieval Spain*, 37, 40, 43–44; Wolfram, 197–202, 209–12.

17. Vives, 107–522.

18. My translation of "La liturgie mozarabe a dans la liturgie gallicane une soeur, que nous font aisément reconnaître comme telle les particularités de son caractère et les traits généraux de sa physionomie. Mais, s'agit-il d'une soeur aînée ou d'une soeur cadette?" *LM*, ix.

19. "Prenotandos," nos. 28, 32, 113; Jungmann, *Early Liturgy*, 229–33.

20. Vogel, *Medieval Liturgy,* 35.

21. Josef A. Jungmann, *The Place of Christ in Liturgical Prayer*, trans. Geoffrey Chapman (Collegeville, MN: Liturgical Press, 1989), 86.

22. See Archdale A. King, *Liturgies of the Past* (London: Longmans, Green and Co., 1959), 77n1, citing H. Netzer, *Introduction de la Messe Romaine en France sous les Carolingiens*, 2.

23. Jungmann, *Place of Christ*, 227.

24. See Vogel, *Medieval Liturgy,* 35–36, 38.

25. See *LM*, ix-x; Ramón Gonzálvez, "Los orígenes de la liturgia hispano-mozárabe," *Anales Toledanos* 35 (1998): 34; Pinell, *Liturgia hispánica*, 69.

26. Pinell, *Liturgia hispánica*, 25, and chap. 7.

27. Peter C. Scales, "¿Cuál era la verdadera importancia de la conquista de Tuletwu, capital de los godos?" *Estudios Sobre Alfonso VI*, 1:339.

28. O'Callaghan, *A History of Medieval Spain*, 59. Also Marius Férotin, "L'Ordinatio Regis ou le sacre de rois wisigoths de Tolède au VII siècle," in *Le Liber Ordinum En Usage Dans l'Eglise Wisigothique et Mozarabe d'Espagne du Cinquième Siècle* (Paris: Firmin-Didot, 1904 [hereafter *LO*]), Appendix II, 498–505; Paul A. Jacobson, "Sicut Samuhel Unxit David: Early Carolingian Royal Anointings Reconsidered," *Medieval Liturgy: A Book of Essays*, ed. Lizette Larson-Miller (New York: Garland, 1997), 269–70; Vogel, *Medieval Liturgy,* 183–187; Vives (Toledo IV, canon 75, alludes to the anointing of the king as a reason for the people not to sin against him).

29. Gonzálvez, "Los orígenes," 34.

30. O'Callaghan, *A History of Medieval Spain*, 78.

31. O'Callaghan, *A History of Medieval Spain*, 83. He points out that in other parts of Europe this was not always the case, as it was a period of decay and corruption in many areas.

32. Jordi Pinell, "El misal hispano-mozárabe: Nueva edición revisada," *Phase* 191 (1992): 371. It is important to note that Férotin, an earlier scholar of the rite, does not make this distinction between traditions.

33. On the Mozarabic chapel in the Old Cathedral of Salamanca, see Lamberto de Echeverría, "La Real Capilla Universitaria de San Jerónimo," in *Triduo Sacro en rito hispano antiguo o mozárabe*, gen. ed. Lamberto de Echeverría (Salamanca: Universidad de Salamanca Junta de Capilla, 1980), 2–20. On the efforts in Plasencia, see Cleofé Sánchez Montealegre, "Aprobada la Reforma del Rito Mozárabe," *CM* 22 (1988): 3. Monasteries, such as the former Cistercian monastery at Valdeiglesias (Madrid) also were preserves of the ancient liturgy in the sixteenth century (see *CM* 62 [2005]: 24–28).

34. "Prenotandos," no. 21; for a brief overview of the structure, see Francisco de Sales Córdoba, "Estructura de la misa hispana o mozárabe," *CM* 15 (1985): 4–6.

35. For a comparison of the updated Hispano-Mozarabic rite with the reformed Roman and Ambrosian rites, see Vincent A. Lenti, "Liturgical Reform and the Ambrosian and Mozarabic Rites," *Worship* 68 (1994): 417–26.

36. See Cleofé Sánchez, "La Reforma del Rito Mozárabe," *CM* 18 (1986): 11–12; Balbino Gómez-Chacón, "Sobre la revisión del rito hispano-mozárabe," *CM* 19 (1987): 1–3; Gonzálvez, "Los orígenes," 52–53; Pinell, *Liturgia hispánica*, 186.

37. For six graphs showing the structure of the Hispano-Mozarabic eucharistic celebration as well as other materials pertinent to this book, see Center for the Study of Latino/a Catholicism on the sandiego.edu website.

38. "Prenotandos," no. 23. Also see José Janini, "Misas mozárabes recompuestas por Ortiz," *Hispania Sacra* 34 (1982): 153.

39. King, 152–53. He cites canon 30 of the Council of Agde (506) (153n1).

40. Cf. Robert Cabié, "The Entrance Rites," Martimort, 2:55–56; Gómez-Chacón, "Sobre la revisión," 2; "Prenotandos," nos. 146–47.

41. The *Prælegendum* is only sung during Ordinary Time in accord with the liturgical practice of Tradition B (Seville). Gómez-Chacón, "Sobre la revisión," 2.

42. Cabié, 54.

43. See Vives, canon 13 (p. 196); Mt 26:30; Vogel, *Medieval Liturgy,* 293–97.

44. Gy, Martimort, 1:49; Michael Witczak, "Sacramentary of Paul VI," in *The Eucharist*, vol. 3 of *Handbook for Liturgical Studies*, ed. Anscar J. Chupungco (Collegeville, MN: Liturgical Press, 1999), 146.

45. Cabié, 54; Witczak, 146n5.

46. Josef A. Jungmann, S.J., *The Mass of the Roman Rite: Its Origins and Development (Missarum Sollemnia)* (New York: Benzinger Bros., 1951), 1:356.

47. See Edward Foley, "Overview of Music in Catholic Worship and Liturgical Music Today," *The Liturgy Documents: A Parish Resource*, 3rd ed. (Chicago: LTP, 1991), 273.

48. Hans-Joachim Schulz, *The Byzantine Liturgy: Symbolic Structure and Faith Expression*, trans. Matthew J. O'Connell (New York: Pueblo Pub. Co., 1986), 22.

49. Férotin uses the term found most frequently in the Visigothic sources, *Missa*, for the first prayer. However, he also indicates that the earliest sources do not have a presidential prayer at this point in the liturgy (*LM*, xx, xxxviii). Also see Janini, "Misas mozárabes," 153. Janini notes that Ortiz systematically introduced *Post Gloriam* prayers to the Mozarabic Masses in the *Missale mixtum* (1500).

50. "Prenotandos," no. 31.

51. King, 157–59.

52. Pinell, "El misal hispano-mozárabe, 371.

53. Vogel, *Medieval Liturgy,* 301.

54. My translation of "supplication solennelle et invitation à la prière" (*LM*, xxxix-xl).

55. Ferrer Grenesche interview, 26 June 1996. *Post Gloria* prayers do not appear in this collection; the first oration of the Eucharist is the *Missa*, today called the *oratio Admonitionis* (*LM*, xx, xxxviii).

56. King, 151; Jungmann, *The Mass of the Roman Rite*, 2:152.

57. Enrico Mazza, *The Eucharistic Prayers of the Roman Rite*, trans. Matthew J. O'Connell (New York: Pueblo Pub. Co., 1986), 61–62.

58. Ferrer Grenesche, interview, 26 June 1996.

59. *LM*, xxiv.

60. Also *Inlatio*; it is equivalent to the Greek *anaphora*. Cf. King, 173; *LM*, xxi.

61. Enrique Carrillo Morales, "La pasión en la liturgia mozárabe," in *La Semana Santa dentro del Misterio Cristiano: I Ciclo de Conferencias, marzo 1998* (Toledo: Junta de Cofradías y Hermandades de Semana Santa de Toledo, 1999), 20.

62. See Janini, "Misas mozárabes," 155.

63. King, 173–74.

64. Férotin uses the term *missa secreta* to refer to the Institution Narrative, since this is the name found in the ancient manuscripts. Apparently it was recited in a low voice or done in complete silence by the time the manuscripts were copied in the eleventh century (*LM*, xxiv).

65. See Juan-Miguel Ferrer Grenesche, "La eucaristía en rito hispano-mozárabe," *Toletana* 1 (1999): 59–88.

66. The Eucharistic Prayer's origin is much debated, though the Jewish table blessing *birkat ha-mazon* seems to have been most influential on it. See David N. Power, O.M.I., *The Eucharistic Mystery: Revitalizing the Tradition* (New York: Crossroad, 1995), 101.

67. Peter Cobb, "The Liturgy of the Word in the Early Church," in *The Study of Liturgy*, rev. ed., ed. Cheslyn Jones et al. (New York: Oxford University Press, 1992), 228.

68. Vives, Toledo III, canon 2 (p. 125).

69. Cobb, 228.

70. Vives, 125.

71. Cf. Conferencia Episcopal Española, *Missale Hispano-Mozarabicum: Ordo Missæ—Liber Offerentium* (Toledo: Arzobispado de Toledo, 1991), no. 37 (76) and "Rito Hispano-Mozárabe Ordinario de la Misa" (Toledo: Mozarabic chapel self-published worship-aid booklet, n.d.), 28–29.

72. See W. C. Bishop, *The Mozarabic and Ambrosian Rites: Four Essays in Comparative Liturgiology*, ed. C. L. Feltoe, Alcuin Club Tracts 15 (London: A. R. Mowbray and Co., 1940), 40. Feltoe collected four of Bishop's essays written between the late 1800s and the early 1900s and published this collection originally in 1924; the edition I cite is from 1940. Feltoe cautions in his introduction that some of Bishop's conclusions in his 1906 essay on the Mozarabic Rite are based on work done before Férotin's publication of the

Liber Mozarabicus Sacramentorum; apparently Bishop was unwilling to revise his study after Férotin published his work in 1912 (26).

73. King, 179.

74. Et coniunctio Corporis et Sanguinis Domini nostri Iesu Christi sit sumentibus et potantibus nobis ad veniam, et defunctis fidelibus præstetur ad requiem (*Liber Offerentium,* nos. 41, 79).

75. Vives, canon 18 (p. 198).

76. See Jasper and Cuming, Book VIII, 100.

77. Power, *The Eucharistic Mystery,* 185n2: *Sermo* 73,2, *Corpus Christianorum Series Latina* (CCSL) 103, 307.

78. My paraphrase of "Se entiende que, al concluir la celebración, la mayor bendición que los fieles pueden llevarse consigo es la Eucaristía que han recibido" (Pinell, *Liturgia hispánica,* 183).

79. See Power, *The Eucharistic Mystery,* 184–87.

80. "Prenotandos," no. 140; Janini, "Misas mozárabes," 153n2. Janini identifies the *Post communio* [*sic*] prayers as systematically added by Ortiz.

81. "The solemnities are completed. In the name of our Lord Jesus Christ may our offering be accepted with peace" (*Liber Offerentium,* no. 88).

5. THE STRUCTURE OF THE HISPANO-MOZARABIC LENT

1. See *LMCP*, xxvii–xxxii.

2. Lizette Larson-Miller, "Lent," *New Dictionary of Sacramental Worship,* ed. Peter E. Fink, S.J. (Collegeville, MN: Liturgical Press, 1990), 684.

3. The Latin title of the First Sunday of Lent is "In primo Dominico Quadragesimæ, id est, de carnes tollendas" (*Missale,* 1:175–82).

4. "In secundo Dominico Quadragesimæ, missa de muliere samaritana" (*Missale,* 1:197–204).

5. "In tertio Dominico Quadragesimæ, missa de cæco nato dicenda" (*Missale,* 1:219–25).

6. "In quarto Dominico Quadragesimæ, missa in mediante die festo" (*Missale,* 1:240–46).

7. "In quinto Dominico Quadragesimæ, missa de Lazaro dicenda" (*Missale,* 1:270–76). The *Missale* also offers an alternative set of prayers for this day titled "Appendix: in quinto Dominico Quadragesimæ" (*Missale,* 1:298–303). This implies that the sources had two different Masses for this day proceeding from different areas; the primary set is usually from Tradition B (Seville), whereas the second set is from Tradition A (Toledo).

8. "In Dominico in ramis palmarum" (*Missale,* 1:304–15). The prayers are divided between two liturgical actions: I. "Ordo ad benedicendos ramos" (with antiphons for the procession) (304–7), and II. "Ad missam" (308–15).

9. Vives, canon 49 (p. 99).

10. The Instruction and following two monitions are found in the *Missale Gothicum*, col. 367, lines 20–37; col. 368, lines 6–9; and col. 368, lines 11–15.

11. My translation of "Recitemos de nuevo por tercera vez el texto del símbolo; para que como el símbolo contiene en sí la fe en la divina Trinidad, el mismo número de la repetición concuerde con el misterio de la Trinidad" (Carrillo Morales, "La pasión en la liturgia mozárabe," 26).

12. My translation of "Esta regla de la santa fe, que la Santa Madre Iglesia os transmite ahora, mantenedla con la más firme resolución de vuestra mente; que no surja algún día en vuestro corazón el temor de la duda. Porque si, Dios no lo permita, en esto se duda aunque sea tenuamente [sic], se derrumba todo el fundamento de la fe, y se genera el peligro del alma. Y por tanto, si alguno de vosotros excluye algo de este símbolo, piense que no lo podrá comprender. Crea, más bien, que es verdad todo lo que ha oído. Que Dios todopoderoso ilumine vuestro corazón de tal modo, que entendiendo y creyendo lo que hemos dicho, guardéis la fe recta y brilléis en obras santas, para que por esto lleguéis a la vida bienaventurada. Amén" (Carrillo Morales, "La pasión en la liturgia mozárabe," 26–27).

13. The *Liber Mozarabicus Sacramentorum* and the *Antifonario Visigótico-Mozárabe* of León were also used. See Jaime Sancho Andreu, "El Triduo Sacro en el Rito Hispánico," in *Triduo Sacro*, 50.

14. See *Egeria: Diary of a Pilgrimage*, Ancient Christian Writers 38, trans. George E. Gingras (New York: Newman Press, 1970).

15. See John F. Baldovin, S.J., *The Urban Character of Christian Worship: The Origins, Development, and Meaning of Stational Liturgy* (Rome: Pont. Institutum Studiorum Orientalium, 1987), 111, 251, 263.

16. Scholars of the University of Salamanca identified the scripture passages making up the centonized texts for the Triduum liturgies. See Lamberto de Echeverría, "Introducción," in *Triduo Sacro*, 13–14. The readings in Latin and Spanish for Holy Thursday are found on pages 62–79.

17. *Triduo Sacro*, 70–79.

18. Carrillo Morales, "La pasión en la liturgia mozárabe," 27 (my paraphrase of "humildad más admirable ya al hacerse hombre y al derramar su sangre en la Cruz").

19. For a different version of this rite, see *Triduo Sacro*, 111.

20. Carrillo Morales, "La pasión en la liturgia mozárabe," 28.

21. The texts for the second liturgical action of Holy Thursday can be found in an untitled and unpublished four-page, loose-leaf pamphlet that serves as an addendum to the worship aid provided to worshipers in the section titled "Expoliación del altar" (Toledo: Santa Eulalia y San Marcos Parish, n.d.), 1–2. The *Liber Ordinum* only gives rubrics and an antiphon for this rite (*LO*, 191–92).

22. The verses cited above are my translation of nos. 1 and 4; the responses are my translation of nos. 1, 3, and 4. The official Latin text can be found in *Missale*, 1:339–42.

23. The *Liber Ordinum* gives rubrics and orations for this rite (*LO*, 192–93).

24. *LO*, 192; for the Spanish, see *Triduo Sacro*, 111, 113.

25. Doña María Jesús Jurado Lozano, member, *Hermandad Mozárabe*, Brazo de Damas, parishioner of Santa Eulalia y San Marcos; and Óscar Urbiola Álvarez, fiancé of a Mozarab parishioner of Santa Eulalia, interview by author, Toledo, 2 June 1999.

26. These verses are found in an loose-leaf, four-page pamphlet that serves as an addendum to the worship-aid pamphlet provided to worshipers for the Holy Thursday liturgy. See "Al lavatorio de pies" (Toledo: Santa Eulalia y San Marcos Parish, n.d.), 3–4.

27. "Feria VI in Parasceve," *Missale*, 1:345–51.

28. "Feria VI in Parasceve," *Missale*, 1:352–68.

29. See *Missale*, 1:345–51. Worshipers at Santa Eulalia receive a photocopied, six-page worship aid titled "Triduo Sacro en rito mozárabe: A la hora de Tercia, Exaltación y Adoración de la Cruz" (Toledo: Santa Eulalia y San Marcos Parish, n.d.). Hereafter Worship Aid I.

30. Pinell, *Liturgia hispánica*, 309.

31. *Missale*, 1:352–68. Worshipers at Santa Eulalia receive a photocopied, twelve-page worship aid titled "Triduo Sacro en rito mozárabe" (Toledo: Santa Eulalia y San Marcos Parish, n.d.). Hereafter Worship Aid II.

32. Teodoro González, "Vida Cristiana y Cura Pastoral," BAC 1:582.

33. *Triduo Sacro*, 126–31.

34. Sancho Andreu, "El triduo sacro en el rito hispánico," 51.

35. See Vives, 193; Sancho Andreu, "El triduo sacro en el rito hispánico," 51–52; González, "Vida Cristiana y Cura Pastoral," 574.

36. "Sermo," *Liber Commicus*, 1:275–76.

37. Vives, canon 11 (p. 128); González, "Vida Cristiana y Cura Pastoral," 570; John T. McNeill and Helena M. Gamer, *Medieval Handbooks of Penance: A Translation of the Principal* Libri Poenitentiales *and Selections from Related Documents,* Records of Western Civilization Series 29 (New York: Columbia University Press, 1990 <1938>), 14.

38. Pinell, *Liturgia hispánica*, 312.

39. See Vives, 128, 210, 239.

40. Vives, 193.

41. *Missale*, 1:369–411; the readings are in the *Liber Commicus*, 1:278–320.

42. Some who attend the Easter Vigil at Santa Eulalia receive a booklet titled "Sagrados Oficios de Semana Santa según el antiguo Rito Hispano o Mozárabe" (Toledo: Santa Eulalia y San Marcos Parish, n.d.). It is a photocopy of the Spanish-language texts for the Vigil taken from *Triduo Sacro*.

43. The rubrics say this is to take place in the sacristy (*Missale*, 1:369).

44. My paraphrase of "Los bendecimos (la lámpara y el cirio) por el glorioso misterio de aquella noche, de modo que, santificados con la bendición de la luz, percibamos la gracia sacramental de la resurrección de Cristo, que celebramos en aquella sagrada vigilia" (cited in Pinell, *Liturgia hispánica*, 314).

45. Actually, the *Liber Commicus* offers two sets of readings divided between Year I and Year II. Year I has eleven Old Testament readings, indicating they

come from Tradition B (1:278–96) and Year II has twelve readings, indicating they come from Tradition A (1:296–320). Nonetheless, like many Roman rite parish pastors, the pastor of Santa Eulalia often selects only a minimal number of readings for the liturgy.

46. *Missale*, 1:385–93.

47. My translation of "Aquel cuerpo llevaba, no el desfallecimiento del que muere, sino el amor. En aquellas entrañas no se encerraba la flaqueza, sino la piedad. El estar colgado, es del hombre; el resucitar, es de Dios. . . . Tú clavabas tus delitos [*sic*] en aquellas manos. Mi muerte y tu propia salvación las cosías con aquellos clavos que atravesaban aquellos pies, a los que habría que besar, si fuera posible . . . para que las criaturas, rescatadas, conociesen a su Autor por el cual el hombre, si no hubiese sido rescatado, no habría conocido su perdición. Amén." (This is the Spanish version of the prayers found in *Triduo Sacro*, 201, 203, and reproduced in "Sagrados Oficios.")

48. Called *Cofradía de la Santa Caridad* (Confraternity of Holy Charity) (see Parro, 2:175).

49. Parro, 2:190.

50. Don Jesús Fernández López, retired pastor, part-time assistant, Capitular Archives and Library of Toledo Cathedral, interview by author, Toledo, 27 May 1999.

51. Anscar J. Chupungco, O.S.B., *Liturgical Inculturation: Sacramentals, Religiosity, and Catechesis* (Collegeville, MN: Liturgical Press, 1992), 104–5; Baldovin, 85n9, citing J. Wilkinson, trans., *Jerusalem Pilgrims before the Crusades* (Warminster: Aris and Phillips, 1974), 34.

52. See, among others, Michael S. Driscoll, "Liturgy and Devotions: Back to the Future?" in *The Renewal That Awaits Us*, ed. Eleanor Bernstein, C.S.J., and Martin F. Connell (Chicago: LTP, 1997), 68–70, 73; see also, Mark R. Francis, C.S.V., "Popular Piety and Liturgical Reform in a Hispanic Context," in *Dialogue Rejoined: Theology and Ministry in the United States Hispanic Reality*, ed. Ana María Pineda and Robert Schreiter (Collegeville, MN: Liturgical Press, 1995), 169–74.

53. Crispino Valenziano, "Liturgy and Anthropology: The Meaning of the Question and the Method for Answering It," in *Fundamental Liturgy*, vol. 2 of *Handbook for Liturgical Studies*, ed. Anscar J. Chupungco, O.S.B. (Collegeville, MN: Liturgical Press, 1998), 209–10.

6. THE LIGNUM CRUCIS AND ITS RITUAL SETTING

1. My descriptions are based on videotapes taken during the events described and on my observations as a participant-observer in them. Though most of the references are to the events of 1999, I have returned almost yearly and have found only slight variations to what is described here.

2. See Ronald L. Grimes, *Beginnings in Ritual Studies*, rev. ed. (Columbia: University of South Carolina Press, 1995), 5, 24–25, 38–39.

3. See O'Callaghan, *A History of Medieval Spain*, 43; Keay, 208.

4. On the three cultures and their influence on Toledo, see Olga Pérez Monzón and Enrique Rodríguez-Picavea, *Toledo y las tres Culturas*, Historia del Mundo Para Jóvenes (Madrid: Ediciones AKAL, 1995).

5. *Guía del Toledo Judío* (Toledo: Ediciones Codex, 1990), 18–19; Samuel and Tamar Grand, "Exploring the Jewish Heritage of Spain" (Bilbao: Secretaría de Estado de Turismo, Dirección General de Promoción del Turismo, 1980), 4.

6. See Pérez Monzón and Rodríguez-Picavea, 42–44; Jay Jacobs, ed., *The Horizon Book of Great Cathedrals* (New York: American Heritage Pub., 1968), 264; Antonio Cabrera y Delgado, *Catedral de Toledo*, 2nd ed. (Barcelona: Editorial Escudo de Oro, 1993), 2, 6, 10.

7. Arellano García, *La Capilla Mozárabe*, 14; Cabrera y Delgado, 45–47.

8. For photos of Toledo and various other aspects of the parish of Santa Eulalia and of the processions, see Center for the Study of Latino/a Catholicism on the sandiego.edu website.

9. Francisco de Sales Córdoba, "Las iglesias mozárabes de Toledo," *CM* 11 (1984): 9–10; Ignacio Gallego Peñalver, "La iglesia mozárabe de Santa Eulalia de Toledo," *CM* 17 (1986): 7–9; and Parro, 2:189–91.

10. See Córdoba, "Las iglesias mozárabes de Toledo," 9. In November 2006 the church was temporarily closed for worship due to dangerous cracks in the western wall. The church repairs were to be completed by Holy Week 2008. As a result, Sunday Mass in the Hispano-Mozarabic rite for the parishioners of Santa Eulalia y San Marcos was moved to the Capilla de la Virgen del Sagrario in the Toledo cathedral until the building could be rededicated for worship.

11. For a description of Visigothic, Mozarabic, and Mudéjar architecture, see Xavier Barral i Altet, *The Early Middle Ages: From Late Antiquity to A.D. 1000*, Taschen's World Architecture Series (Cologne: Benedikt Taschen Verlag GmbH, 1997), 99–117.

12. A. Arellano, "La Parroquia Mozárabe de Santa Eulalia," *CM* 6 (1982): 12.

13. Enrique Carrillo Morales, "Las Reliquias de Santa Eulalia," *CM* 20 (1987): 3. "Now from the apse of the presbyterium presiding over the entire church is Christ crucified, the highest symbol of the love of the Father, to whom alone is due honor and glory in the church." My translation of "Ahora desde el ábside del presbiterio preside todo el templo Cristo crucificado, símbolo extremo del amor del Padre, a quien solo se le debe honor y gloria en la Iglesia."

14. "Necrologías," *CM* 22 (1988): 16, the statue carved in 1987.

15. See Mario Arellano García, "Santa Eulalia: ¿De Mérida o Barcelona?" *CM* 20 (1987): 10.

16. Ferrer Grenesche, *Los Santos*, 52.

17. The Archeological Museum of Madrid contains part of the so-called treasure of Guarrazar, found in a field near Toledo in the mid-1800s after centuries of having been hidden, probably at the time of the Arab invasion. See Gisela Ripoll and Isabel Velázquez, *Historia de España: La Hispania visigoda. Del rey Ataúlfo a Don Rodrigo*, Historia 16 Temas de Hoy, vol. 6 (Madrid: Ediciones Temas de Hoy, S.A., 1995), 43, 51, 74–75; Barral i Altet, 100.

18. Joan Carroll Cruz, *Relics* (Huntington, IN: Our Sunday Visitor, 1984), 1–8. Also see Theresa Sanders, "Relics," in *Modern Catholic Encyclopedia* (1994).

19. Baldovin, 46–48; T. Jerome Overbeck, S.J., "Cross," in *New Dictionary of Sacramental Worship*, ed. Peter E. Fink, S.J. (Collegeville, MN: Liturgical Press, 1990), 304–5; Cruz, 38–39; H. Chirat, "Cross, Finding the Holy," and E. Lussier, "Sepulcher, Holy," in *New Catholic Encyclopedia* (1967).

20. Cruz, 3, 39–40; Baldovin, 111.

21. Baldovin, 46, 49, 50, 52, 53, 54, 100; Cruz, 40; W. E. Kaegi, Jr., "Heraclius, Byzantine Emperor," in *New Catholic Encyclopedia* (1967).

22. See *Egeria*, 126, 238–39nn, 255–57nn; see also "Introduction," 13, 38, 43.

23. Cruz, 40–41; Overbeck, 305.

24. Reilly, *The Kingdom of León-Castile under King Alfonso VI, 1065–1109*, 305.

25. Reilly, *The Kingdom of León-Castile under King Alfonso VI, 1065–1109*, 305, 308: in 305n8 he cites Julio Puyol y Alonso, ed., "Las crónicas anónimas de Sahagún," *Boletín de la Real Academia de la Historia* 76 (1920), 116–17.

26. *Francisco de Pisa, Apuntamientos para la II Parte de la "Descripción de la Imperial Ciudad de Toledo," según la copia manuscrita de D. Francisco de Santiago Palomares, con notas originales autógrafas del Cardenal Lorenzana*, Estudio preliminar, transcripción y notas de José Gómez-Menor Fuentes (Toledo: I.P.I.E.T Diputación Provincial de Toledo, 1976), 64; Parro, 2:176–77n. Parro notes that the *cofradía* continued to take this out from the Convent of the Calced Carmelites until 1810. After 1810 the procession began from the parish Church of La Magdalena. Parro claims that this relic came into the possession of the *cofradía* after 1481; the relic had been found in a wall of Santa Eulalia around that time (190). The *cofradía* still existed in 1857 when Parro published his book.

27. The Good Friday service found in Cisneros was incorporated into the Lorenzana edition of the nineteenth century. See *Missale mixtum* (Cisneros, 1500), "Feria Sexta: In parasceue ad nona(m) pro indulgentia," folios clxxi (front, bottom left col.) through clxxiiii (back); *Missale Gothicum* (Lorenzana, 1854 ed.), "Feria VI In Parasceve," "Ad Nonam pro indulgentia," cols. 403–21.

28. See Lynette M. F. Bosch, *Art, Liturgy, and Legend in Renaissance Toledo: The Mendoza and the Iglesia Primada* (University Park: Pennsylvania State University Press, 2000), 44.

29. Parro, 2:190. Parro claims that the relic found in the wall of Santa Eulalia is the relic that came into the possession of the *cofradía de la Vera Cruz*.

30. Carrillo Morales, "Las Reliquias de Santa Eulalia," 2.

31. See Mario Arellano García, "Lápidas en la parroquia mozárabe de Santa Eulalia," *CM* 43 (1997): 10–11.

32. Arellano García, "Lápidas," 11. He does not say whether the latter parish still owns the pendant or what became of the relic in the other crystal case.

33. Carrillo Morales, "Las Reliquias de Santa Eulalia," 3. My paraphrase and translation of "Hay otro simbolismo, que merece en esta circunstancia destacarse . . . : el hecho de que en un mismo relicario estén un trozo de la cruz

y a los pies las reliquias de la titular de la Parroquia. En la cúspide la cruz y sus pies la mártir." He does not clarify what that symbolism is.

34. I inspected the base on 17 May 1999. The inscription goes around the four sides and reads: (front) FRANCISCVS DE LA PALMA HVRDO HV ECCLAE EVLALIAE ROR; (right) PVERI AD VITAM MIRACVLOSE REVOCATI; (back) ET PROPRIAE SALUTIS MIRABILITER RECVPERATAE MEMOR; (left) S.S. LIGNUM SVIS SUMPTIB9 ORNABAT A.D. MDCXXXVI. (Francisco de la Palma Hurtado, rector of this church of Eulalia . . . in memory of the boy whose life was returned miraculously . . . and of his own health wondrously recuperated . . . this most sacred wood ornamented from his own resources A.D. 1636—my translation.). Apparently a boy was miraculously cured on Corpus Christi in 1481, and the memory of this event was venerated by Hurtado. See Carrillo Morales, "Las Reliquias de Santa Eulalia," 2.

35. The inscription reads: OSA ET CINERES S. EULALIAE (bones and ashes of Saint Eulalia). Carrillo Morales, "Las Reliquias de Santa Eulalia," 2.

36. For the art and architecture of the baroque era in Spain, see Susan Verdi Webster, *Art and Ritual in Golden-Age Spain* (Princeton, NJ: Princeton University Press, 1998), 59, 82–83.

37. Carrillo Morales, interview by author, Toledo, 17 May 1999.

38. Carrillo Morales, "Las Reliquias de Santa Eulalia," 3. My translation of "En orden a . . . devolver el Lignum Crucis al lugar que le corresponde."

39. Carrillo Morales, "Las Reliquias de Santa Eulalia," 3.

40. Carrillo Morales, "Las Reliquias de Santa Eulalia," 3. My partial translation of "En la capilla del Santísimo, no sólo por las razones históricas ya indicadas, sino litúrgicas, que son sin duda las que sostienen a aquellas, sobre el tabernáculo el Lignum Crucis, que por la veneración singular que le presta la liturgia católica, se asimila y auna con la que presta la Iglesia a la presencia de Jesús Sacramentado."

41. For the origin and use of Spanish crucifixes in Holy Week processions, see Webster, 73, 89–99.

42. "La cruz mozárabe," *CM* 1 (1969): 3.

43. *Constituciones* (1999), art. 4 (19).

44. *Constituciones* (1999), arts. 12 and 20 (22, 23–24).

45. See, for example, K. A. Kitchen, "Serpent, Bronze," in *Illustrated Bible Dictionary*, 3:1422. Kitchen refers to Numbers 21:4–9, John 3:14, and 1 Corinthians 10:9, 11, as the basis for seeing Moses' bronzed serpent as an archetype of the cross.

46. Overbeck, 305.

7. THE RITUAL USE OF THE LIGNUM CRUCIS ON GOOD FRIDAY

1. The description is based on my observations and notes, as well as videotape taken by my research assistants, Roland Morin and Leon Zalewski, at the Santa Eulalia Holy Week services, 1–3 April 1999.

2. Carrillo Morales, interview, 29 May 1999.

3. Victor Turner, *The Ritual Process: Structure and Anti-Structure* (Ithaca, NY: Cornell University Press, 1991), 95–97. Turner includes the concepts of liminality, ritual process, and *communitas* in his notion of social drama.

4. The hymn was composed by F. X. Moreau. Another version under the title "Tú reinarás" is available in the hymnal *Flor y Canto* (Portland, OR: OCP Pub., 1989), no. 194.

5. Turner, 96–97, 126–29. Turner refers to the bonding that takes place among those undergoing the same process, such as an ordeal in a rite of passage.

6. See J. O'Connell, *The Rite of High Mass and Sung Mass,* vol. 3 of *The Celebration of the Mass: A Study of the Rubrics of the Roman Missal* (Milwaukee: Bruce Pub. Co., 1940), 34.

7. O'Connell, 26.

8. Carrillo Morales, interview, 17 May 1999. The Cisneros and Lorenzana Missals also describe a procession with the Lignum Crucis.

9. Morin, *Ad tertiam* videotape, 2 April 1999. My paraphrase and translation of "En esta liturgia he tratado de ser fiel a esta tradición nuestra católica española."

10. Morin, *Ad tertiam* videotape, 2 April 1999; Carrillo Morales, interview, 17 May 1999. My paraphrase and translation of "Cristo dio por rosas, mártires; por azucenas, vírgenes; y por morigerados, violetas."

11. Carrillo Morales, interview, 17 May 1999.

12. Lozano Durán, interview, 2 June 1999. My translation of "Soy pendiente de que no se le olvide nada a Don Enrique ya que tiene esa tendencia."

13. Carrillo Morales, interview, 29 May 1999. See "Vexilla Regis prodeunt," Ad Vesperas Dominicum I Passionis, *Liber Usualis Missæ et Officii Pro Dominicis et Festis cum cantu gregoriano ex editione Vaticana Adamussim excerpto et Rhythmicis Signis in Subsidium Cantorum A Solesmensibus Monachis Diligenter Ornato* (Paris: Desclée et Socii; Rome: S. Sedis Apostolicæ et Sacrorum Rituum Congregationis Typographi, 1958), 575–76.

14. Carrillo Morales, interview, 29 May 1999.

15. John H. McKenna, C.M., "Adoration, Theology of," in *New Dictionary of Sacramental Worship*, 27.

16. Ritual follows a process that takes time and effort, following certain steps in order to be accomplished. See Ronald Grimes, *Reading, Writing, and Ritualizing: Ritual in Fictive, Liturgical, and Public Places* (Washington DC: Pastoral Press, 1993), 6, 8, 17.

17. Lozano Durán, interview, 2 June 1999. My translation of "La manera en que Don Enrique trae el Lignum Crucis con capa y velo significa que es un acto muy importante."

18. Lozano Durán, interview, 2 June 1999. My translation of "Me doy cuenta de que la manera en que se trata el relicario quiere decir que el santísimo y el Lignum Crucis tienen la misma importancia."

19. Lozano Durán interview. My translation of "Hay dos ocasiones que no se pierde Felipe, primero ir de procesión con su custodia y segundo ir de procesión el Viernes Santo con su Lignum Crucis; es como si fuese su santísimo."

20. Carrillo Morales, interview, 19 September 1999.

21. *LO,* 199n1 (he says the council was held in 638; however, Toledo VI was held then); Vives, canon 55 (p. 210) (he gives the correct date of Toledo IV); see also DS 485, 490.

22. Jorge Perales, "The Service of the *Indulgentia*: Light on the Rite of General Confession and Absolution," *Worship* 62 (1988): 140. See also *Ordo Penitentie*, in *LO*, cols. 87–92; *Ordo ad Reconciliandum Penitentem*, in *LO*, cols. 96–100; *LO*, cols. 199–204; the *Oracional Visigótico* (267–68); and the *Liber Misticus* (88–94).

23. See *Missale mixtum*, folios CLXVII–CLXXIIII (see *LMCP*, xxx).

24. The *Liber Ordinum* does not contain the complete service but appears to have only those elements that vary from a typical Nones service during Lent (*LO*, cols. 199–204). The source for the contemporary service is found in the *Liber Misticus*, 88–94.

25. *Triduo Sacro*, 51–52, 117–51.

26. See *Triduo Sacro*, 127.

27. *Triduo Sacro*, 129.

28. *Triduo Sacro*, 131, 133 (Latin version: 130, 132).

29. *LO*, 200–202; Vives, canon 7 (p. 193).

30. *Triduo Sacro*, 133. My translation of "Porque nuestro Señor oirá, de seguro, la voz de nuestra petición, si ve la sincera devoción de nuestra alma."

31. My paraphrase and translation of the beginning of the prayer: "Oh Hijo unigénito de Dios Padre, de quien hace ya muchísimos años cantó este verso el profeta: 'Serás reconocido en medio de dos animales'; eres ciertamente conocido no sólo al estar colgado en la cruz entre dos ladrones, o entre los dos Testamentos." See *Triduo Sacro*, 147; Worship Aid II, 11.

32. Baldovin, 84.

33. *Egeria*, chaps. 30–38 (103–14). See also Baldovin, 55–64; Kenneth Stevenson, *Jerusalem Revisited: The Liturgical Meaning of Holy Week* (Washington DC: Pastoral Press, 1988), 3–8, 15–20.

34. Grimes, *Reading, Writing, and Ritualizing*, 63.

35. Grimes, *Reading, Writing, and Ritualizing*, 63.

36. Grimes, *Reading, Writing, and Ritualizing*, 63–64; Grimes, *Beginnings in Ritual Studies*, 27.

37. Grimes, *Reading, Writing, and Ritualizing*, 63–64.

38. Keay, 162–65. He cites second-century Latin writer Apuleius *(The Golden Ass)* as a source for information about the processions and related practices.

39. Keay, 165.

40. For a survey of the different religions, their practices, and their appeal in the late Roman Empire and in Hispania, see Keay, chap. 7; Sotomayor, "La Iglesia y la España romana," 23–31.

41. For Christian adaptation of pagan practices in the third to fifth centuries, see Herman Wegman, *Christian Worship in East and West: A Study Guide to Liturgical History* (Collegeville, MN: Liturgical Press, 1990), 53; Geoffrey Wainwright, "The Periods of Liturgical History," in *The Study of Liturgy*, rev.

ed., ed. Cheslyn Jones et al. (New York: Oxford University Press, 1992), 63; Jungmann, *Early Liturgy*, chap. 11; Baldovin, 85, 164.

42. Baldovin, 85, citing Wilkinson, *Jerusalem Pilgrims before the Crusades*, 34.

43. Baldovin, 165.

44. Baldovin, 160. In note 75 he cites Ildephonso Schuster, *The Sacramentary (Liber sacramentorum): Historical and Liturgical Notes on the Roman Missal*, 5 vols. (New York: Benzinger Bros., 1924–30), 1:220: "Here was the liturgy moving out into the open to meet the needs of God's family and attract popular attention by song and scenic effect."

45. For the texts of the Council of Elvira, see Vives, 1–15.

46. Baldovin, 158–60.

47. Jaime Lara, "The Liturgical Roots of Hispanic Popular Religiosity," in *Misa, Mesa y Musa: Liturgy in the U.S. Hispanic Church*, ed. Kenneth G. Davis, O.F.M.Conv. (Schiller Park, IL: World Library Publications, 1997), 31.

48. Lara, "Liturgical Roots," 29, 31.

49. See *Semana Santa Toledo '99: Programa de Actos y Cultos*, booklet (Toledo: Junta de Cofradías y Hermandades de Semana Santa de Toledo, 1999; *Semana Santa '99 Toledo: Programa de Actos y Cultos*, pamphlet (Toledo: Junta de Comunidades de Castilla-La Mancha, Asociación Provincial de Empresarios de Hostelería de Toledo, 1999). These are the official programs for 1999.

50. Congregation for Divine Worship and the Discipline of the Sacraments, *Directory on Popular Piety and the Liturgy: Principles and Guidelines* (Boston: Pauline Books and Media, 2002), nos. 245–47.

51. Grimes, *Beginnings in Ritual Studies*, 51–53.

52. Descriptions of the groups and *pasos* are in *Semana Santa '99* booklet, 17–19, pamphlet, 7–10. On the development of Spanish *cofradías*, see Antonio Mestre Sanchis, "Religión y cultura en el siglo XVIII español," BAC 4:596–98; Ricardo García-Villoslada, *Historia de la Iglesia Católica: En sus cinco grandes edades: Antigua, Media, Nueva, Moderna y Contemporánea*, vol. 2 of *Edad Media (800–1303): La cristiandad en el mundo europeo y feudal*, 5th ed. (Madrid: BAC, 1988), 852–55.

53. For the link between *cofradías* and their images, see Mestre Sanchis, 596–97.

54. See Roth, *The Spanish Inquisition*, 109–10, 268.

55. *Semana Santa '99* booklet, 19, pamphlet, 10: the programs erroneously say they accompany the Sorrowful Mother. They actually escort the *Hermandad Mozárabe*, as indicated in the pamphlet, 6.

56. Lozano Durán, interview, 2 June 1999.

57. See Marcelo González Martín, "Decreto sobre el 'Lignum Crucis' de la Parroquia Mozárabe de Santa Eulalia y San Marcos," *BOAT* 132 (1976), 208–9; repr. *CM* 20 (1987): 4–5.

58. See *Semana Santa '99* booklet, 15.

59. Jurado Lozano, interview, 2 June 1999.

60. *Constituciones* (1984), art. 5; *Constituciones* (1999), arts. 14, 25.

61. Jurado Lozano family, interview, 2 June 1999. My combination and translation of statements made by different members of the family: "Es un acto de recogimiento. Significa acompañar al Lignum Crucis. Es completar la penitencia."

62. Arellano García, interview, 20 May 1999. My translation of "Es el elemento más importante de la procesión de Viernes Santo puesto que es la reliquia auténtica de la cruz. Lo demás es solamente imágenes."

63. Cf. *Constituciones* (1984), arts. 1, 5; *Constituciones* (1999), art. 13.

64. Bernard J. F. Lonergan, *Method in Theology* (Toronto: University of Toronto Press, 1971), 64.

65. Lonergan, 32.

66. Rev. Thomas Knoebel, academic dean, Sacred Heart School of Theology, Hales Corners, WI, to author, 4 January 2000. Narrative reflecting on the ritual use of the Lignum Crucis. Transcript in the hand of Rev. Thomas Knoebel.

67. See *Semana Santa '99* booklet and pamphlet for the schedule of liturgical events and processions (Monday, 15 March through Easter Sunday, 4 April 1999).

68. Arellano García interview, 20 May 1999. My translation of "Llevar el *Lignum Crucis* en procesión es hacer un homenaje público aunque hay un acto en la iglesia. En la iglesia es más íntimo ya que solamente los que están allí veneran la reliquia, pero cuando vamos de procesión se convierte en un acto de fe público."

8. CHRISTOLOGICAL CONTROVERSY AND OTHODOXY

1. Harold O. J. Brown, *Heresies: The Image of Christ in the Mirror of Heresy and Orthodoxy from the Apostles to the Present* (Garden City, NJ: Doubleday, 1984), 165, 459n6. Also see J. N. D. Kelly, *Early Christian Doctrines*, 2nd ed. (New York: Harper and Row, 1979), 375–77, 386–90.

2. See *The Correspondence of Pope Gregory VII: Selected Letters from the Registrum*, trans. Ephraim Emerton, Records of Western Civilization Series (New York: Columbia University Press, 1990 <1932>).

3. O'Callaghan, *A History of Medieval Spain*, 81; Vives, 456 (a summary of Julian's *Confessione fidei* is in the *acta* of Toledo XV [688]). Also see PL 96.525–36.

4. Vives, 449–74.

5. John C. Cavadini, *The Last Christology of the West: Adoptionism in Spain and Gaul 785–820* (Philadelphia: University of Pennsylvania Press, 1993), 1, 24. Cf. Juan Manuel Sierra, "Contexto teológico y espiritual del rito hispano-mozárabe," in *Curso de Liturgia Hispano-Mozárabe*, ed. Juan-Miguel Ferrer Grenesche (Toledo: Estudio Teológico de San Ildefonso, Seminario Conciliar, 1995), 113. Sierra gives 794 for the Council of Frankfurt.

6. Cavadini, 24, 80–81, 83, 105.

7. J. N. Hillgarth, "Priscillian" and "Priscillianism," in *New Catholic Encyclopedia*, 2nd ed. (2003), 11:719–20. Also Manuel Sotomayor, "El priscilianismo," BAC 1:233–72; Sierra, 101–2.

8. Salisbury, 192; Sotomayor, "El priscilianismo," 238.

9. Vives, canons 1, 2, 7 (pp. 16–18).

10. Anne M. Clifford, "Creation," in *Systematic Theology: Roman Catholic Perspectives*, ed. Francis Schüssler Fiorenza and John P. Galvin (Minneapolis: Fortress Press, 1991), 1:214.

11. Salisbury, 192–93.

12. J. Stevenson, ed., *Creeds, Councils, and Controversies: Documents Illustrative of the History of the Church A.D. 337–461* (London: S.P.C.K., 1978 <1966>, 153–54.

13. Salisbury, 214. In 226n90 she cites as the source of her speculation Henry Chadwick, *Priscillian of Avila* (Oxford: Oxford University Press, 1976), 233.

14. Hillgarth, "Priscillianism."

15. Sierra, 102.

16. Hillgarth, "Priscillianism"; cf. Sierra, 101.

17. Regarding the Spanish church's concerns about Priscillianism, see Eugenio Romero-Pose, "Trasfondo teológico del III Concilio de Toledo," in *Concilio III de Toledo: XIV Centenario 589–1989*, 361.

18. Vives, canon 21 (pp. 25–26); eighteen anathemas (pp. 26–28); profession of faith by Priscillianist bishops (pp. 28–33).

19. "Commonitorium de errore Priscillianistarum et Origenistarum," in *Paulus Orosius, The Seven Books of History against the Pagans*, trans. Roy J. Deferrari (Washington DC: CUA Press, 1964), xv, xvi. Orosius wrote this letter to Saint Augustine, who responded by writing *Contra Priscillianistas et Origenistas*. See PL 42–43.665–89 for Orosius's letter to Augustine; PL 42–43.670–89 for Augustine's letter to Orosius.

20. Sotomayor, "El priscilianismo," 256, 261–64, 268.

21. Vives, 65–69.

22. Salisbury, 200, 201, 206, 214–15, 236–37. Regarding the incorporation of pagan practices into liturgy, see Jungmann, *Early Liturgy*, 164–66.

23. See *LO*, 63–64, 162–64, 166–70; González, "Vida Cristiana y Cura Pastoral," 608–11.

24. Pinell, *Liturgia hispánica*, 25, 27, 28–29; "Prenotandos," *Missale* 1, nos. 1, 2, 3, 6, 9; González, "Vida Cristiana y Cura Pastoral," 579–85.

25. M. L. Cozens, *A Handbook of Heresies*, abridged ed. (New York: Sheed and Ward, 1928), 30–31.

26. Cf. Walter Kasper, *Jesus the Christ* (New York: Paulist Press, 1976), 176.

27. Brown, 116.

28. Cf. J. N. D. Kelly, *Early Christian Creeds*, 3rd ed. (London: Longman Group, 1972), 296–98; Manuel Sotomayor, "El donatismo y la crisis arriana. Osio de Córdoba, Potamio de Lisboa y Gregorio de Granada," BAC 1:196.

29. Stevenson, *Creeds, Councils, and Controversies*, 160–61; the legislation is found in the *Codex Theodosianus*. Stevenson provides translations of "The Edict on the Profession of the Catholic Faith, 380" (*Cod. Theod.* XVI 1.2) and "The Effective Prohibition of Paganism, 391" (*Cod. Theod.* XVI 10.10).

30. Brown, 138.

31. Wolfram, 22, 74, 75–85; Jones, 169–70.

32. Wolfram, 84–85; Wolfram cites Auxentius (*Max. diss.* 63) (413n 331); Wilhelm Streitberg, *Die gotische Bibel*, vols. 1 and 2, 6th ed. (Darmstadt, 1971), 1:xvii; cf. Adolf Lippold, "Ulfila," in *Realencyclopädie der classischen Altertumswissenschaften* (RE), II (Stuttgart, 1893ff.), 524–26.

33. Jones, 207; José Orlandis Rovira, "El significado del Concilio III de Toledo en la Historia Hispánica y Universal," in *Concilio III de Toledo: XIV Centenario 589–1989*, 326–27.

34. Vives, Toledo III, anathemas 12, 13, and 14 (p. 119): Anathema 12 states: "Quiquumque Patrem et Filium et Spiritum Sanctum honore et gloria et divinitate separat et disiungit, anathema sit."

35. Vives, Toledo III, anathema 16 (p. 119): "Quiquumque libellum detestabilem duodecimo anno Leovigildi regis a nobis editum, in quo continetur Romanorum ad hæresem Arrianam transductio, et in quo gloria Patri per Filium in Spiritu Sancto male a nobis instituta continetur; hunc libellum si quis pro vero habuerit, anathema sit in æternum."

36. Vives, canon 2 (p. 125); Jordi Pinell, "Credo y comunión en la estructura de la misa hispánica según disposición del III Concilio de Toledo," *Concilio III de Toledo: XIV Centenario 589–1989*, 333–42.

37. Vives, 118–21.

38. See DS 150, 470; Kelly, *Early Christian Creeds*, 358–67.

39. Brown, 222. Also see Catherine Mowry LaCugna, "The Trinitarian Mystery of God," in Schüssler Fiorenza and Galvin, *Systematic Theology*, 1:184n89.

40. Cavadini, 1; Brown, 95.

41. Brown, 222.

42. See Vives, 345, 346–54.

43. Cavadini, 6.

44. Cavadini, 4.

45. Cavadini, 19; *Elipandi Epistolæ Ad Megetium Hæreticum* (PL 96.859–67).

46. Though Beatus's tract against Elipandus brought attention to the controversy, he is better remembered for the illuminations in his "Commentary on the Apocalypse" *(Beati in Apocalipsin libri duodecim)* than for his theology. This latter book was written about ten years before the Adoptionist controversy (c. 774–83); it was recopied often, so that it could be re-illustrated, thus generating a genre called the *Beatus*. See John W. Williams, "Orientations: Christian Spain and the Art of Its Neighbors," in *Art of Medieval Spain A.D. 500–1200*, ed. John P. O'Neill (New York: Metropolitan Museum of Art, 1993), 19; Achim Arbeiter and Sabine Noack-Haley, "The Kingdom of Asturias," in *The Art of Medieval Spain* (New York: Metropolitan Museum of Art, 1993), 113.

47. Cavadini gives the name of this bishop as Heterius (25, 45, 167n8, 169n16). Brown gives the name as Etherius (223). The Spanish version is Eterio (Rivera Recio, "La iglesia mozárabe," 40). None gives dates for him.

48. Cavadini, 27–31, 36.

49. Cavadini, 34–35; *Elipandi Epistolæ* (PL 96): III, *Ad Carolum Magnum* (867–69); IV, *Ad Albinum* (871–74); and V, *Ad Felicem Nuper Conversum* (880–82).

50. Cavadini, 36–37. Philippians 2:6–7 is key to Elipandus's theology.

51. Cavadini, 35.

52. Cavadini, 71. Also see Rivera Recio, "La iglesia mozárabe," 38.

53. Cavadini, 71–72.

54. Cavadini, 96–102. Also see Sierra, 114.

55. Cavadini, 100.

56. Brown, 224–25.

57. Cavadini, 2–4, 69–70.

58. See *Elipandi Epistolæ*, IV: *Ad Albinum* (PL 96.874–75).

59. Alcuin, *Adversus Elipandum Hæresin* (PL 101.17–120; 119–230) and *Adversus Elipandum, liber secundum* (PL 101.257–70).

60. O'Callaghan, *A History of Medieval Spain*, 187.

61. Walker, 25–26.

62. PL 96.893–1032.

63. Cavadini, 3.

64. Cavadini, 3.

65. Sierra, 99.

66. See, among others, Haines, 33; Brown, 226; O'Callaghan, *A History of Medieval Spain*, 186; Rivera Recio, "La iglesia mozárabe," 33–37.

67. Cavadini, 68–70, 105. Also see Vicens Vives, 30n2.

68. Colomina Torner, interview, 23 September 1999; Sánchez, interviews, 28 June 1996 and 24 September 1999. Also see José Janini, "Libros Litúrgicos mozárabes de Toledo conquistador," in *Estudios Sobre Alfonso VI*, 49, 24–25; Jaime Colomina, "Hacia la actualización del rito mozárabe," *CM* 11 (1984): 1–3; Cleofé Sánchez Montealegre, "De 5 de Enero de 1500 a 17 de Noviembre de 1991," *CM* 31 (1991): 100–102. Also see *CM* 32 (1992): passim.

69. Balbino Gómez-Chacón, "La última revisión del rito hispano-mozárabe," *CM* 32 (1992): 130–33. He states that the commission has attempted to present a new *Missale* that would be as close to a new critical edition as possible.

9.   THE CHRISTOLOGY AND SOTERIOLOGY OF THE TEXTS

1. *LO*, xvi–xvii.

2. Worship Aid I and Worship Aid II.

3. *Semana Santa '99* booklet and *Semana Santa '99* pamphlet.

4. *Missale* 1 (1991) and the *Liber Commicus* 1 (1991). Also, *LO*, LXXXIIII—Ordo de VI Feria in Parasceve, 193–204; and *LMCP*.

5. Worship Aid I, 1. The title page states that the official texts are in "Feria VI in Parasceve," *Missale*, 1:345–51.

6. Worship Aid I, 3. My translation.

7. Worship Aid I, 4–5.

8. The *Missale*, 1:345, suggests that verses 1–4 and 5–8 of Psalm 113 can be sung between the antiphons above if the procession route is long *(Si iter longior est, vv. 1–4 et 5–8 psalm 113 In exitu Israel psallere potest inter antiphonas)*. However, as noted, Don Enrique chose a recently composed hymn to sing instead.

9. Worship Aid I, 5. My interpretation of "El Verbo en ti clavado, muriendo nos rescató/ Extiende por el mundo/ tu Reino de salvación/ Impere sobre el odio/ Aumenta en nuestras almas/ tu Reino de santidad/ Su cruz nos lleve al cielo,/ la tierra de promisión."

10. "Mirad el glorioso leño, del que hace algún tiempo pendieron los miembros de Cristo Salvador, redentores del mundo. Venid a postraros aquí, presentando con lágrimas vuestras peticiones" (Worship Aid I, 6). "Ecce lignum gloriósum, in quo dudum pensa sunt Christi Salvatóris mundum rediméntia. Fletu producéntes omnes preces hic prostérnite" *(Missale*, 1:345).

11. *Missale*, 1:142–43.

12. *Missale*, 1:143. Take note that the Latin says *continentes* (the pure); D. Enrique in his oral explanation of the ritual used the word *penitentes* (penitents) instead. I use the word *pure* as found in the documents.

13. *Missale*, 1:143: "Hæc ad illum, per minístros voluntátis eius apóstolos, confécta óperis sui pensa transmísit."

14. *Missale*, 1:346–49: "Versus de Ligno Domini." See also *LO*, 195–99: Férotin lists two hymns for the veneration of the cross; this is the second of the two.

15. *Liber Usualis*, 575–76.

16. Carrillo Morales, interview, 29 May 1999. See also Enrique Carrillo Morales, *Música y Capellanes Mozárabes: Discurso de apertura del Curso 1991–1992* (Toledo: Seminario Conciliar, Estudio Teológico de San Ildefonso, 1991), 6–8, 20–21.

17. Joseph Connelly, *Hymns of the Roman Liturgy* (London: Longmans, Green and Co., 1957), 80.

18. *Liber Usualis*, 576: *Te, fons salútis Trínitas, Colláudet ómnis spíritus: Quíbus Crúcis victóriam Largíris, ádde praémium.*

19. "God reigned on the tree." Connelly, 80. The latter verse is in the *Liber Usualis*, but the former is not.

20. *Apologia prima pro Christianis (Apol. 1, 41)* (PG 6.391).

21. For example, the three antiphons at the onset of the *Ad tertiam* liturgy appear in the *Antifonario Visigótico-Mozárabe de la Catedral de León*, ed. Louis Brou and José Vives, Monumenta Hispaniæ Sacra, Serie Litúrgica, vol. V, 1 (Barcelona-Madrid: Consejo Superior de Investigaciones Científicas, Instituto P. Enrique Flórez, 1959), fol. 166 v, 271–72; *Missale*, 1:345.

22. *Liber Usualis*, 575: "Quæ vulneráta lánceæ Mucróne díro, críminum Ut nos laváret sórdibus, Manávit unda et sánguine."

23. Jaroslav Pelikan, *Jesus through the Centuries: His Place in the History of Culture* (New York: Harper and Row, 1987), 100–101.

24. Worship Aid I, 6–8.

25. *Missale*, 1:350.

26. Worship Aid I, 7. My translations of "Feraz y poderoso, para nosotros o dulce madero, que llevas en tus ramas frutos tan nuevos" (verse 4) and "Extiendes tus ramas adornadas con flores nuevas" (verse 5).

27. Worship Aid I, 6. My translation of "Humilde en su amor piadoso. . . . hecho víctima por nosotros, de las fauces del lobo arrancó a sus oveja [*sic*] el sagrado cordero."

28. Worship Aid I, 6. My translation of "Con sus manos traspasadas, de la calamidad al mundo redimió, y tras sus despojos el camino de la muerte cerró."

29. Worship Aid I, 6. My translation of "Aquí la mano ensangrentada forjó aquella llave, que a Pablo y a Pedro de su culpa de la muerte arrancó."

30. Worship Aid I, 7. My translation of "Entre tus brazos está colgada la vid, de la que fluyen sabrosos vinos purpúreos como sangre."

31. Worship Aid I, 8: "Señor Jesucristo, glorioso creador del mundo, que sinedo [*sic*] el esplendor de la gloria, igual al Padre y al Espíritu Santo, y has permitido clavar al patíbulo de la cruz tus manos gloriosas." Cf. *LO*, 199; *Missale*, 1:351: "Dómine Iesu Christe, glorióse cónditor mundi, qui cum sis splendor glóriæ, æquális Patri Sanctóque Spirítui, carnem inmaculátam assúmere dignátus es, et gloriósas tuas sanctas palmas in crucis patíbulum permisísti confígere."

32. Worship Aid I, 8: "Te has dignado asumir una carne inmaculada." *Missale*, 1:351: "Carnem inmaculátam assúmere dignátus es." *LO*, 190: "Carnem inmaculatam adsumere digantus es."

33. Worship Aid I, 8: "ten misericordia de nosotros manchados por la culpa, oprimidos por los pecados."

34. Worship Aid I, 8: "para que merezcamos en estas solemnidades sagradas, estar inmaculados ante tí [*sic*]."

35. "Feria VI in Parasceve, Ad nonam pro indulgentia," *Missale*, 1:352–68; *Liber Commicus*, 1:256–77; *Triduo Sacro*, 117–51; "Sagrados Oficios," 30–34; Worship Aid II. The *Missale* and *Liber Commicus* give texts for Year I and Year II. The worship aid used at Santa Eulalia follows Year I, as does the presider's worship aid, "Sagrados Oficios." This follows Janini's critical edition of the texts from Toledo found in *LMCP*, 88–94.

36. "Sagrados Oficios," 30; *Triduo Sacro*, 117; *LO*, 194; *Missale*, 1:352. The official text reads: "Eo vero die, hora nona, signum sonat; et hora legitimæ Nonæ ingrediendum est ad officium, quando legimus Christum in cruce positum emisisse spiritum. Et discinctis religiosis omnibus, lignum sanctæ Crucis levatur a diacono in patena ad præparatorium, precedendo celebrantem ante Evangelium sine cooperturio. Ingressus in ecclesia fit sub silentio, et mox ut ipsum Lignum positum fuerit super altare, et celebrans cum ministris ascenderint ad sedes, a lectore incipiatur prima lectio (anno primo), vel imponatur a celebrante versus "Popule meus" (anno secundo)."

37. Cf. Worship Aid II, 1; *Triduo Sacro*, 117; "Sagrados Oficios," 30. These give Proverbs 9:24–27 instead of 3:24–26, as found in *LMCP*, 88, and *Liber Commicus*, 1:256.

38. "Porque el Señor será tu confianza y preservará tu pie de quedar preso" (Prv 3:26). Cf. NAB and NRSV—the former uses the word *security* in place of *confidence*. See *Triduo Sacro,* 117; "Sagrados Oficios," 30.

39. *Liber Commicus,* 1:258–59.

40. My translation of "El justo, mi siervo, justificará a muchos, y cargará con las iniquidades de ellos." Cf. "Out of his anguish he shall see light;/ he shall find satisfaction through his knowledge./ The righteous one, my servant, shall make many righteous,/ and he shall bear their iniquities" (Is 53:11, NRSV).

41. *Liber Commicus,* 1:260–61.

42. "Sagrados Oficios," 34. *Triduo Sacro,* 125: "¿No hay entre vosotros algún prudente capaz de ser juez entre hermanos? En vez de esto, ¿pleitea el hermano contra el hermano, y esto ante los infieles? Ya es una mengua que tengáis pleitos unos con otros. ¿Por qué no preferís sufrir la injusticia? ¿Por qué no ser despojados? Cf. "And this is what some of you used to be. But you were washed, you were sanctified, you were justified in the name of the Lord Jesus Christ and in the Spirit of our God" (1 Cor 6:11, NRSV).

43. "Sagrados Oficios," 34. *Triduo Sacro,* 125, where in Spanish it is given as 1 Cor 6:12: "Y algunos érais [*sic*] esto, pero habéis sido lavados, habéis sido santificados, habéis sido justificados en el nombre del Señor Jesucristo y por el Espíritu de nuestro Dios."

44. *Triduo Sacro,* 127–31; "Sagrados Oficios," 35–37; *Liber Commicus,* 1:261–64.

45. My translation of "El que lo vio da testimonio, y su testimonio es verdadero. Y nosotros creemos que esto es verdad, y creyendo, tendremos vida en su nombre" (attributed to Jn 20:30–31). The Spanish version appears to be a gloss on John 20:30–31. Cf. "Now Jesus did many other signs in the presence of his disciples, which are not written in this book. But these are written so that you may come to believe that Jesus is the Messiah, the Son of God, and that through believing you may have life in his name" (John 20:30–31, NRSV). Cf. *Liber Commicus,* 1:264: "Et qui vidit, testimónium perhíbuit, et verum est testimónium eius. Et nos crédimus, quia verum est, ut credéntes vitam habeámus in nómine eius."

46. *Liber Commicus,* 1:257.

47. Cf. *Liber Commicus,* 1:259: Ps 21:2–3; 7–23. The English translation of the verses provided in the body of the paragraph is mine.

48. Vives, canon 7 (p. 193).

49. *LO,* 200–201; *Liber Commicus,* 1:275–77.

50. "Sagrados Oficios," 38; *Triduo Sacro,* 133. My translation of the response.

51. "Sagrados Oficios," 37; *Triduo Sacro,* 131. My paraphrase of "Hoy, Dios nuestro Señor, puso en la balanza el precio de nuestra salvación, y con su muerte humana redimió al mundo entero."

52. "Sagrados Oficios," 37; *Triduo Sacro,* 131. My paraphrase of "El que no tenía pecados propios, llevó dignamente los ajenos."

53. "Sagrados Oficios," 37; *Triduo Sacro*, 131. "Entregué mis espaldas a los que me herían y no escondí mi rostro ante las injurias y salivazos" (Is 50:6, English translation from NRSV).

54. "Sagrados Oficios," 38; *Triduo Sacro*, 133. My translation of "recibió nuestros males, para darnos sus bienes."

55. "Sagrados Oficios," 38; *Triduo Sacro*, 133. My translation of "Pues, ¿qué voy a decir de la piedad de aquél [*sic*], que, para que nadie desespere, recibe en su paraíso al ladrón que, al morir, le confiesa?" The word *confesar* can mean "to confess," "to acknowledge," "to proclaim," or "to give witness to."

56. "Sagrados Oficios," 38; *Triduo Sacro*, 133: my translation of "Porque nuestro Señor oirá, de seguro, la voz de nuestra petición, si ve la sincera devoción de nuestra alma."

57. Vives, canon 7 (p. 193): "Ideoque oportet eodem die mysterium crucis, quod ipse Dominus cunctis adnuntiandum voluit, prædicare, atque indulgentiam criminum clara voce omnem populum postulare, ut poenitentiæ compunctione mundati venerabilem diem dominicæ resurrectionis remissis iniquitatibus suscipere mereamur, corporisque eius et sanguinis sacramentum mundati a peccato sumamus."

58. See Worship Aid II, 4–10. Cf. "Annus primus," *Missale*, 1:352–60; *Triduo Sacro*, 133–45; "Sagrados Oficios," 38–44.

59. Worship Aid II, 4; "Sagrados Oficios," 38; *Triduo Sacro*, 133. My translation of "Roguemos a Dios nuestro Señor que se digne concedernos indulgencia para nuestros crímenes y perdón para nuestros pecados."

60. Worship Aid II, 4; "Sagrados Oficios," 39; *Triduo Sacro*, 135; *Missale*, 1:353.

61. Worship Aid II, 5; "Sagrados Oficios," 39–40; *Triduo Sacro*, 135, 137 (the subject of the petitions shifts from "us" to "those").

62. Worship Aid II, 6; "Sagrados Oficios," 40; *Triduo Sacro*, 137. My translation of "cuya preciosa sangre fue atormentada por los judíos, mofada por los ingratos y crucificada al igual que la de los ladrones."

63. Worship Aid II, 6. My translation of "pero ¿no es admirable entender que también manara agua?"

64. Worship Aid II, 6. My translation of "Esta es ciertamente el agua que, manando de su cuerpo, sirve para regenerar y dar vida nueva a los que habíamos muerto en Adán."

65. Worship Aid II, 6. "Through your mercy, our God, who lives with God the Father, and reigns with the Holy Spirit, forever and ever." My translation of "Por tu misericordia, Dios nuestro, que vives con Dios Padre, y reinas con el Espíritu Santo, por los siglos de los siglos."

66. Worship Aid II, 7. My paraphrase of "Para ello, extendiste en la cruz tus propias manos, para devolvernos piadoso, al árbol de la vida; del que Adán no mereció comer, por el pecado de la prevaricación; tu cruz, oh Dios, que es el árbol de la vida, vivifique a cuantos gusten de ella."

67. Worship Aid II, 8–9; "Sagrados Oficios," 42–43; *Triduo Sacro*, 141, 143; *Missale*, 1:357–58 (Ps 50:3–21).

68. Vives, canon 15 (pp. 197–98). Although the latter decrees that the *Gloria* be recited after the joyful psalms, *Missale* (vol. 1) and *LO* indicate it is to complete Psalm 50 in this liturgy.

69. Worship Aid II, 11. My paraphrase of "Eres ciertamente conocido no sólo al estar colgado en la cruz entre dos ladrones, o entre los dos Testamentos; sino también al oscurecerse el sol, al apagarse el día, al temblar la tierra; Tú, Cristo, bajaste a los infiernos, y los sepulcros de los santos se abrieron. Pedimos tu misericordia, para que podamos entender cuánto es lo que, ya resucitado, nos vas a dar en tu reino, tú, que al morir, nos resucitaste del infierno para la gloria."

70. Worship Aid II, 11–12.

71. See Gail Ramshaw-Schmidt, *Christ in Sacred Speech: The Meaning of Liturgical Language* (Philadelphia: Fortress Press, 1986), 6–18, 84–85; Paul Ricoeur, *Interpretation Theory: Discourse and the Surplus of Meaning* (Fort Worth: Texas Christian University Press, 1976), 62–63; David Tracy, *Plurality and Ambiguity: Hermeneutics, Religion, Hope* (Chicago: University of Chicago Press, 1994), 73, 76–77, 79, 90, 96, 101.

72. Manuel Lanza Alandi, "Introducción," *Semana Santa '99* booklet, 2. My translation of "Desde la Junta de Cofradías y Hermandades de Toledo os invitamos a todos los de buena voluntad a compartir con nosotros, en nuestras iglesias, en el gran templo, en nuestra Catedral, la Liturgia del Amor del Padre de la Misericordia y del Sacrificio del Hijo. Después, en las calles, acompañar o simplemente contemplar el paso de los desfiles procesionales en los que cada hermandad o cofradía pondrá su oración, su silencio, su devoción. Muy conscientes de que lo que les mueve ha quedado atrás, en la celebración de los Santos Oficios o de una Hora Santa celebrada en el silencio de un convento recoleto, en la meditación sosegada del supremo acto de la Redención, acompañando el dolor de la Madre y siempre confiados en el mensaje del discípulo amado: *Deus Cáritas est*, Dios es Amor."

73. Agustín Conde Bajén, "Carta del Alcalde," *Semana Santa '99* booklet, 1. My translation of "Toledo y la Semana Santa han conseguido en los últimos años un punto de encuentro del que todos nos sentimos muy satisfechos. La ciudad, con sus callejuelas, plazas y cobertizos, ofrece un escenario espectacular para resaltar la magnificencia de los cortejos procesionales, que nos permiten disfrutar de las mejores piezas del arte religioso toledano. Son días en que la belleza y los más sinceros sentimientos se adueñan del ambiente toledano. Lo mejor de nuestra tradición vuelve a la calle. . . . Yo animo a todos los toledanos a participar en estos festejos y expreso mi respeto para quienes viven estos días de intensa intimidad religiosa."

74. See González Martín, "Decreto Sobre el 'Lignum Crucis,'" 208.

75. González Martín, "Decreto Sobre el 'Lignum Crucis,'" 208. My paraphrase of "Ponderadas por Nos las razones aducidas, y deseando por Nuestra parte fomentar la piedad y devoción de los Fieles, considerando suficientemente probada la autenticidad de mencionada Reliquia del 'Lignum Crucis' y la gran devoción profesada en siglos pasados."

76. González Martín, "Decreto Sobre el 'Lignum Crucis,'" 208. My paraphrase of "Deberán observarse las normas litúrgicas referentes al 'Lignum Crucis' y el orden que Nos aprobamos en documento aparte."

77. Sierra, 99.

10. THE SPIRITUALITY OF THE CROSS

1. See, e.g., Kevin W. Irwin, *Context and Text: Method in Liturgical Theology* (Collegeville, MN: Liturgical Press, 1994), 44–46; Mary Collins, "Critical Questions for Liturgical Theology," *Worship* 53 (1979): 302–17; Robert Taft, "What Does Liturgy Do? Toward a Soteriology of Liturgical Celebration: Some Theses," *Worship* 66 (1992): 194–211; Dwight Vogel, "Liturgical Theology: A Conceptual Geography,"in *Primary Sources of Liturgical Theology: A Reader*, ed. Dwight W. Vogel, 3–14 (Collegeville, MN: A Pueblo Book, The Liturgical Press, 2000), 5–13.

2. See, e.g., Maxwell E. Johnson, *The Rites of Christian Initiation: Their Evolution and Interpretation* (Collegeville, MN: Liturgical Press, 1999); Edward Yarnold, *The Awe-Inspiring Rites of Initiation* (Slough, UK: St. Paul, 1971).

3. Alexander Schmemann, *Introduction to Liturgical Theology*, trans. Asheleigh E. Moorhouse (Crestwood, NY: St. Vladimir's Seminary Press, 1986), 9.

4. Schmemann, 11.

5. Margaret Mary Kelleher, O.S.U., "Liturgy: An Ecclesial Act of Meaning," *Worship* 59 (1985): 490–91.

6. Lozano Durán, interview, 2 June 1999. My translation of "Es un trozo de la cruz de Jesús. Es como si llevaríamos a Cristo de procesión, por eso va bajo palio. Es el único que va bajo palio como el Santísimo. Las demás son solamente imágenes y no tienen mucho valor espiritual aunque son preciosas."

7. *LO*, no. 33.

8. Carrillo Morales, interview, 17 May 1999. My translation of "Seguimos el ejemplo de la Iglesia de Jerusalén tal como lo describe Eteria [*sic*]."

9. Worship Aid I, 8; *Missale*, 1:351. My translation of "Qui vivis cum Deo Patre et Sancto Spíritu, unus Deus regnans in sæcula sæculorum. Amen."

10. Cf. Worship Aid II, 6, 8, and 11; *Missale*, 1: 355, 356, 360. The Spanish is "Por tu misericordia, Dios nuestro, que vives con Dios Padre, y reinas con el Espíritu Santo, por los siglos de los siglos. Amén." The Latin text for the first two prayers reads: "Per misericordiam tuam, Deus noster, qui vivis cum Deo Patre, et regnas in sæcula sæculorum. Amen." The Latin text for the third prayer reads "Quia multum miséricors est Dóminus noster Iesus Christus, vivens cum Patre et regnans cum Spíritu Sancto in sæcula sæculorum. Amen." Clearly the Spanish is an adaptation that combines the two forms into one.

11. For regulations regarding the role of the Holy See and bishops in the designation of any form of worship as liturgy, see *SC*, no. 22; Instruction *Inter Oecumenici* (26 September 1964), 26.

12. Cf. *SC*, no. 22; Decree on the Pastoral Office of Bishops, *Christus Dominus* (28 October 1965), nos. 11, 15.

13. See Congregatio Pro Cultu Divino, "Hispaniæ Dioecesium," Prot. n. 203/86, *Missale,* 1:7–8; Ángel Card. Suquía Goicoechea, Archbishop of Madrid, President of the Conferencia Episcopal Española, "Decreto," *Missale*, 1:9; "Normas de Aplicación del Misal," sect. IV of "Prenotandos," *Missale* 1:57–58.

14. Lonergan, 64.

15. Lonergan, 32.

16. Lonergan, 73.

17. Kelleher, "Liturgy: Ecclesial Act of Meaning," 482.

18. Kelleher, "Liturgy: Ecclesial Act of Meaning," 483n7, citing Yves M. J. Congar, "L'Ecclesia ou communauté chrétienne, sujet intégral de l'action liturgique," in *La Liturgie après Vatican II* (Paris: Cerf, 1967), 256.

19. Kelleher, "Liturgy: Ecclesial Act of Meaning," 482.

20. Kelleher, "Liturgy: Ecclesial Act of Meaning,"486n23, citing Lonergan's notion of community, *Method in Theology*, 79.

21. Kelleher, "Liturgy: Ecclesial Act of Meaning," 494.

22. José Miranda Calvo, interview, 23 March 2000. My translation of "Es símbolo de nuestra fe católica, no hay nada mejor por ser un trozo del Lignum Crucis; nada más puede representar el sacrificio de nuestro redentor."

23. Miguel Pantoja, interview, 21 March 2000. My translation of "Es una demostración de fe que se manifiesta en la calle." The impersonal *se* in Spanish can designate individual or group action depending on the context. From the context of the question and discussion, Pantoja was referring to a group demonstration of faith.

24. See USCCB, "Popular Devotional Practices: Basic Questions and Answers," issued November 12, 2003.

25. Peter W. Williams, *Popular Religion in America: Symbolic Change and the Modernization Process in Historical Perspective* (Englewood Cliffs, NJ: Prentice-Hall, 1989), 5.

26. Charles H. Lippy, *Being Religious American Style: A History of Popular Religiosity in the United States* (Westport, CT: Praeger, 1994), 2.

27. Ann Taves, *The Household of Faith: Roman Catholic Devotions in Mid-Nineteenth-Century America* (Notre Dame, IN: University of Notre Dame Press, 1986), 27–28, 89.

28. *Conclusiones*, vol. 2 of *La Iglesia en la Actual Transformación de América Latina a la Luz del Concilio*, Bogotá/Medellín Conference, 1968 (Bogotá: Consejo Episcopal Latinoamericano [CELAM], 1984), chap. 6, nos. 1–15, and chap. 9, no. 15; *La Evangelización en el Presente y en el Futuro de América Latina-Puebla* (Bogotá: Consejo Episcopal Latinoamericano [CELAM], 1984), nos. 444–69, 910–15, 935–37, 959–63; John Paul II, *The Church in America—Ecclesia in America: On the Encounter with the Living Jesus Christ: The Way to Conversion, Communion, and Solidarity in America*, Post-Synodal Apostolic Exhortation (Washington DC: USCC; 1999), no. 16.

29. Luis Maldonado, "Popular Religion: Its Dimensions, Levels, and Types," *Concilium* 186 (1986): 3.

30. *The Hispanic Presence: Challenge and Commitment* (December 1983) and *National Pastoral Plan for Hispanic Ministry* (November 1987), in NCCB, *Hispanic Ministry: Three Major Documents*, bilingual ed. (Washington DC: USCC, 1995), 1–21, 59–98.

31. Rev. Luis Munilla, S.D.S., former provincial superior, Spanish Pro-Province of the Society of the Divine Savior, interview by author, Milwaukee, Wisconsin, 15 April 2000. Also see Luis Maldonado, *Religiosidad Popular: Nostalgia de lo Mágico*, Epifanía 8 (Madrid: Ediciones Cristiandad, 1975), 343–44, and idem, "Liturgy as Communal Enterprise," *Reception of Vatican II*, ed. Giuseppe Alberigo, Jean-Pierre Jossua, and Joseph A. Komonchak, trans. Matthew J. O'Connell (Washington DC: CUA Press, 1987), 313.

32. Virgil Elizondo, "Popular Religion as Support of Identity: A Pastoral-Psychological Case-Study Based on the Mexican American Experience in the USA," *Concilium* 186 (1986): 36.

33. Orlando O. Espín, "Popular Catholicism among Latinos," in *Hispanic Catholic Culture in the US*, ed. Jay P. Dolan and Allan Figueroa Deck, S.J., 308–59. See also, Orlando O. Espín, *The Faith of the People: Theological Reflections on Popular Catholicism* (Maryknoll, NY: Orbis Books, 1997).

34. Espín, *The Faith of the People*, 112.

35. Arturo Pérez, *Popular Catholicism: A Hispanic Perspective/El Catolicismo Popular: Una perspectiva hispana*, American Essays in Liturgy 9 (Washington DC: Pastoral Press, 1988).

36. Pérez, *Popular Catholicism*, 7. He cites *La Evangelización en el Presente y en el Futuro de América Latina-Puebla*, nos. 444, 913.

37. Arturo J. Pérez, "The History of Hispanic Liturgy since 1965," in Dolan and Figueroa Deck, *Hispanic Catholic Culture in the US*, 365.

38. *Catechism of the Catholic Church*, 2nd ed. (Washington DC: USCC, 1994, 1997, pt. 2, chap. 4, art. 1, nos. 1667–79.

39. For the importance of ordinary food and its link to the Eucharist see "Ade Bethune," in *How Firm a Foundation: Voices of the Early Liturgical Movement*, comp. Kathleen Hughes, R.S.C.J. (Chicago: LTP, 1990), 33–35.

40. Cf. "William Leonard," in Hughes, *How Firm a Foundation*, 170–71; Rosa María Icaza, "Prayer, Worship, and Liturgy in a U.S. Hispanic Key," in *Frontiers of Hispanic Theology in the United States*, ed. Allan Figueroa Deck, S.J. (Maryknoll, NY: Orbis Books, 1992), 136–37.

41. For Mary's role in Hispanic spirituality since earliest times, see Ferrer Grenesche, *Los Santos*, 132–33, 138–39; Jaime Colomina Torner, "Jesús, Dios y Hombre, Hijo de María, en los textos eucarísticos hispanomozárabes," *Ephemerides Mariologicæ* 49 (1999): 147–70.

42. "Feria V in Cena Domini," *Missale*, 1:334: "crux salvíficat, sanguis emáculat, caro sagínat."

43. "In Nativitate Domini," *Missale*, 1:143: "*Animan suam pro illa pósuit*, suscéptæ et calcátæ mortis spólia in dotem illi regnatórus victor exhíbuit" (my emphasis).

44. "V Dominico Paschæ," *Missale,* 1:500: "Fácito nos, omnípotens Deus, ut carnáli devícta concupiscéntia, *veráciter gloriémur in cruce tua*" (my emphasis).

45. "In Diem Inventionis Sanctæ Crucis," *Missale,* 2:339: "Christe Dei Filius, in cuius nómine per Crucis mystérium omne genu fléctitur."

46. My paraphrase and translation of "Per ipsum apud te sit nostri ieiúnii parsimónia acceptábilis, qui nos tibi reconciliávit per oblátum sui sacrifícium córporis: ut ligno crucis suæ in huius mundi procellósa fluctuatióne portémur, et ad eum, repúlsis vítiis ac repléti virtútibus, veniámus" (*Missale,* 1:211). The Masses of the second week of Lent also make references to the theme of the Second Sunday of Lent *(missa de muliere samaritana)*, "Jesus, the one who gives life-giving water to the sinner."

47. My translation of "elevatísque in cruce mánibus, et sacrifícium vespertínum pepéndit in ligno, et benefícium matutínum surgens præbuit e sepúlcro." "In Nocte Sancta, Vigilia Paschalis," *Missale,* 1:407.

48. The feast of the Holy Cross is celebrated on 3 May. See "In Diem Inventionis Sanctæ Crucis," *Missale,* 2:339–46.

49. Illatio, "In V Dominco Paschæ," *Missale,* 1:501.

50. Cf. *Constituciones* (1984), 17, and *Constituciones* (1999), art. 6.

51. Ferrer Grenesche, *Los Santos,* 14. My paraphrase and translation of "Se componen unas Misas en las que desde la Oratio Adnonitionis [*sic*] de los Dípticos hasta la Bendición . . . se nos narra la vida o el martirio de un santo, destacando los datos más maravillosos en los que se manifiesta en él el Reino traído por Jesucristo y la victoria de éste sobre el mundo."

52. Ferrer Grenesche, *Los Santos,* 14. My paraphrase and translation of "No se olvida a Cristo en la Plegaria Eucarística, Cristo está presente en el santo. El santo recoge el don de Dios en Cristo y con su vida lo hace alabanza a gloria de Dios."

53. "In Diem Sanctæ Eulaliæ Emeritensis, Virginis et Martyris," *Missale,* 2:131.

54. "In Diem Sanctæ Eulaliæ, Virginis et Martyris, Barcinonis," *Missale,* 2:284.

55. Cf. Segundo Galilea, *Religiosidad Popular y Pastoral Hispano-Americana* (New York: Centro Católico para Hispanos del Nordeste, 1981), 15, 41–43, 51–52; Jaime Lara, "Las imágenes de Jesucristo populares en Latinoamérica," in *Religiosidad Popular: Las Imágenes de Jesucristo y la Virgen María en América Latina* (San Antonio, TX: Instituto de Liturgia Hispana, 1990), 15.

56. Roberto S. Goizueta, "A Matter of Life and Death: Theological Anthropology Between Calvary and Galilee," *CTSA Proceedings* 53 (1993): 3 (emphasis added). Also see Roberto S. Goizueta, "The Symbolic World of Mexican American Religion," in *Horizons of the Sacred: Mexican Traditions in U.S. Catholicism,* ed. Timothy M. Matovina and Gary Riebe-Estrella, S.V.D., 119–38 (Ithaca, NY: Cornell University Press, 2002).

57. Goizueta, "A Matter of Life and Death," 4.

58. Goizueta, "A Matter of Life and Death, 5.

59. Luis de León, *The Names of Christ,* The Classics of Western Spirituality Series (New York: Paulist Press, 1984), 119.

60. De León, 131. Also see William Wroth, *Images of Penance, Images of Mercy: Southwestern "Santos" in the Late Nineteenth Century* (Norman: University of Oklahoma Press, 1991), 6.

61. See Pascual González, *Chicotá pá Sevilla* (Sevilla: Ediciones Giralda, 1993), 52. Also see Lara, "Imágenes de Jesucristo," 22.

62. Lara, "Imágenes de Jesucristo," 19.

63. See Jaime Sancho Andreu, "Ritos de la infancia y la adolescencia en el antiguo rito hispánico," in *Psallendum: Studi offerti al Prof. Jordi Pinell i Pons*, ed. Ildebrando Scicolone, O.S.B., Studia Anselmiana 105, Analecta Liturgica 15 (Rome: Pontificio Ateneo S. Anselmo, 1992), 207–45; *LO*, VI: "Oratio super eum, qui capillos in sola fronte tondere uult" (37–38); *LO*, VII: "Oratio super paruulum, quem parentes ad doctrina offerunt" (38–39); and *LO*, XII: "Ordo super eum qui barbam tangere cupit" (43–46); Isidore of Seville, *De ecclesiasticis officiis, liber secundus*, PL 83.810c-812b; and *Ritual del Matrimonio*, nos. 149, 169, 177.

64. See, e.g., Virgilio Elizondo, *Christianity and Culture: An Introduction to Pastoral Theology and Ministry for the Bicultural Community* (San Antonio, TX: Mexican American Cultural Center, 1975, 1983), 137–40; Gilberto M. Hinojosa, "Mexican-American Faith Communities in Texas and the Southwest," in *Mexican Americans and the Catholic Church, 1900–1965*, ed. Jay P. Dolan and Gilberto M. Hinojosa (Notre Dame, IN: University of Notre Dame Press, 1994), 13, 19–23; Timothy M. Matovina, *Tejano Religion and Ethnicity: San Antonio, 1821–1860* (Austin: University of Texas Press, 1995), 39–45.

Selected Bibliography

PRIMARY SOURCES

Published Works

"El Concilio III de Toledo. Texto Crítico." *Concilio III de Toledo: XIV Centenario 589–1989*, 13–38. Toledo: Arzobispado de Toledo, 1991.

"Homilía de S.S. Juan Pablo II en la Basílica de San Pedro durante la Misa en Rito Hispano-Mozárabe." *Boletín Oficial del Arzobispado de Toledo* 148 (1992): 275–79.

"Introduction." *General Instruction of the Roman Missal*, 4th ed. (1975), nos. 6–9. In DOL 208, nos. 1381–84.

"Normas de Aplicación del Misal," Section IV. "Prenotandos," *Missale Hispano-Mozarabicum*, 1:57–58. Toledo: Arzobispado de Toledo, 1991.

"Rito Hispano-Mozárabe Ordinario de la Misa." Toledo: Mozarabic Chapel self-published worship-aid booklet, n.d.

"Vexilla Regis prodeunt." Ad Vesperas Dominicum I Passionis. In *Liber Usualis Missae et Officii Pro Dominicis et Festis cum cantu gregoriano ex editione Vaticana Adamussim excerpto et Rhythmicis Signis in Subsidium Cantorum A Solesmensibus Monachis Diligenter Ornato*, 575–76. Paris: Desclée et Socii; Rome: S. Sedis Apostolicae et Sacrorum Rituum Congregationis Typographi, 1958.

Agobard, Bishop of Lyon. *Tract against Felix*. PL 104.49–70

Alcuin. *Adversus Elipandum, liber secundum*. PL 101.257–70.

———. *Adversus Elipandum Hæresin*. PL 101.17–120; 119–230.

Archidiócesis de Toledo. "Concediendo el Traslado del Culto de las Parroquias Mozárabes de San Marcos y sus Filiales San Torcuato y Santa Eulalia del Templo de la Trinidad al Reconstruido de Santa Eulalia, y de la Consagración del Altar Mayor de esta Iglesia." Prot. no. 214/73. Photocopy provided by Don Jaime Colomina Torner, 11 May 1999.

Augustine of Hippo. *Contra Priscillianistas et Origenistas*. PL 42–43.670–89.

Barriga-Planas, J. R. *El Sacramentari, Ritual i Pontifical de Roda*. Barcelona: Fundació Salvador Vives Casajuana, 1975.

Beatus. *Adversus Elipandus*. PL 96.916 A II-917 C6.

———. *Apologeticus*. PL 96.893–1032.

223

Breviarium Gothicum ad debite persolvendum divinum officium secundum regulam beatissimi Isidori arciepiscopi hispalensis, ed. Francisco Antonio de Lorenzana. Madrid, 1775. PL 86.

Breviarium secundum regulam beati Ysidori dictum mozarabes: maxima cum diligentia perfectum et emendatum per reverendum in utroque iure doctorem dnm. alfonsum ortiz canonicum toletanum. Toledo: Petri Hagembach impensis Melchioris Gorricii, 1502.

Brou, Louis, and José Vives, eds. *Antifonario Visigótico-Mozárabe de la Catedral de León*. Monumenta Hispaniæ Sacra. Serie Litúrgica, vol. V, 1. Barcelona-Madrid: Consejo Superior de Investigaciones Científicas, Instituto P. Enrique Flórez, 1959.

Capellanes de la Capilla del Corpus Christi. *Rito Hispano-Mozárabe: Ordinario de la Misa*. Toledo: Instituto de Estudios Visigótico-Mozárabes, Delegación Diocesana de Liturgia, 1996.

Catechism of the Catholic Church. 2nd ed. Rev. in accord with the official Latin text promulgated by Pope John Paul II. Washington DC: USCC, 1994, 1997.

Celebrazione Eucaristica in Rito Ispano-Mozarabico presieduta dal Santo Padre Giovanni Paolo II, Basilica Vaticana, 28 Maggio 1992. Vatican City: Ufficio delle Celebrazioni Liturgiche del Sommo Pontefice, [1992].

Christus Dominus, Decree on the Pastoral Office of Bishops (1965). Vatican Council II. *AAS* 58 (1966), 673–96; ConstDecrDecl 277–321. Translated by ICEL.

Code of Canon Law, Latin-English ed. Translation prepared under the auspices of the Canon Law Society of America. Washington DC: Canon Law Society of America, 1983; a translation of *Codex Iuris Canonici*, 1983, by Libreria Editrice Vaticana, Vatican City.

Code of Canons of the Eastern Churches, Latin-English ed. Translation prepared under the auspices of the Canon Law Society of America. Washington DC: Canon Law Society of America, 1992; a translation of *Codex Canonum Ecclesiarum Orientalium*, auctoritate Ioannis Pauli PP. II promulgatur, Rome: Typis Polyglottis Vaticanis, 1990.

Colomina Torner, Jaime, trans. and ed. *Misa Mozárabe del Corpus Christi*. Toledo: self-published worship booklet, 1974.

Conferencia Episcopal Española. "Prenotandos." *Missale Hispano-Mozarabicum*, 1:15–58. Toledo: Arzobispado de Toledo, 1991.

———. *Missale Hispano-Mozarabicum*. 2 vols. Toledo: Arzobispado de Toledo, 1991.

———. *Missale Hispano-Mozarabicum: Liber Commicus*. 2 vols. Toledo: Arzobispado de Toledo, 1991–1994.

———. *Missale Hispano-Mozarabicum: Ordo Missae—Liber Offerentium*. Toledo: Arzobispado de Toledo, 1991.

Congregation for Divine Worship and the Discipline of the Sacraments. *Directory on Popular Piety and the Liturgy: Principles and Guidelines*. North American ed. Boston: Pauline Books and Media, 2002.

————. "Instruction (fourth)." *The Roman Liturgy and Inculturation: "Fourth Instruction for the Right Application of the Conciliar Constitution on the Liturgy" (nos. 37–40).* Vatican English text. In *Origins* 23 (1994): 745–56.

Congregatio Pro Cultu Divino. "Hispaniæ Dioecesium." Prot. no. 203/88. *Missale Hispano-Mozarabicum*, 1:7–8. Toledo: Arzobispado de Toledo, 1991.

————. "Decretum Hispaniæ Dioecesium, Decretum Congregationis, quo Missale Hispano-Mozarabicum confirmatur—Die 17 iulii 1988 (Prot. 203/88)." *Notitiæ* 24 (1988): 671–72.

Constituciones de la Ilustre y Antiquísima Hermandad de Caballeros Mozárabes de Nuestra Señora de la Esperanza, de la Imperial Ciudad de Toledo, Capítulo de Toledo. Toledo: Arzobispado de Toledo, parroquias Mozárabes de San Marcos y de Santas Justa y Rufina, 1966, rev. 1984 and 1999.

Constituciones de la Ilustre y Antiquísima Hermandad de Caballeros y Damas Mozárabes de Nuestra Señora de la Esperanza, de la Imperial Ciudad de Toledo. Toledo: Arzobispado de Toledo Parroquias Mozárabes de San Marcos y de Santas Justa y Rufina, 1966, rev. 1999.

Correspondence of Pope Gregory VII: Selected Letters from the Registrum. Translated with Introduction and notes by Ephraim Emerton. Records of Western Civilization Series. New York: Columbia University Press, 1990 <1932>.

de Echeverría, Lamberto, gen. ed. *Triduo Sacro en rito hispano antiguo o mozárabe.* Salamanca: Junta de Capilla, Universidad de Salamanca, 1980.

Documents on the Liturgy 1963–1979: Conciliar, Papal, and Curial Texts. Prepared by ICEL. Collegeville, MN: Liturgical Press, 1982.

Egeria: Diary of a Pilgrimage. Ancient Christian Writers 38. Translated by George E. Gingras. New York: Newman Press, 1970.

Elipandus. *Elipandi Epistolæ Ad Megetium Hæreticum.* PL 96.859–67.

————. *Elipandi Epistolæ, III: Ad Carolum Magnum.* PL 96.867–69.

————. *Elipandi Epistolæ, IV: Ad Albinum.* PL 96.871–75.

————. *Elipandi Epistolæ, V: Ad Felicem Nuper Conversum.* PL 96.880–82.

————. *Epistola Episcoporum Hispaniæ ad Episcopos Franciæ.* PL 96.120–24.

Férotin, Marius. *Le Liber Mozarabicus Sacramentorum et les Manuscrits Mozarabes.* Monumenta Ecclesiæ Liturgica 6. Paris: Firmin-Didot, 1912.

————. *Le Liber Ordinum En Usage Dans l'Église Wisigothique et Mozarabe d'Espagne du Cinquième Siècle.* Monumenta Ecclesiæ Liturgica 5. Paris: Firmin-Didot, 1904.

González Martín, Marcelo. "Decreto sobre el 'Lignum Crucis' de la Parroquia Mozárabe de Santa Eulalia y San Marcos." *BOAT* 132 (1976): 208–9; repr. *CM* 20 (1987): 4–5.

————. "Presentación." *Missale Hispano-Mozarabicum*, 1:10–12. Toledo: Archidiócesis de Toledo, 1991.

Isidore of Seville. *De ecclesiasticis oficiis, liber secundus.* PL 83.809–14.

Janini, José (J.), ed. *Liber Missarum de Toledo.* 2 vols. Serie Litúrgica, fuentes III, IV–VIII. Toledo: Instituto de Estudios Visigótico-Mozárabes, 1983.

————. *Liber Missarum de Toledo y Libros Místicos.* 2 vols. Toledo: Instituto de Estudios Visigótico-Mozárabes, 1982–83.

————. *Liber Misticus de Cuaresma y Pascua (Cod. Toledo, Bibl. Capit. 35.5).* Serie Litúrgica, Fuentes II. Toledo: Instituto de Estudios Visigótico-Mozárabes, 1980.

————. *Liber Ordinum Episcopal (Cod. Silos Arch. del Monasterio, 4).* Studia Silensia 15. Burgos: Abadía de Silos, 1991.

————. "La sagrada liturgia en rito hispano-mozárabe." Homilia die 28 maii 1992 habita, infra Missam Ritu Hispano-Mozarabico celebratam in Basilica Vaticana. *Notitiæ* 28 (1992): 386–90.

Julian of Toledo. *Apologeticum fidei.* PL 96.525–36.

Lorenzana, Francisco Antonio. "Carta de S. Exca. Sobre Rito muzárabe y biblioteca general de esta Sta. Iglesia." Toledo 7 de mayo de 1781. Transcription by Mario Arellano García. *CM* 62 (2004): 21–23. Original found in the Archivo de la S.I.C.P., Toledo. Tomo 84, fol. 234 al 238. Actas Capitulares.

Migne, J. P., ed. *Patrologiæ Cursus Completus.* Series Latina. Paris-Mountrouge: 1844–64.

————. *Patrologiæ Cursus Completus.* Series Græca. Paris-Mountrouge: 1857– .

Missæ Gothicæ et Officii muzarabici dilucida expositio, a D.D. Francisco Antonio Lorenzana, Archiepiscopo Mexicano, et a D. D. Francisco Fabian et Fuero, Episcopo Angelopolitano, Ad usum percelebris Sacelli Muzarabum, in alma Ecclesia Toletana Hispaniarum Primate ab Emmo. Cardinali Ximenez de Cisneros erecti. Editio novissima jussu et aprobatione Illmi. D. D. Santos ab Arciniega, Vicarii Capitularis, huius Archidiæceseos Gubernatoris, et Archipresbyteri dignitate in hac Ecclesia Primate præditi, facta. Toledo: Typis Severiani Lopez Fando et filii, 1775. Appendix to *Liber Missarum de Toledo,* 1:554–79.

Missale Gothicum secundum regulam beati Isidori Hispalensis Episcopi, jussu Cardinalis Franciscii Ximenii de Cisneros in usum Mozarabum prius editum, denuo opera et impensa Eminentissimi Domini Cardinalis Franciscii Antonii Lorenzanæ recognitum, et recussum ad Excellentiss. et Eminentiss. Principem et D. D. Ludovicum Borbonium, Archiepiscopum Tolentanum, Hispaniarum Primatem. Rome, 1804. Aoud Antonium Fulgonium.

Missale Gothicum secundum regulam beati Isidori Hispalensis Episcopi, jussu Cardinalis Franciscii Ximenii de Cisneros in usum Mozarabum prius editum, denuo opera et impensa Eminentissimi Domini Cardinalis Franciscii Antonii Lorenzanæ recognitum, et recussum ad Excellentiss. et Eminentiss. Principem et D. D. Ludovicum Borbonium, Archiepiscopum Tolentanum, Hispaniarum Primate, 1804. PL 86.

Missale mixtum secundum regulam beati Isidori dictum Mozarabes. Museo del Hospital de la Santa Cruz, Toledo, Inventorio General número 1324. Toledo: Petri Hagembach impensis Melchioris Goricii, 1500.

Moreau, F. X. "Tú reinarás." *Flor y Canto*, hymn no. 194. Portland, OR: OCP, 1989.

National Conference of Catholic Bishops (NCCB). *National Pastoral Plan for Hispanic Ministry* (November 1987). In NCCB, *Hispanic Ministry: Three Major Documents*, bilingual ed., 59–98. Washington: USCC, 1995.

———. *Hispanic Presence: Challenge and Commitment* (December 1983). In NCCB, *Hispanic Ministry: Three Major Documents*, bilingual ed., 1–21. Washington: USCC, 1995.

Ordinario de la Misa del Rito Hispano-Mozárabe—Oferencio. Traducción aprobada *ad experimentum* para la Capilla Mozárabe y Archidiócesis de Toledo por el Emmo. y Rvdmo. Sr. Cardenal Arzobispo de Toledo, Primado de España, Dr. D. Marcelo González Martín, Superior Responsable del Rito Hispano-Mozárabe. Toledo: Arzobispado de Toledo, 1991.

Orientalium Ecclesiarum. Decree on the Eastern Catholic Churches (1964). Vatican Council II. *AAS* 57 (1965): 76–85; ConstDecrDecl 223–240. Translated by ICEL.

Padrón de las Nobles Familias de Caballeros Mozárabes de Toledo según la parroquia de origen por "ius familiae" de este rito de Stas. Justa y Rufina y Sta. Eulalia y S. Marcos. Toledo: Instituto de Estudios Visigótico-Mozárabes de San Eugenio, 1982.

Paulus Orosius: The Seven Books of History against the Pagans. Translated by Roy J. Deferrari. Fathers of the Church Series 50. Washington: CUA Press, 1964.

Roman Missal. Revised by decree of the Second Vatican Council and published by authority of Pope Paul VI. *The Sacramentary,* approved for use in the Dioceses of the United States of America by the National Conference of Catholic Bishops and confirmed by the Apostolic See. Eng. Translation prepared by ICEL. New York: Catholic Book Pub. Co., 1985.

Sacred Congregation for Divine Worship. "Instruction (third)." *Liturgicæ instaurationes: On the Orderly Carrying Out of the Constitution on the Liturgy* (1970). *AAS* 62 (1970): 692–704; *Notitiæ* 7 (1971): 10–26. Translated by ICEL.

Sacred Congregation of Rites (Consilium). "Instruction (first)." *Inter Oecumenici: On the Orderly Carrying Out of the Constitution on the Liturgy* (1964). AAS 56 (1964): 877–900. Translated by ICEL.

———. "Instruction (second)." *Tres abhinc annos. On the Orderly Carrying Out of the Constitution on the Liturgy* (1967). *AAS* 59 (1967): 442–48; *Notitiæ* 3 (1967): 169–94. Translated by ICEL.

Sacrosanctum Concilium (Constitution on the Sacred Liturgy) (1963). Vatican Council II. AAS 56 (1964): 97–138; ConstDecrDecl 3–69. Translated by ICEL.

Semana Santa Toledo '99: Programa de Actos y Cultos. Toledo: Junta de Cofradías y Hermandades de Semana Santa de Toledo, 1999. Booklet.

Semana Santa '99 Toledo: Programa de Actos y Cultos. Toledo: Junta de Comunidades de Castilla-La Mancha, Asociación Provincial de Empresarios de Hostelería de Toledo, 1999. Pamphlet.

Suquía Goicoechea, Ángel Card., Archbishop of Madrid, President of the Conferencia Episcopal Española. "Decreto." *Missale Hispano-Mozarabicum,*

1:9. Toledo: Conferencia Episcopal Española Arzobispado de Toledo, 1991.

USCCB (United States Conference of Catholic Bishops). "Popular Devotional Practices: Basic Questions and Answers." Washington DC: USCCB, November 12, 2003.

Vives, José, Tomás Marín Martínez, and Gonzalo Martínez Díez, eds. *Concilios Visigóticos e Hispano-Romanos*. España Cristiana 1. Barcelona-Madrid: Consejo Superior de Investigaciones Científicas Instituto Enrique Flórez, 1963.

Unpublished Works

"Al lavatorio de pies." Toledo: Santa Eulalia y San Marcos Parish, n.d. Pamphlet for Holy Thursday liturgy.

"Expoliación del altar." Toledo: Santa Eulalia y San Marcos Parish, n.d. Pamphlet for Holy Thursday liturgy.

"Triduo Sacro en rito mozárabe." Toledo: Santa Eulalia y San Marcos Parish, n.d. Pamphlet for *Ad nonam pro indulgentia* liturgy (Worship Aid II).

"Triduo Sacro en rito mozárabe: A la hora de Tercia, Exaltación y Adoración de la Cruz." Toledo: Santa Eulalia y San Marcos Parish, n.d. Pamphlet for *Ad tertiam* liturgy (Worship Aid I).

Colomina Torner, Jaime. "Actualización del Rito Hispano-Mozárabe—Datos y fechas." A manuscript provided by interviewee describing the activities leading to the actualization of the rite, 25 September 1999.

———. Mozarabic rite pastor of San Marcos, Toledo, to Archbishop Marcelo González Martín, 1 October 1973. TL. Photocopy provided by Colomina Torner, 11 May 1999.

Morin, Roland. *Ad nonam* service. Good Friday, 2 April 1999 (videotape).

———. *Ad tertiam* service. Good Friday, 2 April 1999 (videotape).

"Sagrados Oficios de Semana Santa según el antiguo Rito Hispano o Mozárabe." Toledo: Santa Eulalia y San Marcos Parish, n.d. Booklet photocopied from *Triduo Sacro en rito hispano antiguo o mozárabe*, gen. ed. Lamberto de Echeverría. Salamanca: Junta de Capilla, Universidad de Salamanca, 1980.

Zalewski, Leon. *Ad nonam* service. Good Friday, 2 April 1999 (videotape).

———. *Ad tertiam* service. Good Friday, 2 April 1999 (videotape).

SECONDARY SOURCES

"Jornadas sobre liturgia hispánica." *BOAT* 139 (1983): 252–53.

"La cruz mozárabe." *CM* 1 (1969): 3.

"Los mozárabes de Toledo." *CM* O (1968): 1–6.

"Necrologías." *CM* 22 (1988): 16.

"Noticias Mozárabes. *CM* 3 (1970): 11

"Nuestro Sr. Arzobispo." *BOAT* 128 (1972): 3ff.

"Sobre los Diezmos de las Parroquias Mozárabes de Toledo." *CM* 6 (1982): 3–4.

Abalos, David T. *Latinos in the United States: The Sacred and the Political.* Notre Dame, IN: University of Notre Dame Press, 1986.

Aldazábal, José. "Bibliografía." In *Liturgia hispánica*, ed. José Aldazábal, 13–21. Biblioteca litúrgica 9. Barcelona: Centre de Pastoral Litúrgica, 1998.

———. "La misa en el rito hispano-mozárabe revisado." *Phase* 175 (1990): 57–77.

———. "Presentación." In *Liturgia hispánica*, ed. José Aldazábal, 9–12. Biblioteca litúrgica 9. Barcelona: Centre de Pastoral Litúrgica, 1998.

Arbeiter, Achim, and Sabine Noack-Haley. "The Kingdom of Asturias." In *The Art of Medieval Spain A.D. 500–1200*, 113–19. New York: Metropolitan Museum of Art, 1993.

Arellano, A. "La Parroquia Mozárabe de Santa Eulalia." *CM* 6 (1982): 12.

Arellano, Alicia. "¿Quiénes somos?" *CM* 34 (1993): 10.

Arellano García, Mario. *La Capilla Mozárabe o del Corpus Christi.* Toledo: Instituto de Estudios Visigótico-Mozárabes de San Eugenio, 1980.

———. "Indice alfabético de autores." *CM* 26 (1989): 16–20.

———. "Introducción." *Apéndice no. 3. Padrón de las Nobles Familias de Caballeros Mozárabes de Toledo según la parroquia de su origen por "ius familiae" de este rito, de Stas. Justa y Rufina y Sta. Eulalia y S. Marcos.* Toledo: *CM* (1995): 1.

———. "Lápidas en la parroquia mozárabe de Santa Eulalia." *CM* 43 (1997): 7–13.

———. "Nuevos Datos Sobre el Lignum Crucis." *CM* 20 (1987): 10.

———. "Santa Eulalia. ¿De Mérida o Barcelona?" *CM* 20 (1987): 10–13.

Arevalus, Faustinus (Faustino Arévalo). "Notæ Ad Missale Gothicum," cols. 1295–96. *Missale Gothicum secundum regulam beati Isidori Hispalensis Episcopi, jussu Cardinalis Franciscii Ximenii de Cisneros in usum Mozarabum prius editum, denuo opera et impensa Eminentissimi Domini Cardinalis Franciscii Antonii Lorenzanæ recognitum, et recussum ad Excellentiss. et Eminentiss. Principem et D. D. Ludovicum Borbonium, Archiepiscopum Tolentanum, Hispaniarum Primatem.* Rome, 1804. Aoud Antonium Fulgonium.

Baldovin, John F., S.J. *The Urban Character of Christian Worship: The Origins, Development, and Meaning of Stational Liturgy.* Orientalia Christiana Analecta 228. Rome: Pont. Institutum Studiorum Orientalium, 1987.

Barral i Altet, Xavier. *The Early Middle Ages: From Late Antiquity to A.D. 1000.* Taschen's World Architecture Series. Cologne: Benedikt Taschen Verlag GmbH, 1997.

Barrero García, Ana María. "La política foral de Alfonso VI." In *Estudios Sobre Alfonso VI y la Reconquista de Toledo,* Serie Histórica 4. Toledo: Instituto de Estudios Visigótico-Mozárabes, 1987. 1:115–56.

Bell, Catherine M. *Ritual: Perspectives, and Dimensions.* New York: Oxford University Press, 1997.

———. *Ritual Theory, Ritual Practice*. New York: Oxford University Press, 1992.

Bernard, Jessie. "Community: Community Disorganization." In *International Encyclopedia of the Social Sciences*, ed. David L. Sills, 3:163–69. New York: Macmillan Co. and Free Press, 1968.

Bishop, W. C. *The Mozarabic and Ambrosian Rites: Four Essays in Comparative Liturgiology*. Edited by C. L. Feltoe. Alcuin Club Tracts 15. London: A. R. Mowbray and Co.. 1940.

Bosch, Lynette M. F. *Art, Liturgy, and Legend in Renaissance Toledo: The Mendoza and the Iglesia Primada*. University Park: Pennsylvania State University Press, 2000.

Brown, Harold O. J. *Heresies: The Image of Christ in the Mirror of Heresy and Orthodoxy from the Apostles to the Present*. Foreword by George H. Williams. Garden City, NJ: Doubleday, 1984.

Burman, Thomas E. *Religious Polemic and the Intellectual History of the Mozarabs, c. 1050–1200*. Brill's Studies in Intellectual History 52. Leiden: E. J. Brill, 1994.

Cabié, Robert. "The Entrance Rites." In Martimort, 2:55–56.

Cabrera y Delgado, Antonio. *Catedral de Toledo*. 2nd ed. Barcelona: Editorial Escudo de Oro, 1993.

Carrillo Morales, Enrique. *Música y Capellanes Mozárabes: Discurso de apertura del Curso 1991–1992*. Toledo: Seminario Conciliar, Estudio Teológico de San Ildefonso, 1991.

———. "La pasión en la liturgia mozárabe." In *La Semana Santa dentro del Misterio Cristiano: I Ciclo de Conferencias, marzo 1998*, 7–30. Toledo: Junta de Cofradías y Hermandades de Semana Santa de Toledo, 1999.

———. "Las Reliquias de Santa Eulalia." *CM* 20 (1987): 2–3.

Cavadini, John C. *The Last Christology of the West: Adoptionism in Spain and Gaul 785–820*. Philadelphia: University of Pennsylvania Press, 1993.

Chupungco, Anscar J., O.S.B. *Liturgical Inculturation: Sacramentals, Religiosity, and Catechesis*. Collegeville, MN: Liturgical Press, 1992.

———. *Liturgies of the Future: The Process and Methods of Inculturation*. New York: Paulist Press, 1989.

Clifford, Anne M. "Creation." In *Systematic Theology: Roman Catholic Perspectives*, ed. Francis Schüssler Fiorenza and John P. Galvin, 1:195–248. Minneapolis: Fortress Press, 1991.

Cobb, Peter. "The Liturgy of the Word in the Early Church." In *The Study of Liturgy*, rev. ed., ed. Cheslyn Jones, Geoffery Wainwright, Edward Yarnold, S.J., and Paul Bradshaw, 219–29. New York: Oxford University Press; London: S.P.C.K., 1992 <1978>.

Colbert, Edward P. *The Martyrs of Córdoba (850–859): A Study of the Sources*. The Catholic University of America Studies in Mediaeval History, New Series 17. Washington: CUA Press, 1962.

Collins, Mary. "Critical Questions for Liturgical Theology." *Worship* 53 (1979): 302–17.

————. "Language, Liturgical." In *New Dictionary of Sacramental Worship*, ed. Peter E. Fink, S.J., 651–61. Collegeville, MN: Liturgical Press, 1990.

Collins, Roger. *Early Medieval Spain: Unity in Diversity, 400–1000*. New York: St. Martin's Press, 1983.

Colomina Torner, Jaime (Colomina). "1992: Toledo mozárabe en Roma." *Toletum* 28 (1992): 153–59.

————. "Don Marcelo y la Comunidad Mozárabe." *CM* 61 (2004): 15–19.

————. "Hacia la actualización del rito mozárabe." *CM* 11 (1984): 1–3.

————. "Jesús, Dios y Hombre, Hijo de María, en los textos eucarísticos hispanomozárabes." *Ephemerides Mariologicæ* 49 (1999): 147–70.

————. "El Lignum Crucis de la parroquia mozárabe de Santa Eulalia." *CM* 20 (1987): 5–9. Repr. of "El Lignum Crucis de la parroquia mozárabe de Santa Eulalia." *BOAT* 132 (1976): 247–51.

Concilio III de Toledo: XIV Centenario 589–1989, 13–38. Toledo: Arzobispado de Toledo, 1991.

Connelly, Joseph. *Hymns of the Roman Liturgy*. London: Longmans, Green, and Co., 1957.

Córdoba, Francisco de Sales (Córdoba Sánchez-Bretaño). "Estructura de la misa hispana o mozárabe." *CM* 15 (1985): 4–6.

————. "Jornada del Foso (807)." *CM* 8 (1982): 8.

————. "La civilización del reino visigodo español." *CM* 5 (1981): 3.

————. "La cultura mozárabe y su difícil supervivencia." *CM* 24 (1989): 7–9.

————. "Las iglesias mozárabes de Toledo." *CM* 11 (1984): 9–10.

Córdoba Bravo, F. de Sales. "Aspectos del Arte Mozárabe (continuación)." *CM* 36 (1994): 9–12.

Cozens, M. L. *A Handbook of Heresies*. Abridged ed. New York: Sheed and Ward, 1928.

Cruz, Joan Carroll. *Relics*. Huntington, IN: Our Sunday Visitor, 1984.

Dávila, José Antonio (or Dávila García-Miranda or J. A. Dávila y García Miranda). "La calidad Mozárabe en la Descendencia." *CM* 3 (1970): 3–5.

————. "La Nobleza e Hidalguía de las familias Mozárabes de Toledo." *Revista Hidalguía* 75 (March-April 1966): 257ff.

————. "Más sobre lo mismo." *CM* 57 (2003): 12–17.

————. "Una nueva etapa en la comunidad mozárabe toledana." *CM* 30 (1991): 63–75.

de Echeverría, Lamberto. "La Real Capilla Universitaria de San Jerónimo." In *Triduo Sacro en rito hispano antiguo o mozárabe*, gen. ed. Lamberto de Echeverría, 2–20. Salamanca: Universidad de Salamanca, Junta de Capilla, 1980.

de las Cagigas, Isidro. *Los Mozárabes*. Minorías étnico-religiosas de la Edad Media española 1. Madrid: Consejo Superior de Investigaciones Científicas, Instituto de Estudios Africanos, 1947.

de las Heras y Borrero, Francisco Manuel. *Apuntes Sobre Instituciones Nobiliarias en España*. Colección Persevante Heráldica Borgoña. Madrid: Prensa y Ediciones Iberoaméricas, 1994.

de León, Luis. *The Names of Christ*. Translated and introduction by Manuel Durán and William Kluback. The Classics of Western Spirituality Series. New York: Paulist Press, 1984.

de Mora Ontalva, José María. "Nuevo Boletín de liturgia hispánica antigua." *Hispania Sacra* 26 (1973): 209–37.

Deck, Allan Figueroa. "The Spirituality of United States Hispanics: An Introductory Essay." In *Mestizo Christianity: Theology from the Latino Perspective*, ed. Arturo J. Bañuelas, 224–35. Maryknoll, NY: Orbis Books, 1995.

Delattre, Roland A. "Ritual Resourcefulness and Cultural Pluralism." *Soundings* 61 (1978): 281–301.

Denzinger, Henricus, and Adolfus Schönmetzer. *Enchiridion Symbolorum: Definitionum et Declarationum de Rebus Fidei et Morum*, ed. xxxiv emendata. Freiburg im Breisgau: Verlag Herder KG, 1967.

Díaz y Díaz, M. C. (Manuel C.). "Breves notas sobre los mozárabes de Toledo." In *Estudios Sobre Alfonso VI y la Reconquista de Toledo* (1989): 3:11–24.

Domínguez del Val, Ursicino, O.S.A. "Características de la Patrística hispana en el siglo VII." In *La Patrología Toledano-visigoda, XXVII Semana Española de Teología (Toledo, 25–29 Sept. 1967)*, 5–36. Madrid: Consejo Superior de Investigaciones Científicas, Patronato "Menéndez Pelayo," Instituto "Francisco Suárez," 1970.

Domínguez Ortiz, Antonio, ed. *Historia de España*. 12 vols. Barcelona: Editorial Planeta, 1988–90.

Donghi, Antonio. *Actions and Words: Symbolic Language and the Liturgy*. Translated by William McDonough and Dominic Serra. English text edited by Mark Twomey and Elizabeth L. Montgomery. Collegeville, MN: Liturgical Press, 1997. Originally published in Italian as *Gesti e Parole: Un'iniziazione al linguaggio simbolico*. Vatican City: Libreria Editrice Vaticana, 1993.

Donin, Hayim Halevy. *To Pray as a Jew: A Guide to the Prayer Book and the Synagogue Service*. N.p.: Basic Books, 1980.

Driscoll, Michael S. "Liturgy and Devotions: Back to the Future?" In *The Renewal That Awaits Us*, ed. Eleanor Bernstein, C.S.J., and Martin F. Connell, 68–90. Chicago: LTP, 1997.

Driver, Tom E. *The Magic of Ritual: Our Need for Liberating Rites that Transform Our Lives and Our Communities*. San Francisco: Harper San Francisco, 1991.

Elizondo, Virgilio P. (Virgil). *Christianity and Culture: An Introduction to Pastoral Theology and Ministry for the Bicultural Community*. San Antonio, TX: Mexican American Cultural Center, 1975.

———. "Popular Religion as Support of Identity: A Pastoral-Psychological Case-Study Based on the Mexican American Experience in the USA." *Concilium* 186 (1986): 36–43.

———. "The Sacred in the City." In *San Fernando Cathedral: Soul of the City*, ed. Virgilio P. Elizondo and Timothy M. Matovina, 87–97. Maryknoll, NY: Orbis Books, 1998.

Espín, Orlando. *The Faith of the People: Theological Reflections on Popular Catholicism*. Maryknoll, NY: Orbis Books, 1997.

———. "Pentecostalism and Popular Catholicism: Preservers of Hispanic Catholic Tradition?" *ACHTUS Newsletter* 4 (1993): 10–12.

Estudios sobre Alfonso VI y la Reconquista de Toledo, Actas del II Congreso Internacional de Estudios Mozárabes (Toledo, 20–26 Mayo 1985), 4 vols. Serie Histórica 5. Toledo: Instituto de Estudios Visigótico-Mozárabes, 1987–1990.

Fernández Collado, Ángel. "Canonización de D. Ricardo Plá Espí." *CM* 33 (1992): 155–56.

———. "El caminar de un rito vivo y desconocido." *CM* 44 (1997): 5–15.

———. "Situación económica de las parroquias mozárabes de Toledo en 1822." *CM* 17 (1986): 6–7

Fernández Conde, J. "La Iglesia en el reino astur-leonés." BAC II-1:64–83.

Férotin, Marius. "L'Ordinatio Regis ou le sacre des rois wisigoths de Tolède au VII siècle." Appendix 2:498–505. In *Le Liber Ordinum En Usage Dans l'Eglise Wisigothique et Mozarabe d'Espagne du Cinquième Siècle*. Monumenta Ecclesiæ Liturgica 5. Paris: Firmin-Didot, 1904.

Ferrer Grenesche, Juan-Miguel. "La eucaristía en rito hispano-mozárabe." *Toletana* 1 (1999): 59–88.

———. *Los Santos del Nuevo Misal Hispano-Mozárabe*. Toledo: Estudio Teológico de San Ildefonso, seminario conciliar, 1995.

Fletcher, Richard. *Moorish Spain*. Berkeley and Los Angeles: University of California Press, 1992.

Francis, Mark R., C.S.V. "Popular Piety and Liturgical Reform in a Hispanic Context." In *Dialogue Rejoined: Theology and Ministry in the United States Hispanic Reality*, ed. Ana María Pineda and Robert Schreiter, 162–77. Foreword by Donald Senior, C.P. Collegeville, MN: Liturgical Press, 1995.

Francis, Mark R., and Arturo J. Pérez-Rodríguez. *Primero Dios: Hispanic Liturgical Resource*. Chicago: LTP, 1997.

Francisco de Pisa, Apuntamientos para la II Parte de la "Descripción de la Imperial Ciudad de Toledo," según la copia manuscrita de D. Francisco de Santiago Palomares, con notas originales autógrafas del Cardenal Lorenzana. Estudio preliminar, transcripción y notas de José Gómez-Menor Fuentes. Toledo: I.P.I.E.T Diputación Provincial de Toledo, 1976.

Galilea, Segundo. *Religiosidad Popular y Pastoral Hispano-Americana*. New York: Centro Católico para Hispanos del Nordeste, 1981.

Gallego Peñalver, Ignacio. "La iglesia mozárabe de Santa Eulalia de Toledo." *CM* 17 (1986): 7–9

García-Rivera, Alex. "Communion and Community: The Language of the Sacraments." In *Languages of Worship/El lenguaje de la liturgia*, ed. Raúl

Gómez, S.D.S., 38–44. Chicago; LTP; Washington DC: Instituto Nacional Hispano de Liturgia, 2004.

García-Villoslada, Ricardo. *Historia de la Iglesia Católica: En sus cinco grandes edades: Antigua, Media, Nueva, Moderna y Contemporánea.* Vol. 2 of *Edad Media (800–1303): La cristiandad en el mundo europeo y feudal.* 5th ed. Madrid: BAC, 1988.

García-Villoslada, Ricardo, and Bernardino Llorca. *Edad Nueva: La Iglesia en la época del Renacimiento y de la Reforma católica.* Vol. 3 of *Historia de la Iglesia Católica.* 3rd ed. Madrid: BAC, 1987.

Geertz, Clifford. *The Interpretation of Culture: Selected Essays.* New York: Basic Books, 1973.

———. "Religion as a Cultural System." In *Anthropological Approaches to the Study of Religion,* ed. Michael Banton, 1–46. London: Tavistock, 1966.

Glick, Thomas F. *Islamic and Christian Spain in the Early Middle Ages.* Princeton, NJ: Princeton University Press, 1979.

Goizueta, Roberto S. "A Matter of Life and Death: Theological Anthropology between Calvary and Galilee." *CTSA Proceedings* 53 (1993): 1–20.

Gómez-Chacón, Balbino (G.-Chacón). "Editorial." *CM* 4 (1981): 1.

———. "Sobre la revisión del rito hispano-mozárabe." *CM* 19 (1987): 1–3.

———. "La última revisión del rito hispano-mozárabe." *CM* 32 (1992): 126–35.

González, Pascual. *Chicotá pá Sevilla.* Sevilla: Ediciones Giralda, 1993.

González, Teodoro. "La Conversión de los Visigodos al Catolicismo." In *La iglesia en la España visigoda y romana,* vol. 1 of García-Villoslada, *Historia de la Iglesia en España,* 402–21. Madrid: BAC, 1979.

———. "Organización de la Iglesia Visigoda." BAC 1:491–535.

———. "Paganismo, judaísmo, herejías y relaciones con el exterior." BAC 1:663–99.

———. "Vida Cristiana y Cura Pastoral." BAC 1:564–611.

González González, Julio. "Los mozárabes toledanos desde el siglo XI hasta el Cardenal Cisneros." In *Historia Mozárabe, Primer Congreso Internacional de Estudios Mozárabes: Toledo, 1975,* 79–90. Serie C, no. 1. Toledo: Instituto de Estudios Visigótico-Mozárabes de San Eugenio, 1978.

González Mohíno, Félix. "El Canto Hispano-Mozárabe. Aproximación a su Estudio." In *Curso de Liturgia Hispano-Mozárabe,* ed. Juan-Miguel Ferrer Grenesche, 127–36. Toledo: Estudio Teológico de San Ildefonso, Seminario Conciliar, 1995.

Gonzálvez Ruiz, Ramón (Gonzálvez). "El arcediano de Toledo Joffré de Loaysa y las parroquias urbanas de Toledo en 1300." In *Historia Mozárabe, Primer Congreso Internacional de Estudios Mozárabes: Toledo, 1975.* Serie C, no. 1. Toledo: Instituto de Estudios Visigótico-Mozárabes de San Eugenio, 1978, 91–148.

———. "Cisneros y la Reforma del Rito Hispano-Mozárabe." A talk presented at the International Colloquium on the Bible and the Spanish Renaissance: Cardinal Ximénez de Cisneros (1436–1517) and the Complutensian

Polyglot, Loyola University, Chicago, 10–13 June 1999. Text provided by
        author.
———. "Noticias sobre códices mozárabes en los antiguos inventarios de la
        Biblioteca Capitular de Toledo." In *Historia Mozárabe, Primer Congreso
        Internacional de Estudios Mozárabes: Toledo, 1975*, 45–78. Serie C, no.
        1. Toledo: Instituto de Estudios Visigótico-Mozárabes de San Eugenio,
        1978.
———. "Los orígenes de la liturgia hispano-mozárabe." *Anales Toledanos* 35
        (1998): 33–54.
———. "The Persistence of the Mozarabic Liturgy in Toledo after A.D. 1080."
        In *Santiago, Saint-Denis, and Saint Peter: The Reception of the Roman
        Liturgy in León-Castile in 1080*, ed. Bernard F. Reilly, 157–85. New York:
        Fordham University Press, 1985.
Gracia, Jorge J. E. *Hispanic/Latino Identity: A Philosophical Perspective*.
        Malden, MA: Blackwell, 2000.
Grand, Samuel and Tamar. "Exploring the Jewish Heritage of Spain." Pamphlet.
        Bilbao: Secretaría de Estado de Turismo, Dirección General de Promoción
        del Turismo, 1980.
Gray, Ann, and Jim McGuigan, eds. *Studying Culture: An Introductory Reader*,
        2nd ed. London: Arnold; New York: Oxford University Press, 1993, 1997.
Grimes, Ronald L. *Beginnings in Ritual Studies*. Rev. ed. Columbia: University
        of South Carolina Press, 1995. Originally published by University Press
        of America, 1982.
———. *Reading, Writing, and Ritualizing: Ritual in Fictive, Liturgical, and Public
        Places*. Washington DC: Pastoral Press, 1993.
———. *Ritual Criticism: Case Studies in Its Practice, Essays on Its Theory*.
        Columbia: University of South Carolina Press, 1990.
Gy, P. M. "History of the Liturgy in the West to the Council of Trent." In
        Martimort, 1:45–61.
Haines, C. R. *Christianity and Islam in Spain: AD 756–1031*. New York: AMS
        Press, 1972; repr. of London: Kegan Paul, Trench, and Co., 1889.
Harvey, L. P. *Islamic Spain, 1250 to 1500*. Chicago: University of Chicago Press,
        1992 <1990>.
Higueruela Del Pino, Leandro. "Don Francisco Antonio de Lorenzana, Cardenal
        Ilustrado." *Toletum* 23 (1989): 169–89.
Hillgarth, J. N. "El Concilio III de Toledo y Bizancio." In *Concilio III de Toledo:
        XIV Centenario 589–1989*, 297–306. Toledo: Arzobispado de Toledo, 1991.
———. s.v. "Priscillian" and "Priscillianism." In *New Catholic Encyclopedia*,
        2nd ed. (2003), 11:719–20.
*Historia Mozárabe, Ponencias y Comunicaciones presentadas al I Congreso
        Internacional de Estudios Mozárabes: Toledo, 1975*. Serie C, no. 1. Toledo:
        Instituto de Estudios Visigótico-Mozárabes de San Eugenio, 1978.
Hoffman, Lawrence A. *Beyond the Text: A Holistic Approach to Liturgy*. Jewish
        Literature and Culture Series. Series ed., Alvin Rosenfeld. Bloomington:
        Indiana University Press, 1987. Midland Book ed., 1989.

Hughes, Kathleen, R.S.C.J., comp. and intro. *How Firm a Foundation: Voices of the Early Liturgical Movement*. Chicago: LTP, 1990.

Icaza, Rosa María. "Prayer, Worship, and Liturgy in a U.S. Hispanic Key." In *Frontiers of Hispanic Theology in the United States*, ed. Allan Figueroa Deck, S.J., 134–53. Maryknoll, NY: Orbis Books, 1992.

Irwin, Kevin W. *Context and Text: Method in Liturgical Theology*. Collegeville, MN: Liturgical Press, 1994.

———. *Models of the Eucharist*. Mahwah, NJ: Paulist Press. 2005.

Jacobson, Paul A. "Sicut Samuhel Unxit David: Early Carolingian Royal Anointings Reconsidered," in *Medieval Liturgy: A Book of Essays*, ed. Lizette Larson-Miller, 267–303. Garland Medieval Casebooks 18 and Garland Reference Library of the Humanities 1884. New York: Garland Pub., 1997.

Janini, José. "Libros Litúrgicos mozárabes de Toledo conquistado." In *Estudios Sobre Alfonso VI y la Reconquista de Toledo* (1990): 4:9–25.

———. "Misas mozárabes recompuestas por Ortiz." *Hispania Sacra* 34 (1982): 153–63.

Janini, José, and Ramón Gonzálvez, with the collaboration of A. M. Mundó. *Catálogo de los Manuscritos Litúrgicos de la Catedral de Toledo*. Patronato "José María Quadrado," del Consejo Superior de Investigaciones Científicas 11. Toledo: Diputación Provincial, 1977.

Jasper, R. C. D., and G. J. Cuming. *Prayers of the Eucharist: Early and Reformed*. Texts translated and edited with commentary. 3rd ed., rev. Collegeville, MN: Liturgical Press, 1990.

Johnson, Maxwell E. *The Rites of Christian Initiation: Their Evolution and Interpretation*. Collegeville, MN: Liturgical Press, 1999.

Jones, A. H. M. *Constantine and the Conversion of Europe*. Medieval Academy Reprints for Teaching 4. Toronto: University of Toronto Press; Medieval Academy of America, 1978, repr. 1989. First published by Macmillan Co., 1948.

Jungmann, Josef A., S.J. *The Early Liturgy to the Time of Gregory the Great*. Translated by Francis A. Brunner, C.SS.R. University of Notre Dame Liturgical Studies 6. Notre Dame, IN: University of Notre Dame Press, 1980. Originally published in 1959.

———. *The Mass of the Roman Rite: Its Origins and Development (Missarum Sollemnia)*. Vol. 1. Translated by Francis A. Brunner, C.SS.R. New York: Benzinger Bros., 1951.

———. *The Place of Christ in Liturgical Prayer*. Translated by Geoffrey Chapman. Collegeville, MN: Liturgical Press, 1989.

Jurado Puñal, Felipe. "Los mozárabes en la septimania francesa." *CM* 61 (2004): 22–24.

Kasper, Walter. *Jesus the Christ*. New York: Paulist Press; London: Burns and Oates, 1976. Originally published in German as *Jesus der Christus*. Mainz: Matthias-Grünewald-Verlag, 1974.

Kavanagh, Aidan. *On Liturgical Theology: The Hale Memorial Lectures of Seabury-Western Theological Seminary, 1981*. New York: Pueblo Pub. Co., 1984.

Keay, S.J. *Roman Spain*. Exploring the Roman World 2. Berkeley and Los Angeles: University of California Press/British Museum, 1988.

Kelleher, Margaret Mary, O.S.U. "Liturgical Theology: A Task and a Method." *Worship* 62 (1988): 2–25.

———. "Liturgy: An Ecclesial Act of Meaning." *Worship* 59 (1985): 482–97.

———. "Liturgy as a Source for Sacramental Theology." *Questions Liturgiques* 72 (1991): 25–42.

———. "Ritual Studies and the Eucharist: Paying Attention to Performance." In *Eucharist: Toward the Third Millennium*, ed. Martin F. Connell, 51–64. Chicago: LTP, 1997.

Kelly, J. N. D . *Early Christian Creeds*, 3rd ed. London: Longman Group, 1972 <1950>.

———. *Early Christian Doctrines*. 2nd ed. New York: Harper and Pub., 1979 <1960>.

Kilmartin, Edward J., S.J. *Eucharist in the West: History and Theology*. Edited by Robert J. Daly, S.J. Collegeville, MN: Liturgical Press, 1998.

King, Archdale A. *Liturgies of the Past*. London: Longmans, Green and Co., 1959.

Kluckhohn, Clyde. "Universal Categories of Culture." In *Anthropology Today: An Encyclopedic Inventory*, ed. Alfred L. Kroeber, 507–23. Chicago: University of Chicago Press, 1953.

Knoebel, Rev. Thomas, academic dean, Sacred Heart School of Theology, Hales Corners, WI. To author. 4 January 2000. Narrative reflecting on the ritual use of the Lignum Crucis. Transcript in the hand of Rev. Thomas Knoebel.

LaCugna, Catherine. "Can Liturgy Ever Again Become a Source for Theology?" *Studia Liturgica* 19 (1989): 1–13.

———. "The Trinitarian Mystery of God." In *Systematic Theology: Roman Catholic Perspectives*, ed. Francis Schüssler Fiorenza and John P. Galvin, 1:151–92. Minneapolis: Fortress Press, 1991.

Lanza Alandi, Manuel. "Introducción." In *Semana Santa Toledo '99: Programa de Actos y Cultos*, 2. Toledo: Junta de Cofradías y Hermandades de Semana Santa de Toledo, 1999. Booklet.

Lara, Jaime. "Las imágenes de Jesucristo populares en Latinoamérica." In *Religiosidad Popular: Las Imágenes de Jesucristo y la Virgen María en América Latina*, 15–30. San Antonio, TX: Instituto de Liturgia Hispana, 1990.

———. "The Liturgical Roots of Hispanic Popular Religiosity." In *Misa, Mesa y Musa: Liturgy in the U.S. Hispanic Church*, ed. Kenneth G. Davis, O.F.M.Conv., 25–33. Schiller Park, IL: World Library Publications, 1997.

Larson-Miller, Lizette. "Lent." In *New Dictionary of Sacramental Worship*, ed. Peter E. Fink, S.J., 680–87. Collegeville, MN: Liturgical Press, 1990.

Lechner, R. F. "Braga, Rite of." In *New Catholic Encyclopedia* (1967).

Leclercq, Henri, and Fernand Cabrol. "Mozarabe (La Liturgie)." In *Dictionnaire d'Archéologie Chrétienne et de Liturgie*, Tome Deuxième-A, ed. Fernand Cabrol and Henri Leclercq. Paris: Librairie Letouzey et Ané, 1935.

Lenti, Vincent A. "Liturgical Reform and the Ambrosian and Mozarabic Rites." *Worship* 68 (1994): 417–426.

Lippy, Charles H. *Being Religious American Style: A History of Popular Religiosity in the United States.* Westport, CT: Praeger, 1994.

Loewe, William P. *The College Student's Introduction to Christology.* Collegeville, MN: Liturgical Press, 1996.

Lonergan, Bernard J. F. *Method in Theology.* Toronto: University of Toronto Press (for the Lonergan Research Institute of Regis College), 1971.

Maldonado, Luis. *Religiosidad Popular: Nostalgia de lo Mágico.* Epifanía 28. Madrid: Ediciones Cristiandad, 1975.

———. "Popular Religion: Its Dimensions, Levels, and Types." *Concilium* 186 (1986): 3–11.

Martimort, A. G., ed. *The Church at Prayer.* Translated by Matthew J. O'Connell. Introduction by Gerald S. Sloyan. Collegeville, MN: Liturgical Press, 1992.

Martín-Cleto, Julio Porres. "La iglesia mozárabe de Santa María de Alficén." In *Historia Mozárabe, Ponencias y Comunicaciones presentadas al I Congreso Internacional de Estudios Mozárabes Toledo, 1975,* 29–44. Serie C, no. 1. Toledo: Instituto de Estudios Visigótico-Mozárabes de San Eugenio, 1978.

Matovina, Timothy M. *Tejano Religion and Ethnicity: San Antonio, 1821–1860.* Austin: University of Texas Press, 1995.

Matovina, Timothy M., and Gary Riebe-Estrella, S.V.D., eds. *Horizons of the Sacred: Mexican Traditions in U.S. Catholicism.* Ithaca, NY: Cornell University Press, 2002.

Mazza, Enrico. *Eucharistic Prayers of the Roman Rite.* Translated by Matthew J. O'Connell. New York: Pueblo Pub. Co., 1986. Originally published in Italian as *Le Ordierne Preghiere Eucaristiche.* Bologna: Centro Editoriale Dehoniano, 1984.

McKenna, John H., C.M. "Adoration, Theology of." In *New Dictionary of Sacramental Worship,* ed. Peter E. Fink, S.J., 25–28. Collegeville, MN: Liturgical Press, 1990.

McNeill, John T., and Helena M. Gamer. *Medieval Handbooks of Penance: A Translation of the Principal Libri Poenitentiales and Selections from Related Documents.* Records of Western Civilization Series 29. Reprinted with new Introduction. New York: Columbia University Press, 1990 <1938>.

Meseguer Fernández, Juan, O.F.M. "El cardenal Jiménez de Cisneros, fundador de la Capilla Mozárabe," 149–245. *Historia Mozárabe, Ponencias y Comunicaciones presentadas al I Congreso Internacional de Estudios Mozárabes Toledo, 1975.* Serie C, no. 1. Toledo: Instituto de Estudios Visigótico-Mozárabes de San Eugenio, 1978.

Mestre Sanchis, Antonio. "Religión y cultura en el siglo XVIII español." BAC 4:586–743.

Metzger, Marcel. "The History of the Eucharistic Liturgy in Rome." In *The Eucharist*, vol. 3 of *Handbook for Liturgical Studies*, ed. Anscar J. Chupungco, 103–31. Collegeville, MN: Liturgical Press, 1999.

Miranda Calvo, José. "La continuidad cultural Nacional a través de la Mozarabía entre los siglos VIII al XI." *CM* 16 (1986): 1–5.

———. "Los Mozárabes: Su significado histórico (2)." *CM* 39 (1995): 5–9.

———. "Los Mozárabes: Su significado histórico (3)." *CM* 40 (1995): 4–9.

———. "Los Mozárabes: Su significado histórico (4)." *CM* 41 (1996): 13–15.

———. "El Ordenamiento jurídico mozárabe: El Fuero Juzgo." *CM* 19 (1987): 4–5.

———. "Reflexiones sobre la reconstrucción del templo mozárabe de Santa María de Melque." *CM* 28 (1990): 21–23.

Mundó, Anscari M. "Introducción." In *Liber Misticus de Cuaresma (Cod. Toledo 35.2, hoy en Madrid, Bibl. Nac. 10.110)*, ed. José Janini, xiii–xliii. Estudio paleográfico por el Prof. Anscari M. Mundó. Serie Litúrgica, Fuentes I. Toledo: Instituto de Estudios Visigótico-Mozárabes, 1979.

Muñoz Perea, Antonio. "Carta del Hermano Mayor." *CM* 61 (2004): 1–3.

———. "Escrito de nuestro Hermano Mayor." *CM* 62 (2005): 9–10.

Navarro Artiles, Francisco. "Un cantar majorero con raíces mozárabes." *CM* 14 (1985): 8–10.

New Catholic Encyclopedia. 2nd ed. New York: The Gale Group, 2003.

Nine Curt, Carmen Judith. *Non-Verbal Communication in Puerto Rico*, 2nd ed. Cambridge, MA: Evaluation, Dissemination and Assessment Center, 1984.

O'Callaghan, Joseph F. *A History of Medieval Spain*. Ithaca, NY: Cornell University Press, Cornell Paperbacks, 1994 <1975>.

———. "The Integration of Christian Spain into Europe: The Role of Alfonso VI of León-Castile." In *Santiago, Saint-Denis, and Saint Peter: The Reception of the Roman Liturgy in León-Castile in 1080*, ed. Bernard F. Reilly, 101–20. New York: Fordham University Press, 1985.

O'Connell, J. *The Rite of High Mass and Sung Mass*. Vol. 3 of *The Celebration of the Mass: A Study of the Rubrics of the Roman Missal* (Milwaukee: Bruce Pub. Co., 1940).

Orlandis Rovira, José. "El significado del Concilio III de Toledo en la Historia Hispánica y Universal." In *Concilio III de Toledo: XIV Centenario 589–1989*, 325–32. Toledo: Arzobispado de Toledo, 1991.

Ortiz, Alfonso. "Prefatio." In *Missale mixtum secundum regulam beati Isidori dictum Mozarabes*. Museo del Hospital de la Santa Cruz, Toledo, Inventorio General número 1324. Toledo: Petri Hagembach impensis Melchioris Goricii, 1500.

Overbeck, T. Jerome, S.J. "Cross." In *New Dictionary of Sacramental Worship*, ed. Peter E. Fink, S.J. Collegeville, MN: Liturgical Press, 1990.

Palencia, Clemente. "Historia y leyendas de las mujeres de Alfonso VI." In *Estudios Sobre Alfonso VI y la Reconquista de Toledo* (1988): 2:281–304.

Pardo, Andrés. "Don Marcelo y la Liturgia." *BOAT* 142 (1986): 253–58.

Parro, Sixto Ramón. *Toledo en la mano*, 2 vols. Serie 4, Clásicos Toledanos 6. Toledo: Instituto Provincial de Investigaciones y Estudios Toledanos, 1978; repr. of *Toledo en la mano*. Toledo: Severiano López Fando, 1857.

Payne, Stanley G. *Spanish Catholicism: An Historical Overview*. Madison: University of Wisconsin Press, 1984.

Pelikan, Jaroslav. *Jesus through the Centuries: His Place in the History of Culture*. New York: Harper and Row, 1987. Originally published by Yale University Press, 1985.

Peñarroja Torrejón, Leopoldo. *Cristianos Bajo El Islam: Los mozárabes hasta la reconquista de Valencia*. Monografías históricas 4. Madrid: Gredos, 1993.

Perales, Jorge. "The Service of the *Indulgentia*: Light on the Rite of General Confession and Absolution." *Worship* 62 (1988): 138–53.

Pérez, Arturo (J.). *Popular Catholicism: A Hispanic Perspective/El Catolicismo Popular: Una perspectiva hispana*. American Essays in Liturgy 9. Washington DC: Pastoral Press, 1988.

———. "History of Hispanic Liturgy since 1965." In *Hispanic Catholic Culture in the US: Issues and Concerns*, ed. Jay P. Dolan and Allan Figueroa Deck, S.J., 360–408. Notre Dame, IN: University of Notre Dame Press, 1994.

Pérez de Urbel, Justo, O.S.B., and Atilano González y Ruiz-Zorrilla. *Liber Commicus*. Monumenta Hispaniæ Sacra, Serie Litúrgica 2. Madrid: Consejo Superior de Investigaciones Científicas, Escuela de Estudios Medievales, 1950.

Pérez Monzón, Olga, and Enrique Rodríguez-Picavea. *Toledo y las tres Culturas*. Historia del Mundo Para Jóvenes. Madrid: Ediciones AKAL, 1995.

Phan, Peter C., ed. *Directory on Popular Piety and the Liturgy: Principles and Guidelines, A Commentary*. Collegeville, MN: Liturgical Press, 2005.

Pinell, Jordi, O.S.B. (J. Mª. Pinell or Jorge M. Pinell). *Liturgia hispánica*. Edited by José Aldazábal. Biblioteca litúrgica 9. Barcelona: Centre de Pastoral Litúrgica, 1998.

———. "Boletín de Liturgia Hispano-Visigótica (1949–1956)." *Hispania Sacra* 9 (1956): 405–27.

———. "Credo y comunión en la estructura de la misa hispánica según disposición del III Concilio de Toledo." In *Concilio III de Toledo: XIV Centenario 589–1989*, 333–42. Toledo: Arzobispado de Toledo, 1991.

———. "El misal hispano-mozárabe: Nueva edición revisada." *Phase* 191 (1992): 367–80.

———. "Missale Hispano-Mozarabicum." *Notitiæ* 24 (1988): 670–727.

———. "El problema de las dos tradiciones del antiguo rito hispánico. Valoración documental de la tradición B, en vistas a una eventual revisión del Ordinario de la Misa Mozárabe." In *Liturgia y Música Mozárabes: Ponencias y*

Comunicaciones presentadas al I Congreso Internacional de Estudios Mozárabes: Toledo, 1975, 3–44. Serie D, no. 1. Toledo: Instituto de Estudios Visigótico-Mozárabes de San Eugenio, 1978.

———. "Los textos de la antigua liturgia hispánica. Fuentes para su estudio." *Estudios sobre la liturgia mozárabe* (Toledo, 1965): 109–64.

Plácido Suárez, Domingo. "El Bajo Imperio." In *La España romana y visigoda (siglos III a.C.-VII d.C.)*, vol. 2 of *Historia de España*, gen. ed. Antonio Domínguez Ortiz, 315–410. Barcelona: Editorial Planeta, 1988; 3rd ed., 1989.

Power, David N., O.M.I. *The Eucharistic Mystery: Revitalizing the Tradition.* New York: Crossroad, 1995.

———. *Unsearchable Riches: The Symbolic Nature of Liturgy.* Collegeville, MN: Liturgical Press, 1984.

Puyol y Alonso, Julio, ed. "Las crónicas anónimas de Sahagún." *Boletín de la Real Academia de la Historia* 76 (1920): 116–17.

Ramis, Gabriel. "Liturgia Hispano-Mozárabe Boletín Bibliográfico (1977–1992)." *Ecclesia Orans* 11 (1994): 107–20.

Ramos-Lissón, Domingo. "Los laicos y el III Concilio de Toledo." In *Concilio III de Toledo: XIV Centenario 589–1989*, 343–56. Toledo: Arzobispado de Toledo, 1991.

Ramshaw-Schmidt, Gail. *Christ in Sacred Speech: The Meaning of Liturgical Language.* Philadelphia: Fortress Press, 1986.

Reglá, Juan. "Isabel II." In *(15) El siglo XVIII, (16) el siglo XIX, y (17) el siglo XX*, vol. 2 of *Historia de España Ilustrada*, 788–829. Barcelona: Editorial Ramón Sopena, 1972.

Reilly, Bernard F. *The Contest of Christian and Muslim Spain 1031–1157.* A History of Spain, gen. ed. John Lynch. Cambridge, MA: Blackwell, 1995 <1992>.

———. *The Kingdom of León-Castilla under King Alfonso VI, 1065–1109.* Princeton, NJ: Princeton University Press, 1988.

———. *The Kingdom of León-Castilla under Queen Urraca, 1109–1126.* Princeton, NJ: Princeton University Press, 1982.

———. "Alfonso VI: Conqueror, Politician, Europeanizer." In *Estudios Sobre Alfonso VI y la Reconquista de Toledo* (1987): 1:13–30.

Ricoeur, Paul. *Interpretation Theory: Discourse and the Surplus of Meaning.* Fort Worth: Texas Christian University Press, 1976.

Ripoll, Gisela, and Isabel Velázquez. *Historia de España. La Hispania visigoda. Del rey Ataúlfo a Don Rodrigo.* Historia 16 Temas de Hoy, vol. 6. Madrid: Ediciones Temas de Hoy, S.A., 1995.

Rivera Recio, Juan Francisco. "Formas de convivencia y heterodoxias en el primer siglo mozárabe," 3–16. *Historia Mozárabe: Ponencias y Comunicaciones presentadas al I Congreso Internacional de Estudios Mozárabes, Toledo, 1975.* Serie C, vol. 1. Toledo: Instituto de Estudios Visigótico-Mozárabes de San Eugenio, 1978.

———. "La iglesia mozárabe." BAC II-1:21–60.

———. "La supresión del rito mozárabe y la introducción del romano." BAC II-1:275–85.

Rodríguez Marquina, Javier. *Genealogías Mozárabes: Ponencias y Comunicaciones presentadas al 1 Congreso Internacional de Estudios Mozárabes: Toledo, 1975,* vol. 1 of *Linajes Mozárabes de Toledo, en los siglos XII y XIII.* series B, no. 1. Toledo: Instituto de Estudios Visigótico-Mozárabes de San Eugenio, 1981.

Romero, C. Gilbert. *Hispanic Devotional Piety: Tracing the Biblical Roots.* Faith and Cultures Series. Maryknoll, NY: Orbis Books, 1991.

Romero Castelló, Elena, and Uriel Macías Kapón. *The Jews and Europe: 2,000 Years of History.* New York: A Henry Holt Reference Book, Henry Holt and Co., 1994.

Romero-Pose, Eugenio. "Trasfondo teológico del III Concilio de Toledo," 357–374. In *Concilio III de Toledo: XIV Centenario 589–1989.* Toledo: Arzobispado de Toledo, 1991.

Roth, Cecil. *The Spanish Inquisition.* New York: W. W. Norton, 1964; reissued 1996.

Roth, Norman. *Jews, Visigoths, and Muslims in Medieval Spain: Cooperation and Conflict.* New York: E. J. Brill, 1994.

Roura Aulinas, Lluís. "La guerra de la Independencia." In *La transición del Antiguo al Nuevo régimen (1789–1874),* vol. 9 of *Historia de España,* 3rd ed., gen. ed. Antonio Domínguez Ortiz, 137–77. Barcelona: Editorial Planeta, 1989 <1988>.

Ruiz, Teófilo F. "Burgos and the Council of 1080." In *Santiago, Saint-Denis, and Saint Peter: The Reception of the Roman Liturgy in León-Castile in 1080,* ed. Bernard F. Reilly, 121–30. New York: Fordham University Press.

Ruiz Torres, Pedro. "Economía y sociedad en la crisis del Antiguo régimen." In *Historia de España,* 3rd edition, 12 vols., general editor Antonio Domínguez Ortiz, 9:9–89. Barcelona: Editorial Planeta, 1988–90.

Sainz Saiz, Javier. *Arte Prerrománico en Castilla y León.* León: Ediciones Lancia, 1996.

Salisbury, Joyce E. *Iberian Popular Religion 600 B.C. to 700 A.D.: Celts, Romans and Visigoths.* Texts and Studies in Religion 20. Lewiston, NY: Edwin Mellen Press, 1985.

Sánchez Montealegre, Cleofé (Sánchez). "Aprobada la Reforma del Rito Mozárabe." *CM* 22 (1988): 1–3.

———. "Celebración del Matrimonio en rito Mozárabe en Toledo." *CM* 29 (1990): 43–44.

———. "De 5 de Enero de 1500 a 17 de Noviembre de 1991." *CM* 31 (1991): 100–102

———. "El lenguaje es la liturgia mozárabe." *CM* 23 (1988): 1–3.

———. "La Liturgia, razón de ser de la Mozarabía." *CM* 18 (1986): 1–2.

———. "La Reforma del Rito Mozárabe," *CM* 18 (1986): 11–12.

Sancho Andreu, Jaime. "Ritos de la infancia y la adolescencia en el antiguo rito hispánico." In *Psallendum: Studi offerti al Prof. Jordi Pinell i Pons,* ed.

Ildebrando Scicolone, O.S.B., 207–45. Studia Anselmiana 105, Analecta Liturgica 15. Rome: Pontificio Ateneo S. Anselmo, 1992.

———. "El Triduo Sacro en el Rito Hispánico," 49–54. In *Triduo Sacro en rito hispano antiguo o mozárabe*, gen. ed. Lamberto de Echeverría. Salamanca: Junta de Capilla, Universidad de Salamanca, 1980.

Scales, Peter C. "¿Cual era la verdadera importancia de la conquista de Tuletwu, capital de los godos?" In *Estudios Sobre Alfonso VI y la Reconquista de Toledo* (1987): 1:339–52.

Schmemann, Alexander. *Introduction to Liturgical Theology*. Translated by Asheleigh E. Moorhouse. Crestwood, NY: St. Vladimir's Seminary Press, 1986.

Schulz, Hans-Joachim. *The Byzantine Liturgy: Symbolic Structure and Faith Expression*. Translated by Matthew J. O'Connell. New York: Pueblo Pub. Co., 1986. Originally published in German as *Die byzantinische Liturgie*. Trier: Paulinus-Verlag, 1980.

Sierra, Juan Manuel. "Contexto teológico y espiritual del rito hispano-mozárabe." In *Curso de Liturgia Hispano-Mozárabe*, ed. Juan-Miguel Ferrer Greneche, 97–126. Toledo: Estudio Teológico de San Ildefonso, Seminario Conciliar, 1995.

Simonet, Francisco Javier. *Historia de los mozárabes de España, deducida de los mejores y más auténticos testimonios de los escritores cristianos y árabes*. 4 vols. Madrid: Ediciones Turner, 1999; repr. of 1903 ed. by Manuel Gómez Moreno.

Sobrequés Vidal, S. *Hispania: Síntesis de Historia de España*. 9th ed. Revised and updated by Joaquim Nadal Carreras. Barcelona: Editorial Vicens-Vives, 1979.

Sotomayor y Muro, Manuel. "El concilio de Granada (Iliberri)." BAC 1:81–119.

———. "El donatismo y la crisis arriana. Osio de Córdoba, Potamio de Lisboa y Gregorio de Granada." BAC 1:187–232.

———. "La Iglesia hispana en la época de transición." BAC 1:372–400.

———. "La Iglesia hispana en el imperio romano del siglo IV." BAC 1:166–86.

———. "La Iglesia y la España romana." BAC 1:7–34.

———. "Poetas, historiadores y viajeros. Invasiones germánicas." BAC 1:311–71.

———. "El priscilianismo." BAC 1:233–72.

———. "Sobre los orígenes del cristianismo en Hispania." BAC 1:120–65.

———. "Los testimonios históricos más antiguos del cristianismo hispano." BAC 1:35–80.

Stevenson, J., ed. *Creeds, Councils, and Controversies: Documents Illustrative of the History of the Church A.D. 337–461*. London: S.P.C.K., 1978 <1966>.

Stevenson, Kenneth (W.). *Jerusalem Revisited: The Liturgical Meaning of Holy Week*. Washington DC: Pastoral Press, 1988.

———. *To Join Together: The Rite of Marriage*. Studies in the Reformed Rites of the Catholic Church 5. New York: Pueblo Pub. Co, 1987.

Suárez Fernández, Luis. "Toledo, 1085: Un cambio para la convivencia." In *Estudios Sobre Alfonso VI y la Reconquista de Toledo* (1987): 1:157–64.

Sullivan, Lawrence E. "Sound and Senses: Toward a Hermeneutics of Performance." *History of Religions* 26 (1986): 1–33.

Swaan, Wim. *The Gothic Cathedral*. With a historical introduction, "The Cathedral in Medieval Society," by Christopher Brooke. New York: Park Lane, 1984.

Taft, Robert, S.J. *Liturgy of the Hours in East and West: The Origins of the Divine Office and Its Meaning for Today*. Collegeville, MN: Liturgical Press, 1986.

———. "What Does Liturgy Do? Toward a Soteriology of Liturgical Celebration: Some Theses." *Worship* 66 (1992): 194–211.

Taves, Ann. *The Household of Faith: Roman Catholic Devotions in Mid-Nineteenth-Century America*. Notre Dame, IN: University of Notre Dame Press, 1986.

Terrero, José. *Geografía de España*. Barcelona: Editorial Ramón Sopena, 1956.

Tobar, Dora E. "El lenguaje de la cultura hispana y la liturgia." In *Languages of Worship/El lenguaje de la liturgia*, ed. Raúl Gómez, S.D.S., 63–77. Chicago: LIP; Washington DC: Instituto Nacional Hispano de Liturgia, 2004.

Tracy, David. *Plurality and Ambiguity: Hermeneutics, Religion, Hope*. Chicago: University of Chicago Press, 1994. Originally published by Harper SanFrancisco, 1987.

Turner, Victor. *Dramas, Fields, and Metaphors: Symbolic Action in Human Society*. Symbol, Myth, and Ritual Series, gen. ed. Victor Turner. Ithaca, NY: Cornell University Press, 1974.

———. *Ritual Process: Structure and Anti-Structure*. Ithaca, NY: Cornell University Press, 1991. Originally published by Aldine Pub. Co. in 1969.

———. "Passages, Margins, and Poverty: Religious Symbols of Communitas" (part I). *Worship* 46 (1972): 390–412.

Valenziano, Crispino. "Liturgy and Anthropology: The Meaning of the Question and the Method for Answering It." In *Fundamental Liturgy*, vol. 2 of *Handbook for Liturgical Studies*, ed. Anscar J. Chupungco. Collegeville, MN: Liturgical Press, 1998.

Vicens Vives, Jaime. *Approaches to the History of Spain*. 2nd ed., rev. Translated and edited by Joan Connelly Ullman. Berkeley and Los Angeles: University of California Press, 1970 <1967>. Originally published in Spanish as *Aproximación a la historia de España*, Barcelona: Editorial Vicens-Vives, 1952. English translation based on the 2nd edition published by Editorial Teide, 1960, for the Centro de Estudios Históricos Internacionales, Universidad de Barcelona.

Vizuete Mendoza, J. Carlos. "La reforma gregoriana en Castilla a través de las disposiciones conciliares." In *Estudios Sobre Alfonso VI* (1988): 2:321–35.

Vogel, Cyrille. *Medieval Liturgy: An Introduction to the Sources*. Revised and translated by William G. Storey and Niels Krogh Rasmussen, O.P., with the assistance of John K. Brooks-Leonard. Washington DC: The Pastoral Press, 1986; rev. from *Introduction aux sources de l'histoire du culte chrétien au moyen age*, 1981.

Vogel, Dwight W. "Liturgical Theology: A Conceptual Geography." In *Primary Sources of Liturgical Theology: A Reader*, ed. Dwight W. Vogel, 3–14. Collegeville, MN: Liturgical Press, 2000.

Vrijhof, Pieter Hendrik, and Jacques Waardenburg. *Official and Popular Religion: Analysis of a Theme for Religious Studies*. The Hague: Mouton Pub., 1979.

Wainwright, Geoffrey. "The Periods of Liturgical History." In *The Study of Liturgy*, rev. ed., ed. Cheslyn Jones, Geoffrey Wainwright, Edward Yarnold, S.J., and Paul Bradshaw, 61–67. New York: Oxford University Press; London: S.P.C.K., 1992 <1978>.

Walker, Rose. *Views of Transition: Liturgy and Illumination in Medieval Spain*. British Library Studies in Medieval Culture. Toronto: University of Toronto Press, 1998; 1st pub. London: British Library, 1998.

Ward, Anthony, S.M., and Cuthbert Johnson, O.S.B. "Présentation." In *Le Liber Ordinum en Usage Dans L'Église Wisigothique et Mozarabe de'Espagne du Cinquième au Onzième Siècle*, 9–27. Réimpression de l'édition de 1904 et supplément bibliographie générale de la liturgie hispanique préparés et présentés par Anthony Ward, S.M. et Cuthbert Johnson, O.S.B. Rome: Centro Liturgico Vincenziano-Edizioni Liturgiche, 1996.

Watt, W. Montgomery. *A History of Islamic Spain*. With additional sections on literature by Pierre Cachia. Edinburgh: University Press, 1967 <1965>.

Webster, Susan Verdi. *Art and Ritual in Golden-Age Spain*. Princeton, NJ: Princeton University Press, 1998.

Wegman, Herman. *Christian Worship in East and West: A Study Guide to Liturgical History*. Translated by Gordon W. Lathrop. Collegeville, MN: Liturgical Press, 1990 <1985>. Originally published in Dutch as *Geschiedenis van de Christelijke Eredienst in het Westen en in het Oosten*. Gooi en Sticht bv, Hilversum, 1976.

Williams, John W. "Orientations: Christian Spain and the Art of Its Neighbors." In *Art of Medieval Spain A.D. 500–1200*, ed. John P. O'Neill, 13–25. New York: Metropolitan Museum of Art, 1993.

Williams, Peter W. *Popular Religion in America: Symbolic Change and the Modernization Process in Historical Perspective*. Englewood Cliffs, NJ: Prentice-Hall, 1989.

Williams, Raymond. "Culture is Ordinary." In *Studying Culture: An Introductory Reader*, 2nd ed., ed. Ann Gray and Jim McGuigan, 5–14. London: Arnold; New York: Oxford University Press, 1993, 1997. Originally published in *Convictions*, ed. N. McKenzie, 1958; repr. in R. Williams and R. Gable. *Resources of Hope: Culture, Democracy, Socialism*. London: Verso, 1989.

Witczak, Michael. "Sacramentary of Paul VI." In *The Eucharist*, vol. 3 of *Handbook for Liturgical Studies*, ed. Anscar J. Chupungco, 3:133–75. Collegeville, MN: Liturgical Press, 1999.

Wolfram, Herwig. *History of the Goths*. Translated by Thomas J. Dunlap. Berkeley and Los Angeles: University of California Press, 1988. First paperback printing 1990, new and completely revised from the 2nd German ed.; 1st published in Munich by C. H. Beck'sche Verlagsbuchhandlung, Oscar Beck, 1979.

Wroth, William. *Images of Penance, Images of Mercy: Southwestern "Santos" in the Late Nineteenth Century*. Norman: University of Oklahoma Press; Colorado Springs, CO: Colorado Springs Fine Arts Center, 1991.

Wybrew, Hugh. "Ceremonial." In *The Study of Liturgy*, rev. ed., ed. Cheslyn Jones, Geoffrey Wainwright, Edward Yarnold, S.J., and Paul Bradshaw, 485–93. New York: Oxford University Press; London: S.P.C.K., 1992 <1978>.

Yarnold, Edward. *The Awe-Inspiring Rites of Initiation*. Slough, UK: St. Paul, 1971.

N.B.: For a more complete bibliography, including a listing of unpublished primary sources, see the Center for the Study of Latino/a Catholicism website.

Index

247